THE CRIMEAN WAR

THE
CRIMEAN WAR

CLIVE PONTING

Chatto & Windus
LONDON

Published by Chatto & Windus 2004

2 4 6 8 10 9 7 5 3 1

First published in Great Britain in 2004 by
Chatto & Windus
Random House, 20 Vauxhall Bridge Road,
London SW1V 2SA

Random House Australia (Pty) Limited
20 Alfred Street, Milsons Point, Sydney,
New South Wales 2061, Australia

Random House New Zealand Limited
18 Poland Road, Glenfield,
Auckland 10, New Zealand

Random House (Pty) Limited
Endulini, 5A Jubilee Road, Parktown 2193, South Africa

The Random House Group Limited Reg. No. 954009
www.randomhouse.co.uk

A CIP catalogue record for this book is available from the British Library

ISBN 0 7011 7390 4

Papers used by The Random House Group Limited are natural, recyclable products
made from wood grown in sustainable forests; the manufacturing processes
conform to the environmental regulations of the country of origin

Typeset by SX Composing DTP, Rayleigh, Essex
Printed and bound in Great Britain by
Biddles Ltd, King's Lynn

Contents

Preface

Most British people remember the Crimean War for the heroic disaster of the Charge of the Light Brigade and the selfless devotion of Florence Nightingale. Myths, such as the shipload of left boots, are still widely believed even though they never happened. Britons may also be dimly aware of the war through pub and street names such as Alma and Inkerman and items of clothing such as a balaklava, cardigan and raglan.

The true reasons for the war, who was allied with whom, why it was fought in the Crimea, how it was fought and its outcome are now largely lost in obscurity. The war has become a byword for inefficiency and incompetence (as though these were unique to this war) and it has come to be seen as an historical irrelevance. Now, 150 years after the outbreak of the war, it is time to re-evaluate this war and return it to its place as the most important and devastating conflict fought in the century between 1815 and 1914.

The 'Crimean War' is a misnomer for a conflict which was fought from the Arctic to the Pacific and which affected nearly every state in the world. The allies (Britain and France) did not choose to undertake a siege of Sevastopol in Crimea which lasted for a year – that happened as a result of poor planning, military incompetence and stiff Russian resistance. Britain certainly did not want to fight such a war, because the army it could maintain was about a quarter of the size of the French army and its influence over strategy reflected this disparity. The British had hoped and planned that the Royal Navy would be their chief weapon and that the main theatre of operations would be in the Baltic. There they hoped to destroy the Russian fleet and possibly even attack and capture St Petersburg.

The 'Crimean War' was not a title known to contemporaries, who for some time after the war ended in 1856 referred to it as the 'Russian War' or 'The Great War with Russia'. It was the only modern war that Britain ever fought against Russia and it demonstrated that it was impossible for either the greatest land power or the greatest sea power in the world to inflict a decisive defeat on the other. The title 'Crimean War' came into general use gradually in the late nineteenth century and was part of the establishment of a consensus about that war that has remained, in many essentials, almost unchanged until the present day.

The war of 1854–56 was rapidly considered to be a mistake that should never be repeated. Britain had fought in alliance with its traditional enemy France to support an ... Islamic power (the Ottoman empire) which was almost universally considered to be corrupt and condemned to inevitable extinction by the march of progress. (A progress that was exemplified by perceived British superiority to all other powers in morals, economics, technology and politics.) The war was viewed as the outcome of poor diplomacy and the unexpected escalation of a trivial dispute over the minutiae of Christian church politics in Palestine into a quarrel between the great powers of Europe. The Crimean War came to be seen as the outstanding example of why wars should not be fought.

This assessment is wrong. Although the diplomatic quarrel did begin over a religious dispute, it very rapidly became a contest for power and influence in the Ottoman empire that seriously affected the strategic interests of all the major European powers. The diplomacy that led up to the war was clumsy but, in the last resort, the war was fought because Russia, France and Britain thought their vital interests were at stake.

The results of the Crimean War also seemed to be disappointing. Russia, Britain's main rival for world power in the mid-nineteenth century, was only slightly checked by the war. The peace treaty was certainly not a victors' peace. The British blamed the French for making peace too soon and ignored the fact that they could not have continued the war on their own with any real chance of success. The British, Palmerston in particular, might dream about a harsh peace but, despite their industrial and technological supremacy over the other European powers, they lacked the military and naval force to impose such a settlement. The war remained a limited one and, not surprisingly, the peace treaty reflected its limited nature. Had the war continued into 1856, it might well have expanded into a full-scale European war that would have had incalculable consequences and would certainly have led to a major redrawing of the map of Europe. Such a major conflict did not occur for a number of reasons. Diplomacy still operated during the war and kept war aims limited. Austria, the main 'neutral', was able to act as a bridge between the two sides, and Napoleon III kept a very realistic perspective on what he wanted.

The British decided that they would rather forget the Crimean War because in nearly every respect it was a failure. It had raised a number of very real and potentially damaging questions. It had raised doubts about the competence of the small aristocratic group that provided the leadership of the army, about the ability of the governing political elite and about the efficiency of the British system of government. In the first half of 1855 there were powerful demands for a major restructuring of British institutions. They were contained, but after the war the small governing group in Britain naturally preferred to let these troublesome questions fade away and be forgotten. They, and others, could return to a comforting complacency about the superiority of the British way of doing things. Military incompetence could be accepted because limited reforms and success in colonial wars against technologically inferior people seemed to show that it would not happen again.

More comforting myths came to dominate the accepted view of the war. The stupidity of the orders that led to the charge of the Light Brigade could be played down ('their's not to reason why') and the blind courage of those involved brought to centre stage ('the noble six hundred'). The other redeeming feature of the war could be the selfless heroism of Florence Nightingale, who was portrayed as the incarnation of Victorian female virtues – the caring 'mother' and healer who struggled against stupidity, but took on a role considered suitable for a woman.

The 'Crimean War' (the title is retained simply because it is now too familiar to change) became the forgotten war. For the British it was an aberration because it was the only time the country was involved in a European war between 1815 and 1914. It was a lesson to be learnt – Britain should steer clear of Europe and concentrate on its imperial glories. In fact that was the wrong lesson to draw. Britain was a European power and it could not ignore what happened on the continent. The Crimean War also showed that Britain could not simply be a maritime power – the Royal Navy helped protect trade and the empire, but it could not make a significant contribution in a European conflict. If Britain wanted to have any real influence over the conduct of such a war it had, whether it liked it or not, to provide a major army. It was a painful lesson that had to be learnt all over again in 1914.

Eye-witnesses

The Crimean War is one of the first major wars for which a substantial number of first-hand accounts have survived. They provide vivid descriptions of the fighting and the conditions in the Crimea and often a surprisingly blunt view of the army leadership. Rather than provide a second-hand, paraphrased account of the war, I decided to include extracts from these accounts throughout the story. They will be found in 'boxes' at appropriate points in the narrative. I have retained the idiosyncratic spelling, grammar, punctuation and capitalisation of the originals. The war is followed through the experiences of a number of men. A very short biographical note on the chief contributors can be found below.

William Howard Russell

He was born in 1820 near Dublin and educated at Trinity College, although he did not graduate. He dabbled in journalism and in 1841 was a correspondent for *The Times* on the elections in Ireland. He read for the Bar, taught mathematics and was also a parliamentary reporter for *The Times* from 1843. He acted as a correspondent in the Schleswig-Holstein wars and was then sent by *The Times* to cover the war in the east.

Although he became famous as the first 'war correspondent', and his despatches were later seen as having a major impact on opinion in Britain about the war, Russell's reports have to be treated with caution. He was, like most of his contemporaries, anti-Ottoman (the Turks were grubby, cowardly Orientals) and virulently anti-French. From some of his descriptions of the battles it would be hard to believe that the French took any part in them. It is also obvious that he cannot have seen for himself all of the events he purports to describe. The identity of his informants is unknown and their reliability is difficult to assess. Russell was also away from the Crimea during the most crucial time in the dreadful winter of 1854–55. He left on 7 December and spent Christmas at Constantinople living in considerable luxury before returning at the end of the month.

Not surprisingly, his reports reflect the prevailing attitudes of the British upper-middle-class readership of *The Times*. They tell his readership what it wanted to hear about the war. Russell was close to Raglan, whom he rarely criticised, but fell out of favour with Codrington when he became

British commander in the autumn of 1855. Russell blamed Codrington for the British failure at the Great Redan during the final attack on Sevastopol. He left the Crimea in early December 1855 and was replaced by the Constantinople correspondent of *The Times*.

After the Crimean War he covered numerous other conflicts – the American Civil War, the Austro-Prussian and the Franco-Prussian Wars – before retiring in 1882. He stood unsuccessfully as a Conservative candidate for Parliament, founded the *Army and Navy Gazette* and was knighted in 1895. He died in 1907.

Roger Fenton

Born in 1819, Fenton came from a manufacturing and banking family and his father was Liberal MP for Rochdale in the 1830s. He studied in London and Paris, where he took up the new technology of photography. He returned to London in 1844, became a solicitor, but kept up his interest in photography and was a founder of the Photographic Society in 1853.

Fenton was not the first war photographer – that honour probably falls to Karl Baptist von Szathmari of Bucharest, whose photographs of the 1853 Danube campaign were shown at the Universal Exhibition at Paris in 1855. The British army decided to have an official photographer in the east and chose Richard Nicklin of Dickinson & Co. of New Bond Street, who was contracted for six months at six shillings a day plus food, allowances and a free passage. He left in mid-June 1854 for Varna with sixteen cases of equipment. It is uncertain what happened to him, but he probably drowned off Balaklava in the 'Great Storm' of November 1854. The army replaced him with Ensigns Brandon and Dawson, who were given a month's training with the portrait photographer, J. E. Mayall. The two soldiers left in the spring of 1855 and it is known that their photographs still existed, in a poor condition, in the War Office in 1869. They were subsequently destroyed.

Fenton was financed by Thomas Agnew & Sons of Manchester, who wanted to produce an album suitable for sale to a Victorian audience. His photographs are not an accurate record of the war. He was instructed not to record the horrors of war and his photos are therefore carefully constructed images designed to emphasise certain aspects of the conflict that would be agreeable to his audience. The technology available ruled out action photographs – exposure times were very long and scenes therefore had to be static.

Fenton left in mid-February 1855 with his two alcoholic assistants and a specially converted van that he had bought from a Canterbury wine merchant. It was designed as the men's living, cooking and sleeping quarters and also housed five cameras, 700 glass plates and huge amounts of equipment. Fenton arrived at Balaklava on 8 March and soon found that his letters of introduction from Prince Albert smoothed away the military opposition to his activities. Overall he took nearly 400 usable photographs (the summer heat made processing difficult) before he left after the failure of the allied assault on 18 June. Fenton accompanied the royal visit to Paris in August 1855 and went again the next month to show Napoleon 360 photographs. Nearly all of them were exhibited in London in October and then sold in a limited edition priced at 360 guineas. After the war he continued to work in photography until 1862 when he became a full-time solicitor in London. He died in 1869.

The other eye-witnesses to the war are serving soldiers – their accounts come from either diaries or letters home.

Henry Clifford

Born in 1826, he was the third son of Lord Clifford of Chudleigh. This was a Catholic family and he was educated at Catholic schools and, briefly, the University of Fribourg. He joined the Rifle Brigade in 1846 and served in South Africa before returning to Britain in January 1854. He travelled out to the eastern Mediterranean in July and served as aide-de-camp to Brigadier George Buller, the commander of the 2nd Brigade of the Light Division. In late 1854, after Buller returned to Britain, Clifford worked on the Quartermaster staff of the Light Division. After the Crimea he remained in the army, reaching the rank of Major-General before his death in 1883.

George Frederick Dallas

Born in 1827, he was the fourth son of Captain Robert Dallas. He was educated at Harrow and his family bought his commission as an Ensign in the 46th South Devonshire, Regiment of Foot that was commanded by Lieutenant-Colonel Robert Garrett, a friend of Robert Dallas since the Peninsular War. At the age of twenty-one, 'Fred' Dallas bought a commission as a Lieutenant. His regiment did not travel to the Crimea as a single unit because of a series of courts-martial following a number of notorious and well-publicised incidents. Dallas left on 9 August 1854 with Lieutenant-General Sir George Cathcart, the commander of the 4th

Division. They reached Varna on 2 September, just in time to sail to the Crimea. Dallas landed at Evpatoriya, but did not take part in the battle of the Alma – his under-strength regiment was left behind to clear up the beaches. He was the only 'eye-witness' to serve throughout the Crimean campaign – he was in the last party to leave after peace was signed and he did not arrive back in Britain until 5 August 1856.

After the Crimea Dallas served at Gibraltar and Hong Kong and was in India during the 'mutiny' of 1857, but took no part in the fighting. He went on to half-pay in 1861, married and finally sold his commission in 1876. His children were taught by a then obscure local music teacher, Edward Elgar. Dallas died in 1888.

George Palmer Evelyn

Born in 1823, Evelyn was the son of an army officer who had fought at Waterloo. After education at Cheam School he joined the Rifle Brigade and served in North America and South Africa. He left the army in the early 1850s, but served as an officer in the Royal Surrey Militia. He travelled east in December 1853 as either a freelance reporter or an officer with the Ottoman army (it is impossible to discover which). He left the Danube front (which he found too dull) in March 1854 and returned to Britain for militia training. He left again for the east in July and briefly visited Varna. In early September he was appointed as a British liaison officer with the Ottoman forces, but appears never to have joined them. After Inkerman he was bored with the prospect of a long siege at Sevastopol and a Crimean winter and left for home on 25 November 1854. He settled down in Surrey, married and continued to serve in the militia. He died in 1889.

Temple Godman

He was born in 1832 into a wealthy Surrey landed family and was educated at Eton. He joined the 5th Dragoon Guards in 1851 as a Cornet – the commission cost £840. He bought his promotion to Lieutenant in March 1854 and to Captain just over a year later. (The latter promotion cost £3,225 – about £150,000 at today's prices.) His regiment left from Cork in late May 1854 and reached Varna in early June. They did not sail with the main convoy to the Crimea, and Godman did not land at Balaklava until 1 October. His regiment formed part of the Heavy Brigade. He left, with most of the rest of the cavalry, in November 1855 to spend the winter at Scutari. When peace was signed he travelled to Jerusalem and Cairo before returning to Britain in late June 1856. After the Crimea he rose to the rank of Colonel by 1876 before retiring in 1882. He died in 1912.

George Lawson

Born in 1831, Lawson was the son of a London wine merchant. He began training as a medical student at King's College in 1848 and qualified in 1852. He volunteered for military service as a doctor in early 1854 and left Woolwich, after brief training, in early March. He stayed at Gallipoli until late June before moving to Varna, where he contracted typhoid fever in mid-July and was ill until late August. He was nearly invalided home, but did sail to the Crimea. In May 1855 Lawson contracted fever again (probably typhus this time) and sailed home in June, arriving in August. He never fully recovered from these illnesses, but worked as a doctor (specialising in eye treatment) until his death in 1903.

George Newman

He was born in 1828 in Runcorn, but his early life is a mystery. He could speak French and probably learnt the language working as a navvy building railways with the many British contractors operating in France. He joined the 23rd Regiment of Foot, Royal Welch Fusiliers at Winchester on 8 February 1849 and sailed for the Crimea on 5 April 1854. At the battle of Inkerman he was part of an isolated detachment under Lieutenant James Duff that was surprised by a group of Russians appearing suddenly out of the mist. Newman and eleven other men were taken prisoner.

He was a prisoner of war for almost a year and was marched from Sevastopol to Simferopol, Perekop, Melitopol and Kharkov to Voronezh, where he arrived in the middle of February 1855. Here he was allowed free access to the town and was well paid teaching English to a Russian lady. He planned to escape but was selected for a prisoner exchange and taken to Odessa in August. Newman rejoined his regiment at the end of October and left the Crimea in mid-June 1856, reaching Portsmouth on 21 July. He left the army on 1 January 1857 just a month before his regiment was due to leave for China. His life after he left the army is unknown. The extraordinary story of his adventures as a prisoner of war was written for his half-brother, William Peerless.

A Note on Names

The transliteration of Russian names seemed to cause the British and French a number of problems. The most obvious one was the use of Sebastopol instead of Sevastopol, through a misunderstanding of the pronunciation of the Russian 'b'. Other mistakes were much worse, with 'Woronzoff' probably winning the prize – it should be Vorontsov – for there is no 'w' in Russian, the 'z' is the wrong sound and 'ff' should be 'v'. It seems to have been the French who introduced an unnecessary 't' at the beginning of Chernaya and Chorgun and in the middle of Kacha and Kerch. It is Balaklava in Russian, and there is no need to introduce a 'c' instead of the 'k' because the sound is the same. Similarly there is no double 'n' at the end of Inkerman.

I have tried to use the standard method for transcribing Russian (the fact that the Crimea is now in the Ukraine is irrelevant in the context of history) adopted in the 1940s. This does produce some slight oddities – Fedyukhin, Evpatoriya and Bakhchisarai – but is, I hope, consistent. At least there is no argument over one of the crucial battles – it is the 'Alma'. No doubt I have made some mistakes in this difficult area and the experts concerned will surely point them out!

Acknowledgments

I would like to acknowledge all those who gave permission for the Eye-Witness extracts and, in particular, Michael Hargreave-Mawson, a fellow member of the Crimean War Research Society, for the use of the papers of his ancestor, 'Fred' Dallas.

List of Maps

List of Illustrations

The Reason Why

The dispute that started the diplomatic slide to the Crimean War began more than six years before the British and French declarations of war on Russia at the end of March 1854. The argument involved the Orthodox, Armenian and Catholic churches disputing control of some of the Christian Holy Places in Palestine. It led to war because of the way the issue was exploited by France and Russia so that eventually the very future of the Ottoman empire was at stake. War could easily have been avoided, but all the powers involved chose, at various times, to escalate the crisis.

The Holy Places

As so often in the history of Christianity, the disputes between the different sects were even more vicious than the Christian quarrels with their monotheistic rivals – Islam and Judaism. In late 1847 the various Christian churches began arguing over the Church of the Nativity in Bethlehem. The Catholics did not hold a set of keys to the main door of the church (only the Orthodox and the Armenians had this privilege) and were, therefore, restricted to the use of an adjoining chapel and entered the church through a side door. The dispute worsened when a silver star with Latin inscriptions went missing. The Catholics suggested, with some justification, that it had been stolen by the Orthodox clergy. They decided to use the 'theft' to raise the wider question of their rights and privileges and appealed to the French government for support.

These arguments were the culmination of an increasing rivalry between the various churches in Palestine. In 1845 the Orthodox Patriarch of Jerusalem moved his residence to the city from Constantinople, and two years later Pope Pius IX sent the Catholic Patriarch back to the city for the first time since 1291. The French government set up their first diplomatic representative in 1843 following the assertion by the Catholic Church of its right to rebuild the Church of the Holy Sepulchre in Jerusalem. As the intra-Christian conflicts escalated, the Ottoman government was forced to move in troops to separate the monks who were fighting around the Holy Sepulchre.

It was not until 1849 that the French government took up the cause of the Catholic clergy. It instructed its Ambassador in Constantinople to demand the 'restoration' of Catholic rights over the Holy Places, which, it argued, were defined in a treaty of 1740 made with the Ottoman government. The French were supported by some of the other Catholic powers of Europe – Portugal, Spain, Sardinia, Naples and Belgium (but not Austria). Belgium added its own demand for the restoration of the tombs of Baldwin and Godfrey (the rulers of the crusader kingdom of Jerusalem in the twelfth century, who came from Flanders). The French demanded that the Catholics should have equal possession of the sanctuary of the Nativity in Bethlehem, that their star should be replaced and they should also be allowed to place a tapestry in the grotto of the church. Second, they should have the right to 'repair' the main cupola of the Church of the Holy Sepulchre in Jerusalem so as to restore the building to its pre-1808 condition (which would remove the Orthodox Pantokrator from the dome). Third, they should also have the right to 'restore' the Tomb of the Virgin at Gethsemane. In response to these demands the Orthodox Patriarch of Jerusalem asserted his right to repair the Church of the Holy Sepulchre, and in making these demands he was supported by the Russian government. The dispute now involved two major European powers each supporting their respective churches (the Russian position was, they argued, supported by a treaty of 1776). The problem was that ultimately the different claims were irreconcilable, as the Russian minister in Constantinople reported to St Petersburg: 'The litigation is as old as it is complicated; no attempt to resolve it has proved successful; the titles are obscure and contradictory.'[1]

The Ottoman government saw little reason to become involved in a petty dispute between 'infidels' as long as it did not threaten their own position. Their main aim was to avoid committing themselves to either side. They played for time and suggested a commission of representatives of the three churches involved, which finally met in Jerusalem on 4 August 1851. Each side argued over the 'rights' supposedly granted in various documents dating back to 1776, 1740, 1686, 1528, 1453 and 636. The commission met until the end of October, when the Ottoman government suspended the talks, which were deadlocked. They decided that the Christians were too intransigent to settle the issue, so they set up their own commission composed of Islamic scholars and in October 1852 attempted to impose a settlement based on the work of these scholars. However, it could not be enforced. The Orthodox clergy refused to hand over the key to the main door of the Church of the Nativity and the Latin star was still missing. The engineer who was to start work on the cupola of the Church of the Holy Sepulchre did not appear and said only that he would consult all three groups before starting work.

By the end of 1852 the obscure dispute over the Holy Places had been rumbling on for five years. There seemed to be no reason why it should not continue in this way for a long time. Yet within six months Russia had invaded part of the Ottoman empire, and in less than a year the Ottoman empire and Russia were at war. By March 1854 Britain and France had joined that war. The conflict between the various Christian churches helped produce the first war between the major European states for forty years. It did so not because of the intrinsic merits of that argument (if there were any), but because the quarrel was deliberately escalated so that in the end fundamental strategic issues were judged to be at stake. The reasons for the Crimean War therefore have to be sought in the wider European situation.

Europe in the mid-nineteenth century

The somewhat surprising French interest in the position of the Catholic Church in Palestine stemmed from the outcome of the 1848 revolution. The revolution in Paris on 24 February that caused the monarch, Louis-Philippe, to flee to Britain was part of a wave of revolutions across Europe that year. Outside France the revolutionary wave was contained and then suppressed. In Paris a republic was proclaimed the day after Louis-Philippe's departure, but it was rapidly subverted by Louis Napoleon (the probable son of Napoleon Bonaparte's brother – his legitimacy was disputed). He became the Bonapartist heir in 1832 and attempted two badly botched coups in 1836 and 1840. In 1848 he was living in exile in Britain and was unable to take immediate advantage of the revolution. He became a Deputy in September 1848 and in December was elected President. Napoleon had considerable support within the army and in November 1851 he was able to make one of his main backers, Saint Arnaud, Minister for War. This was the prelude to a coup on 2 December when Saint Arnaud was able to crush resistance in Paris within a couple of days. Napoleon's long-term aim was to restore the empire of his uncle and this was approved by a plebiscite in late November 1852. On 2 December Napoleon was installed as Emperor (taking the title Napoleon III, which emphasised his descent from his uncle) in a ceremony in the Tuileries.

It was Napoleon who directed French policy over the Holy Places from early 1849 and escalated the dispute in order to curry favour with conservative Catholic groups in the period leading up to his coup. The chief reason, however, was diplomatic. Ever since the Congress of Vienna in 1815, France had been constrained by the so-called 'Concert of Europe'. This was a grouping of the conservative autocracies of Russia, Austria and

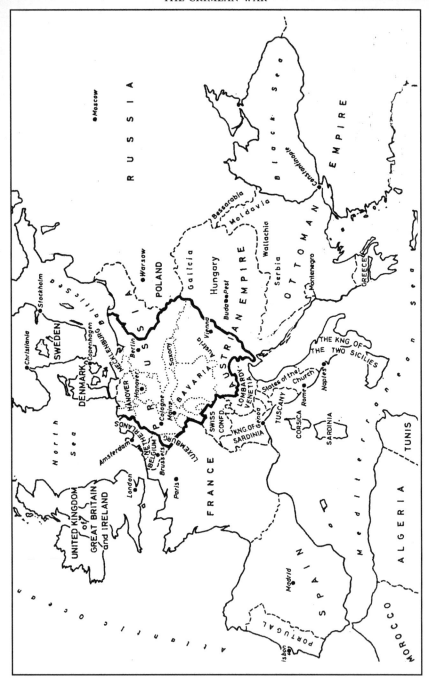

Map 1: Europe in the early 1850s

Prussia aimed at maintaining the 1815 settlement and, more important, defeating moves towards liberalism in Europe. It was still operating in 1849 when the Russian army supported the Habsburgs in putting down revolutionary movements in Austria and Hungary and re-establishing Austrian control over its Italian provinces (Lombardy and Venetia). All French governments since 1815 had tried to increase their room for manoeuvre in European diplomacy, but with only limited success. Napoleon did little more than place a greater emphasis on this effort. He realised that the Holy Places dispute could bring diplomatic gains. It would probably increase French influence in the Levant and, by backing the Catholic cause, would also split Catholic Austria and Orthodox Russia and therefore weaken the Concert of conservative powers. As Napoleon III's Foreign Minister told a friend:

> The question of the Holy Places and everything affecting them was of no importance whatever to France. All this Eastern Question which provoked so much noise was nothing more for the imperial government than a means of dislocating the continental alliance which had tended to paralyze France for almost half a century.[2]

France was the traditional enemy of Britain, and Napoleon's rise to power rekindled old emotions stemming from the wars of 1793–1815 (some of the British politicians in power in the 1850s were old enough to have served in the governments of that period). Following Napoleon's assumption of the imperial title in late 1852, the new government led by Lord Aberdeen expected war – not with Russia but with France. However, the main threat to Britain's strategic position came from Russia. The result was a contest between the world's greatest sea power and the world's strongest land power. They came into conflict in a number of regions across the globe ranging from the Arctic (the rivalry over the fur trade between the Hudson's Bay Company and the Russian-American Company, which still controlled Alaska) to the Pacific and from East Asia to the Baltic. However, the key area where the two powers collided was in the Near East. Russia had not yet conquered the Muslim states of Central Asia and so its threat to British control of India was prospective rather than immediate. However, they did clash over Persia, the Gulf, Afghanistan and, most important of all, the future of the Ottoman empire. Russia was the main expansionist power in the area in the late eighteenth century (it secured control of the Crimea in 1783) and in the early nineteenth century (as it slowly took control of the Caucasus region). Any further expansion of Russian power towards Constantinople would threaten British interests in the eastern Mediterranean and a push into

Persia would threaten the Gulf area. Both regions were regarded as vital for communications with India.

The Ottoman empire was the dominant power in the Near East – it still stretched from the frontiers of Hungary across all of the Balkans (except for the tiny kingdom of Greece), through Anatolia, the Levant and the Arabian peninsula to the frontiers of Persia. In theory it also controlled the North African coast (apart from Algeria), although in practice the rulers of this area were autonomous.

The so-called 'Eastern Question' remained of little importance in European diplomacy throughout the 1830s and 1840s apart from one significant development. The Straits Convention of 1841 closed the Dardanelles to warships of all states as long as the Ottoman empire was at peace. This not only stopped the Russian fleet from reaching the Mediterranean, but also ensured that Britain and France (the two powers with the strongest fleets in the Mediterranean) could not threaten Russian control of the Black Sea.

Given the vital strategic position of the Ottoman empire, its internal government was regarded as a fundamental issue for the other European powers. The empire was a multi-national, multi-religious unit that was governed through a high degree of autonomy for local groups and with only limited central government from Constantinople. The key feature was the *millet* system, under which each major religious group collected its own taxes on behalf of the central government and had jurisdiction over civil cases involving its own members. The heads of each of these groups (such as the Orthodox Patriarch of Constantinople) were responsible to the central administration and their appointment was subject to the veto of the Sultan. At the local, village level (nearly all villages were composed of a single religious group) leaders were elected and formed the local administration. The main religious groups that had their own *millet* were the Orthodox Church (which made up nearly one-third of the population of the empire), the Armenians and the Jews. The Catholics were too small to merit separate status and the minuscule Protestant population was granted a *millet* of its own in 1850 only as a favour to Britain.

The Ottoman empire had begun a major process of reform and modernisation in the 1820s and this had produced an effective army equipped with modern weapons. However, administrative reform was, potentially, extremely destabilising. Increasing centralisation threatened the power of local groups that had governed the empire for more than 400 years. Abolition of the *millet* system (which would produce a common citizenship) threatened Muslim supremacy within the empire. Britain tended to favour modernisation and the abolition of the *millet* system because it had nothing to gain from the latter. Russia, however, tried to exploit the existing *millet* system to its own advantage by supporting the Orthodox Church.

Russia was by far the largest of the European states and had been expanding westwards since the time of Peter the Great in the early eighteenth century. However, it was economically backward and a large proportion of its people were serfs owned by either the landowners or the state. Its government was an autocracy and policy was decided by Tsar Nicholas I, who had taken the throne in 1825 and savagely suppressed a military revolt aimed at liberalising some elements of the Russian state. Nicholas was a strong believer in autocracy, yet was easily swayed by his advisers who were old and mainly from a military background. The exception was the Foreign Minister Count Nesselrode who held the post from the late 1820s. He was a Baltic German who never spoke Russian correctly and was, remarkably, a member of the Anglican Church. Since 1829 he had advocated a policy of allowing a weakened Ottoman empire to survive so that a strong state did not threaten Russia's southern frontier.

Russia was in a poor condition by the late 1840s. It was continually threatened by peasant revolts and by nationalist uprisings in areas such as Poland and the Caucasus. The arbitrary system of government was only just able to keep control, and increasingly draconian censorship had been imposed from 1846 in an attempt to keep out ideas that might threaten its fragile stability. Most of Nicholas's advisers were out of touch with reality and still believed that Russia was a strong, prosperous state that could dominate Europe.

Russia creates a crisis

In late 1852 Russia escalated the Holy Places dispute, which had been rumbling along for five years. It did so for a number of reasons. First, the Ottoman decision in late November to grant the keys of the Bethlehem church to the Catholics seemed to favour France. Second, a revolt began in Montenegro following the imposition of an Ottoman governor as a replacement for the local ruler. Russia saw itself as the protector of the Orthodox population in these circumstances. Third, Napoleon's proclamation of the Second Empire and his assumption of the title Napoleon III at the beginning of December seemed a direct threat to the monarchical principle. The other European powers soon accommodated themselves to the new reality, but Nicholas was less willing to do so. Fourth, and perhaps most important, a despatch was sent from Constantinople by the Ambassador, Ozerov, on 13 December. This enclosed an appeal for support from the Orthodox Patriarch in Constantinople couched in emotional terms that suggested the end of the Church was nigh. Ozerov backed up this appeal by suggesting that a much stronger Russian policy was now necessary.

Russian policy was decided in the first days of 1853. Nesselrode argued for a continuation of his cautious policy. He did, however, go along with Nicholas's suggestion that a special envoy should be sent to Constantinople in an attempt to browbeat the Ottoman government into accepting Russian terms over the Holy Places dispute. Prince A. S. Menshikov, who had been a governor of Finland and Minister of the Navy since 1830, was selected for the role. He was a poor choice for a crucial diplomatic mission – apart from being old and ill, he was arrogant and extremely tactless. Nicholas also decided that Menshikov's mission was to be backed up by the threat of force. Two army corps were to be secretly mobilised and plans made to move them rapidly from Odessa and Sevastopol so as to capture Constantinople before the British and French could react. (In practice the Russian military could not carry out such an operation, but Nicholas was kept in the dark about this crucial fact.)

Nicholas also drew up a plan for a full-scale partition of the Ottoman empire. Russia was to gain the Principalities (roughly modern Romania and Moldova) and the northern part of what is now Bulgaria. Serbia and the rest of Bulgaria were to be independent. Austria was to be compensated by gaining Epirus and the Salonika area (even though these were claimed by the tiny independent state of Greece). Egypt and perhaps Cyprus and Rhodes would go to Britain, with France gaining Crete and the Aegean islands. Constantinople was to be a 'free city', though it would have a Russian garrison. The Ottoman empire was to be relegated to Anatolia. Almost nothing in this scheme would have been acceptable to the other European powers. The Tsar's plan makes no mention of the dispute over the Holy Places, which only increases the suspicion that it was no more than a convenient issue that might enable Russia to realise its longer-term ambitions.

The Menshikov mission

Prince Menshikov arrived in Constantinople on board the steamship *Thunderer* on 28 February 1853. He was accompanied by a large entourage of naval and military officers. His instructions were drafted earlier in the month, probably by the Tsar himself. The first part dealt with the Holy Places dispute. All concessions to the Catholics, apart from possession of the keys to the front door of the Church of the Nativity in Bethlehem, were to be withdrawn. The Sultan was to confirm all former grants to the Orthodox Church, create special rights for the Patriarch of Jerusalem and allow a new church and hospice to be built in the city under the control of the Russian Consul. These were extreme demands and, if granted by the Sultan, would have been seen as a humiliation for Napoleon III (which is what Nicholas wanted). Menshikov was instructed to offer the Ottomans a defensive alliance if they felt threatened by the French as a result of meeting the Russian demands.

It is unlikely that the Ottomans (let alone the French) could have accepted these terms. However, Menshikov's instructions contained a further crucial item. The Sultan was to issue a formal *sened* to confirm the status of the Orthodox Church and Russia's right to protect the Orthodox subjects of the Sultan. This demand was a fundamental attack on the sovereignty of the Ottoman empire and would, if implemented, give the Russians the right to intervene over the position of one-third of the Ottoman population and turn the empire into a subordinate state.

Menshikov was instructed that his demands were non-negotiable (Nicholas assumed that Britain was so anti-Bonapartist that it would not support France). He was to use bribery if necessary and present his demands shortly after his arrival. If the Russian demands were not accepted, Menshikov was to leave immediately. He failed to carry out his instructions and allowed the negotiations to drag on for almost three months. Because of poor communications, the governments in Paris and London were unaware of the demands the Russians were making. However, they suspected that Menshikov was determined to pressurise the Ottoman government. On 19 March Napoleon (supported only by Persigny, the Minister of the Interior) ordered the Mediterranean fleet, commanded by Admiral Aaron Regnault de la Suisse, to move from Toulon to Salamis near Athens. Napoleon hoped to force the British into similar action. At a meeting the next day a group of British ministers decided against sending the Mediterranean fleet eastwards from its base at Malta.

Menshikov was aware of the French military moves by 24 March and began to advise caution on St Petersburg. He suggested that Ottoman intransigence should be met not with an attack on Constantinople, but by the occupation of the Principalities (roughly modern Romania). The Russians had taken similar action in 1829–34 and 1848–51 without any adverse reaction from London and Paris. Menshikov was told to continue his mission as previously instructed.

On 8 April the Ottoman Grand Council met. Knowing that they had the tacit support of the British and French, they rejected Menshikov's draft *sened*. Menshikov asked for instructions and was told by St Petersburg to repeat the Russian demands. In parallel, negotiations over the narrower

Holy Places dispute were continuing in Constantinople. By early May they had reached a compromise acceptable to all. There was to be an Orthodox porter on the main door of the church in Bethlehem, but he was not to stop Catholic access. The Orthodox Patriarch was unable to regulate Catholic use of the Tomb of the Virgin, but the Catholics were limited to a daily service lasting not more than ninety minutes and this could only take place after both the Orthodox and Armenian services. The Ottomans would reconstruct the cupola of the Holy Sepulchre church in Jerusalem and the Orthodox clergy could make 'observations' about how this was to be done. The problem was that the original dispute over the Holy Places was no longer the central issue. On 5 May Menshikov gave the Ottomans an ultimatum. They were to accept the Russian demands for a wider authority over the whole Orthodox population within five days.

There is no need to follow the details of the complex diplomatic negotiations in Constantinople over the next two weeks. The government in Constantinople was clear that the Russian demands could not be accepted. The most that the Ottomans would offer was a reaffirmation of the status quo in the Holy Places (which favoured the Orthodox Church) and a *firman* setting out the *existing* privileges of the Orthodox Church. (A *firman* was an internal document granted by the Sultan and did not carry the significance of an international agreement contained in a *sened*.)

These terms were rejected by Menshikov on 18 May. He had left the embassy a week earlier and was now living on his steamboat *Thunderer*. The rest of the embassy (apart from the commercial section) was evacuated and on 21 May Menshikov set sail for Odessa. His mission had been a total failure and had served only to worsen the Russian position. On 22 May the eagles decorating the gates and façade of the Russian embassy were taken down, watched by a silent crowd of Orthodox Christians. The Russians had little support from the Orthodox population of Constantinople – they were content with their position in the Ottoman empire and did not want closer supervision by the Russian government.

The decision for military action

The consequences of the Tsar's ill-thought-out policy were now clear. Russia had made extreme demands, but with no idea of how they could be enforced. The Ottomans had rejected these demands and Nicholas regarded this as a severe blow to his prestige. He gave the Ottomans a final chance to accept the Russian terms under the clear threat that, if they refused, Russia would occupy the Principalities. If the ultimatum was rejected, the Principalities would not only be occupied but also declared independent (though obviously under Russian tutelage). Constantinople would be blockaded. Further military action was judged to be too risky because of the likely presence of the British and French fleets in the area.

The Ottoman government had also begun its own military preparations. A new state bank was founded in late May to organise the financing of a war. A short-term loan of £450,000 was raised on the London market. On 18 May all navy and army reserves were to be put on a war footing and mobilisation started. This process would take about three months to complete because of the size of the empire. The Ottoman government, even before it received the Russian ultimatum of 31 May, suspected that the Principalities would be occupied, but decided not to go to war over the issue because they were not yet ready.

In Constantinople the British Ambassador, the anti-Russian Viscount Stratford, quickly grasped the real nature of Menshikov's demands. He told London:

> If a treaty were to be concluded . . . the spiritual supremacy over the members of the Greek church would be entirely transferred to the Emperor of Russia. [These] functions not being limited to spiritual matters only, but extending also to temporal concerns, Russia would also interfere in all the temporal affairs of that Church.[3]

The government in London was much slower to understand what was happening. They had taken little interest in the dispute over the Holy Places because it did not involve a Protestant church (if anything they were sympathetic to the Orthodox position). However, Menshikov's departure was a clear sign of impending trouble and it concentrated their minds.

Aberdeen remained cautious and reluctant to make any moves that increased the likelihood of war. This partly reflected his hatred of the Ottomans and Muslims in general (a view he shared with most of his colleagues). In February he told Lord John Russell, 'These barbarians hate us all and would be delighted to take their chance of some advantage, by embroiling us with the other powers of Christendom.'[4] As the crisis deepened at the end of May he wrote to Sir James Graham, First Lord of the Admiralty, 'I should as soon think of preferring the Koran to the Bible, as of comparing the Christianity and civilization of Russia to the fanaticism and immorality of the Turks.'[5]

The British government was unsure what to do. The only military force it had available was the Mediterranean fleet, still at Malta. The hardliners (Lord Palmerston and Lord John Russell) wanted to send the fleet through the Dardanelles to Constantinople, even though this would be a clear breach of the 1841 convention because the Ottoman empire was still at peace. Aberdeen preferred to do nothing. The majority had no clear policy. The first step towards military intervention was taken on 31 May when Stratford in Constantinople was granted authority to summon the fleet if he thought it necessary. Once this power had been given, the fleet inevitably had to be moved nearer to Constantinople. On 2 June the Cabinet agreed that the Mediterranean fleet should leave Malta for Besika Bay near the southern entrance to the Dardanelles. The next day Napoleon ordered the French fleet to leave Salamis.

In many ways this compromise was the worst possible decision. As a gesture it was bound to alienate the Russians. Yet it provided no extra security for Constantinople – a Russian force could still sail there from Sevastopol in less time than the French and British fleets would take to arrive from Besika. (The fleets were 190 miles from Constantinople and the first third of the journey would have to be made against adverse winds and currents.) The Earl of Clarendon, Secretary of State for Foreign Affairs, told the Prime Minister that the government had little choice but to do something:

> I recommend this as the least measure that will satisfy public opinion and save the government from shame hereafter, if, as I firmly believe, the Russian hordes pour into Turkey from every side. It may do some good to ourselves, which should not be our last consideration.[6]

However, the Cabinet decided that a Russian occupation of the Principalities would not be treated as a declaration of war on the Ottoman empire – negotiations would continue.

Military action

During June there was little diplomatic activity as the consequences of the failure of the Menshikov mission were played out. The orders to the British Mediterranean fleet arrived in Valetta late in the evening of 7 June and it dropped anchor in Besika Bay early on the morning of 13 June, with the French ships arriving from Salamis that evening. (The stay in the bay was a disaster. Ships ran aground, there was an outbreak of malaria and the vessels were anchored in such a way that they could not use their guns.) The Russian ultimatum was delivered on 9 June and rejected by the Ottoman government on 16 June. The next day the archives of the Russian embassy were moved to Odessa. Ten days after that the final orders were issued to the Russian troops concentrated along the south-western frontier with the Ottoman empire – they were to invade the Principalities on 2 July.

On 2 July 1853 about 50,000 Russian troops of the 4th and 5th Corps, commanded by Prince Gorchakov, crossed the frontier into the Ottoman empire. On 15 July they reached Bucharest where Gorchakov set up his headquarters. He was instructed not to cross the Danube and not to deploy troops near Serbia (the Tsar thought either action would alienate Austria). The Russians soon established control over the Principalities. News of the occupation reached Constantinople on 7 July, but the Ottomans decided they needed more time to complete military preparations. They were wary about further negotiations – they knew the Russians opposed direct talks and were worried that any intervention by the other European powers would only compromise their position. They decided to play for time. The defences of Constantinople were improved – four battleships and eight frigates were moved into position and thirteen forts with more than 300 guns were fully manned. The ruler of Egypt sent 10,000 troops, three battleships and six other vessels by the middle of August, and the Bey of Tunis despatched a fleet of four frigates and a steamer.

The failure of diplomacy

Ottoman reservations about how they would be treated by the other European powers were fully justified. The Russian escalation of the crisis began a frantic round of diplomatic activity, much of it centred on Vienna. The Austrians began to play a central part in the negotiations because their interests were directly affected by the developing crisis. They opposed any expansion of Russian influence in the Balkans, and the occupation of the Principalities involved an area of key strategic importance for the Austrians. Austria wanted a diplomatic settlement because war would present it with an unpalatable series of choices. It did not want to see a Russian victory, yet if it allied with France and Britain it would probably gain little and be left isolated to face the hostility of Russia after the war. France was also Austria's enemy because Napoleon seemed likely to favour an Italian revolt to drive Austria out of the north of the country. The Austrian Foreign Minister, Buol, therefore chaired a conference of Ambassadors in Vienna (Britain, France and Prussia took part) in an attempt to find a compromise proposal that would satisfy the Russians and avoid war.

The common thread in these talks was that the four European powers (together with Russia) ought to settle the issues between themselves and give the Ottomans no alternative but to accept the outcome. They believed without question in their right to negotiate in what they decided was the best interests of the Ottoman empire, and were shocked when they discovered that the Ottomans had a different view of the matter.

By the end of July 1853 the talks in Vienna had produced a 'compromise' plan, even though Buol already knew that the terms were not acceptable to the Ottomans. Russia accepted the plan on 6 August. It did so for three reasons. First, the proposals were almost an endorsement of the Russian terms that Menshikov had put to the Ottomans. Second, they seemed like an Austrian ultimatum, and the Russians did not want to alienate Austria. Third, Russia expected the other powers to force the Ottomans to accept the proposals.

The Ottomans thought the Vienna proposals gave away all of the position they had established during the negotiations with Menshikov. In mid-July they told the Ambassadors of France, Britain, Austria and Prussia that they would not alter their position 'never to make a diplomatic engagement with Russia relative to the privileges of the Greek Church' because such an action would be 'a death sentence for the Ottoman Empire'.[7] The Ottoman government rejected the Vienna note on 18 August and suggested its own redraft, which was in turn rejected by Russia.

The European governments, in particular the British, could not understand the differences between the Vienna and Ottoman proposals. They failed to see why the Ottomans should object to supranational control of their religious and secular affairs. In addition they believed the Ottomans should gratefully accept the terms that the Christian powers had negotiated on their behalf. During August they lost patience with the government in Constantinople. On 5 August Clarendon told Aberdeen, 'I begin to think we shall have as much trouble with the Turks as with the Russians.'[8] Three weeks later Clarendon said, 'The Turks seem to be getting more stupid and obstinate every day.'[9]

However, the British soon began to realise that they faced an awkward dilemma. They had supported the Ottomans so far and moved the fleet. Could they now retreat without losing face merely because the Ottomans would not accept the Vienna note? After all, the threat from Russia was still real. As Clarendon told Lord Cowley, the Ambassador in Paris:

> If we abandon Turkey which we should have a right to do so [sic] on her rejection of our advice we make her at once the prey of Russia which Austria would then join, if we support her it will be in her wrong and against our own advice . . . I have at no time felt more uneasy about the final solution than I do at this moment.[10]

Gradually opinions within the Cabinet began to harden as they realised that they could neither force the Ottomans to accept the Vienna note nor abandon them in the face of the Russian threat.

In September the diplomatic situation deteriorated still further. A Berlin newspaper published a note written by a Russian Foreign Office official, Labenski, about the Vienna and Ottoman proposals. This made it clear that the Russians interpreted the Vienna note as giving them the right to interfere in the internal affairs of the Ottoman empire. These developments left the British government in an even more awkward situation. They decided that since they could not force the Ottomans to accept the Vienna note, they would, in the last resort, have no choice but to support them in whatever policy they adopted. They could not be seen to give way in the face of Russian pressure and they could not afford to wait until the Russians and Ottomans were at war before moving the fleet to Constantinople, even though this would mean breaching the Straits Convention of 1841. As Clarendon put it, breaking the treaty was 'far preferable to anything like a retreat'.[11] As an interim measure two British and two French warships were moved to Constantinople under the guise of delivering important messages. On 19 September the French proposed that both fleets should now move to protect the Ottoman capital and three days later the British agreed.

Events in Constantinople during September demonstrated just how little control the British and French had over the drift to war. The Ottoman government decided that acceptance of the Russian demands (even as marginally modified by the other European powers) would give Russia an effective protectorate and mark the end of the empire as an independent state. General resentment was also expressed about the humiliating way in which all the Christian powers treated the Ottomans. The consensus was that they had little alternative but to fight and that, although there was no guarantee of British and French support, it was likely that they would, eventually, provide help. This would represent the most favourable possible circumstances for a war with Russia. On 29 September Sultan Abdul-Mejid accepted the recommendation for war; 40,000 army reservists were mobilised. War was not declared – instead, on 8 October Russia was given an ultimatum to evacuate the Principalities within two weeks. The British and French Ambassadors waited until the expiry of the Ottoman ultimatum before requesting the British and French fleets to move to Constantinople. Instructions were sent to Besika Bay on 20 October and the fleets began to move two days later. Because of bad weather it was nearly a week before they arrived at the Ottoman capital.

In London the Prime Minister, Aberdeen, looked back over the events of the previous months and realised just how far the British had been manipulated by the Ottomans. He told the Chancellor, William Gladstone:

The Turks, with all their barbarism, are cunning enough, and see clearly the advantages of their situation. Step by step they have drawn us into a position in which we are more or less committed to their support. It would be absurd to suppose that, with the hopes of active assistance from England and France, they should not be desirous of engaging in a conflict with their formidable neighbour. They never had such a favourable opportunity before, and may never have again.[12]

Queen Victoria took a similar view, telling Clarendon, 'we have taken on ourselves in conjunction with France all the risks of a European war without having bound Turkey to any conditions with respect to provoking it'.[13] The failure of British diplomacy was complete.

On 7 October the Cabinet held its first meeting for six weeks. They agreed that the fleet could move from Constantinople into the Black Sea once Russia attacked Ottoman territory. The problem for the British and French was that they had no idea what sort of war Russia and the Ottomans would fight and what their own strategy would be if they joined the war. They were not even formally allied with the Ottomans or with each other. How could they ensure the security of the Ottoman empire let alone fight Russia?

War

The Russians ignored the Ottoman ultimatum and made no effort to withdraw from the Principalities. Tsar Nicholas I told Menshikov (now in command of Russian naval forces in the Black Sea) that the Ottoman fleet was to be destroyed if it left Constantinople. Russian troops were not to cross the Danube, but an attack in the Caucasus region was to be launched with the aim of capturing Kars, Ardahan and Bayezid. Orders from Constantinople reached the Ottoman commander, Omer Pasha, at Shumla late on 22 October. He was to start military operations immediately. Omer Pasha was a remarkable example of the multi-national nature of the Ottoman empire. He was a Croat, Michael Lattas, who had joined the Austrian army but deserted in 1828 after he committed a minor offence. He emigrated to Ottoman territory, converted to Islam and adopted his new name. He spoke three languages fluently and became a tutor to the Sultan. He then joined the Ottoman army and achieved rapid promotion. He was a Colonel by 1839 and soon established himself as the most able of all the Ottoman commanders.

The Ottoman army was successful in the first military operations. There had been skirmishes along the Danube front from early September, and on the day war was declared the Ottomans captured the St Nicholas fort. Their main aim, however, was to stop any Russian thrust towards Serbia, which might start a revolt by the Orthodox population. On 27 October 10,000 Ottoman troops crossed the Danube and captured Kalafat, the key to the route to Serbia. Russian troops were under orders to do no more than contain any Ottoman advance. A week later on 2 November more Ottoman troops crossed the Danube and captured the quarantine house at Oltenitsa. This was the first stage of an intended operation aimed at recapturing Bucharest. The local Russian commander decided to ask his superior, General P. A. Dannenburg, for instructions. By the time orders to attack arrived on 4 November the Ottoman troops were well entrenched. A badly directed Russian attack left 970 soldiers dead or wounded. However, the Ottomans did not have enough troops for an attack on Bucharest and decided to withdraw from Oltenitsa on 15 November. The Russians were more successful on the Caucasus front. On 1 December a Russian force of 10,000 troops under General V. I. Bebutov defeated a far larger Ottoman army at the battle of Başgedikler. The survivors fled to the city of Kars.

The most significant action took place at sea. The Ottomans, knowing they had the British and French fleets to back them up, began a series of missions in the Black Sea. In early November the large frigate *Nuzretieh* left Constantinople with Admiral Slade (the British adviser to the Ottoman navy) on board. The conditions on the ship during a severe winter storm were terrible. The crew survived on a diet of biscuits, rice, olives and water, and had only summer clothing to wear. Gratings were fitted over the hatchways to stop them going below deck, even after several inches of snow fell on 11 November. The ship eventually returned to Constantinople without having encountered any Russian vessels. The main Ottoman fleet sailed in mid-November for Sinope, the only decent harbour on the north Anatolian coast. The problem was that this anchorage was only about 200 miles from the main Russian naval base of Sevastopol, but over twice that distance from Constantinople. Russian ships were spotted, but the fleet stayed at Sinope even after four steam frigates passed through on their way back to Constantinople from convoying supplies to Ottoman troops on the Caucasus front. They could have escorted the fleet back to base. The Russian ships under Admiral Nakhimov waited until six large warships and two frigates arrived from Sevastopol as reinforcements. Even then the Russian ships were outgunned by the Ottoman ships, although the latter were anchored in the bay and unable to fire all of their guns. The shore batteries at Sinope were also ineffective – some of the guns in the forts dated back to the fifteenth century when the Genoese had controlled the area. The Russians attacked at 11.30 a.m. on 30 November. The only surprise was that it took them nearly two hours to destroy the Ottoman fleet. The Russians lost no ships and only thirty-eight dead and 235 wounded. Ottoman losses are unknown – some sailors swam ashore and deserted. Altogether the toll may have been as high as 4,000 men. Much of the town was destroyed during the bombardment, although the Russians were careful to aim at the local quarter and not the European sector. Only one Ottoman ship, *Taif,* was able to escape and brought news of the battle to Constantinople on 2 December.

The initial operations of the Russian-Ottoman war now came to an end. Fighting had begun very late in the campaigning season and winter made significant operations impossible. The armies along the Danube front stayed in their winter quarters, and storms across the Black Sea made any substantial naval activity too dangerous. Initial success along the Danube made the Ottomans less willing to compromise. Despite victories at Sinope and Başgedikler, the Tsar wanted a major military success to restore Russian prestige.

The destruction of the Ottoman fleet at Sinope produced outrage in the British and French capitals. It was denounced as a 'massacre', even though it was a perfectly normal operation of war. Both governments were under pressure to take some action to restore their credibility. The British Cabinet was badly divided. Palmerston resigned as Home Secretary, ostensibly about Lord John Russell's proposals concerning electoral reform. (He rejoined the Cabinet within a fortnight.) Russell was himself urging a tough policy, and Aberdeen suspected that he and Palmerston wanted to bring down the government over the issue. The British were also under pressure from the French, who advocated allowing the allied fleets to undertake offensive operations in the Black Sea. The British Cabinet agreed to this policy after a five-and-a-half hour meeting on 22 December. The Cabinet knew that this decision would, almost inevitably, lead to war with Russia. The Russians could not allow the British and French to establish naval supremacy in the Black Sea, although they were disobliging enough not to declare war on Britain and France.

During this hiatus, although Britain and France were actively preparing for war against Russia, there was one last chance for diplomacy to work. The French certainly seemed to be trying to avoid a war. Indirect contacts with Russia were under way in Paris via the Saxon minister, Baron Seebach, who was Nesselrode's son-in-law. British suspicions seemed to be confirmed when Cowley was unable to stop Napoleon III sending a personal letter to Nicholas I on 29 January 1854. In it he suggested a mutual withdrawal of forces – Russia would evacuate the Principalities and the British and French fleets would leave the Black Sea. Then there would be a Russian-Ottoman peace treaty that would be submitted to the four 'neutral' powers (Britain, France, Austria and Prussia) for approval. The Tsar refused to consider a proposal that might well have split Britain and France.

On 12 January 1854 the British and French Ambassadors in St Petersburg informed the Russian government of the instructions given to their navies in the Black Sea: Russian ships would be treated as hostile if they ventured out of port. This was a provocative policy and designed to be so. On 6 February the Russian Ambassadors in Paris (Kiselev) and London (Brunnow) suspended diplomatic relations and left for home. The British and French Ambassadors (Seymour and Castelbajac) in St Petersburg were then instructed to leave. The Tsar acted first by expelling Seymour. As a gesture, Castelbajac was awarded the Order of St Andrew and his wife was given a present by the Tsarina.

The final actions in the drift to war were played out in slow time because the British did not want the conflict to start until the Royal Navy could operate in the Baltic at the end of March as the winter ice broke up. On 27 February the British and French governments issued an ultimatum to Russia to withdraw from the Principalities – they had made no formal protest, nor taken any action eight months earlier when Russia had invaded. They could not even agree on the date by which the Russians were to do this. Britain asked for withdrawal by 15 April, France by 30 April. Because diplomatic relations had been suspended, the documents had to be taken by courier across Europe and did not arrive in St Petersburg until 14 March. The Russians were given six days in which to reply but did not bother to do so. On 12 March a general alliance between Britain, France and the Ottoman empire was signed. The formal British and French declarations of war on Russia were made on 27 and 28 March. On 12 April the 'old enemies' Britain and France signed an offensive and defensive alliance to last for the duration of the war.

In February 1853 (just before Menshikov arrived in Constantinople) the Prime Minister, Aberdeen, told Lord John Russell: 'we ought to regard as the greatest misfortune, any engagement which compelled us to take up arms for the Turks.'[14] Yet within a year this was exactly what Britain was doing, and in alliance with the one power it regarded as its real enemy – Napoleonic France. A deeply disillusioned Aberdeen, who too easily discounted the determination of Russia to secure a religious and secular domination over the Ottoman empire, reflected on the failure of his government's policy:

> The independence and integrity of Turkey was a phrase which had no meaning . . . Peace might have been made half a dozen times over

if Turk more reasonable and not under the influence of fanatical party acting in the belief that, having England and France to back them, it was a grand opportunity for them to fight Russia.[15]

2

Strategy

The powers involved in the general war that began at the end of March 1854 had very different military capabilities stemming from their different traditions, societies and economies. In addition they all faced major strategic dilemmas in trying to fight an effective war and in defining their war aims. The Crimean War was shaped by the fact that neither Russia nor the allies could inflict a devastating defeat on their opponent.

In the early 1850s the great wave of industrialisation that was to transform nearly all European societies by the end of the century was still in its initial stages. Britain, the most industrially developed of all the European states, still had about half its population living in the countryside even though it produced half the world's industrial output, consumed two-thirds of the world's coal production and made five-sevenths of the world's steel. Britain had 6,600 miles of railways, more than the rest of Europe combined, but steam power was still in its infancy in many areas – Britain had twenty times more sailing ships than steam-powered ones. Britain was far wealthier than any other state in Europe – its income per head was probably three times that of Russia – but its population at twenty-six million was smaller than that of France or Austria and less than half that of Russia. Although Russia was by far the largest European state, it was poor and economically backward – it had only 400 miles of railways (all around St Petersburg and Moscow).

European armies and navies

Although Russia had the largest army in the world with a peacetime strength of well over one million its effectiveness was low. The French army had almost doubled in size since 1847 to a strength of about 450,000. It was by far the best-equipped and trained army in Europe. It also had extensive combat experience from the long wars fought since 1830 to secure control of Algeria. The British army was, in theory, slightly larger than that of France, but the biggest part was the Indian army with its indigenous contingent that was unavailable for service elsewhere. Britain had only about 100,000 men for colonial and home defence.

At sea, Britain was the predominant naval power. The Royal Navy was larger than those of Russia and France combined, although the latter matched it technologically. The problem for Britain was that two-thirds of the Royal Navy was deployed outside home waters and the Mediterranean – it was scattered around the globe in West Africa, the Cape, South America, the Caribbean, the Pacific and in South-East Asia. The Russian fleet was at a low technological level and, although it was capable of overawing minor powers, it could not take on either the British or French fleets.

All navies were affected by the rapid changes in technology following the development of the first steam-powered ships in the early 1820s. The earliest were paddle steamers and therefore of limited military effectiveness. It was the development of the screw propeller that marked a significant step forward. The first steam battleship with a screw propeller, *Napoleon,* was under construction in France in 1848, followed by the British *Agamemnon* the next year. Both ships were launched in 1852. By the outbreak of war the British had eight and the French nine such ships in operation – they were the only ones in the world. Each of these ships could carry 90–100 guns. The main problem lay in the armour of these vessels. Iron ships had been rejected as impracticable in the 1840s and so the new steam-powered ships had wooden hulls with only light armour protection. This meant that although they were faster, more manoeuvrable and better armed than sailing ships, they were still highly vulnerable to the fire of coastal fortresses. This was particularly the case following the development of the explosive artillery shell that replaced the cannon ball.

Although the Royal Navy was by far the largest in the world, it was in a poor state. Ships were under-manned in peacetime and there was no reserve from which crews for the additional ships needed in war could be found. Most captains recruited their own crews from whatever source they could. The press gang was still legal, though in practice not used. (Smugglers could be, and were, impressed for five years.) Men still served in bare feet and their pay was usually months, if not years, in arrears. There were no formal arrangements for shore leave (it was a privilege, not a right), but men could leave a ship when its tour of duty ended. The men received no benefits and there was no chance of promotion to officer. Discipline was harsh, with flogging commonplace. About 2,500 men deserted every year. Most officers joined as children – some were under ten and served as 'captain's servants', but the more normal recruitment age was thirteen as a Midshipman. (In June 1854, just after the outbreak of war, the dominant figure of the Royal Navy in the early twentieth century, Admiral 'Jacky' Fisher, joined as a Midshipman.) All of the senior commanders were old – promotion was strictly by seniority and Admirals usually died in service. At a junior level only a few officers had any experience of warfare.

European armies – technology

The key technology that fundamentally affected the battles of the Crimean War was the invention of an effective rifle. Until the 1840s European armies were still using weapons that were little more than variants of the musket first used in the sixteenth century. These were of very limited range and, because they were muzzle-loading, their rate of fire was low. The rifle was known, but its use was restricted to snipers because its increased accuracy did not compensate for the very low rate of fire. It was the development by the French of the Minié rifle in the late 1840s that proved to be crucial (the British adopted the weapon in 1851). This rifle was easy to use and reliable and its bullet was capable of much greater penetration than existing weapons. In the Napoleonic Wars only about one bullet in 450 had any effect. In the Crimea this figure was reduced to one in sixteen. The key advantage of the new weapon was its much greater range of least 800 yards.

The infantry now had a weapon that significantly changed the balance on the battlefield. Cavalry took about three minutes to cover 800 yards, yet in this time the infantry would be able to fire between twelve and sixteen times, all with effective bullets. The maximum range of field artillery was about 600 yards, but now they could be put under infantry fire. Although breech-loading artillery would soon change this position, the Crimean War was fought with weapons which meant that the cavalry and artillery operated under severe difficulties on the battlefield. Possession of the Minié rifle was, therefore, the key to success even though tactics were only slowly changing to take account of the new weapon. By the outbreak of war all of the French and most of the British infantry were equipped with the weapon. However, Russia had just 6,200 rifles for an army of well over one million men. They would be fighting at a severe disadvantage.

Cavalry remained, for social reasons, the elite part of all armies, but its effectiveness was severely limited. Although equipped with the long lance this was of limited use and the sword was useful only once the cavalry had broken up infantry formations. The new revolver (demonstrated by Colt at the Great Exhibition in 1851) was too heavy and not very reliable. The cavalry charge depended on little more than discipline and courage. In the British army galloping was forbidden until within 250 yards of the enemy and the charge was only sounded when forty yards away, so as to retain maximum shock and impact. The limitations of cavalry as a weapon were painfully apparent to British and French commanders – the cavalry were kept to the flanks (where they might be able to charge the enemy from side-on) and their main function was reconnaissance. Their major disadvantage (as became apparent to the British in the winter of 1854–55) was the huge amount of forage they required. Although artillery were under a severe disadvantage facing infantry equipped with rifles, they were still effective against cavalry. In a cavalry charge lasting about eight minutes (as happened at Balaklava in October 1854) the artillery could fire almost twenty rounds – more than enough to cause very heavy casualties.

The British army

The French army was undoubtedly the most effective in Europe. The British army was, in terms of its organisation and methods (if not its technology), far behind its new ally. Since 1815 the army had not been organised to fight a European war – its role was primarily the defence of India and the colonies and home defence against an expected French invasion. Until his death in 1852 the Duke of Wellington dominated the army either directly or through subordinates who had served with him in Spain and at Waterloo. They were unwilling to challenge his ideas or change his methods. His influence was particularly malign during the 1840s when he served as Commander-in-Chief. He was increasingly senile, showed little interest in the quality of the troops or their training and resisted all change.

Soldiers enlisted for twenty-one years (only four years less than the serfs of Russia) and, if they survived, received a pension of one shilling a day. Over half of all recruits came from Scotland and Ireland and joined because of poverty and the lack of any alternative employment. Usually they received just two meals a day – a monotonous and unbalanced diet of one pound of meat and one pound of bread (the rest they had to buy and cook themselves). Married men lived with their wives and children in dormitory-style barracks, but few wives could accompany the men on overseas tours (which usually lasted for more than ten years). The main activity in peacetime was drinking – on average one in eight soldiers was arrested every month for drunkenness. Discipline was harsh. Flogging was still the rule, although the maximum number of strokes that could be imposed was fifty (it had been 1,200 in the 1820s). Deserters were still branded on recapture. At any one time 3,000 soldiers were in military prison – they were kept in solitary confinement and did ten hours' hard labour a day. Not surprisingly nearly 2,000 men a year deserted, almost all of them new recruits.

The officers of the army were drawn overwhelmingly from landed and titled families. A private income was essential, and dress, behaviour and code of conduct were the most important aspects of an officer's life. Pay was poor (only Russian officers were paid less), but officers could retire on half-pay after just three years' service and still be promoted without serving in the army. In the early 1830s there were nearly 10,000 officers on half-pay compared with fewer than 7,000 serving in the army. The scheme was little more than a state subsidy to the landed class. Commissions and promotion could be bought in the infantry and cavalry. A regulation price was fixed in 1821 but usually ignored. To buy the rank of Lieutenant in the infantry cost £1,000, that of Lieutenant-Colonel £7,000. Guards regiments were more expensive (and socially exclusive) because they normally only served at home and had about eight times more chance of promotion. Promotion in the infantry and cavalry was normally by purchase rather than merit – about half of all officers had bought their promotions. The result was that inexperienced and ineffective officers from wealthy families promoted themselves over the heads of their more experienced and able, but less wealthy, colleagues. The purchase system did not apply in the artillery and engineers where promotion was by seniority. This produced a different problem – by 1854 half the Lieutenant-Colonels in the Royal Artillery were aged over sixty and in the Royal Engineers the proportion was two-thirds. About half of the full Colonels had joined the army in the eighteenth century. These two regiments were the only ones where a military education was required. However, such officers could not serve as staff officers with commanders. The prevailing attitude towards education was exemplified by the Duke of Wellington when he gave evidence to a parliamentary committee in 1836. He thought military education was 'unsound' and said he preferred 'the education usually given to English gentlemen'.[1]

Given the class nature of the officer corps, ordinary soldiers did not normally become officers. The Duke of Wellington argued that such men 'do not make good officers . . . they are not persons that can be borne in the society of the officers of the Army; they are men of different manners altogether'.[2] The officers had minimal contact with ordinary soldiers, little sense of duty towards them and generally despised them. As Henry Clifford (the third son of Lord Clifford of Chudleigh) wrote in October 1855:

> What a mistake to over-pay a *soldier*! You must not look upon a soldier as a responsible agent, for he is not able to take care of himself, he must be fed, clothed, looked after like a child and given just enough to make him efficient as a part of the great machine for

War. Give him one farthing more than he really wants, and he gives way to his brutal propensities and immediately gets '*drunk*'. Taken from the outcasts of Society . . . He is only kept in order by strict discipline.[3]

The major problem for the army was the lack of organisation and infra-structure for contemporary warfare, particularly against other European powers. Although there were small groups of officers who argued for reform, in general complacency ruled. In 1853 full-scale manoeuvres were conducted for the first time at Chobham camp. They were a disaster, with officers unable to control their units and no clear lines of command. No test was made of the support and logistic services. Nevertheless, the *United Service Magazine* commented:

> How is it that after forty years of peace, the organization of our troops should be so much more perfect than it was after some twenty years of constant warfare? Most soldiers degenerate – ours have improved in every way.[4]

The experience of warfare in the Crimea proved these remarks to be hopelessly optimistic. Eighteen months later, after nine months of war, Prince Albert painted a gloomy picture of the real state of the British army:

> We have . . . no general staff or staff corps; – No field commissariat, no field army department; no ambulance corps, no baggage train, no corps of drivers, no corps of artisans; no practice, or possibility of acquiring it, in the combined use of the three arms, cavalry, infantry, and artillery; – No general qualified to handle more than one of these arms, and the artillery kept as distinct from the army as if it were a separate profession.[5]

The Ottoman army

Until British and French forces could move to the east, the Ottomans had to rely on their own resources in fighting Russia. The army had been reorganised and modernised in the 1830s. Conscription for a five-year period provided the *nizam* or front-line army, which totalled about 150,000 men. In 1853 plans were laid to recruit an extra 75,000 front-line troops, but these took time to implement. Reservists served for seven years and formed the *redif*, which was the same size as the *nizam*. In addition there were the armies from the provinces that numbered about 700,000, but these were of low quality and were not normally used outside their own provinces. The final part of the army comprised the irregulars or *bashi-bazouks*. These were mainly cavalry units who received arms and ammunition, but no uniforms or pay – they lived off the loot they acquired. Overall the total effective strength of the Ottoman army (excluding most of the provincial forces) was about 400,000.

The regular army was well armed. About a quarter of the infantry were equipped with the latest rifles – a much higher proportion than in the Russian army. The artillery had the latest British and French guns and was as effective as any in the world. The Ottoman army was strong defensively and showed itself well able to cope with the Russian attack in the early summer of 1854. However, it lacked the strength to defeat the numerically superior Russian army. The main problem area in the Ottoman army lay in support and organisation. The troops were only paid intermittently and supplies of food regularly broke down, leaving the troops to fend for themselves.

Russian forces and strategy

Russia had by far the largest army of all the European powers, but much of it was ineffective. In total the regular army numbered just over one million men, which was about the maximum the country could support because of the low productivity of its serf-based agriculture. About 80,000 serfs were conscripted every year and served for twenty-five years. It was effectively a life sentence and the sole reward was that the soldier and his family gained their freedom from serfdom at the end of service (a major reason why general conscription could not be implemented). A large proportion of the recruits did not survive to gain their freedom – in the twenty years before the outbreak of the Crimean war more than one million army recruits died as a result of disease, campaigns in the Caucasus, desertion and in training.

As in the British army, discipline was harsh and soldiers spent most of their time drilling on the parade ground. Junior officers were not allowed to exercise any initiative and therefore the Russian army was inflexible on the battlefield. It still marched in the old-fashioned oblong column, which was easy to control, but poor in combat because only the first two ranks could engage the enemy. Like the British army, it also lacked an effective general staff for planning and command. In both armies staff functions were provided by a small group of officers (mainly aides-de-camp) around the commander who were usually chosen for their social connections. The commanders themselves were, like their counterparts in the British army, old and generally incompetent. The Russian commander in Europe was Field Marshal Ivan Paskevich, a seventy-two-year-old veteran of the 1812 campaign against Napoleon. He was indecisive, but respected by Nicholas I. The commander in the Crimea, Prince Alexander Menshikov, proved to be as poor a General as he was a diplomat. His replacement, Prince Michael Gorchakov, was probably even worse.

In the Russian army these weaknesses were exacerbated by technological backwardness, especially in the infantry, which was mainly equipped with smooth-bore, muzzle-loading muskets, some of which still used the ancient flintlock rather than percussion system. These weapons had a range of little more than 200 yards compared with four times that for the British and French rifles. In addition they could only fire about two rounds a minute at most – about half the rate of the modern rifle. This meant that the Russian infantry was at a severe disadvantage in combat – it had to rely on the bayonet, assuming it ever got near enough for close combat. However, the Russian artillery was as modern and effective as that of the British, French and Ottomans.

The technological inferiority of the Russian army was made worse by major logistic and strategic problems. The huge size of the country and its appalling communications system – there were no railways south of Moscow – meant that it was very difficult and extremely time-consuming to move troops around from one area to another. In addition a large part of the army had to be used for internal political control and suppression of the frequent peasant uprisings. A significant part of the army also had to be used for training the annual recruit levy and maintaining communications. The result was that little more than half of the army could be deployed for operations. Many of these had to be used for static defence. About 270,000 were stationed around St Petersburg in case of a British or French attack on the capital. Another large garrison had to be left in Poland to deal with any revolt by the local population and to combat any Austrian invasion from Galicia if they joined the war. This meant that only about 50,000 troops could be deployed in the Crimea and it would take many months for reinforcements (if they could be spared) to march across Russia to assist them.

From the autumn of 1853 the Russians tried to increase the size of the army by levying six extra drafts of serfs from all of the provinces. By October 1854 nearly 340,000 men had been drafted, and this rose to more than 460,000 by the spring of 1856. This was almost twice the normal rate of recruitment and could not be sustained for long without risking widespread peasant discontent and opposition from the landowners who were losing the workforce on their estates. The men also took a long time to train and deploy to the front line. Serfs were not, under a law dating back to 1742, allowed to volunteer for the army – the permission of their landlord, who owned them, was required. This prohibition was repeated in an order of the Tsar in March 1854. However, the next month an order was issued for the recruitment of a naval militia to defend the Baltic coast. The volunteers would serve until November when the freezing over of the Baltic would make them redundant. Rumours about the recruitment of a militia spread across the countryside, where the peasants believed that if they volunteered they would, like army recruits, be freed from serfdom, even though they would only serve for the duration of the war. Tens of thousands of peasants walked to cities across the country to volunteer; they were immediately returned to their estates. Others moved on Moscow, where more than 1,400 had been imprisoned by July 1854. The city jails were full, the authorities ran out of leg-irons for the peasants and the imperial riding school had to be used as a temporary jail. By the late summer the movement was over and the peasants were returned to serfdom.

Given their poor military capabilities, Russian strategic options were bound to be limited. The occupation of the Principalities in the summer of 1853 was successful, but it was unclear whether a further advance across the Danube was feasible. Nevertheless Nicholas I decided that this was the only feasible military option in the spring of 1854 before the British and French armies were available for operations. Given the technological inferiority and relative size of the Russian navy, it could not challenge the British and French fleets. It could not venture out of port and could only be used for the immediate defence of strategic points such as Sevastopol in the Crimea and Kronstadt near St Petersburg. Overall Russian strategy would be defensive. Its main asset was the sheer size of the country and the difficulty that its opponents would face in trying to achieve a major strategic victory. The crucial doubt concerned how long the country could sustain a substantial war before social and economic problems produced a major crisis.

British and French war aims

In the spring of 1854 the two new allies tried to decide what their objectives would be in the war with Russia. In public Clarendon said, 'We enter upon the war for a definite object. It is to check and to repel the unjust aggression of Russia . . . and to secure a peace honourable to Turkey.'[6] These were minimum and negative aims designed to stop Russia gaining Constantinople, thereby making the Black Sea a Russian lake, allowing it to dominate the Caucasus and giving its fleet access to the Mediterranean. In private Clarendon told Aberdeen, 'The war was undoubtedly, defensive in its character at the commencement . . . but now England and France have taken part in it on European grounds and for the defence of Ottoman territory, the character of the war is changed, and we are fighting for a state of things which will render peace durable.'[7] The Prime Minister was, however, suspicious about grandiose and vague ideas. He told a colleague, 'I have recently heard much of securing the independence of Europe, the progress of civilization, and the overthrow of barbarism. These are objects too vague to be easily understood, or practically to regulate our proceedings.'[8]

The two politicians with the widest war aims were Napoleon III and Palmerston. To some extent Napoleon had already achieved his diplomatic aims before the war started – a break-up of the Austria–Russia axis and an alliance with Britain. He certainly had wider strategic aims, but whether they could be achieved in any likely war with Russia was more doubtful. Napoleon dabbled with the idea of creating an independent Poland, with Prussia gaining territory in north Germany as compensation. His main objective was to weaken Austria in northern Italy, where Lombardy and Venetia would pass to Sardinia (France would, as 'compensation', gain Nice and Savoy from Sardinia). Austria would be compensated with the Principalities even though the war was supposedly being fought for Ottoman independence and integrity. Palmerston put a similarly far-reaching scheme to his Cabinet colleagues on 19 March, a week before the war officially began. He advocated giving Finland and the Åland Islands to Sweden, and the 'German' provinces of Russia along the Baltic coast to Prussia. In addition an independent kingdom of Poland would be established. The Principalities and the Mouths of the Danube would go to Austria – which would, however, lose northern Italy, which would either become independent or part of Sardinia. The Crimea and Georgia would go to the Ottomans as compensation for the loss of the Principalities, and the Caucasus would either become independent or be under nominal Ottoman control.

The two schemes were remarkably similar, but neither could be achieved unless Russia suffered a major defeat. How this was to be accomplished was unclear. France and Britain could not inflict such a defeat on Russia on their own. Palmerston wanted to use his scheme to tempt other powers – Austria, Prussia and Sweden – into the war. A major Austrian and Prussian land attack into western Russia might be sufficient to achieve such a comprehensive victory. Palmerston told Clarendon in January 1854 that 'it would certainly be necessary to summon Austria and Prussia to declare themselves and to take one side or the other'.[9] However, neither

Napoleon nor Palmerston considered whether these powers would be willing to fight such a major war in order to bring about a radical reconstruction of the European order. They were essentially conservative powers with a strong interest in the status quo. Without the assistance of Austria and possibly Sweden, it was difficult to see how Britain and France could achieve a major victory over Russia.

British and French war plans

Neither the British nor the French had a clear idea how they were to fight a war with Russia. Inevitably, a major area of operations would have to be around Constantinople and the Black Sea to ensure that the Ottomans were not defeated. The British, not surprisingly, preferred a naval strategy and expected their major campaign to be in the Baltic during the summer of 1854. The French preferred a land strategy, but the British realised they could make little contribution in this area. Nevertheless when Napoleon offered the British overall command of the British and French fleets, with France taking control on land, the British rejected the idea.

The British began building up a fleet to send to the Baltic in the winter of 1853–54, but the problem was finding an adequate army to send to the east (the Ottomans were promised in February 1854 that British and French forces would be sent). At the end of January the Cabinet agreed to the recruitment of 10,000 extra sailors, 3,000 marines and 12,000 soldiers. Twelve regiments were recalled from the colonies as troops began to leave for Malta and the east at the end of February. The government had no idea how many troops would be needed. Russell thought a force of 10,000 (half-French and half-British) would be more than enough to defend Constantinople. Other estimates suggested 50,000 would be the absolute minimum. At the end of April the government agreed to add another 15,000 men to the army and 5,000 to the Royal Navy. But these were notional figures for which money was provided – it was unclear whether the necessary men could actually be recruited. The French with their much stronger and more professional army were able to provide seasoned troops and commanders from Algeria as the core of their force being sent to the east.

The first stage of Anglo-French strategy was relatively easy to decide. Constantinople and the surrounding area would have to be secured and only then could wider operations be contemplated. At the end of January the seventy-two-year-old General Sir John Burgoyne (the illegitimate son of the General Burgoyne who surrendered at Saratoga during the American War of Independence), the Inspector-General of Fortifications, travelled to the east via Paris. In the French capital he and Napoleon agreed on the priority of defending Constantinople. Burgoyne was accompanied on his mission by two French Colonels – Charles-Prosper Dieu and Paul-Joseph Ardant. Once the trio arrived at Constantinople, their estimate of how many troops would be required rose rapidly from 9,000 to nearly 90,000 (two-thirds of which would have to be French because the British could not find many more than 30,000 troops at most).

Meanwhile Britain, as a naval power, was most interested in the destruction of the Russian naval base at Sevastopol, which was seen as the key to Russian power in the area. Graham, the First Lord of the Admiralty, who was central to the evolution of British strategy, told Clarendon at the beginning of March:

> My opinion from the beginning is in unison with the Emperor's. The Dardanelles must be secured; a position in front of Constantinople fortified covering both the city and the Bosphorous; but *the* operation which will be ever memorable and decisive, is the capture and destruction of Sevastopol. On this my heart is set: the eye tooth of the Bear must be drawn: and 'til his fleet and naval arsenal in the Black Sea are destroyed there is no safety for Constantinople, no security for the peace of Europe.[10]

However, Graham had already made it clear to his Cabinet colleagues that Britain's ability to determine strategy would be limited by its lack of a large army. He was, he told them, 'anxious to abate any extravagant expectation' that by naval means alone it was possible to 'humble the pride of Russia or strike any decisive blow'. He added, 'It is not in the power of England to strike a decisive blow to the heart of Russia in either of these seas [Baltic and Black]'.[11] A naval reconnaissance of Sevastopol carried out in early January by Captain James Drummond on board *Retribution* reported 'the fortifications so strong as opposed to ships that it would be impossible to enter the Harbour and destroy the ships at anchor without the almost certain destruction of the attacking force'.[12] The base could only be captured by an army – and how that army was to be landed and sustained in the Crimea was unclear.

The great advantage the British and French had in despatching forces to the east was the use of steamships from Marseilles to the Bosphorous. The voyage took about twelve to sixteen days (one-fifth of the normal time for sailing ships) whereas the Russians took months to march troops to the Crimea. Graham, who thought fighting alongside the French was 'unnatural', refused to use British ships to transport French troops. He told Clarendon, 'It may not be amiss to let them [the French] feel that armies in perfect fighting order are not carried across seas without immense difficulty and enormous cost.'[13] (It was obvious which sea Graham had in mind.)

During February and March, as troops moved east, no decision had yet been made on how they would be used once they had landed somewhere near the Dardanelles, probably at Gallipoli. One possibility was to move them to the Danube front to support Ottoman troops. The port of Varna seemed to be a possible base. When Burgoyne arrived in Constantinople he inspected the defences of the city and was satisfied with the Ottoman system. He left on 9 March for Varna. It took him one and a half days to travel the fifty-six miles to Shumla in a four-horse open carriage provided by Mr Colquhoun, the former British Consul at Bucharest. Burgoyne held a series of discussions with Omer Pasha, the Ottoman commander, and recommended Varna as a suitable base for British and French forces. He reported that 'it was a healthy country; that it would be easy to obtain there any amount of supplies'.[14] This assessment was soon to be proved wildly optimistic.

The commanders of the British and French forces left in mid-April, although their instructions were still hopelessly vague. On 12 April Napoleon told Marshal Saint Arnaud, 'Either march and meet the Russians on the Balkans, or take possession of the Crimea or, again, disembark at Odessa or at any point on the Russian coast of the Black Sea.'[15]

The next day the Secretary of State for War, the Duke of Newcastle, sent the British commander, Lord Raglan, his instructions:

> I fear you will think [your instructions] less full and explicit than you desire – but the more I have been compelled to think upon the subject the more I have become convinced that any attempt to lay down any detailed plan of action for your guidance (even if I were capable of making one) would hamper your discretion.[16]

Meanwhile Burgoyne did write a detailed memorandum for Raglan following his visit to the east. Once a firm base at Gallipoli was established and Constantinople was secured, it would be possible to think about offensive operations. Burgoyne thought, correctly, that Ottoman forces would be able to contain the Russian offensive along the Danube. Varna was a possible base, but Burgoyne then gave a warning about operations in the Crimea:

> With regard to any attack on Sebastopol, it can have little strength as a fortress, and its fate will depend upon the power of obtaining

firm possession of the Crimea, an attack on which must be well considered before it is undertaken. No operation is of such doubtful issue as the landing in an enemy's country for the purpose of conquest. Modern, and British history in particular, is full of disastrous failures in the attempt, and those which have succeeded have been, generally, most hazardous.[17]

Burgoyne's warning was, within a few months, to be ignored with dreadful consequences.

3

The Baltic: 1854

The British, as in the past, preferred to rely on their financial and economic strength, fight a naval war and leave their ally to fight the Russian army. The declaration of war on Russia had been timed to coincide with the break-up of the winter ice in the Baltic, and the British decided that it was here that they would fight their major campaign in 1854. Indeed for the first five months of the war it was the scene of the only real fighting between the allies and Russia.

The problem the British faced was in providing an effective force to fight in the Baltic. They lacked suitable ships, were unable to provide trained crews and the commanders available to them were of poor quality. The Royal Navy's most efficient unit – the Mediterranean fleet – was required for operations in the Black Sea. The fleet that sailed for the Baltic did contain some modern warships – five steam battleships, four steam blockships, four screw frigates and three paddle-driven frigates – but they were far from ideal for operations in the shallow waters they would encounter. To cope with these conditions a fleet of minimal-draught gunboats and mortar ships was needed, but the Admiralty disliked these vessels and had always preferred to use its resources to increase prestige by building battleships. In the year prior to the outbreak of war no attempt was made to order shallow-draught ships, and half-hearted attempts to buy some gunboats being built for Brazil in the shipyards along the Thames came to nothing. Graham, the First Lord of the Admiralty, spent the summer of 1853 touring the defences of the Channel Islands (designed to deal with a French attack) and thought that gunboats could be bought in Sweden and Denmark when the fleet arrived there.

The British had only very limited intelligence about Russian defences in the Baltic area. For example, it took them six months to discover that the Russian squadron at Reval had moved to Sveaborg in the autumn of 1853. Captain John Washington visited Denmark, Sweden and Russia in August and September 1853 and gained some basic information. The Russians, surprisingly, were willing to show him round the defences of their main naval base in the Baltic – Kronstadt near St Petersburg. British charts of the area were inadequate and there were no surveying vessels or crews available.

The fundamental British problem lay in providing crews for the ships of the Baltic fleet. Although the power to press-gang men into the navy still

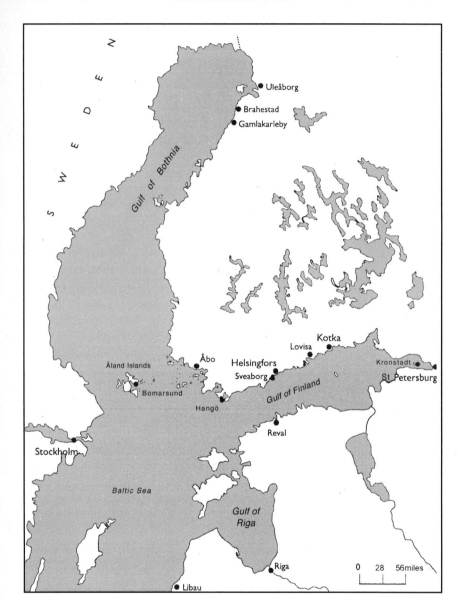

Map 2: The War in the Baltic

existed, the government decided it was too unpopular to use. Few men would transfer from the merchant navy because conditions in the Royal Navy were so bad. This meant that the government had to rely on a motley collection of volunteers and old reservists drafted unwillingly from coastguard units. Creating efficient crews in a short period of time was an almost impossible task. At the end of May 1854 Captain Byam Martin of the *Nile* wrote:

> It is a melancholy thing to see the poor old men . . . dragged from the coastguard stations to man the navy. They are too old to learn, and too stiff to move; sending them aloft would be murder . . . I was more than ever struck with the badness of the crew of this ship; so many infirm old creatures and so many raw uncouth savages from inland! It is a hopeless task.[1]

The situation on one ship was typical. *Monarch* sailed with just eight trained able seamen out of a crew of 850. When the ship left for the Baltic it was described as 'badly manned . . . abominably so. None are fit to go into action.'[2] No reinforcements could be sent to the Baltic because no more men could be found to provide crews. The commander of the Baltic fleet was advised to try and recruit extra men at Swedish and Danish ports. When *Cumberland* returned from three years on the North American station, the crew demanded a period of shore leave. Instead they were given three months' pay and towed out to sea by the Admiralty yacht *Black Eagle* and forced to sail to the Baltic. When other ships returned from long spells abroad, the crews were paid off and disbanded in order to avoid a repetition of these events. For several months the Baltic fleet had to spend its time undertaking exercises – ships could not keep station and there were numerous collisions until basic seamanship was mastered.

These problems were exacerbated by the choice of commander for the expedition. Because of the size of the fleet, and the participation of French units, the government decided that only a full Admiral or Vice-Admiral would be appropriate. Only two Admirals were available. The seventy-nine-year-old Lord Dundonald volunteered, but was rejected because the Cabinet felt he was on the verge of insanity. The command was offered to Sir William Parker, who had commanded the Mediterranean fleet until 1852, but he declined, arguing that he was too old at seventy-three. His decision meant that the choice lay between two Vice-Admirals. Sir George Seymour, the commander of the North American and West Indies squadron, could not be recalled in time. This left the sixty-seven-year-old Sir Charles Napier as the only option. No minister was happy with this choice. Napier was short-tempered, abusive and had an over-developed sense of his personal honour. These qualities were made worse by his alcoholism. It was for exactly these reasons that he had been passed over for command of the Mediterranean fleet in 1852. However, the government was not prepared to promote a junior officer over him and he was therefore the only choice available. Graham, who had known Napier since 1814, consoled himself by hoping that Napier's reputation for insubordination might turn him into a second Nelson. He was to be sorely disappointed.

The strategic situation

Potentially the Baltic could be an area of significant Russian weakness because of the threat of a Polish revolt. However, St Petersburg was heavily defended with about one-third of the combat battalions of the Russian army deployed in the area. In total there were more than 270,000 men to defend the Baltic region. In these circumstances any landing by an allied army would probably result in failure. Such a prospect was only theoretical because the allies did not have an army available for such an operation. The small British army was already deploying to the east and the French 'Army of the North' at Boulogne lacked transports and could only provide about 10,000 men for limited attacks.

The Russians expected to have to defend the Baltic (British intentions were hardly a secret) and they started preparations in early 1854. On paper the Russian navy looked impressive – the Baltic fleet was composed of 196 ships including twenty-five major warships. However, there were no steamships and training was so poor that the fleet could not operate as a unit. Apart from the gunboats that might provide some coastal protection, the fleet was ordered to stay in port. This meant that Russian defences were concentrated around their two main, fortified bases – Kronstadt and Sveaborg (modern Suomenlinna in Finland). However, these bases were not well defended. Some of the guns at Sveaborg dated back to the 1790s and the local foundries could only make two guns a day. As Rear Admiral Matyushkin reported:

> Materially and in the art of using our artillery we belong to the last century . . . if the enemy knew that we have at our disposal only nine guns firing shell and few other guns we have and the weakness of the wall they would be able to destroy everything this autumn . . . But Sveaborg's undeserved reputation has led the enemy to postpone their attack until they receive more reliable information . . . Very few

of our projectiles will reach the enemy, but on our side a good deal will be burned and destroyed.[3]

Nevertheless some precautions could be taken. Coastal lighthouses were extinguished and navigational markings were removed or deliberately misplaced. A new telegraph line was installed from Kronstadt to Hangö and observation posts set up along the Finnish coast – they were manned by five men with two horses kept permanently saddled. A major limitation on Russian preparations was their fear of revolt as British and French forces approached. In early March the Tsar decided that all non-Russian and non-Orthodox landlords should be deported from the Baltic area. The order was eventually cancelled after the German nobility organised 'spontaneous' patriotic demonstrations and sent their sons as 'volunteers' to the Russian army. In Finland the government decided it was safe to establish a small marine corps of 500 men to crew a force of gunboats, and in June 1854 a temporary militia was set up to meet any allied landings.

Sweden and Denmark

Given the limited allied capabilities, it was extremely unlikely that a purely naval operation could inflict a significant defeat on Russia. The key to a successful Baltic campaign therefore appeared to lie with Sweden and Denmark. Of the two states, Sweden was by far the most important and it seemed possible that it could be tempted to join the war. It had lost Finland and the Åland Islands to Russia in 1809 and it had a long-standing quarrel with its neighbour over Finnmark, the area of northern Norway bordering Finland (Norway being still part of Sweden at this time). Sweden had a very effective navy – more than 350 gunboats that could provide exactly what the British needed – and an army of some 120,000 men that would pose a real threat to Russia, particularly in Finland. The Swedish government was badly divided over what policy to adopt. The liberals, the press and Crown Prince Oscar were strongly anti-Russian and favoured joining the allies, particularly if the right terms could be obtained. However, King Oscar I was much more cautious. He did not trust the British and French, believing – with some justification – that they would leave Sweden in the lurch to face a hostile Russia after the war was over. Before joining the war he wanted not just firm guarantees of allied support, both diplomatic and military, but also the assurance of Austria joining the allies to create a wider European war that would ensure a major defeat for Russia.

The position of Denmark was even more difficult. Like Sweden it was internally divided, with the conservatives sympathetic to Russia because of

Russian support for Denmark in its recent war with the German states over Schleswig and Holstein. A treaty of 1852 also gave the Russians the key role in the selection of a new Danish royal family if the current line died out, as seemed likely. Liberal elements in the country tended to favour the allies. Denmark was weak militarily and could not afford to take part in any war. Economically it was dependent on Britain, particularly for its coal supplies, and it still feared a repetition of the British attacks on Copenhagen in 1801 and 1807. Equally it feared Prussia. If Prussia joined Russia in the war, it might repeat its recent attack, but if Prussia joined Britain and France, it might be rewarded with Danish territory.

During the spring and summer of 1853, as the prospect of war between Britain, France and Russia grew, the two Scandinavian states consulted about what they could and should do. In March Sweden told its neighbour that its policy would be one of neutrality, that it might fight Russia (though any such decision would be put off for as long as possible), but that it would never join Russia in a war with Britain. In the middle of June the Danish Royal Council, chaired by King Frederick VII, decided that the only possible policy was neutrality. On 26 October both states declared their intention to remain neutral. However, the exact terms on which this would be done were still to be settled. Denmark and Sweden decided they had little choice but to open their ports to belligerent ships, even though this would be a pro-allied move, with the Russian fleet confined to port. Russia complained about this policy in public, but privately told the Danish government that it understood why the decision had been made. The Danish government took only limited military measures so as not to alarm Prussia. About 20,000 troops were concentrated in Zealand to deal with any British attack, but there was no call-up of reservists or use of conscription. Danish pilots did act for British warships until they were stopped by their government, and four Danish officers did serve with the French navy in the Baltic until they were recalled. The Swedes kept their main forces – nineteen major warships under Admiral von Krusenstjerna and 6,500 regular troops reinforced by a 10,000-strong militia – concentrated around Gotland.

The main allied aim was to see whether they could gain Sweden's support for the 1854 campaign. In the last week of March, as the British fleet sailed towards the Baltic, the French envoy in Stockholm, Charles-Victor Lobstein, opened negotiations with King Oscar I. He was joined on 25 April by Sir Charles Napier, commander of the Baltic expedition. The most the British and French would offer was a return of the Åland Islands and the King rejected this as grossly inadequate. Negotiations resumed in mid-June when Oscar I met two French envoys, Colonel Blanchard and Captain Karth. The French asked Sweden to provide 60,000 troops and

200 gunboats to support allied operations. The King asked for a sub-stantial subsidy to finance the Swedish war effort and 60–70,000 allied troops. Blanchard (without any authority from Paris or London) offered a subsidy of six million francs a month and an army of 100,000 troops – there was no possibility that the latter could ever be provided. However, when it seemed possible that Austria might join Britain and France in the war, the Swedish government discussed its strategic options during a four-day conference at the beginning of July. General Carl Gustav Löwenhjelm produced a plan for landing 60,000 troops in Latvia, but Oscar thought the Swedish public would demand the 'liberation' of Finland. Eventually Sweden's terms were put to the allies. They were a 'return' of Finland, a guarantee of the new enlarged Sweden, and a subsidy of five million francs a month. Sweden would require 60,000 French troops to fight alongside its army in Finland, Austria was to join the war (and agree to the enlargement of Sweden) and Sweden was to participate as a full member of the peace conference. In return, Sweden offered to provide 60,000 troops, four major warships and 192 gunboats. The French were prepared to negotiate on this basis, the British were not – they were not keen on detaching Finland from Russia, correctly guessed that Austria would not join the war and resented the French taking the lead in the negotiations. The allies were, however, agreed that the campaigning season was now too far advanced for Sweden to offer anything substantial for 1854 and any decision should therefore be postponed until the 1855 campaign took shape.

The fleet departs

The war in the Baltic would, therefore, be conducted by the British and French navies with only limited military support and no other allies. Its chances of success were slim. Nevertheless it left in a blaze of enthusiasm and optimism. On 7 March 1854 a dinner was held at the Reform Club for Admiral Napier, and grandiose speeches from Palmerston, Graham and Napier himself all promised success and a decisive defeat for Russia. When the fleet sailed from Spithead on 10 March (slightly ahead of schedule because the British Consuls in the Baltic reported an early break-up of the winter ice) it was seen off by Queen Victoria and Prince Albert. Napier was on board his flagship, the 131-gun *Duke of Wellington*, in command of forty-four vessels with a total of more than 2,000 guns. Success seemed assured, as *The Times* reported:

We have equipped and despatched from our shores an armament

such as the world has never seen equalled, and not unworthy of that
supremacy which we claim to hold upon the ocean . . . It must not be
supposed that the fleet which we are thus sending from our shores
exhausts our naval strength . . . our dockyards and private establishments could enable us to show the world results at least twice as
great as those the last few months have yielded . . . The power and
fortunes of England sail with her navy. That force . . . must exercise
an important influence upon the future history of a reign hitherto
unprecedentedly prosperous and peaceful. Whatever betides, we
have sent out stout ships, manned by stout and willing hearts,
propelled by the same agency which has so incalculably increased
our internal resources, and commanded by a gallant Admiral who is
not likely to lose any opportunity that may present itself of having
his name inscribed in the book of fame with those of Nelson and the
other heroes whose victories have established our supremacy upon
the seas.[4]

By 20 March the fleet was anchored just south of Copenhagen and ready
to begin operations.

The first task was to secure the Danish Sound against any attempt by
Russia to move its fleet into the North Sea to attack British shipping and
possibly even threaten Britain itself. The Russians had neither the capa-
bility nor the intention of carrying out any such operation, although
Napier was ordered to use force to stop them even before the official
declaration of war. On 29 March, following the outbreak of war, Napier
was ordered to declare a close blockade of the Russian coast so that
merchant shipping could be captured. He was also to carry out a reconnaissance of the major Russian fortifications (in early March a British
frigate, *Miranda*, had navigated through the fog and ice as far as Reval),
but Napier took no immediate action.

Within a couple of weeks the campaign had developed into a stalemate.
The Russian fleet wisely avoided a major action by staying in port. The
wooden ships of the allied fleet were too vulnerable to fire from coastal
batteries to risk a major attack on the Russian fortified bases. Much of the
time in April was spent trying to turn the British fleet into an effective
fighting force. In the first week the crew of the flagship *Duke of
Wellington* rioted off Copenhagen and destroyed the mess utensils.
Desertion rates were high. Progress was slow. The Captain of *Royal
George*, Edward Codrington, reported at the end of April that 'method,
arrangement, lead, and above all, nerve is wanting'.[5] Napier rapidly
alienated his senior commanders by his methods. Captain Henry Keppel
wrote to his sister Polly at the end of May that Napier 'frequently says he

is much too old for this sort of work and most assuredly speaks the truth when he says so. As it is, he is irritable, finds fault with everybody and everything and is most unjust in his censures.'[6] The suspicion grew among his senior officers that Napier's heavy drinking was badly affecting his performance.

Meanwhile the logistics for the operation were being established. The British encountered, for the first time, a major problem with the new steam-powered warships – the need for huge quantities of coal to keep them operational. A coaling base was set up in the sound between Gotland and the small island of Fårö (Sheep Island). The area had deep, sheltered water and was away from the main area of operations. Buildings were erected and within a few weeks nearly a hundred colliers and twenty supply ships were at the base. A large number of locals were employed and the base provided considerable short-term prosperity for a poor, isolated community. The negative effects were discovered later in the year when an outbreak of cholera led to the deaths of more than a hundred merchant seamen and an unknown number of locals. Communications with the fleet were set up through a weekly Foreign Office courier to Danzig, where despatches were exchanged every Friday. Private letters (including those from Graham at the Admiralty to Napier) went via the normal Post Office channels and naval transports, at a cost of one penny each. Graham was worried about the reports from the fleet giving details of its operations. What he did not know was that Napier himself was acting as a correspondent for *The Times*. At the end of April Napier wrote to the Editor, John Delane, asking for his local correspondents to get in touch because 'I will be able to give them news from time to time'. However, Napier was worried about the safety of his own correspondence, telling Delane, 'Be cautious in alluding to this letter – the news you get can always come from your own correspondent. Direct to me for the present to Copenhagen under cover to Mr Ryan, for I believe my letters are opened.'[7]

Early operations

Napier sailed from Kioge off the Danish coast on 12 April and four days later was at the entrance to the Gulf of Finland. Poor weather affected the area until the end of the first week of May, and Napier used this as an excuse for inaction. He claimed that he was justified in this by the fact that in 1808–09 the British fleet had not entered the Gulf until July, forgetting that he was now equipped with steam-powered ships that could overcome the unfavourable conditions. However, his orders from Graham at the

Admiralty advised caution and gaining control of the Gulf of Finland as a first objective. Graham added:

> I by no means contemplate an attack either on Sweaborg [sic] or Cronstadt [sic]: I have great respect for stone walls, and have no fancy for running even screw line-of-battle ships against them because the public here may be impatient . . . you must not risk the loss of the fleet in an impossible enterprise.[8]

Although Graham was being cautious, some action beyond the establishment of a blockade was expected from the Baltic fleet.

Napier decided to conduct a series of raids on the towns along the Gulf of Finland. In the orders he was given on 29 March, Napier was told, 'on no account to attack defenceless places and open towns, but to confine your efforts to the reduction of forts and batteries'.[9] Rear-Admiral Sir James Plumridge, who conducted the operation, ignored these orders. George Giffard, the Captain of Plumridge's flagship, the paddle frigate *Leopard*, said that the aim was 'to show the people the misery war caused for all sides'.[10] The result was a wave of destruction in the coastal towns. On 16 May Libau (Liepaja in Latvia) was attacked and local ships towed away to provide prize money for the crews. Brahestad (modern Raahe) was burnt to the ground on 30 May, followed two days later by Uleåborg (Oulu) at the head of the Gulf of Bothnia. Tornea was burnt and destroyed on 8 June. In most of the attacks British casualties were minimal, but the attack on Gamlakarleby (Kokkola) on 7 June went badly wrong. Plumridge undertook the attack with two ships (*Vulture* and *Odin*) and when their small boats headed for the shore, they came under fire from Russian infantry and Finnish militia. British losses were fifty-two men killed, wounded and taken prisoner and the boat from *Vulture* was captured (it can still be seen in Kokkola).

Overall the operation was a disaster. Although Plumridge continually referred to the population of the towns as Russian, they were overwhelmingly Finnish and therefore potentially unsympathetic to the Russians. The destruction of their towns, and in particular of the small sailing ships and fishing boats on which the locals relied for their livelihood, merely increased Finnish resentment of the British. Goods worth an estimated £400,000 (about £20 million at today's prices) were destroyed. Most of these items belonged not to the Russians, but to British merchants who traded in the area. *The Times* was deluged by letters of protest. Napier tried to disown the operation, but his popularity started to fall rapidly.

The Baltic: 1854

Kronstadt

By early June, almost three months after the fleet left Britain, little had been achieved – even the blockade was only partially enforced. Officers in the Baltic fleet were losing confidence in Napier almost as rapidly as the government. Keppel wrote to his brother-in-law on 6 June, 'The gallant old [Napier] . . . has lost lately, by his vacillating conduct and evident reluctance to advance, much of that confidence we had in him when we started, he is too old and too prejudiced to ancient warfare to make proper use of and appreciate the wonderful power of steam.'[11] The French fleet of twenty-six ships under Vice-Admiral Alexandre Parseval-Deschênes reached the entrance to the Gulf of Finland on 12 June. At the same time a series of private yachts, owned by various members of the British elite, also joined the fleets to watch any action that might take place. Among them were *Gondola* (Lord Euston), *Esmerelda* (Lord Lichfield), the steam-powered *Vesta* (Lord Newborough, together with his cook and his mistress disguised as a 'housemaid') and *Pet* (Reverend Robert Hughes). In addition a number of other ships carrying personal supplies of food for the officers of the fleet arrived. Much of their time was spent pleasantly exchanging visits and dinners with the French officers.

On 20 June Napier sent a gloomy report to Graham. He had established the blockade and had carried out a reconnaissance of Sveaborg (this was an exaggeration), but the base could not be captured without strong military support. He suggested that he might sail to Kronstadt, but the Russian fleet would not give battle and ships would be unable to destroy the fortifications (as Graham himself had recognised at the beginning of May). The other possibility was an attack on Bomarsund, the main base on the Åland Islands. While London considered these possibilities, the British and French Admirals decided they had better do something other than cruise around the entrance to the Gulf of Finland. On 22 June the two fleets began the move to Kronstadt, where they arrived four days later. The allied ships (which had no charts of the area) found they could not approach from the north because the water was too shallow, while the southern passage was through a narrow, winding channel protected by eight forts with about 1,000 guns. The fleet took soundings and made some charts. The Russian court, including the heir apparent (Nicholas's son Alexander) and his wife, came out from nearby St Petersburg to watch. A young maid-of-honour, Anna Tiutcheva, recorded in her diary, 'I am very grateful indeed to the English for providing us with an excuse for such a pleasant outing.'[12] After a few days of desultory activity the British and French fleets withdrew, having achieved almost nothing.

Bomarsund

Captain B. J. Sulivan conducted a reconnaissance of the Åland Islands in early June and his report was sent to London by Napier as part of his message of 20 June. On 2 July Graham told Napier that the Cabinet had considered the state of the operations and, 'being of the opinion that the presence of the Allied Fleet in the Baltic must be marked by some result', had proposed a series of joint operations to the French. Graham went on, 'I am disposed to begin with Bomarsund, but you and the French Admiral must decide.' This base was important because it could be held as a bargaining counter to be used with the Swedes, but an attack on Sveaborg was another possibility.[13] Napier and Parseval-Deschênes agreed that Bomarsund should be the objective, but they had to wait until troops arrived from France.

The French troops from the 'Army of the North' began embarking at Calais on 16 June when 5,000 men left on four British sailing battleships, each towed by British paddle steamers. (The French had to pay the British for this operation.) Three days later another 4,000 men left on six transports and an iron-hulled merchant ship, *Prince*. Two French battleships carried the siege artillery and the engineers. The commander, General Baraguay d'Hilliers, travelled out later on Napoleon III's private yacht *Reine Hortense*. The British abandoned the blockade of the Gulf of Bothnia and Admiral Plumridge moved his ships to the north of the Åland Islands to intercept any Russian reinforcements. The ships carrying the troops arrived off the islands at the end of July, where they met up with the allied fleet. (Napier was instructed that the four battleships that had been towed from Calais were not to be risked in the shallow waters around Bomarsund and were to return to Britain immediately.) On 2 August all the British and French senior officers sailed round Bomarsund on a reconnaissance on board the *Reine Hortense*. They discovered that the Russian defences were minimal. The islands had been ceded by Sweden in 1809, but the Russians had not begun to construct any fortifications until 1829. Although the ultimate aim was to threaten Stockholm, by 1854 only three of the fourteen planned fortified towers had been completed and they provided no coherent defence. The islands had a garrison of just over 2,000 men commanded by Major-General J. A. Bodisko, but they had been cut off for months by the British blockade and were short of ammunition and food.

The last part of the French forces arrived on 5 August. The 9,000 French troops were joined by a small force of 900 British marines. They started landing, without resistance, shortly after 3 a.m. on 8 August. (The Russians had already withdrawn their troops from the earth fort on

Grinkarudden and brought all their forces within the stone towers.) The bulk of the French troops – the Chasseurs de Vincennes, the 2nd Light Infantry Regiment and the 3rd, 48th and 51st Regiments – landed on the south of Bomarsund, while the 2,000 remaining French troops and the British marines landed on the north. Two days later the artillery were landed (the French had fifty horses, but the British relied on sailors to haul the guns). During the operation the Royal Navy ship *Penelope* ran aground in front of the Russian forts. It was under fire for almost four hours from 11.30 a.m. and could only be refloated after all the guns and equipment had been thrown overboard. A number of British Captains left their battleships, which were supposed to be guarding against any sortie by the Russian fleet, and went ashore to watch the fighting. They either hired or commandeered carts and carriages and camped out on the island to follow the siege.

On 14–15 August two outposts surrendered, bringing the French guns within 800 yards of the main fortress. Thirteen battleships and frigates moved into position offshore. The bombardment on the morning of 16 August was sufficient to produce a Russian surrender by 1 p.m. Drunken Russian troops looted the officers' quarters before the French arrived to restore order. Overall casualties in the operation were slight. The British lost three killed and thirteen wounded, the French thirty-eight killed and wounded. The Russian casualties are unknown, but are likely to have been higher than those of the allies. The British and French also had to deal with just over 2,000 prisoners of war. The women attached to the garrison were left on the island and were subsequently picked up by a Russian paddle steamer. Some of the men remained behind too – they were left to starve by the local population who hated the Russians. The rest were divided between the British and French. Eventually some 360 prisoners were sent to Lewes in Sussex. Fifteen officers were allowed to live in the town on parole, while the men were accommodated in the reconstructed prison. (Twenty-eight died before they were released in 1856.) Although the British and French always referred to these men as 'Russian', they were nearly all Finns and Åland islanders from the local militias.

The capture of Bomarsund was, apart from any impact it might have on domestic opinion, an irrelevance. The British and French already knew that the Swedish price for entering the war was one they were not prepared to pay and therefore the islands could not be used as a bargaining counter. They were offered to Sweden on 19 August, but King Oscar declined the gift. He believed that taking them would simply alienate the Russians who might counter-attack during the winter, once the Baltic froze. (The Swedes did, however, organise tourist trips to the islands from Stockholm for what was left of the summer.) The only option left to the allies was to destroy the remaining fortifications. Ships were moved in, but even at a range of just 500 yards were unable to accomplish any significant destruction. The towers of Prästö and Notvik were blown up by the army, followed, on 2 September, by the main fort. The French troops then withdrew. The allied operations left the local population in a precarious position. The administration collapsed after the allies took the local sheriff, Carl Lignell, prisoner and refused to release him. After the withdrawal of the troops the filth they left behind caused an outbreak of cholera, which killed about 150 locals. The Russians were soon able to re-establish control. By early September they had a spy on the islands (Lieutenant Gadelli, an Ålander by birth).

The end of the campaign

After the capture of the Åland Islands there was still at least six weeks available for operations before the weather deteriorated. The Admiralty wanted some action, probably an attack on Sveaborg, in order to placate public opinion. The problem was that this would require troops. The British and French commanders decided against any such attack, although the two engineer officers attached to the force thought such an operation was feasible. They were probably wrong because the allies lacked the shallow-draught armoured bombardment vessels to attack the fortifications from close range. The debate was academic because the French army commander, Baraguay d'Hilliers, had already on 28 August asked for transports to take his troops back to France. Not knowing of the decisions made in the Baltic, on 12 September the Admiralty ordered Napier to consult the French about an attack on Sveaborg. By the time the message arrived, the French troops had already left for home.

The 'campaign' continued for a few more weeks, but accomplished nothing. The Admiralty still wanted action and on 4 October ordered Napier to attack Sveaborg as soon as Kronstadt froze (within a couple of weeks) and before the ice reached the Finnish port. Napier did come up with a plan for a bombardment, but did not implement it – he just wanted to leave the Baltic. Criticism of his conduct was growing within the fleet and, more importantly, in London. On 4 October Delane, the Editor of *The Times*, warned him, 'your conduct in the Baltic has caused extreme dissatisfaction to the Government and to the public . . . eclipse, if you can, the glory of the capture of Sebastopol [these reports were untrue] by the destruction of Kronstadt. Unless you do something of the kind you are a lost man.'[14]

Delane's warning was accurate. The fleet began to withdraw from the

Baltic to Kiel in the third week of October. A few ships were left at the Gulf of Finland, but they were withdrawn a month later after two of them collided. On 1 December Napier was ordered home by the Admiralty. He returned to Spithead, the scene of his triumphal departure nine months earlier, on 16 December and was ordered to strike his flag six days later. The First Sea Lord, Admiral Berkeley, began a series of private consultations with the Captains of the Baltic fleet about Napier's performance and whether he had lost their confidence. The overwhelming response was that he had done so. Captain Codrington told Berkeley, 'I at once say that he decidedly had lost it. With most of them this took place at a very early period, as soon as the personal observations of a few weeks had dispelled the unfounded estimate which they had naturally been led to form of him from mere popular opinion.'[15] Napier was refused any honour at the end of the campaign. He further alienated the Admiralty by using his position as an MP (he was elected for Southwark in 1856) until his death in November 1860 to try to salvage his reputation and justify his conduct of operations.

Whatever Napier's personal failings, and they were substantial, he was used as a scapegoat by the Admiralty and by politicians such as Graham to disguise general inadequacies and failings. Despite the British belief, well attested in *The Times* report on the sailing of the Baltic fleet, that it had the greatest navy in the world, there were, in practice, substantial weaknesses. Although ships were available, there were major problems in manning and creating an effective Baltic fleet from the motley collection of aged coastguards and raw recruits. The ships to which the Royal Navy had access were of little use for operations in the Baltic. Large battleships were the pride of the fleet, but they could contribute little if the Russian navy stayed in harbour. Wooden ships could not attack coastal fortifications – the shore batteries would destroy them before they could cause any substantial damage to stone forts. The only way these forts could be attacked was by armoured, shallow-draught ships capable of shelling from short range and withstanding bombardment. The British did not have such vessels. Given these restrictions (which were admitted by Graham himself when he told Napier not to risk the fleet attacking fortifications), there was little that a Baltic operation could achieve.

The inferior Russian fleet stayed in its harbours and so no decisive battle was possible. The main Russian bases of Kronstadt and Sveaborg could not be attacked. The fleet was left to cruise around the Baltic attacking a few undefended towns and villages along the Finnish coast and destroying mainly British property. The attack on Bomarsund was successful because the defences were so inadequate, but it achieved nothing of strategic importance. Napier's problem was that he had deliberately played up the chances of substantial success. When he, the Admiralty and the public were brought up against the realities of naval warfare using the equipment available in 1854, he paid the price.

4

The War in the East

Long before Britain and France declared war on Russia at the end of March 1854 they had decided that their first task was to keep the Ottomans in the war and to ensure Constantinople was not captured. This required not just a naval presence in the Black Sea (which existed from late 1853), but an army. The early spring of 1854 was spent organising the two expeditionary forces and selecting the commanding officers.

The French expeditionary force

The French had the second-largest army in Europe – more than 600,000-strong by 1855. Although nominally a conscript army, it was in practice largely professional because conscription could be avoided by the rich and powerful through a system that allowed them to buy a proxy recruit from the poor and unemployed. Its other strength was that both the troops and Generals were battle-hardened by the long campaigns in Algeria. In the first three months of the war more than 30,000 troops were removed from Algeria to form the bulk of the units sent to the east. That expeditionary force, the *Armée d'Orient,* was originally intended to be about 6,000-strong, but by March 1854 nearly 35,000 troops were on their way to the eastern Mediterranean. At its peak in the summer of 1855 the French had an army of 120,000 in the Crimea and, because units were regularly rotated more than 300,000 troops served in the east.

Most of the French troops left from Toulon and Marseilles and both ports were scenes of great confusion in the spring of 1854. Communication from Paris was provided by telegraph, and the railway from the capital was almost complete apart from two small gaps. These were filled by transport along the Saône, although this was left to private enterprise to organise. Had the river frozen over in the winters of 1854–55 and 1855–56 (as it often did), French supplies to the Crimea would have collapsed. In the spring of 1854 the troops left southern France by steamer ahead of all their equipment and had only enough rations for eight days. They were, therefore, incapable of undertaking operations for some time. The last major item to join the army was the siege train, which was left behind at Toulon and did not arrive in the east until mid-July.

Napoleon III was generally popular in the army – mainly because of his name rather than his military competence. However, few of the army leaders were Bonapartists (especially those from Algeria) and he selected the commanders of the expeditionary force on the basis of their loyalty rather than their ability. Napoleon chose as the overall commander Marshal Achille Le Roy de Saint Arnaud, who had played the key role during the coup of 1851. He was a colourful character. Born in 1789 as Arnaud Jacques Le Roy, he had lived under a variety of other names before adopting his army name in 1841. In the 1820s he fought in the Greek War of Independence, worked in London as a fencing and dancing master, fled the city to escape his debts and worked as a comedian under the name of 'Floridor' in Belgium. He joined the French army in February 1831 and started his long service in Algeria in 1836. From Napoleon's point of view his main assets were political reliability and his ability to speak fluent English. His major disadvantage was his rapidly deteriorating health. Before he left Paris in April 1854 he was diagnosed with angina and intestinal cancer and given four months to live. He insisted on leading the army, believing that he had enough time to achieve the great success that would crown his career.

The obvious candidate to succeed Saint Arnaud was the forty-five-year-old François Canrobert. He came from a military family and had served in the infantry since 1828. He had obeyed Saint Arnaud's orders in the 1851 coup and by the spring of 1854 was regarded as a reasonably loyal follower of Napoleon. His military ability was, however, limited even though he was given command of the 1st Division. Apart from Napoleon's son, Prince Jerôme, who commanded the 3rd Division during 1854, the other divisional commanders were competent professionals. The 2nd Division was commanded by the forty-four-year-old General Pierre Bosquet, who was still on political 'probation' – he had been a student leader of the 1830 revolution and a strong republican in 1848–51. The 4th (reserve) Division was under General Élie Forey, who had been promoted for his support of the 1851 coup.

The British expeditionary force

The British had much greater difficulty than the French in putting together an expeditionary force from the various regiments in Britain and those that could be recalled from the colonies. In total it numbered about 27,000, but this number was very difficult to sustain and the size of the force declined rapidly through casualties (mainly from disease). A major problem was finding any Generals with experience of European warfare or even colonial wars. Although no French commander was older than fifty-five, the British could find only one divisional infantry commander aged under sixty, and he was the thirty-four-year-old Duke of Cambridge who was chosen to command the 1st Division solely because he was Queen Victoria's cousin.

The man chosen as commander-in-chief was the sixty-six-year-old Lord Raglan. He was born in 1788, the youngest of the eleven sons of the Duke of Beaufort. He joined the army as a Cornet in the 4th Light Dragoons – his commission was bought when he was a fifteen-year-old at Westminster School. In 1810 he became military secretary to Sir Arthur Wellesley (later Duke of Wellington) and married his niece. His whole career thereafter was determined by his relationship with Wellington. He was an administrator in the army for forty years – mainly with Wellington at the Horse Guards in London. He was MP for Truro for seven years, but never spoke in the House of Commons. Although he lost his right arm at Waterloo he had, before 1854, never commanded as large a unit as a battalion in the field. The expeditionary force was to be his first independent command. Raglan, in the traditions of mid-nineteenth-century patronage, appointed four of his nephews as his personal staff and aides-de-camp. He was chosen as commander less for his military ability and more for his social position, his ability to speak French and the lack of any obvious alternative. The Secretary of State for War, the Duke of Newcastle, did not agree with the choice, but was overruled by the Cabinet. Newcastle's doubts were to be fully borne out by events. Many of the problems of the expedition to the east and the subsequent campaign in the Crimea stemmed from Raglan's total lack of experience of modern warfare and his inability to exercise effective command.

The 2nd Division was commanded by Sir George de Lacy Evans, a veteran of the Peninsular War who had been on half-pay since 1818. He had fought with the British auxiliaries during the Carlist wars in Spain and was, therefore, the only British commander with even the remotest experience of European war. The 3rd Division was under General Sir Richard England, who had fought in Afghanistan and the Cape. The 4th Division was commanded by Sir George Cathcart. He held the dormant commission to replace Raglan in the event of the latter's death, but Raglan refused to have him as one of his inner group of advisers and kept the 4th Division away from the action.

The other senior officers had many of the same faults, in particular inexperience and age. The sixty-four-year-old General Sir George Brown, who was appointed to lead the Light Division, was probably the most unpopular infantry officer in the army. The choice of most unpopular officer in the cavalry was a close race between Lord Lucan, the overall commander, and his brother-in-law the Earl of Cardigan who commanded the Light Brigade. Lucan, who had served with Menshikov when he commanded Russian troops in the war with the Ottomans in 1828, had retired on half-pay as a Lieutenant-Colonel in 1837, but had reached the rank of Major-General by 1851 and came out of retirement in 1854 to take charge of the cavalry. One problem that might have been regarded as a slight drawback was that he did not know modern cavalry drill or the words of command. Cardigan had become an MP at the age of twenty-one and bought all his promotions to reach Lieutenant-Colonel by the age of thirty-three. A vain, egotistical man, his army career was marked by constant controversy, disputes and a duel that resulted in a trial before his peers in the House of Lords. Lucan and Cardigan hated each other and were barely on speaking terms. Lucan was determined to exercise his command as Cardigan's senior officer, while Cardigan used Raglan to try to undermine Lucan's authority.

The other Generals in the army were an undistinguished group. The Adjutant-General, Estcourt, had never seen battle, had been on half-pay as a Lieutenant-Colonel after 1843, but was promoted to Brigadier in February 1854 when he took up his post. The Quartermaster-General, Airey, had similarly not experienced war and had only held various regimental and staff jobs. He was given his job because he was military secretary to the sixty-nine-year-old Commander-in-Chief, Lord Hardinge. Probably the most competent General was the seventy-two-year-old Sir John Burgoyne, whom we have already seen undertaking a preliminary reconnaissance in Constantinople and Varna (he did not join the expeditionary force until August).

EYE-WITNESS
THE VOYAGE TO THE EAST

George Lawson, doctor
He left Woolwich on 10 March 1854 and sailed on board the *Cape of Good Hope*, taking seventeen days to reach Malta.
'We breakfast every morning pretty punctually at ½ past 8 . . . the tables are well covered, we have eggs and bacon, rump steak, pigeons, duck, cold hashed meat, ham and in fact everything you can pile upon the table in the shape of eatables. At 12 o'clock is grog time; spirits and wine and biscuits are set on the table, and at 4 o'clock we dine, a dinner quite equal to any which you could get at any hotel. At 7 we have tea and at ½ past 8 grog again, and at 10 we all go to bed . . . to be ready to begin the same process again at ½ past 8 the following morning.'

Temple Godman, officer

He left Cork on 28 May 1854 sailing on *Himalaya*, a P&O screw-propelled steamship. He went via Malta to Varna, where he arrived on 11 June.

'They do not feed us very well on board. I am getting used to being crowded in our cabin – there is not much room to spare with three in it. All our men were very ill at first, and you can't fancy anything more wretched than they were, strewn all over the floor and deck as thick as peas, so very ill they could not move; they have none of them got any hammocks, but sleep where they can.'

Frederick Dallas, officer

He sailed with Lieutenant-General Sir George Cathcart, commander of the 4th Division, leaving on 9 August 1854 and reaching Varna on 2 September.

16 August: 'We have been getting along very satisfactorily, wind and weather in our favour . . . every sail out & the screw working her best, we literally tore through the water. Today is certainly hot, the wind gone down and the sea like glass.'

18 August: 'Our voyage has not continued so successfully. Yesterday morning we had come in sight of Africa with a very heavy wind in our teeth & we made little way all day. At night we attempted to go thro' the Straits but the wind increased to a Gale & after hours of fighting against it & making no way we were driven back into the Atlantic again . . . we are drifting about at the mercy of the winds and waves.'

Initial plans

When Saint Arnaud left Paris he was instructed by Napoleon to look after the troops and 'only to engage them in a military action with extremely favourable chances'.[1] His first task was to create a defensive position at Gallipoli from which he would, if necessary, be able to advance into the Balkans to support Ottoman forces. If forced to retreat by the Russians, he was to leave the defence of Constantinople to the Ottomans and move back to Gallipoli. He was not to cross the Danube unless Austria joined the war on the Russian side. He could, in consultation with Raglan and the Ottoman commander, Omer Pasha, consider a landing in the Crimea or near Odessa. On the day Raglan left for Paris and the east as commander (10 April), he was given his orders by Newcastle. His 'first duty' was, like Saint Arnaud, the defence of Constantinople. If no Russian threat emerged, then he was to prepare for operations against Sevastopol and make 'careful but secret inquiry into the present amount and condition of the Russian Force in the Crimea and the strength of the Fortress of Sevastopol'.[2] Napoleon III was thinking along similar lines. He told Saint Arnaud: 'If you decide to take the Crimea, the initiative for it will come not from England but from me who sees in the conquest of this peninsula the only means of striking an effective blow against Russia and of having a victory on our hands.'[3]

EYE-WITNESS
THE BRITISH AT GALLIPOLI

George Lawson

'Of all the uncivilised, uncultivated, miserable places you have ever seen or heard of, I should think Gallipoli would surpass all. They seem to be at least 3 centuries behind any place I have ever seen . . . The houses are all miserable wooden things, more like very old country barns with a few red tiles on the top . . . The six Medical Staff (myself included) are quartered in what is considered one of the best sort of houses. It is very clean, with whitewashed walls . . . the structure of the house is so slight that the landlady requested we should not bring up all our luggage, in case we should break the floor thro' . . . We have no chairs or table but a sort of broad platform about one foot from the ground, on which you are supposed to sit in Turkish fashion . . . the nights have been most dreadfully cold . . . we lost three of the 93rd Highlanders in one night. Two of them were brought home very drunk, in fact perfectly insensible, and placed in their tents. In the morning they were found dead and quite cold . . . The officers go about town in a most dishabile style; straw hats and wideawakes are the fashion, with white trousers . . . One feels inclined to do nothing but drink lemonade and eat ices which . . . we have in abundance, of course manufactured by the French.'

As the British and French forces began to arrive at Gallipoli, where they established their base, they faced two major problems. The first was organising the expeditionary force, which arrived piecemeal. Saint Arnaud wrote to his brother that the French army was 'not set up, nor organised, having neither its artillery, its cavalry, its ambulance, its train, its transport, nor its provisions', and that 'the English army is no more advanced than we'.[4] It was to take weeks to create an effective force capable of undertaking operations. The second problem was that neither army had any reliable intelligence about Russian forces either along the

Danube or in the Crimea. The British did not even have adequate maps of the area where they would operate. Major Thomas Jervis, who had retired from the Bombay Engineers of the East India Company, did have copies of the Russian army map of the Crimea and the Austrian army map of the European part of the Ottoman empire. The Treasury at first refused Raglan's request to purchase them, but eventually agreed to spend £48 on having them copied. The only map of the Dobrudja region that could be found was a geological one that was given to Raglan by the publisher John Murray. Apart from this hopelessly inadequate map, Raglan had almost no information about the Danube/Balkan area of operations where the British army was expected to deploy.

EYE-WITNESS
THE BRITISH ENCOUNTER THE FRENCH ARMY AT GALLIPOLI

William Russell, *The Times*, war correspondent

'The French came first, and like all first comers, they were the best served.' Russell could only watch the 'ceaseless activity of the French with the daily arrival of their steamers and the admirable completeness of all their arrangements in every detail – hospitals for the sick, bread and biscuit bakeries, waggon trains for carrying stores and baggage – every necessary and every comfort, indeed, at hand, the moment their ships come in . . . They understand things much better than we do. The way in which they have provided for the soldiers is wonderful. They seem to have thought of everything, they have even brought machines for roasting the coffee and grinding it . . . They have now landed a great quantity of artillery, and are practising at a target in the morning. They have an immense number of horses and have brought forage for them, and commissariat provisions for their troops – thus to a great extent rendering themselves independent of the country. They are also much quicker in their movements. They will, almost, land from their transport vessels 2,000 men and have them encamped 2 miles away, while we are looking for boats.'

The Greek problem

As British and French troops were deploying to the eastern Mediterranean, their governments were acting to try and control a potentially embarrassing problem with the Greek government. In 1833 Greece became the first country to gain its independence from the Ottoman empire. However, it ruled only the Peloponnese, the area around Athens and Thebes and some of the Aegean islands – large areas with Greek-speaking populations (in particular Epirus, Thessaly and Macedonia) lay outside the small independent state. The major European powers had forced a Bavarian monarchy on the country, and King Otho I ruled either as an autocrat or in conjunction with a series of corrupt politicians who sought support from one of the three 'protecting powers' – Russia, France and Britain. The one policy that united Otho and all Greeks in the weak and indebted state was the aim of incorporating the Greek Orthodox population of the Ottoman empire into a 'Greater Greece'.

Greece was always anti-Ottoman and was also sympathetic to the Russians in their backing for the Orthodox Church. The Greek government was bound to see a Russian war with the Ottomans as potentially a repeat of their war of independence, when the great powers had forced the Ottomans to make concessions, and therefore as an opportunity to seize more territory. Any conflict between the Greeks and the Ottomans would pose enormous problems for Britain and France, given their alliance with the latter. A classically educated generation tended to romanticise the modern Greeks as the direct descendants of the ancient Greeks. How far could Britain and France go in taking action against a Christian country trying to 'liberate' its fellow Greeks from what many saw as tyrannical Islamic rule?

Many in the British political elite despised the Ottomans, and Islam in general. The issue of Greece, Ottoman rule and British support for the Ottoman empire was therefore highly sensitive. One of the strongest opponents of the war, John Bright, wrote to *The Times*:

> We are building up our Eastern policy on a false foundation – namely the perpetual maintenance of the most immoral and filthy of all despotisms over one of the fairest portions of the earth which it has desolated, and over a population it has degraded but has not been able to destroy.[5]

Within the government there were also doubts, expressed by that most Christian of politicians, Gladstone, to his anti-Ottoman Prime Minister, Aberdeen. In November 1853 Gladstone told his colleague, 'It is not to be thought of that England should aid the Ottoman power in keeping or putting down its Christian subjects.'[6] In February 1854, just before war was declared, Gladstone recorded a conversation with Aberdeen:

He said how could he bring himself to fight for the Turks? I replied we were not fighting for the Turks, but we were warning Russia off the forbidden ground. That if indeed we undertook to put down the Christians under Turkish rule by force then we should be fighting for the Turks – but in this I for one could be no party.[7]

In practice the British had to suppress these sensibilities in the interests of supporting their ally.

Fighting along the Greek-Ottoman border began in the spring of 1853 as the crisis over the 'Holy Places' and the Menshikov mission deepened. Brigandage was endemic along the borders in Epirus and Thessaly, but it escalated in March 1853, just as the Russian Admiral Kornilov, who was part of the Menshikov mission, arrived in Athens on board the warship *Bessarabia*. Within a month the Greek government had organised 2,000 men to join the border fighting. This was a dangerous policy to adopt, but the Greeks were under the illusion that Britain and France would support them, as in the 1820s. In practice the two powers were never prepared to allow this small, bankrupt state to jeopardise their wider aims. In early June 1853 the British minister in Athens, Wyse, formally warned the Greek government that Britain had 'much reason' to complain of Greek behaviour, that the government was 'creating false hopes' in the Greek people and had 'displayed a want of judgement as well as knowledge of the policy of the Great Powers of Europe, who have never been more firmly determined than at the present time, to maintain the integrity and independence of the Turkish Empire'.[8]

Despite this warning, and two others later in the summer of 1853, Otho continued with his risky policy. His aim seems to have been to bolster his declining popularity by pursuing a policy that was favoured in his adopted country. In mid-August he wrote to his father in Bavaria, 'I believe the matter will result in war . . . I am convinced that Divine Providence has decided the enlargement of Greece.'[9] Otho wrote to his brother that 'it was the duty of all Christians in Europe to fight for their co-religionists who were downtrodden by the Crescent'.[10] In the autumn of 1853 the fighting widened when a Greek army officer, Lambros Beikos, crossed the frontier in Epirus with 300 men, and his colleague, Theodore Ziakas, did the same in Thessaly. In late January 1854 Greek frontier police led by Colonel Pierrako, the son of a prominent nationalist politician in Athens, crossed the border in Epirus. On 1 March one of King Otho's aides-de-camp, Lieutenant-General Hatzi-Petros, led more than 500 men across the border in Thessaly. The revolt among the Greek population of the two areas grew rapidly and seemed to presage a repeat of the war of independence of the 1820s. The British and French ignored the popular basis of the revolt and, with some justification, blamed the Greek government.

The Greek revolt meant that the Ottomans now faced the prospect of a three-front war – along the Danube and in the Caucasus against Russia, and in the south against Greece. The British and French decided they could not allow the Greeks to weaken their ally. Their warships escorted Ottoman troops to put down the revolt. On 13 February 1854 Britain, France, Austria and Prussia sent a joint note to Otho warning him not to get involved in the insurrection. (The Austrians had their own reasons for not wanting to see a wider Christian revolt across the Balkans.) In London Clarendon backed up this warning by telling the Greek Ambassador, Tricoupli, that his government:

> Had now to choose between the goodwill of England and France and the blockade of Athens, as the two Governments, while engaged in defending the Ottoman territory from Russian aggression, would certainly not tolerate that the Greek subjects of the Sultan should be excited to rebel against his authority, in consequence of measures sanctioned by the Greek Government.[11]

Napoleon III told Otho, that he would 'consider any attack directed against the Ottoman Empire as being directed against France herself'.[12] The British and French ministers in Athens were given the authority to call up the fleets and impose a blockade.

On 6 March Clarendon instructed Wyse in Athens to tell the Greek Prime Minister, Andreas Paicos, that:

> As friendly advice has not been wanting but has been disregarded, as the connivance of the Greek Court and Government with the hostile movement against Turkey is now beyond question, and as Her Majesty's Government and that of the Emperor of the French are determined that their policy shall not be thus thwarted; the Greek Government must be prepared for the consequences of its own acts . . . the responsibility will rest upon the Greek ministers who have shown themselves to be ignorant or careless of the true interests of their own country.[13]

The next day the Ottoman minister in Athens, Nechet Bey, delivered a forty-eight-hour ultimatum demanding that the Greek government find and punish those involved in the revolt and censor the press to stop anti-Ottoman propaganda. The British and French ministers made it clear they supported the Ottoman demands. The Greek government did not comply and diplomatic relations were broken off three days later. War between Greece and the Ottomans seemed likely. The Greek government was warned by the allies that its shipping would be stopped and any arms found would be confiscated. Despite strong advice from his relatives in Bavaria, Otho decided to continue with his policy.

In early April the British, French, Austrians and Prussians agreed on the measures to be taken against Greece. On 10 May the British and French told the Greek government that, since it was in default on the interest charged on the 1832 international loan that financed the Greek state, they would not allow government revenue to finance the insurrection against the Ottomans. They would, therefore, take steps to control Greek government revenue. Greece was to declare its neutrality and withdraw its troops from the frontier areas. Three days later British and French warships blockaded the port of Piraeus and shortly afterwards 6,000 French troops, together with a British infantry regiment, landed to enforce these demands. Otho had little choice but to submit. He sacked the pro-Russian government and appointed a pro-allied government under Alexander Mavrokordatos, the Ambassador in Paris.

Mavrokordatos did not arrive back in Athens until late July 1854 and, accepting the realities of the situation, asked the British and French ministers what they thought 'ought to be the policy of the government before he formally accepted office'.[14] By then Greek troops had already withdrawn from the frontier regions and diplomatic relations with the Ottomans had been restored. Mavrokordatos was forced to issue an apology, give security guarantees and pay an indemnity to the Ottomans. The British and French occupation (which was technically illegal because the third guaranteeing power, Russia, did not consent) continued. The French troops brought cholera to Piraeus during the summer of 1854 and it spread to Athens, killing about 40,000 people. Allied troops were not withdrawn until February 1857 when the Greek government accepted an international commission to control its finances.

Although official Greek support for the Russians was ended by the Anglo–French occupation, Greek volunteers did fight with the Russian forces. By the summer of 1854 there were more than 1,000 men in two battalions fighting Ottoman forces along the Danube frontier. Most of these troops came from the Greek areas that had revolted – Epirus, Thessaly and Macedonia. Later the men were split into six companies serving with different regiments in the 5th Infantry Division. New recruits joined at Odessa in early 1855 and the Greek troops moved to the Crimea where they joined the garrison at Sevastopol. At the end of the war the volunteers were left stranded at Odessa. In June 1856 more than 300 men sailed back to Piraeus but, under British and French pressure, the Greek government refused to let them land. They were all resettled in Russia.

Russian operations

During the spring of 1854, while French and British forces were still deploying to the east, Russia held the strategic initiative. However, its options were limited, mainly because of fears that Austria might join Britain and France. In February the Austrians rejected Russian suggestions that they might like to invade Serbia and Bosnia and begin a de facto joint partition of the Balkans. The Austrians were worried about long-term Russian aims and their occupation of the Principalities. On the other hand, if Austria did enter the war on the allied side, then the Russian position would be very vulnerable – they would have to fight in the Principalities and face an Austrian invasion from Galicia into Poland and the possibility of a Polish revolt. Nevertheless Nicholas I decided in early February that a campaign along the Danube was the best available option. The aim was to capture key Ottoman fortresses, open up communications with Serbia where a revolt could be encouraged, and provide a better defensive position against an expected French and British landing at Varna.

Russian troops under the overall command of the seventy-two-year-old Field Marshal Paskevich crossed the river on 23 March. The attack was concentrated in the north-east sector around Galatz and Ismaila. About 45,000 troops under General Alexander Lüders moved south into Dobrudja and by the end of March had captured the forts of Tulchea, Isacchea, Matchin and Babadagh. By early April Russian forces were along the line Rasova–Kustendje. Their casualties in the fortnight's fighting were relatively light – 201 dead and 510 wounded. From this situation they were in a good position to turn the Ottoman defences at the key point of Silistria. They did not do so because Paskevich opposed the attack and argued for a withdrawal from the Principalities. He was worried that Austria would join the war and turn the Russian flank. His orders not to go beyond Matchin were ignored because they arrived too late to stop Lüders's operations. In the third week of April Paskevich decided to take personal control of the Danube campaign from his headquarters at Bucharest. His pessimistic and cautious attitude was to determine future policy.

The key to the campaign was the fortified town of Silistria. In the

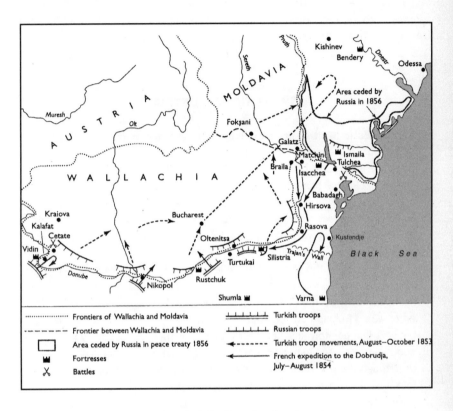

Map 3: The Danube front

1828–29 war with the Ottomans it had taken Russian troops six months to capture the town, but in the intervening twenty-five years its defences had been increased by an outer ring of ten new forts. The Russian siege began on 5 April, directed by General Karl Schilder and his assistant Lieutenant-Colonel Eduard Totleben. Reinforcements were also brought up from Lüders's army.

EYE-WITNESS
THE SIEGE OF SILISTRIA

Captain Butler, British liaison officer with the Ottoman forces in Silistria
He described the town in the early weeks of siege.
'With the exception of a small guard-room at the Stamboul gate, which Mustapha Pasha has appropriated for his own quarters, there is not a bomb-proof building in the whole place: the inhabitants take refuge in caves (which they had constructed for the purpose underground) directly the siege commenced. The town appears quite deserted; nothing but soldiers and dogs to be seen.'
During May 1854 the attacks intensified as the Russians tried to take the fortress.
'No alarm was given till the enemy was actually in the redoubt. The first to enter was a Russian officer, who cut down a Turkish lieutenant of artillery, but was immediately knocked over with a handspike and killed by the men about. A fierce hand-to-hand conflict ensued with the enemy, who clambered up through the embrasures and over the ramparts. They were driven back into the ditch, where a terrific slaughter took place. Numbers of the townspeople went out and cut off the heads of the slain to bring in as trophies, for which they hoped to get a reward; but the savages were not allowed to bring them within the gate. A heap of them, however, were left for a long time unburied just outside the gate.'

A full-scale bombardment began on 10 May, but the 12,000 troops inside the town were not cut off – they were able to bring up supplies and reinforcements because Paskevich decided that a complete encirclement was impossible. At the end of May a Russian assault on the key outer fort of Arab-Tabia was beaten off. The Russian casualties were 317 dead and 623 wounded (most of whom died shortly afterwards). On 9 June Paskevich fell over when an Ottoman shell exploded nearby. He hurt his shoulder in the fall and used this as an excuse to leave the siege and return to Warsaw. On 20 June the fort of Arab-Tabia was captured and the final assault on Silistria was set to start at 4 a.m. on 21 June. Two hours before the attack was due it was called off – Paskevich ordered the troops to lift the siege and recross the Danube. This was the result of an order sent by the Tsar on 13 June. Russian casualties during the siege were 419 dead and 1,783 wounded. Leo Tolstoy was with the Russian troops as they retreated. He noted in his diary that they took with them:

> Nearly 7,000 Bulgar families . . . to save them from the ferocity of the Turks – a ferocity which I've been obliged to believe in despite my incredulity. As soon as we left the various Bulgar villages that we were occupying, the Turks moved in and, except for the women young enough for a harem, massacred everyone they found there.[15]

On 24 June the last Russian troops crossed the Danube and destroyed the only remaining bridge. Why had they retreated just when success seemed likely? They withdrew not as a result of Ottoman – still less French and British – military pressure, but because of Austrian diplomatic moves.

Austrian intervention

In the spring of 1854 Austria faced a very unpalatable situation. On 21 March the Foreign Minister, Buol, sent the Emperor, Franz Josef, a long paper setting out the problems. If Russia were successful in the war, its power and influence over the Ottomans and in the Balkans would expand, severely damaging Austrian interests. However, if France and Britain were successful without Austrian support, they might well back Piedmont in a 'liberation' of northern Italy from Austrian rule. Austria did not want to join either side and was not strong enough economically to fight a long war. Nevertheless it needed to be involved in the diplomacy of the war and in the peace settlement in order to defend its interests.

Buol argued that the most beneficial policy for Austria was to try to end the war as quickly as possible. This could best be done, he argued, by giving carefully limited support to Britain and France in order to restrict their war aims. Austria would suggest that it might join the allies in certain circumstances (but would never give an absolute guarantee of doing so) while working hard to ensure that it never had to join the war on Russia. The mere threat that it might do so could be enough to get the Russians to compromise. This was a policy that would require considerable diplomatic finesse, but it was one that accurately reflected Austrian weakness. It was unpalatable to the conservative groups in Vienna who argued (correctly) that in the long term Austrian interests could never be identical with those of France and Britain. Their suggestion of joining Russia was, however, equally unworkable because of the long-term divergence of interest between the two countries over the fate of the Ottoman empire and the Balkans. Franz Josef reluctantly accepted Buol's advice. For the next two years Austria tried to keep close to Britain and France by suggesting that it might join the war, while at the same time carefully avoiding committing itself to any specific conditions under which it would attack Russia. As Buol put it after the war, 'Did you really believe that Austria could have risked joining the war without risking universal war and revolution and thus the final ruin of her Empire?'[16] Although Austrian policy was probably the best possible, it eventually alienated France, Britain and Russia, leaving the country in a very weak position at the end of the war.

The first Austrian action was to secure an alliance with Prussia, a state equally divided about how to react to the war. A minority was prepared to join Britain and France in the expectation of making gains in Poland and Lithuania. This policy was too revolutionary for the conservatives, including King Wilhelm IV, who favoured Russia. However, Prussia could not join Russia without risking French intervention in Germany, a British blockade and probable Austrian intervention to regain Silesia, lost almost a hundred years earlier. It too therefore decided on a policy of neutrality. On 20 April 1854 Austria and Prussia signed an offensive/defensive alliance. This alliance was also open to the smaller German states such as Bavaria, Saxony and Württemberg, who joined at the end of May. The Austrian-Prussian alliance contained a secret clause allowing Austria to demand Russian withdrawal from the Principalities under the threat of force – Prussia was required to join in a war only if Russia incorporated the Principalities or if its troops crossed into the Balkans.

Austria had very direct interests in the Principalities, particularly in the exclusion of Russian influence and in securing navigation along the Danube to the Black Sea. Austrian military preparations began in late March when the 3rd Army in Hungary (next to the Principalities) was put on a war footing. In the middle of May the 5th Army in Galicia (facing Poland) was fully mobilised. Following these preparations the Austrians decided at the end of May that they were in a position to issue an ultimatum to the Russians. Its terms called for an immediate halt to military operations south of the Danube and for Russia to fix an early date (which was left unspecified) for a withdrawal from the Principalities. The ultimatum did not call for a parallel withdrawal of French and British military and naval forces from the area (as the conservatives in Vienna wanted) and was therefore one-sided. The Russians were told that Austria would seek an agreement with the Ottomans for a joint occupation of the Principalities. The British and French did not like the ultimatum for two reasons. First, it had no time limit for a withdrawal, and second, an Austrian occupation of the Principalities would act as a barrier to allied troops engaging the Russians. Their main hope was that any Austrian move into the area would involve them in war with Russia and make them de facto allies.

The Austrian ultimatum was sent to St Petersburg on 3 June. The Tsar was shocked. Until now he had counted (despite the lack of evidence to support his view) on Austrian benevolent neutrality. His initial reaction – especially when he saw the Austrian Ambassador, Esterházy, three days after the ultimatum was delivered – was to fight. However, his advisers convinced him that such a policy would be madness. Prince Alexander Gorchakov was sent to Vienna with a conciliatory reply, while orders were sent to call off the siege of Silistria and for Russian forces to retreat back over the Danube. The Austrians refused to negotiate over the terms of the ultimatum and eventually the Russians agreed to withdraw from the Principalities that they had occupied a year earlier. Meanwhile, on 14 June the Austrians reached an agreement with the Ottomans (the Convention of Boyadji-Köi) on a joint occupation of the Principalities.

Russian withdrawal

After abandoning the siege of Silistria the Russians began to withdraw from south of the Danube. This brought about serious fighting with a fierce battle around Giurgevo on 5–7 July, but otherwise the retreat was orderly with Ottoman and Austrian forces moving in behind the Russians. (The Austrians ensured their forces never came into contact with the Russians so as to avoid any possible conflict.) The Russians had now returned to their starting line in the spring of 1854 (apart from the fortresses of Tulchea, Isaccea and Matchin, which they continued to hold until October). The withdrawal from the Principalities began on 24 July and produced a contest between the Ottoman and Austrian forces to secure the key positions. The order for Austrian troops to move into Wallachia was not given until 17 August and they did not cross the frontier for another five days. By that time the small Ottoman force under Halim Pasha, which had reached Bucharest on 8 August, had been reinforced by a complete division. Austrian troops under General Coronini entered the city on 6 September. There then followed a race to occupy Moldavia. Ottoman forces reached Braila five days ahead of the Austrians in the third week of September, but the latter, operating from Transylvania, reached Galatz first. On 2 October Austrian troops occupied Iaşi, the capital of Moldavia. However, they had to allow

Ottoman troops to pass through their lines to reach the Bessarabian frontier with Russia.

Russian forces were now inside their own frontier for the first time since the summer of 1853. The Austrian occupation of the Principalities caused considerable friction. They wanted to replace any Russian protectorate with one of their own. However, they faced major problems in that they had almost no support from the local population. They had to declare martial law in their areas in May 1855 to suppress discontent. They also faced the problem of the numerous Polish and Hungarian nationalists who served with the Ottoman army encouraging their fellow nationals in the Austrian army to desert. Ottoman troops refused to withdraw from Bucharest and the Austrians had to accept a division into zones of occupation. Although the Austrian military wanted to annex the Principalities, Buol preferred a more cautious policy and hoped to secure general European agreement to Austrian aims. There was no hope that he would be successful. Once it was apparent that they would not attack the Russians, the British and French made their opposition to Austrian policy clear. The French favoured a union of the Principalities and eventual independence, while the British were content with a weak overall Ottoman sovereignty as long as their trade interests were protected. The issue would have to be resolved at any peace conference.

French and British operations

Until troops arrived in the east the fighting between allied and Russian forces was confined to naval operations using the ships that had been in the area since the summer of 1853. On 9 April 1854 the British frigate *Furious* arrived off Odessa to evacuate the Consul. A sloop under a white flag went into the port where the crew was informed that the Consul had already left. As the sloop returned to the frigate, shots were fired from the fort, probably at *Furious*, which was out of range. When the British and French commanders, Admirals Dundas and Hamelin, heard about these events they decided (with little justification) that the Russian action was a breach of international law. A group of nine war steamers, a frigate and six rocket boats under Captain Jones was sent to Odessa, where they arrived on 21 April. Jones demanded the release of all British and French ships in the port (they were legally detained) and the handing over of all Russian ships as reparations for the events of 9 April. The Governor of the city naturally rejected these demands. The next day the allied ships bombarded the port and the city from 6.30 in the morning until 5 p.m. and caused heavy destruction, but with only a handful of allied casualties. Other bombardments of forts along the eastern Black Sea coast were also carried out, but with little impact because the Russians had evacuated them in March. On 4 April the Admiralty instructed Dundas to start a blockade of the Black Sea, but Hamelin had no instructions from Paris and did not join the action until the end of May. The problem was that the British and French did not have sufficient forces to institute a close blockade and Dundas's alternative suggestion of a distant blockade at the Bosphorous was ruled to be illegal by the British and French governments. The result was that the blockade was highly ineffective. Only fifty-four ships were captured during the whole of 1854 and they were nearly all small coastal vessels with an average displacement of just thirty-five tons each.

By the middle of May 1854 there were 30,000 French and 20,000 British troops assembled around Gallipoli and the Dardanelles. The first part of the allied plan had been achieved – Constantinople appeared to be secure. How were these troops now to be used? An allied war council of Saint Arnaud, Raglan, Omer Pasha (the Ottoman commander) and Riza Pasha (the Ottoman Minister of War) reviewed the situation on 19 May. The main pressure on the Ottomans came from the Russian attack across the Danube and in the siege of Silistria, where the Ottomans were heavily outnumbered. Omer Pasha thought (correctly) that the town might hold out only for another six weeks at best. The conference therefore agreed that the French and British armies should move to Varna on the Black Sea coast. The problem was the lack of transport. The first French troops of the 2nd Division under General Bosquet had to march from Gallipoli to Adrianople and eventually all the way to Varna, which took almost a month. The other French troops and the British army moved by sea. The first units arrived at Varna on 1 June to find that there was no harbour and that all disembarkation had to take place onto the beach. By the middle of the month Saint Arnaud had transferred his headquarters from Gallipoli, but it was mid-July before most of the troops arrived. By then there were about 130,000 allied troops in the Varna region (60,000 Ottoman, 50,000 French and 20,000 British).

**EYE-WITNESS
THE FRENCH AND BRITISH AT VARNA**

Temple Godman
'Varna is a horrid town, the houses of wood, scarcely any shops, and more dirty than any Irish village I ever saw, a few cafés, in which you see sullen-looking Turks cross-legged in clouds of smoke.'

Henry Clifford, officer

'Houses are made of wood, two stories in height, some few with glass windows, but most without, red tiles to the houses, the streets paved with stone and slanting to the centre, which forms a sort of large drain, into which is emptied all sorts of filth . . . In trying to get out of the way of a dead dog the other day, I found my foot on a dead rat. The streets are never cleaned in any way, so the stench beats anything I have ever smelt.'

Temple Godman

'There is a very unusual complaint here: everyone has too much money. We get our pay every day, and as mine is 13s 6d a day, it soon mounts up, and I have got £49 . . . Our men do not know what to do with their pay; some send it home, but those who have no families think nothing of giving 2s for a bottle of porter when they can get it. Their rations and living altogether does not cost them more than 1½d or 2d a day.'

William Russell

'The conduct of the men, French and English, seemed characterized by recklessness verging on insanity. They might be seen lying drunk in the kennels, or in the ditches by the road-sides, under the blazing rays of the sun, covered with swarms of flies.'

Harry Blishen, British infantryman

'We were drilled incessantly during the time we were there; in fact almost harassed to death; and I am sorry to say we lost several men through the effect. We were drilled to give the young generals [officers] an insight into what they would have to do on the field . . . the French have such an advantage over us; you will never see an inexperienced subaltern in their service.'

Margaret Kirwin, wife of Private John Kirwin of the 19th Foot

'There was a report that the Russians were coming down on us. At once all the women were moved to the rear. We marched on up to Devna and remained for a fortnight. There I bought a little wash tub, and carried my cooking things in it. This was the whole of my baggage which I carried on my head during the march. I also had a water bottle and a haversack to carry biscuits in . . . On the march the men kept falling out from the heat and they kept me busy giving them drinks. When we got to Monastne the washing duty fell to me . . . I stood in the midst of the stream from 6 a.m. to 7 p.m. washing. The Colour Sergeant would not keep account and some men paid and some did not, so that I was left with very little for my trouble. The men were dying fast of the cholera and black fever and were buried in their blankets. No sooner had we moved up country than the Turks opened the graves and took the blankets. After this we buried them without covering, save for branches and brambles . . . From my hardships, standing in the river washing, I took two internal complaints and thought I was dying; the men made a shade for me with boughs.'

Temple Godman
'The only amusement we have is shooting hawks and crows . . . The other amusement is dog hunting, all go out in the most fantastic dresses, and whip a half-wild dog out of the bush, and then have a grand hunt, to the great astonishment of the solemn old Turks, who stand by, looking fearfully disgusted at our wickedness.'

William Russell
'I rode into Varna camp this morning, but so changed was the appearance of the principal streets by the restless activity and energy that I could not recognise them. Old blind side walls had been broken down, and shops opened, in which not only necessaries, but even luxuries could be purchased . . . Wine merchants and sutlers from Algiers, Oran, Constantine, Marseilles, Toulon, had set up booths and shops, at which liquers, spirits and French country wines [were sold] . . . The natives had followed the example. Strings of German sausages, of dried tongues, of wiry hams, of bottles of pickles . . .'

The allies had almost no information about what was happening along the Danube front. In early May Raglan employed Captain Lintorn Simmons of the Royal Engineers, who had been travelling privately in the area since the autumn of 1853, reporting to the British Ambassador in Constantinople and liaising with Omer Pasha. For a fee of £100 Simmons agreed to create a network of agents in the area to report on Russian strengths and movements. However, he found this an almost impossible task because the area was depopulated. The outcome was that his estimates of Russian strengths were little more than guesses – not surprisingly he over-estimated their numbers by about half. On 25 June Raglan ordered Cardigan to undertake a cavalry reconnaissance to establish whether the Russians had withdrawn from south of the Danube. He took 190 men of the 8th Hussars and 13th Light Dragoons and a troop of Ottoman lancers. The expedition achieved nothing other than to demonstrate Cardigan's incompetence. He took seventeen days to accomplish what could have been done in little more than a week and returned with no useful intelligence. He refused to allow the men to carry tents or spare clothes, and the lack of water and forage led to the loss of eighty horses with most of the others left permanently unfit for cavalry work. Four days after Cardigan's return the job had to be done again, this time by twelve men of the Royal Horse Artillery who, after a short reconnaissance, returned with the required information. Nevertheless Cardigan regarded the operation as a personal triumph, partly because he had eaten 'almost the same food as the men'.[17] When the Light Brigade (which Cardigan commanded) moved to Yeni-Bazaar he had his two marquees pitched in the shade of the only two trees on the plateau, took over the only well and posted sentries to stop the men using the water. A month later he was promoted to Major-General. The men were highly critical of his performance. Captain Shakespear of the Royal Horse Artillery thought Cardigan was 'the most impractical and most inefficient cavalry officer in the service. He may do all very well when turned out by his valet in the Phoenix Park, but there his knowledge ceases. We are all greatly disgusted with him.'[18]

By the time most of the troops had arrived at Varna, the allies knew that Russian troops were withdrawing from south of the Danube and would shortly be evacuating the Principalities. For six weeks the allied armies were to remain largely inactive at Varna while it was decided what to do next. The first problem they faced was growing friction between the commanders. There was considerable mutual antipathy in the French command, especially over Prince Napoleon, and in particular over his exact role and military competence. (The Duke of Cambridge refused to see him because he was a social upstart.) In early August the Prince left for Constantinople claiming that he was unwell. Saint Arnaud threatened to send him back to France in disgrace and the Prince eventually returned to his command. The main problem the British faced was the mutual antipathy between Lucan and Cardigan. Raglan tended to undermine Lucan's authority as overall commander of the cavalry by dealing direct with Cardigan. It was only after Lucan's formal protest that Raglan confirmed that Lucan was Cardigan's senior officer. Because Cardigan had been promoted following his inept handling of the reconnaissance, Lucan now had to be promoted to Lieutenant-General to make his superior status clear. Cardigan continued to resent his loss of independence.

The major crisis the allied armies had to face almost as soon as they arrived at Varna was an outbreak of cholera on 12 July. The disease had only reached Europe in the early 1830s (brought from India and Central Asia by Russian troops operating in the Balkans) and it thrived in the insanitary conditions in the major cities where drinking water and sewage mixed freely. Cholera arrived at Varna with French troops from Marseilles. Given the heat, poor water supplies and lack of sanitation, it spread rapidly. Within a month the French had lost more than 5,000 troops and British casualties rose from fewer than twenty in June to more than 850 by August.

EYE-WITNESS
CHOLERA STRIKES THE ALLIED ARMIES AT VARNA

Assistant surgeon Cattell, 5th Dragoon Guards

There were only limited supplies of drinking water, but 'the horses were watered there and kept it constantly muddy, the Infantry washed their clothes and bathed in it, and to add to the mischief, butchers found it convenient to throw offal into it.'

William Russell

'Horrors occurred here every day which were shocking to think of. Walking by the beach one might see some straw sticking up through the sand; and on scraping it away with his stick be horrified at bringing to light the face of a corpse which had been deposited there with a wisp of straw round it, a prey to dogs and vultures. Dead bodies rose up from the bottom in the harbour and bobbed grimly around in the water or floated in from the sea and drifted past the sickened gazers on board the ships – all buoyant, bolt upright, and hideous in the sun.'

Henry Clifford

'Our life in Camp was from the first monotonous and without interest of any sort. The Cholera came at a time when all were low spirited and disgusted with the tiresome life we are leading and it has had a very great effect on the spirits of both Officers and men.'

Harry Blishen

'We have harder work against the cholera, dysentery and lake fever, than we should have had against five times our number of the enemy in Russia. The number of deaths with us and the French has been fearful . . . many of my comrades . . . being in robust health one hour, and the next hour groaning in the agonies of death.'

Temple Godman

'Nearly all our officers have been ill with fever and ague . . . The heat is so great, and the food so bad we have no chance of picking up strength after illness, and there are only a few bottles in the hospital, as they will allow us to carry hardly any medicine.'

Under pressure from Napoleon III about the lack of military action, and with cholera spreading rapidly, Saint Arnaud decided to disperse his forces and mount an expedition into the Dobrudja. He thought there might be about 10,000 Russian troops in the area, but he had little idea of the environment that the troops would face. Both Omer Pasha and Raglan wisely refused to participate.

The first French troops left Varna on 21 July headed by a new unit, the *spahis d'Orient*, a makeshift cavalry force composed of about 2,500 *bashi-bazouks* recruited from the Ottomans and commanded by General Yusuf. Immediately behind was the 1st Division led by General Espinasse (Canrobert was away). The last units to leave on 23 July were the 2nd and 3rd Divisions. By the time these units left, cholera had broken out among the leading troops. By the end of the month about 150 men were dying every day as the expedition trudged through the inhospitable Dobrudja region with its numerous marshes. Some of the *bashi-bazouks* deserted and began looting the villages. When the first troops began returning in the early days of August, having accomplished nothing during the expedition, the casualty figures were dreadful. Only 300 *spahis* reached Varna and the 2nd and 3rd Divisions had lost nearly 400 men to cholera by the time they returned to base on 9 August. The heaviest casualties were in the 1st Division, which came back on 18 August with nearly 2,000 men dead from cholera. Saint Arnaud defended the action by claiming, with some justification, that even more might have died had they remained in the overcrowded Varna area. The failure of the expedition gave the British the opportunity to sneer at the French and, in particular, Saint Arnaud's low origins. Clarendon told Lord John Russell, 'St Arnaud ought to be hung for that expedition to the Dobdrudja wh[*sic*] was undertaken without Raglan's knowledge [untrue] & for the purpose of getting a little separate glory – and it has ended in separate disgrace.'[19] Palmerston thought, 'what sensible man would have imagined that a man who had passed his Early Life as an actor could all of a sudden become a great General'.[20] (Saint Arnaud had far more experience of warfare than any British General.) Clarendon thought Saint Arnaud was a 'charlatan'.[21]

While much of the French army was away, conditions at Varna

continued to deteriorate. Cholera spread to the ships offshore – more than 400 men of the Royal Navy died of the disease and another 4,500 were affected by severe diarrhoea.

EYE-WITNESS
AN ATTACK OF CHOLERA

Roger Fenton, war photographer

Fenton came down with cholera just as he was leaving the Crimea in late June 1855. His account is one of the few to describe the speed of a cholera attack. He was lucky in having only a mild dose, for most sufferers died. His home-made remedy was probably the best available at the time.

'I felt unwell being attacked with diarrhoea . . . We had nearly got outside the harbour when I began to vomit, and felt it was not from seasickness. By nine o'clock I was bad with cholera, and there was no doctor on board. Everybody advised me to take different medicine. I tried rhubarb and peppermint but could not keep it in my stomach, so I got them to make me some rice water and mixed lime juice with it, and while it was preparing drank as much lime juice and water as ever I could, vomiting it all up again every ten minutes but drinking again so as to keep up the supply of fluid to the blood. At half past ten cramp began in my legs and I had to held upright and rubbed; in a short time it began in my arms and fingers, which began to turn blue. I could hardly breathe and felt my eyes staring very much . . . At noon I felt the tide was turned, for my fingers recovered their colour and the cramp became less violent. I had kept on drinking rice water, and by night the diarrhoea was stopped, though the cramp continued until the middle of the next day.'

On 10 August a major fire broke out in the town after French officers tried to close a spirit shop. A huge amount of supplies was destroyed, including 19,000 pairs of shoes, most of the cavalry sabres and large amounts of the biscuits that formed the basis of British army rations. Luckily the ammunition stores were saved. The French blamed Greek saboteurs for the outbreak and bayoneted five Greeks to death.

EYE-WITNESS
THE GREAT FIRE AT VARNA

George Lawson
'Last night about half-past 7 o'clock a fire broke out in a French wine shop near the Port Gate – spread with rapidity – burned for many hours notwithstanding the efforts of many thousand soldiers employed to arrest its progress, and consumed nearly one-sixth of the town. It broke out in the immediate neighbourhood of the great magazines of grain, stores and gunpowder of the two armies . . . The English grain and biscuit stores were consumed and the French lost a great part of their army stores. The large powder magazines containing an enormous quantity of powder, which are injudiciously situated in the most crowded part of town, were preserved with great difficulty. This morning the town presents a scene of desolation not often witnessed; and last night the conduct of the soldiers, both French and English, was very discreditable, and even today the cases of brutal intoxication present themselves in every direction. From the quantity of property scattered about, the appearance of the place is that of a town taken and sacked.'

Charles Addington, British officer
'The French worked well at first, but when they discovered a store of brandy &c they became so excited by drink that they were more like demons than human beings. They broke into the houses and in many cases shamefully ill-treated the inhabitants. A band of them amused themselves with throwing some unfortunate Greeks into the hottest part of the fire.'

Cornet Fisher, 4th Dragoon Guards
'There is not a shop left open . . . for the very reason that there is nothing left to sell; although not half the town is destroyed by fire, the whole is sacked. Our gallant generals adhered to their usual policy and did nothing, although there are troops enough to have kept order . . . The English, according to all accounts, behaved very well, confining themselves strictly to getting as drunk as possible on the liquor which was washing all over town . . . The ration biscuits burn beautifully, and will not be put out . . . There is not a Turk to be seen anywhere . . .'

By the last week of August, British and French operations in the east had achieved nothing apart from the loss of several thousand men to cholera. Although Constantinople was secure, it had never really been under threat. In the five months the allied armies had been in the east they had not fought the Russians – indeed, they had hardly seen them. The Russian retreat from the Principalities had been achieved partly by Ottoman resistance, but mainly through Austrian diplomatic pressure. That retreat had produced a strategic stalemate. If the British and French armies wanted to fight the Russians, they would have to pass through the Principalities, which were partially occupied by the neutral Austrians. The other problem was that it was now late in the campaigning season – autumn was rapidly approaching and the weather was likely to deteriorate badly in little more than six weeks or so. What could the allied armies achieve in that time that would avoid the 1854 campaign turning into even more of a fiasco?

5

Varna to the Alma

The idea of an attack on the Crimea with the objective of capturing the naval base of Sevastopol had been part of British and French strategic thinking from early 1854. It was a commonly held assumption that this operation would follow the initial campaign to secure Constantinople. However, it was far from clear how this was to be achieved. By late June, when the politicians in London and Paris knew that Russian troops were retreating from south of the Danube and would be evacuating the Principalities, the pressure to move to the Crimea in the hope of achieving some success in the 1854 campaign became overwhelming.

On 23 June Napoleon III sent orders to Saint Arnaud that some military action was needed. He told his commander, 'I don't see anything else to be done than taking the Crimea . . . means must be found to land a great stroke before the bad season begins.'[1] In this message he was probably influenced by the British view that had been sent to Cowley, the Ambassador in Paris, six days earlier. The Foreign Secretary, Clarendon, told Cowley that despite their 'miserably deficient' information about the Crimea, the majority of ministers felt 'we ought not to be hanging about Varna or the Danube' and that the army should move across the Black Sea.[2] The main advocate of such a course was the First Lord of the Admiralty, Graham. As early as the second week of May he told Raglan, 'I only know what is most desirable; and the destruction of the Russian Fleet and the Capture of Sebastopol are the blows which would knock down, and win the battle in the shortest time and with the greatest certainty.'[3] On 28 June the Cabinet discussed and agreed the orders to be given to Raglan. They formally endorsed the despatch the next day after dinner when most members slept while Newcastle read out the document. Raglan was told that the war was now taking on a 'new character' and that he should not advance into Dobrudja. The allied governments agreed on an attack on Sevastopol unless 'upon mature reflection', Raglan and Saint Arnaud felt otherwise. Newcastle added that there was 'no prospect of a safe and honourable peace' without the capture of Sevastopol and that 'nothing but insuperable impediment . . . should be allowed to prevent the early decision to undertake these operations'.[4]

The instructions from London reached Varna on 17 July. Raglan discussed the despatch with General Sir George Brown, who asked him what information he had about Sevastopol. 'His answer was that he had no information whatever!' Brown said that they normally asked themselves what Wellington would have done in the circumstances, and he was sure the Duke would not undertake such an operation. However, he added:

> You had better accede to the proposal and come into the views of the Government, for this reason, that it is clear to me . . . that they have made up their minds to it at home, and that if you decline to accept the responsibility, they will send some one else out to command the army, who will be less scrupulous, and more ready to come into their plans.[5]

The next day a formal allied war council met. Present were Saint Arnaud, Raglan and the two naval chiefs from each side, Admirals Dundas and Lyons for the British and Hamelin and Bruat for the French. Dundas and Hamelin were opposed to the operation, arguing (correctly) that the fortifications at Sevastopol were too strong to be attacked from the sea. Nevertheless the meeting concluded that they had little choice but to go ahead with a landing in the Crimea, given the strength of feeling in London and Paris. It was decided to carry out a preliminary reconnaissance.

British and French intelligence

A reconnaissance expedition left Varna at 4.30 a.m. on 20 July and reached the Crimea two days later. The main officers involved were General Canrobert and Brigadier Louis-Jules Trochu from the French army and General Sir George Brown representing Raglan. Admiral Sir Edmund Lyons provided the naval input. The ships investigated Sevastopol harbour and it was agreed that an attack from the sea was impossible. Brown told Raglan that the defences were 'completely unassailable from the sea and I should think an attack on Portsmouth child's play to it'.[6] If a direct attack was ruled out, then the only alternative was to land an army near Sevastopol. The expedition sailed east along the coast and looked at Balaklava bay. It then moved north and identified a possible landing site at the mouth of the River Kacha about four miles north of Sevastopol. The expedition returned on 28 July, but had achieved little because it rarely got closer than about three miles from shore.

The other information available to the allied commanders was patchy and unreliable. Raglan was given two travelogues (both published in 1835) before he left London: *Journal of Crimean Travels* by Lord de Ros (who was Quartermaster-General at Varna, but invalided home before the landings in the Crimea) and *Journal of the Crimea* by Major-General Macintosh. Neither contained much more than basic information about the fortifications around Sevastopol. In London Raglan also met the travel writer Laurence Oliphant, who published *The Russian Shores of the Black Sea* in the autumn of 1852. Oliphant grossly over-estimated the seaward defences of Sevastopol, but then added, 'there is nothing whatever to prevent any number of troops landing a few miles to the South of the town . . . and marching down the main street to . . . sack the town and burn the fleet'.[7] This view did have an influence over British and French operations, as did Oliphant's judgement about the harbour at Balaklava: 'Any vessel, however large, having once made its way through the dangerous entrance, may ride out the severest storm upon its unruffled waters.'[8] Despite these dubious assessments, Oliphant did give a very accurate picture of the Crimean climate:

> Except during four months in the year, the climate alone offers obstacles almost insurmountable to the movements of large bodies of men; the roads are impassable for pedestrians in spring and autumn, and in winter the severity of the weather precludes the possibility of troops crossing the dreary steppes.[9]

This view was, however, contradicted by another work of which Raglan was aware – *Russia* by J. G. Kohl, published in 1844. This argued that the Crimea had a very mild climate because it was protected from the cold north wind and open to the warm south wind. This was partly true, but Kohl painted too glowing a picture when he wrote, 'it enjoys . . . an exceedingly mild climate, which allows the vine, the olive, the laurel, the pomegranate, and in short all the fruits of an Italian sky to come to perfection'.[10] These views were endorsed by Newcastle, who wrote to Raglan that he had information from a Dr Lee who had lived 'many years ago' on the Crimean coast. Lee told him that the winter around Sevastopol was 'remarkably salubrious, mild and agreeable'.[11] Experience was to show very soon just how false these views were.

The British and French commanders had little or no information about the size and effectiveness of the Russian forces in the Crimea and their ability to defeat any allied landing. Nevertheless, with no obvious alternative available and under pressure from their governments, they decided to go ahead. Raglan informed Newcastle of the decision, saying:

> The descent on the Crimea is decided upon more in deference to the views of the British government than to any information in the pos-

session of the naval and military authorities, either as to the extent of the enemy's forces, or to their state of preparation.[12]

It was a highly dubious basis on which to risk the French and British armies so late in the campaigning season. Preparations were now put in hand to find the necessary shipping and plan the voyage across the Black Sea.

Russian preparations

Russia had taken the Crimea from the Ottomans in 1783 and Sevastopol became the chief port, naval base and fortress in 1804. The main fortifications were planned and built after 1834 under the direction of Admiral Lazarev. However, by the outbreak of war these works were still incomplete. The sea defences were excellent, as the British and French quickly discovered. These forts were built of stone (three were on the north side of the bay, five on the south) and they contained 571 guns. Sevastopol could not be attacked successfully from the sea.

The real weakness lay in the inadequate and incomplete land defences. The plan agreed in the 1830s called for eight bastions along an arc of about six miles. By late 1853 only one had been completed. Following the outbreak of war, work was speeded up in the spring and summer of 1854. However, activity was limited by the lack of resources (there were only enough tools stored in Sevastopol for 200 men) and by a lack of direction from the commander, Menshikov, on his return from the failure of his diplomatic mission in Constantinople. He believed that he had until the spring of 1855 before any allied attack would take place. Some improvements were made – by September 1854 Bastions 6, 7 and 8 on the south side were in good condition – but much remained to be done. Number 5 was no more than a stone barracks with some cannon behind it, and its main walls could only withstand musket fire. The Malakhov was just a stone tower that would probably collapse if its guns were fired. Number 3 was no more than a field battery of seven guns, while numbers 1 and 2 were only field fortifications. On the south side there were just 145 cannon, many of them obsolete. The defences on the north side were even weaker, with no fortifications on the high ground that dominated the area. When Colonel Totleben arrived from directing the attack on Silistria, Menshikov refused to allow him to undertake any major works. The main achievement of the summer of 1854 was the construction of a direct road from Sevastopol to Inkerman bridge – this was to be the main route along which supplies and reinforcements reached the city throughout the siege of 1854–55.

The Russians were able to organise some reinforcements for the Crimea during 1854. The 17th Infantry Division left Nizhni-Novgorod on 2 December 1853 and, after marching about ten miles a day, five days a week, finally arrived in Sevastopol at the end of April 1854. Later they were joined by the 16th Infantry Division, which spent the summer marching from Yaroslavl. These two marches demonstrate the weakness of the Russian system caused by their lack of railways. Nevertheless, by early September 1854 the population of about 45,000 in Sevastopol was defended by some 38,000 troops aided by 18,000 seamen, many of whom had left their ships and were working on the land fortifications. In addition there were another 12,000 troops in the eastern Crimea guarding Feodosia and Kerch.

Despite indications that the allies might attack, Menshikov remained optimistic. He believed the French and British armies were in a weak state after the outbreak of cholera and the fire at Varna. The Russian commanders thought that the allies could not land more than 30,000 troops and that they could be defeated with the forces available. They believed it was more likely that no more than a raid would take place. On 12 September Menshikov wrote to General Annenkov in St Petersburg, 'My suppositions have been completely borne out; the enemy would never dare to make a landing, and because of the present late season a descent is impossible.'[13] Within a few days his illusions were to be shattered.

Allied doubts

As the planning for the expedition to the Crimea got under way in late July doubts about its feasibility rapidly increased. Where would the troops land? Could they do so in the face of Russian opposition? How could they be sustained without a port to act as a base? Could they defeat the Russian army and then capture Sevastopol? If not, was a siege a practical possibility? If this failed, what would happen to the troops during the winter? Could the army be evacuated if defeat seemed inevitable?

General Sir George Brown told Raglan of his reservations in mid-July, but then advised undertaking the attack because it was what the government wanted. Others were much clearer in setting out their doubts. General Sir John Burgoyne, the engineer in charge of fortifications, who had visited Varna in the spring, was asked by Newcastle on 11 August to go out to Varna and give Raglan some advice on the technical problems involved in the expedition. He left the next day. En route he wrote a long paper headed 'Thoughts on an Attack upon Sebastopol', which he sent to Raglan by messenger on 21 August while he was still at Piraeus. He advised that since Sevastopol could not be captured by a quick naval attack, a landing some distance from the port would be necessary and the Russian army would then have to be defeated in battle. He noted the problems the British had faced in such amphibious landings in the past, in particular the fiascos at Walcheren in the 1790s and Egypt in 1801. Although landing the infantry would not be a major problem, the real difficulty would be getting the artillery, cavalry and provisions ashore. This would take at least a day, during which the army would be very vulnerable to a Russian attack. He advised that any landing should take place about three to four days' march from Sevastopol, possibly at Evpatoriya. Privately, Burgoyne did not expect his advice to be listened to. On 29 August, shortly after his arrival in Varna, he wrote home:

> It is not expected that *I*, coming out so late, and under the repute rather of a professional Engineer than otherwise, should have any opportunity of expressing any opinion upon the great project; nor have I, and I am glad that I have not, for I must confess that I do not understand on what sound principle it is undertaken.[14]

Burgoyne pointed out that almost no attention had been paid to the likely strength of Russian forces and that the allies would not be able to land and support an army that had a decisive superiority in numbers.

Even before his advice was available to Raglan, Brigadier Tylden of the Royal Engineers gave Raglan the most cogent possible reasons not to undertake the expedition. He argued that, even if the landing and the initial battle with the Russians were successful, major problems would remain unsolved:

> The army must proceed to the attack of a fortress which, from its position, cannot be *invested* by the force at our command, with the strength of which we are totally unacquainted, except from a reconnaissance taken at a distance of more than two miles at sea. The besieging army will be liable to attack at all times in front, flank and rear; it will, therefore, be necessary, in the first instance, to throw up strong entrenchments for its security, which *must* occupy many days, even if unmolested; whereas, the fortress is so situated that supplies and reinforcements can be thrown in at any and every moment. It is an established fact in a war that a weak fortress, which from its extent or other causes, cannot be invested is much more difficult, and takes longer time to capture than one of much greater artificial strength which can be invested . . . It is my opinion that the projected attack on Sebastopol, with our present resources at command, is

eminently hazardous and will, at least, require a longer time to effect, than the present advanced season will allow.[15]

All of Tylden's doubts were soon found to be fully justified.

Other commanders, apart from Brown, Burgoyne and Tylden, shared these doubts. The Quartermaster-General, General Sir Richard Airey, one of Raglan's most trusted advisers, felt that although Sevastopol was the right objective, any attack should wait until the spring. Sir George Cathcart, commander of the 4th Division, wrote to his wife as the expedition sailed towards the Crimea:

> We know nothing of the enemy's force & the season is so far advanced that even a protracted success would be more dangerous to British interests & almost worse than a defeat – The British Army would probably be reduced to nothing & we have not another to replace it.[16]

Despite these clear doubts and warnings from most of the senior British commanders, and the lack of any clear plan concerning what to do once the troops were ashore, Raglan decided to continue with the attack on the Crimea and Sevastopol. It was a disastrous decision and shaped the nature of the war for the next year. It would have been much wiser for the allied armies to wait to mount their invasion in the spring. They would have had a secure, easily supplied base during the winter. Then they would have been able to undertake the attack with a long spell of good weather ahead – the Russians would not have been able to move in major reinforcements during the winter. Instead everything was now hazarded on a risky invasion and a decisive attack on Sevastopol within little more than a month. Did the allies have the forces for such an attack, and were their commanders prepared to take risks and make bold decisions to achieve their aims?

Unlike the senior military men in the Crimea, the politicians in London were optimistic and already planning what to do after the fall of Sevastopol when, all were agreed, the fortifications would be destroyed immediately. Palmerston thought the 30,000 Russian prisoners of war who would be captured should be left to walk to Odessa, although most would die of exposure or starvation. The Crimea would be given back to the Ottomans, probably with Georgia, Circassia, the Sea of Azov and the mouths of the Danube. He told Clarendon, 'an adverse critic might say catch and kill your bear before you determine what you will do with his skin, but I think our bear is as good as taken'.[17] Aberdeen was slightly more cautious, telling Palmerston that 'with Sebastopol entirely razed and the fleet captured, I would not give sixpence for the possession of the Crimea in any political view'.[18] Clarendon was equally confident about the short-term position, though he thought the war would continue even after the fall of Sevastopol. 'After we get Sebastopol the Tsar will retire within his own frontier and defy all Europe. We must then coerce him commercially.'[19]

The expedition sails

The British and French spent most of August trying to organise the expedition to the Crimea. In Constantinople the Agent of Transports, Captain John Christie, secured five small steamers and thirty-four pontoons. The base at Malta was able to provide thirty boats, fifty carts and some mules. The Royal Navy officer in charge, Captain William Mends, was able to find enough steam power for all the ships (including towing the sailing ships) and sufficient space for the infantry and most of the artillery, but only half the cavalry. The French did not have enough space for their cavalry and many of the infantry travelled on their battleships (more than a 1,000 men on each ship). (The 11,000 French troops and the British cavalry that were left behind would sail as soon as ships were available.) The Ottoman forces (more than 7,000 men) were also transported on six battleships. Overall the British used fifty-two sailing ships, twenty-seven steam transports and some of their warships. The French employed more than 200 small sailing ships in addition to their battleships. The British were able to move 22,000 infantry, 1,000 cavalry, 3,000 engineers and sixty field guns. The French forces involved were 25,000 infantry, 2,800 engineers and sixty-eight field guns. It was the largest amphibious operation ever attempted until that moment. It was a major feat to have mounted it in so short a time.

On 20 August the British and French admirals met on the *Ville de Paris*. They agreed that embarkation would start on 28 August and be complete by 2 September. The fleet would sail in two columns – the British to the north and the French and Ottomans to the south. Their main worries were that en route to the Crimea the Russian fleet might attack or that a strong north-east wind would blow, dispersing the ships. Both fears proved groundless. The real problems came in loading the ships. The British were delayed by first loading and then unloading much of the cavalry and 3,000 horses. Ambulance wagons were left behind and surgeons had only one pack-pony per regiment to carry their equipment. There was an allowance of just ten stretchers per regiment. Most of the baggage (including tents for both officers and men) and spare cavalry horses were left behind. About 5,000 horses were simply left to starve to death. When officers tried to stop soldiers' wives from getting on board, there was a near riot and eventually some had to be allowed to accompany the expedition. Many remained in Varna for several weeks. All of the ships were grossly overcrowded. As the ships waited in the bay, the bodies of the dead were weighted down and thrown overboard. However, they broke free of the weights and the decomposing bodies were left to bob around the ships with their heads and shoulders out of the water. The French completed loading on 4 September and put to sea. The British were still waiting for their steamers to arrive. They turned up early on the morning of 5 September, but had to take on coal and water. The British were finally ready to sail on 7 September, five days later than planned.

EYE-WITNESS
EMBARKATION AT VARNA

Temple Godman, officer
'The ships are all told off in their divisions, and immense steam-tugs ply about the bay – all is activity and preparation. The shore is strewn with gun-carts, ammunition, gabions etc., which are being shipped as fast as possible. In the meantime the infantry are concentrating around Varna; and the Light Cavalry are expected tomorrow [28 August]. The soldiers whose spirits have been at a low ebb, as well they might from all this sickness, are now on the rise; and everyone looks forward to the fall of Sebastopol.'

Henry Clifford, officer
'It is a thousand pities our army did not go at Sebastopol on first leaving England when in rude health and full of spirits and enthusiasm. All these have vanished. The papers may tell you what they like but our army is not what it was on leaving England. We have been kept in idleness with hundreds falling round us by cholera and fever and every one feels the greatest debility and repugnance to active exertion of any kind. I hope I may be able to write in a few days and tell you Sebastopol is taken, but I doubt it.'

George Lawson, doctor
'Two days ago [30 August] we were all ordered to embark at 6 o'clock in the morning, the place of embarkation being 2 miles distant. We accordingly had to get up soon after 3.0 a.m. as the tents had to be struck, all the pack horses and arabas [carts] laden, and breakfast to be had. I went down seated on the top of some baggage in a bullock cart, and after remaining on the beach for about 3 or 4 hours, I was told there was not room for me in the vessel. I consequently had to come back and pitch my tent again.'

Frederick Dallas, officer

'We started from Varna on the 5th for Balzick Bay about 10 miles off where we again stopped for all one day and then started and sailed, we imagined, for Sebastopol. We cast anchor in the middle of the sea entirely out of sight of land the day before yesterday [9 September] and here we still are just as near as when we started . . . It seems as if Providence favoured our designs for we have had an almost uninterrupted calm ever since we have been here – the slightest gale would have utterly dispersed us anchored as we are in 30 fathoms of water . . . [we are] waiting in the middle of the Black Sea to be told where to go & no one appearing to know where that may be. One rumour is Odessa and to reasonable people it seems to be the best; that such a place as Sebastopol can be taken in 3 days seems hopeless, and all we know is we are to land with 3 days' provisions and 1 blanket apiece & very cold by the way it will be as the nights are now rather biting.'

The announcement about the expedition was received indifferently in the army, where morale was low after a long period of inaction and the growing number of deaths from cholera. Frances Duberly, the wife of an officer, noted that the orders to embark were received in complete silence: 'there was not a single cheer: we have waited in inaction too long. Sickness and death are uppermost in our thoughts just now.'[20] Temple Godman reported that the 5th Dragoon Guards had been decimated while at Varna. 'We have no colonel, our major is ill at Constantinople, our Senior Captain dead, two lieutenants and a cornet on the sick list, our paymaster gone home, our surgeon dead and quartermaster been ill for six weeks and the vet. Surgeon hardly expected to live'.[21] However, some remained optimistic that the campaign in the Crimea would be short. Cornet Fisher wrote, 'Hurrah for the Crimea, we are off tomorrow; fine country, people very friendly; take Sebastopol in a week or so, and then into winter quarters for the winter.'[22]

The cruise across the Black Sea took seven days. The main decision taken en route was to change the landing site. Saint Arnaud, who was now in the last stages of cancer, lay ill in his cabin on the *Ville de Paris*. He called a conference for 1 p.m. on 7 September as the fleet sailed from Varna. Raglan, with only one arm, was unable to climb the side of the ship and sent his secretary, Colonel Steel, accompanied by Admiral Dundas. Doubts were expressed about landing at the mouth of the Kacha – Russian troops had been seen nearby and the likely destination of the expedition had already been published in the London papers. The French suggested landing at Kaffa (near Yalta in the south of the Crimea) and using this as a winter base for an attack on Sevastopol in the spring. All except Saint Arnaud, who was too ill to move, then crossed to the British ships to see Raglan. He still favoured an early attack on Sevastopol and agreed to conduct a further reconnaissance of the coast accompanied by Canrobert. This revealed that about 30,000 Russian troops were near the River Kacha and the mission decided that it would be better to land further north near Evpatoriya (Burgoyne's original choice for the landing). The main advantage of this landing site was its long beach and the open country immediately around it. The warships ought to be able to protect the troops as they landed. The disadvantage was that Sevastopol was about thirty miles away and the allied armies would have to cross three rivers to reach the city, and at each of them the Russian army would have good defensive positions. The Russians would also be able to move inland and threaten the flank of the allied armies as they marched south. In addition there was no water in the area for the troops and horses to drink. However, there seemed to be no alternative and the expedition was duly diverted away to the north.

EYE-WITNESS
LANDING IN THE CRIMEA

William Russell, *The Times* war correspondent
'Eupatoria lies on a spit of sand . . . Towards the south side were innumerable windmills, and several bathing boxes gaily painted along the beach . . . The country inland was covered with cattle, with grain in stack, with farmhouses. The stubble fields were covered with wild lavender, southernwood and other fragrant shrubs . . . we could see the people driving their carts and busy in their ordinary occupations . . . Now and then some Cossacks were visible, scouring along the roads to the interior. The post carriage from Sebastopol to Odessa also was seen rolling leisurely along.'

George Evelyn, militia officer
'The town . . . is on a low sandy spit, with either the sea or a lake behind – the end of the tongue of land covered with windmills – several dome tops, churches, a tower, a large building a mile or two to the left with immense stacks of hay – people are at work either removing or making it. Wretched little Eupatoria has been summoned, and surrendered.'

William Russell
'The officers of each company first descended, each man in full dress. Over

---

his shoulder was slung his haversack, containing what had been, ere it underwent the process of cooking, four pounds and a half of salt meat, and a bulky mass of biscuit of the same weight. This was his ration for three days. Besides this each officer carried his greatcoat, rolled up and fastened in a hoop round his body, a wooden canteen to hold water, a small ration of spirits, whatever change of underclothing he could manage to stow away, his forage-cap and, in most instances, a revolver. Each private carried his blanket and greatcoat strapped up into a kind of knapsack, inside which was a pair of boots, a pair of socks, a shirt, and, at the request of the men themselves, a forage-cap; he also carried his water canteen, and the same rations as the officer, a portion of the mess cooking apparatus, firelock and bayonet of course, cartouche box and fifty rounds of ball-cartridge for Minié, sixty rounds for smooth-bore arms.'

The landing in the Crimea

On the morning of 14 September allied troops began disembarking from the ships. A French officer went ashore to the town of Evpatoriya under a flag of truce and handed the Mayor a summons to surrender. The Mayor fumigated the document (as Russian health regulations required) and agreed to surrender the town. The main landing took place about ten miles south of Evpatoriya on a long sandy beach. The French started landing at 7 a.m. – by nightfall they had three divisions ashore, with their outposts more than four miles inland. The troops carried six days' rations of biscuits, four days' of meat and one day's water and were sheltered in their tents. The Ottoman troops were also all ashore and accommodated in large tents. The British did not start landing until 9 a.m. and by the evening they were in a chaotic state along the beach. The troops landed carrying three days' rations, wearing their greatcoats and carrying a blanket, a rucksack over their right shoulder and a water keg over their left, just as they had in the Napoleonic Wars. They had no tents and so, when a fierce storm broke on the evening of 14 September, they were left exposed on the beach. General Sir George Brown slept under an upturned cart, but General Sir George de Lacy Evans had arranged for his tent to be brought ashore. The British cavalry did not disembark until the next day, when a heavy swell in the bay made the operation hazardous. Improvised platforms had to be made by lashing boats together, and many horses and guns fell over the side. The beach was a scene of utter confusion, with stores strewn everywhere but no transport to move them. Requisitioning parties were sent out and returned with 350 small carts, sixty-seven camels and 253 horses – grossly inadequate for an army of 27,000.

EYE-WITNESS
THE FIRST DAYS ASHORE

George Evelyn
'The troops passed a dreadful night, as it rained in torrents, and they had no tents – several of our artillery boats were wrecked in the surf . . . Several fellows have been on foraging expeditions to the neighbouring villages, and returned laden with poultry, etc. Horses are offered for sale for five dollars, but all money except Russian is refused.'

George Lawson
'Our vessel was not relieved of its load until the evening; we landed on a sandy beach and had to march about 2 miles. We brought nothing on shore with us excepting our blankets and great coats; a change of clothes was impossible, as I am not allowed carriage or a baggage animal. We all bivouacked for the night; but wood could not be found anywhere to make large fires and the night was a pouring wet one, raining in torrents at times . . . The following night we had tents but were obliged to sleep in large numbers in the tents; and as we have no beds we sleep on the ground and cover ourselves with our blankets, and with some straw stolen from some of the villages . . . We suffer dreadfully from want of water. The first day was very hot; we had nothing to drink but water drained out of puddles from the previous night's rain; and even now the water is so thick, that if put into a glass, you cannot see the bottom of it at all.'

Frederick Dallas
(16 September) 'We have had one or two nights of as good (or bad) roughing it as you can well conceive. The first night it poured so we were completely wet through in about 5 minutes trying to sleep on the sand and a cold wind blowing. Last night it was dreadfully cold and we have only a blanket each and no baggage of any description. We are now waiting for the landing of the Cavalry which presents some difficulties owing to the abrupt shore, and an almost constant swell . . . About the enemy we know nothing.'
(18 September) 'We got tents today so that we shall have our nights at least under cover. The nights we find very cold and the food running short, so the sooner we move the better. Firewood is not to be got & water miles off. The men suffer a good deal, I fancy. As regards ourselves, I find what I always

expected & knew . . . that gentlemen can bear discomfort & privation better than the lower orders. I, to whom all this is new, put up I find with it better than most.'

Jean-Jules Herbé, French infantry officer
'The day we landed, the English officers still had not been able to get cooking equipment ashore due to the rough sea. Deprived of food, they were quite at a loss and we saw three or four of them go past carrying a cow's head without a scrap of meat on it . . . We were about to sit down to eat – bread, soup, boiled beef, salad and dried beans – when I suggested to my comrades we share our meal with these English officers. As graciously as possible I invited them and was accepted on the spot with undisguised satisfaction. Imagine how surprised we were when they tucked in without further ado, taking more than half a dish in one go. They probably hadn't eaten in 36 hours and we would have forgiven them such manners borne of an empty stomach if on leaving they had thanked us. But no, they withdrew haughtily and the next day they passed our tent twice without even saying hello.'

The British sent out a reconnaissance party under Cardigan, but with the same disastrous consequences as his mission at Varna in July. Lieutenant Edward Seager of the 8th Royal Irish Hussars described what happened:

We landed in the Crimea on the 16th September in Calamita Bay, without any opposition and immediately had to march 24 miles into the country on a foolish expedition after some supposed Cossacks we never caught sight of, the whole of our regiment and part of the 13th went under Lord Cardigan, who is always doing something to render the Light Cavalry inefficient. He brought us back to the beach at 11 o'clock, the night very dark, having passed through a salt lake and lost our way, besides putting us through a field day, and a great many other unnecessary movements, we had to link our horses together, and passed the night on the beach in our cloaks.[23]

Another officer noted sarcastically what happened to the infantry on the reconnaissance:

This foraging party was nearly worked to death by his eccentric

Lordship, whose military experience has not been sufficient to teach him that infantry cannot keep up with cavalry, even marching at the walk. The presence of infantry retarded his movements, and prevented him destroying the horses according to his wont. [24]

The French completed their landing on 15 September, but the British were not ready for another three days. Eventually, on the afternoon of 18 September, orders were issued that the armies would begin moving south towards Sevastopol the next morning.

The French were annoyed at British incompetence and the ensuing delays. Saint Arnaud was now gravely ill (although he supervised the French landing on horseback) and keen to enter Sevastopol before he died. The allied armies were lucky that Menshikov failed to take the initiative in attacking them while they were so disorganised. The landings were watched by small groups of Cossacks who kept well away from the allied troops. Late on the evening of 18 September the allies captured a Russian messenger carrying a despatch from the Governor of Sevastopol, which gave details of the poor state of the garrison in the town.

19 September – the march south

Early on the morning of 19 September the allied armies formed up for the march south towards Sevastopol. The four French divisions and the Ottoman troops formed the right wing, with their flank on the coast protected by the allied warships that moved south with the armies. The British were on the left because they had the only cavalry to act as a reconnaissance screen inland. The French, led by the elite Zouaves, were ready at 6 a.m. but had to wait three hours for the British. The march eventually began with bands playing and regimental colours flying. The route lay across open rolling grassland, but almost nothing was seen and the cottages and hamlets were deserted. By late morning, as the heat increased, enthusiasm diminished. Water had been very short since the landing five days earlier, and the British rations of salt pork and biscuit only exacerbated the problem.

**EYE-WITNESS
THE MARCH SOUTH**

William Russell

'The day was warm, and our advance was delayed by the wretched transport furnished for the baggage, an evil which will, I fear, be more severely felt in any protracted operations. Everything not absolutely indispensable was sent on board ship . . . The country beyond the salt lake, near which we were encamped, is perfectly destitute of tree or shrub, and consists of wide plains, marked at intervals of two or three miles with hillocks and long, irregular ridges of hills running down towards the sea . . . It is but little cultivated, except in the patches of land around the infrequent villages built in the higher recesses of the valleys. Hares were started in abundance . . . At last, the smoke of burning villages and farm-houses announced that the enemy in front were aware of our march. It was a sad sight to see the white walls of the houses blackened with smoke – the flames ascending through the roofs of peaceful homesteads – and the ruined outlines of deserted hamlets. Many sick men fell out, and were carried to the rear. It was a painful sight – a sad contrast to the magnificent appearance of the army in front, to behold litter after litter borne past to the carts, with the poor sufferers who had dropped from illness and fatigue.'

Shortly before 2 p.m. the allied troops arrived at the first of the four rivers they had to cross before reaching Sevastopol. This was the Bulganak (at this time of the year no more than a shallow stream) – the British broke ranks and dashed for the water. On the far side of the stream, on the ridges leading back up to the plateau, were about 2,000 Russian cavalry and 6,000 infantry. Cardigan, leading the Light Brigade, did not see the Russians, crossed the river and advanced. A small skirmish followed in which four men were wounded. Raglan ordered the cavalry to retire and they did so, covered by artillery fire. The Russian troops retired to their positions about three miles away across the Alma River, where the allies could now see the bulk of the Russian army in defensive positions. The allied commanders decided to halt near water before the inevitable battle the next day.

After the allies landed on 14 September, Menshikov reacted quickly to the invasion that he had not thought possible. He decided, probably wisely, not to attack the British and French at Evpatoriya, where they would be protected by the guns of the warships. Instead he decided to fight on the line of the Alma River, which was the best defensive position on the road to Sevastopol. Here the Russians could entrench themselves on the heights above the river, a position that would help compensate for their inferior numbers. Menshikov had available about 33,000 troops (including two regiments that arrived on the evening of the 19th after a five-day forced march of 150 miles from Kerch. Overall the British, French and Ottomans landed 61,000 troops and so had a superiority of roughly two to one. Menshikov, who had never before commanded an army and who refused to take advice from his seasoned Generals, adopted a reasonable strategy, but it chanced everything on a single battle. A better strategy would have been to move the Russian army inland to threaten the allied left flank as it marched towards Sevastopol. The British cavalry had inadequate numbers to monitor Russian movements, and the allies – without an effective supply train – would have had to keep close to Evpatoriya and the coast. Harassing attacks could have been very effective.

Raglan set up his headquarters for the night of 19 September in a cottage near the bridge carrying the Evpatoriya–Sevastopol road over the Bulganak. That evening Saint Arnaud rode over from the French lines to discuss strategy for the battle the next day. As the commander of the largest army, it was clearly for Saint Arnaud to take the initiative. He spoke in a mixture of French and English in outlining an attack at 5.30 a.m., with a French onslaught near the coast and the British sweeping round to roll up the Russian right wing. Raglan hardly bothered to speak, which Saint Arnaud took as indicating assent. Raglan assured the French commander of British co-operation and did not offer an alternative plan. He did not tell his divisional commanders of the French plan and he did not have one of his own – his staff would probably have been incapable of drawing up a detailed operational plan. No proper reconnaissance was carried out, and Raglan had no idea of the strength of the Russian army across the Alma.

EYE-WITNESS
THE NIGHT BEFORE THE BATTLE

An anonymous Russian NCO

'That evening a military band played marches near the Commander-in-Chief's grey tent and a choir sang old Russian songs. A number of our men were then detailed for picquets over the river forward of the village and the order was given to put out fires . . . At the evening meal many of the soldiers ate little, and night came on in a weariness of waiting. We could hear the

---

barking of hungry dogs roaming the deserted village down below. As we lay down to sleep, dressed in our field marching order, for the first time there arose a feeling of apprehension and uncertainty.'

The battle that would be fought the next day would be the most crucial of the campaign. The allied troops had landed with no agreed plan of what they were to do. All they knew was that they would have to defeat the Russian army at some point. The chaotic landing had, luckily, not been opposed, but all would now depend on the events of 20 September. If the allies were defeated, the expedition would end in disorder and humiliation because it would be almost impossible to evacuate the defeated army. Success might open the way to Sevastopol but there was no plan for how its capture might be achieved. Not only that, but there was no plan for the battle soon to be fought along the Alma. Raglan had listened to Saint Arnaud's ideas but had no intention of carrying them out – he did not wish to be subordinate to the French, whom he still continued to equate with 'the enemy'. The most likely British attack would therefore be a crude frontal assault on the Russian positions.

6

Alma and After

In accordance with the plan discussed with Raglan the previous evening, French and Ottoman troops were ready to move from their encampment near the Bulganak River shortly after 5.30 a.m. The British were not ready. An hour and a half later the troops were still breakfasting and the officers washing. Rations had not yet been issued. Next the two divisions that were to form the left flank of the march had to be brought into line over very broken ground. Finally, at 10.30, five hours late and after the French advance had been postponed three times, the British were ready to move. The allied armies started to advance with bands playing. Almost immediately the French and British armies began to drift apart, creating a hole in the centre of the advance – it took almost an hour to restore the line. About noon, after covering around three miles, the armies came to a ridge from where they could look down on the Alma valley, which was full of trees and two small hamlets – Almatomak and Burliuk. They stopped for lunch under a cloudless sky as the temperature soared.

While the allied armies ate their rations, Saint Arnaud rode over to Raglan and, together with their entourages, they went to a low mound to look at the Russian positions. Raglan used a special attachment to manipulate his telescope with his one hand. They found that Menshikov had chosen a natural defensive position. The riverbank was steep and high, making it difficult to cross. On the far side there were woods, but then bare slopes rising to the plateau that dominated the valley. A range of hills ran inland from the coast for about two miles to Telegraph Hill (so-called because of the unfinished telegraph station on the summit). The Russians had twenty guns and twelve infantry battalions in this sector. (Special stands had also been erected for the civilian spectators from Sevastopol.) From here the ridge pulled away from the valley in a large curve before reaching Kurgan Hill, the centre of the Russian position. Here the Russians deployed seventy guns and eighteen infantry battalions, including two made up of sailors from the Black Sea fleet. There was also a ridge halfway down to the river with improvised defences, fourteen heavy guns and four battalions of infantry. The British, with a sense of exaggeration, called it the 'Great Redoubt'. A battery of guns and five infantry battalions were deployed across the Evpatoriya–Sevastopol road, the axis of the allied advance. Further back along the road were the reserves – two gun batteries and seven infantry battalions. Menshikov divided the front into three

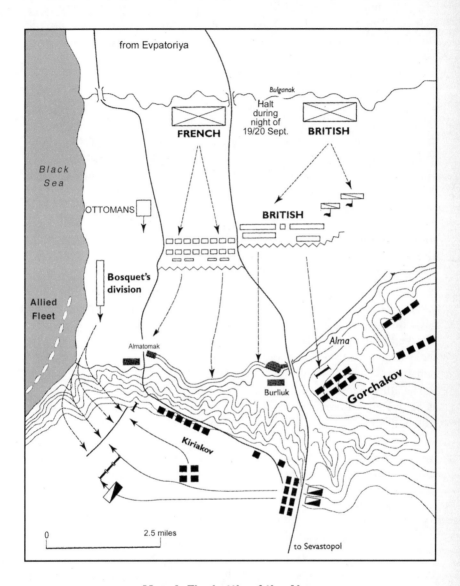

Map 4: The battle of the Alma

sectors of roughly 10,000 men each. Major-General Kiriakov was on the left, including Telegraph Hill. The road was defended by the sixty-four-year-old Prince Gorchakov, who had failed badly in the battles along the Danube earlier in the year. The centre, around the Kurgan, was under Major-General Kvetsinski.

Although superficially strong, the Russian position had a number of weaknesses. The left of the line was nearly two miles from the sea, which would have made a natural flank. Menshikov may have been worried about fire from the allied warships offshore, but he had also been reassured that the cliffs in this area were unscaleable. Although many of the troops had been in position for nearly a week, few trenches or earthworks had been built – the men stood or lay down in columns in the open, forming a dense mass with almost no protection. Menshikov seems to have intended to fight the main battle in the centre, using artillery fire as the allies crossed the river and then following up with a bayonet attack. He had never commanded in battle before and, like the other Russian commanders, had no understanding of the impact that accurate, lethal long-range rifle fire would have on the fighting. He had not destroyed the vineyards, stone walls and houses in the valley, which would provide cover for the allied troops as they descended to cross the river. Menshikov had deployed eight battalions in the vineyards at the bottom of the valley, but they were reserve battalions of recently mobilised conscripts. Even worse, half of them were withdrawn, without authority, to positions higher up and the remainder quickly followed.

The allied plan of attack was still unclear. The British had not deployed as Saint Arnaud intended and had made no effort to move left round the Russian right flank – Raglan thought it was too dangerous because of his lack of cavalry. No decisions were made before the battle started and there was no attempt to co-ordinate French and British actions. Saint Arnaud stuck to his plan of the previous day and assumed the British would make a frontal assault. He rode back to the French positions shortly after 1 p.m.

The opening of the battle – the French attack

The French had discovered not only that the Russian left flank was weakly held, but that there was a path that led up the side of the valley from near the mouth of the Alma to the plateau above. This was an operation with which the French were familiar from their campaigns in Algeria. Bosquet's troops, led by the Zouaves, were to initiate the attack. They dropped their packs as they normally did and descended to the river mouth to cross at a sand bar. They had to move slowly because of the surf. They remained undetected and began the thirty-minute climb up the twisting, narrow path to the summit. The Russians could easily have stopped them at any point. The French troops were not spotted until they reached the top. There they came under Russian artillery fire and took shelter in the scrub just below the summit. The Russians could easily have brought up reinforcements, but subordinate commanders were not allowed to use their initiative and Menshikov did not take seriously the news that the French were on the plateau.

Bosquet, together with General d'Autemarre, 3,000 men and twelve guns, crossed the river by the ford at Almatomak. They climbed up another steep path to the top. It took two hours to drag the guns to the plateau. Long before that had been completed, Saint Arnaud saw that the Zouaves and first parties of Bosquet's troops were on the summit. At about 2.30 p.m., without waiting for the British to move, he ordered a general advance. Saint Arnaud's plan of the previous evening was for Canrobert's division to cross the Alma at the ford below Telegraph Hill and for Prince Napoleon's 3rd Division to cross at the ford below Burliuk. Canrobert's troops crossed the river fairly easily, but found that the lane up the ravine was too narrow for their field guns. They were sent off to the right to use the same path as Bosquet's troops, but it would take time for the guns to be hauled to the top. Canrobert's infantry climbed up the lane under Russian musket and artillery fire, but the advantages of their Minié rifles were soon apparent as the French troops were able to pick off the Russian artillery men who had not taken cover – they were either killed or fled. Canrobert's troops were soon on the edge of the plateau along with the other French troops on their right. Menshikov finally took notice of the French on the summit and realised that his defensive position had been turned. He started moving eight battalions over to his left, but did not order a general attack on the French. He moved with his troops, but accomplished nothing except to put himself out of touch with the overall battle. Meanwhile Prince Napoleon's division, which had moved in eight columns to the bottom of the Alma valley, were pinned down by Russian artillery fire from Telegraph Hill and unable to cross the river. Saint Arnaud had decided to follow the 3rd Division and he was now trapped in a cottage garden near the river.

The British attack

The British began their preparations for an attack shortly after 1 p.m. They normally marched in columns, but attacked in line with each division forming two long lines of 2,500 men stretching almost one mile across.

The complex manoeuvres required to change formation had often been practised on the parade ground, but never under fire. By the end of the process there was confusion in the British line. The Light Division was positioned too close to the 2nd Division, and the 7th Royal Fusiliers of the former were behind the 95th Foot of the latter. This would produce chaos in any attack and attempts were made to move the Light Division to the left and slightly forward. General Sir George Brown was short-sighted and had not seen what had happened, and Raglan, who was higher up and could see, did not issue any orders, hoping matters would sort themselves out. British riflemen moved forward and reached the edge of the grassy slope leading down to the river, where they exchanged fire with Russian skirmishers on the other side.

EYE-WITNESS
THE ALLIES ATTACK

William Russell, *The Times* war correspondent
'The front of the Russian line above us had burst into a volcano of flame and white smoke – the roar of the artillery became terrible – we could hear the heavy rush of the shot, those terrible dumps into the ground, and the crash of trees, through which it tore with resistless fury and force, splinters and masses of stone flew out of the walls . . . the shot came flinging close to me, one, indeed killing one of the two bandsmen who were carrying a litter close to my side . . . It knocked away the side of his face, and he fell dead – a horrible sight . . . Before me all was smoke . . . The rush of shot was appalling and I recollect that I was particularly annoyed by the birds, which were flying about distractedly in the smoke, as I thought they were fragments of shell.'

The Russian Troops
'The English rifle and artillery fire grew in intensity so that our commander Gorev [Tarutinsky battalion] began to move from place to place to escape it . . . until he did this, many soldiers had given way to their terror and were kneeling down, huddled together in groups, calling for help on all that is holy.'
'Our hearts pounded at the sight of the endless mass of [British] troops marching steadily towards us, but when our artillery, which occupied good commanding positions, opened fire, the shells fell short as the enemy was still out of range. Our troops then set alight the village of Burliuk and we became blinded by the smoke which drifted back on us. It would have been

---

wiser, as those with battle experience said at the time, not to have created a smoke screen for the enemy's benefit since this enabled him to fire on us without any loss on his side; but these mistakes were not the last. As the enemy got closer our shells began to blow great holes in his ranks; but the many gaps were immediately closed up and the enemy strode on, apparently indifferent to his losses. Soon afterwards we began to feel the terrible effects of his rifle fire . . . the rifle fire was murderous because each bullet hit its mark; anyone on a horse was an immediate target and many of the field officers became casualties in consequence . . . Our artillery was doing marvellous execution among the enemy . . . but then the guns began to run out of ammunition . . . And so the artillery action ceased almost as soon as it had begun.'

The British lines were a mile from the river, and still overlapping, when Raglan issued the order to halt. He probably did so because he could see the French advance on his right and decided to wait. At the rear, out of range of the Russian guns, the 1st and 3rd Divisions were still in columns – they were halted and told to stand easy. The forward troops of the Light and 2nd Divisions had to lie down under Russian fire for about an hour and a half. For most men this was their first time in action, as Russian artillery fire – mainly round shot that required a direct hit, but some grapeshot – fell among them. The wounded were simply dragged out of line to wait for the bandsmen, who acted as medical assistants, to possibly provide some treatment. It was against orders for any soldier to treat the wounded. By 3 p.m., nearly two hours after the battle began and long after the French troops reached the edge of the plateau, the British had still not crossed the river, were tied down and had achieved nothing. Half an hour after the main French advance started, they requested the British to move and provide some assistance. At 3.05 p.m. Raglan ordered the infantry to advance. However, in Raglan's characteristic fashion, no objective was given and no details were provided.

The British insistence on advancing in a solid line produced further chaos. The overlap between the 7th Royal Fusiliers and the 95th Foot had not been sorted out and was made worse when the 1st Brigade of the 2nd Division veered left, away from the burning houses of Burliuk, and the Light Division slowed up as they picked their way through the vineyards at the bottom of the valley. Eventually the infantry were able to roughly re-form lines on reaching the river, which they crossed holding their rifles and ammunition above their heads. A number fell over and were drowned. The far bank provided cover from the Russian fire above. More chaos ensued as some units formed into squares, expecting a Russian cavalry attack – it would have been a disaster if the Russian artillery had been able to fire at them. Other units were mixed up and did not recognise some of the commanders telling them to advance. Eventually most of the Light Division began climbing the hill towards the Russian artillery position on the lower ridge (the 'Great Redoubt'). About 1,500 Russian infantry were deployed in columns behind the artillery, but only the front ranks could fire their muskets and this was ineffective. The artillery took time to reload and British rifle fire was accurate and deadly.

At around 3.30 p.m. about four British battalions captured the Russian artillery position, but the Russians managed to drag away all but two of their guns. Almost immediately they launched a counter-attack with four battalions of the 31st Vladimir Musketeer Regiment. Exactly what happened next is unclear – the British may have thought the troops were French and held fire – but the outcome was that the retreat was sounded and the British infantry ran back to the river, sheltering under the bank once again. Meanwhile other units were making little progress. The 1st Division, mainly composed of the elite Guards regiments, was commanded by the Duke of Cambridge, but he had never been on active service and had little idea what orders to issue. They moved down to the river in immaculate line behind the Light Division, but stopped short of the vineyards in order not to break the line. It was only after orders from General Airey that the Brigade of Guards continued to advance, crossed the river and formed up on the far side. Just as they did so they were badly affected by the 2,000 or so men fleeing down the hill from the Russian counter-attack. This created a hole in the 1st Division line. Meanwhile the 2nd Division was still pinned down by Russian artillery fire. By about 3.45 p.m. the British had, therefore, achieved little more than the crossing of the Alma River.

The battle of the Alma – the final phase

Shortly before 4 p.m. the French field guns reached the top of the plateau and were able to open fire. They found a mass of Russian soldiers in the open, with no artillery protection and only about 100 yards away. The outcome was a massacre. The Russians retreated back towards Telegraph Hill and came under French artillery fire. The French infantry could deploy under artillery protection and, led by the Zouaves, they were able to capture the telegraph tower. Soon there were nearly 10,000 French troops in the area putting the retreating Russians under heavy fire. The Russian left flank was broken and the battle was effectively decided at this point.

At about this time the British restarted their advance up the hill. The Highland Brigade crossed the river and passed through two battalions of the Light Brigade and began the ascent. When about 300 men of the Light Division tried to fill the gap in the line of the Guards Brigade, Colonel Hood of the Grenadier Guards ejected them – it was not socially acceptable for them to mix with the elite regiments. Under severe pressure from the French on their left, the Russians on the summit were unable to put up much resistance as the British troops climbed up the side of the valley. The 'Great Redoubt' was recaptured and British troops moved on towards the Kurgan Hill as the Russians retreated. Raglan had only ordered the infantry to advance, but the cavalry under Lucan crossed the river on their own initiative and attacked the retreating Russians.

Allied troops now controlled much of the plateau and Russian forces were in full flight along the Sevastopol road. Kiriakov was able to organise a battery of some thirty guns to cover a retreat that was fairly orderly until the troops reached the Kacha River, where they broke and straggled back into Sevastopol. The allies only had the 1,000 British cavalry of the Light Brigade to follow up their success and Raglan ordered them not to advance until artillery support was available. Lucan protested, but Raglan did not bother to reply.

EYE-WITNESS
THE RUSSIAN RETREAT

Lieutenant-General Kvetzenski, 16th Infantry Division
'The mass of English troops, notwithstanding our devastating fire of shot and shell that had made bloody furrows through their ranks, closed up once more and, with new forces, protected by swarms of skirmishing riflemen and supported by a battery firing from behind the smoking ruins of Burliuk, crossed the river and drove back [our troops], forcing our field battery to limber up and depart . . . The English advanced in three columns and threatened to turn my right flank, and the French were coming up on my left wing . . . I then decided that my aim must be to save the regiment and its colours and not the guns . . . then my horse was struck down and I was wounded in the leg. As I was being carried off on a stretcher made of rifles I was hit yet again by a bullet which smashed my arm and rib.'

Colonel V. F. Vinsh, Chief of Staff to Menshikov
'We were amazed to find that our positions to the left of the Sevastopol road had been abandoned and we were astounded all the more because even

the heights behind, which commanded the abandoned positions, were held by nobody. French riflemen were already running up the hill unimpeded, and these, seeing us, opened fire . . . We rode on and, descending into a sheltered hollow, there found General Kiriakov, alone and on foot. When the Commander-in-Chief asked him where were his troops, he merely answered that his horse had been shot from under him!'

Colonel Strogonov
'The enemy took the heights, yet used them only to direct artillery fire on our troops withdrawing from the area of the bridge. He then sat there, rejoicing at his victory over what he imagined to be the advanced guard of our army; his mistake saved us and Sevastopol. For who could have thought that our handful of men *was* the Crimean army . . . our defeated army set off for Sevastopol . . . hardly able to draw breath, hardly able to see reason or come to its senses and understand that this was no nightmare but bitter reality . . . hundreds of wounded had been deserted by their regiments, and these, with heart-rending cries and moans and pleading gestures begged to be lifted into the carts and carriages. But what could I do for them? We were already packed to overloading . . . One man could hardly drag himself along – he was without arms and his belly was shot through; another had his leg blown off and his jaw smashed, with his tongue torn out and his body covered with wounds – only the expression on his face pleaded for a mouthful of water.'

Although the Russians had suffered a major defeat their losses were relatively light – 1,800 dead and 3,900 wounded or missing. The British lost 362 dead and just over 2,500 wounded. French losses were far lower, despite the fact that they had a larger force involved and undertook the most dangerous part of the attack – about 200 killed and 1,200 wounded. The disparity was the result of the greater tactical flair of the French (they did not attack in long lines), the initiative allowed at lower levels of command and their experience of fighting in Algeria.

Alma – the aftermath

EYE-WITNESS
AFTER THE BATTLE – THE WOUNDED

James Peters, Naval Surgeon, HMS *Vulcan*
'No notice was given to me that sick or wounded would be sent here; consequently no preparation was made for their reception. But early next morning a small steamer came alongside with 86 soldiers . . . six of these had been wounded in the cavalry skirmish the night before the battle, and had suffered amputation. No document nor order about them was sent, and I considered that no others were coming, and proceeded to arrange them on the main deck . . . about noon boat after boat came alongside with the sick and the wounded . . . About 6 p.m., finding that there were nearly 500 on board, and that others were alongside, I requested the first lieutenant, in the absence of the commander, to prevent others coming on board . . . the sick and wounded were placed indiscriminately on the decks, to the great risk of the wounded, for with diseases such as cholera and dysentery extensively prevailing, the atmosphere becomes quickly tainted . . . But great distress was experienced from the want of urinals and bed pans, one only of each being on board; and from the want of these, many blankets were thrown overboard by my order when they became foul . . . In conclusion, I would say that, although I do not feel called on to blame any one . . . there can be no doubt that, as from the time the army landed in the Crimea a battle was impending and sickness was very rife, some arrangements should have been made, and certain vessels fitted for the purpose.'

William Russell
'There was more than an acre of Russian wounded when they were brought in to-day . . . They were all infantry . . . When I was looking at the wounded men going off to-day, I could not see an English ambulance. Our men were sent to the sea, three miles distant, on jolting arabas or tedious litters. The French – I am tired of this disgraceful antithesis – had well-appointed covered hospital vans.'

The scene on the battlefield on the evening of 20 September was, of course, chaotic and the allied troops needed time to regroup. The wounded had to be recovered and the dead buried (twenty-four gigantic mounds were dug to accommodate the bodies). The French had a system for collecting the wounded and treating them, but the British did not – they did not even have stretchers. The British wounded were carried down to the mouth of the river, where they were put on small boats that had to move out through the heavy surf to the ships offshore. Here most of them lay on deck before sailing to the base hospital at Scutari near Constantinople. The French who had, as normal, dropped their knapsacks before going into battle, needed time to recover them. During the battle the dying Saint Arnaud spent twelve hours in the saddle and suffered a serious relapse, but he refused to hand over command to Canrobert. The British commanders were still squabbling. Cardigan ensured that he had a tent for his sole use and spent the evening drafting a long letter of complaint to Raglan. He protested that Lucan interfered in the affairs of the Light Brigade. Raglan did not bother to reply for over a week and then made the self-evident point that Lucan, as overall commander of the cavalry, was perfectly entitled to issue orders to his subordinate units and reminded Cardigan that 'all his orders and suggestions claim obedience and attention'. Raglan also told Cardigan that he was 'wrong in every one of the instances cited'.[1]

On the morning after the battle Saint Arnaud informed Raglan that the French were ready to move. The British needed another two days to collect the wounded (the Russians were not dealt with until they had been lying in the hot sun for three days). It was, therefore, not until two hours after sunrise on 23 September that the allied armies resumed their march south. It was another hot march over hills and valleys, and large numbers of men collapsed and died from cholera. Eventually the Kacha valley was reached and, with orchards, vineyards and water available, the British and French troops halted for the night. The Russians had not adopted a 'scorched earth' policy – bridges and houses were not destroyed and crops were left in place.

The Russians were able to use the delay in the allied advance to good effect. After the battle Menshikov moved south and camped on the outskirts of Sevastopol. He decided not to defend the Kacha and Belbek Rivers because it would take time to regroup the Russian forces. Over the next couple of days there was growing disorder in Sevastopol, with drunken troops and sailors roaming through the streets. Admiral Kornilov wanted the Black Sea fleet to set sail and attack the allies – it would almost certainly have been a suicide mission. His deputies wanted to sink the fleet in the harbour and use the sailors to man the land defences. Kornilov rejected their advice. However, Menshikov agreed with this plan. Late on 22 September orders were given for the ships to be sunk in the harbour, and these were carried out the next morning when seven old warships were scuttled in the entrance to the northern bay. The British fleet took no action to stop the Russians. The sinkings were unnecessary because the harbour was well defended by its forts, regardless of the block ships.

Colonel Totleben took charge of the southern defences, mobilising the crews of three frigates on 22 September. Guns from the ships were moved into position, ditches deepened and the civilian population ordered to dig entrenchments. In thirty-six hours more than 100 guns were hauled into defensive positions.

Menshikov decided to move the bulk of the army out of Sevastopol. This was partly to restore discipline over the drunken troops, but also to protect his communications and supply lines to Bakhchisarai and the routes in and out of the Crimea. The move began late on the evening of 24 September along a narrow track through scrub and forest. No flank guards were used because Menshikov did not think he could control the troops. It was a rapid night march that was largely completed by early the next morning. When news of the move reached Simferopol on 26 September, the local Tartar population rose in revolt – they thought the Russians were evacuating the whole of the Crimea. After Menshikov's departure the remaining garrison in Sevastopol was made up of four reserve infantry battalions, four depot battalions and seventeen battalions of sailors who had almost no training in infantry warfare. In total there were 18,000 men in the city. There were twelve guns in place on the north shore. On 26 September many of the units were moved to the south side, which was defended by twenty-seven small-calibre guns. That evening Admiral Kornilov expected the city to fall and blamed Menshikov for leaving Sevastopol almost defenceless:

> The prince ought to be made accountable to Russia for the loss of Sevastopol. If he had not gone – God knows where – we would have been able to defend it. If only I had known that he was capable of such a treacherous act then I never would have agreed to have sunk the ships but would have given battle.[2]

The crucial decision

On the morning of 24 September an allied war council was held to decide what to do after the march south from the Alma to the Kacha River. It was perhaps the most important meeting of the war in the east and the decision taken affected the course of the campaign for the next year. The allies had no idea what the Russians had done since the battle of the Alma and were surprised to find that the rivers had been left undefended. They were confident the Russians had put out most of their forces on 20 September and that the allies had a strong numerical superiority and better equipment. General Burgoyne, one of Raglan's trusted advisers, thought they 'had *highly* over-estimated Russian military power, otherwise the Emperor would never have left this primary substance of his power, Sebastopol and fleet, so meanly protected, after so long warning of our prepared formidable attack. If we succeed in this final object, our government, and that of the French, may fairly dictate their terms as to a very inferior State.'[3] He was optimistic; 'I have great hopes that we may force our way into Sebastopol in a few days, if they [the French], or rather *we* would only act with vigour.'[4]

The only question was therefore how to attack Sevastopol. The logic of allied strategy so far, such as it was, was to attack the city directly from the north. The armies had landed with almost no supplies or equipment, but away from the threat of immediate Russian intervention. The initial battle, which could have resulted in disaster, had been successful. However, the allied armies were too small to fully invest Sevastopol and create an effective siege. If they tried to do so they would be open to attack in their rear by Russian forces from the rest of the Crimea. Winter was little more than a month away at best, and so decisive action was required to capture the city as quickly as possible so as to provide winter quarters.

The initial British meeting on 24 September was dominated by Burgoyne. He had, for the last month, favoured an attack from the south of the city, arguing that the defences on this side were much weaker than those on the north. (In fact the main fort on the north side was held only by a battalion of reserve troops.) He also thought such a move would be a tactical surprise. Raglan preferred an attack from the north, arguing that a march round Sevastopol would be dangerous because of the wooded country and the fact that no maps of the area were available. The army would also lose touch with the fleet and would need time to re-establish its bases in one of the harbours on the south coast of the Crimea. Raglan was correct, but nevertheless allowed Burgoyne to put his plan to the French. When he did so he found strong opposition. Prince Napoleon thought the Russians were demoralised and that the defences on the north side were unlikely to be very effective because there had been almost no time to prepare them. However, Saint Arnaud seems to have been predisposed to accept Burgoyne's ideas because he thought the sunken Russian ships in Sevastopol harbour would make it unusable as a supply base during the winter. On the evening before the meeting, as soon as he heard the news of the Russian action, Saint Arnaud wrote:

> This deed which is a parody of Moscow will cause me some embarrassment. I must think to find some ports for wintering my fleet. This will perhaps change my plan of attack. I will probably go to the South.[5]

Saint Arnaud therefore overruled his advisers and accepted Burgoyne's plan. When Burgoyne returned to the British camp, Raglan had little choice but to accept too. The allied armies were now to embark on a hazardous march around the eastern side of Sevastopol to reach the south side. The move was certainly not expected by the Russians, but it was not a 'tactical surprise' – it was a rejection of the most obvious route for an attack on a very poorly defended city.

The flank march

EYE-WITNESS
THE FLANK MARCH

William Russell

'The country through which we marched was hilly and barren. Amidst steep hillocks covered with thistles, and separated from each other at times by small patches of steppe, wound the road to Sebastopol – a mere beaten track marked with cart-wheels, hoofs, and gun-carriage wheels. We advanced uninterruptedly at an average rate of two and a quarter miles an hour; halting occasionally to rest the troops and allow the baggage-waggons to come up.'

George Evelyn, militia officer

'The most dreadful feature of these marches was the entire absence of any means for conveying the sick. The cholera was in our ranks. Men were often suddenly attacked during the march, and fell to the ground contorted by cramps and spasms. We could give them no help. Their arms were taken from them, and they were left on the parched plains – to die.'

Pyotr Alabin, Russian infantryman

'Those who were in Sebastopol when the Allies moved from the northern to the southern side could not believe their eyes. The defenders of the town, which was weak from the land side, had decided to fight to the very last but no-one held out any hope of staving off the enemy hordes . . . When the Allies moved from a position beneath the northern fortifications, which was defended by two cargo battalions, and a few naval squadrons, to the Chernaya River, nobody could understand what they were thinking of.'

The allied armies resumed their march south at 8.30 a.m. on 25 September. The British were still on the left because they had the only cavalry available for reconnaissance. They crossed the Chernaya River and entered the woodland. The single, narrow path had to be left clear for the cavalry and the artillery, so the infantry had to stagger through the dense oak forest in great heat. Units split up into small groups as they tried to find their way between the trees and the allied armies became a disorganised shambles. The British cavalry were sent forward along the path towards Mackenzie's Farm (the home of the Scottish admiral who had supervised the construction of much of the Sevastopol base in the 1830s). They failed in their primary mission – reconnaissance – because they took the wrong turning at a fork, found it was a dead-end and could not turn round because of the troops behind. The artillery, travelling more slowly, stopped at the fork. Eventually General Airey went forward to the edge of the wood and came out on the Sevastopol–Simferopol road. He was staggered to find that he was facing the rearguard of Menshikov's troops that had left Sevastopol the previous evening. The two armies had been blundering around the same area, but by chance – and the fact that neither had any effective reconnaissance – they had not encountered each other before. The British brought up their artillery and fired a few rounds at the Russians who were leaving the burning farm. Some prisoners were taken, but they were not interrogated and so the British had no idea of Menshikov's march away from Sevastopol. The cavalry finally arrived, but Cardigan refused to take any of the blame for his incompetence, claiming, petulantly, that he was not in charge of the cavalry. They were sent forward on a brief reconnaissance along the road, but achieved nothing. The infantry finally staggered out of the woods in the middle of the afternoon.

EYE-WITNESS
MACKENZIE'S FARM

Captain Shakespear, Royal Horse Artillery
'Suddenly the road turned to the right and to our astonishment a regiment of infantry was formed across the road, front ranks, kneeling within 30 yards of us. They fired a volley but were so bewildered nothing touched us. They bolted into the bush.'

J. Gough Calthorpe, British officer
'The troops were allowed to pillage. In a few moments the ground was

---

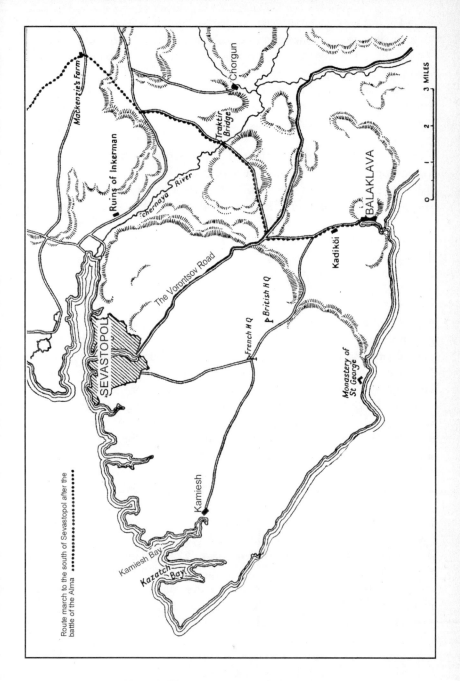

Map 5: The south-west of the Crimea

strewed with every kind of thing . . . handsome Hussar uniforms, rich fur cloaks, every kind of undergarment, male and female. Several wigs I saw being offered for sale, amidst the laughter of the men. French books and novels of an improper kind were not infrequently met with in the baggage of the Russian officers. All these were offered for sale and disposed of to the highest bidder.'

The allied troops spent the night of 25–26 September in a very exposed position on the Fedyukhin Hills. The next day the allied forces continued their march south, but were still in a disorganised state and highly vulnerable. The British artillery was at the front, but had no escort to protect it. The French were often advancing in single file through woods and ravines, but with no idea of the topography of the area. At one point all of the French artillery was in a depression at the entrance to a gorge and within range of Russian artillery in Sevastopol, but the latter took no action – they were preoccupied in constructing defences.

During the march, Saint Arnaud, who had already lived longer than his doctors had forecast in the spring, suffered a major collapse. Not only was his cancer in its final stages, but he also had a violent bout of cholera. He realised he was too weak to carry on and handed over command to Canrobert. It was decided to evacuate Saint Arnaud to Constantinople where his wife was staying and he left the Crimea on 29 September on board the *Berthollet*. He was a disappointed man, telling his doctor, 'I only wanted one thing, to enter Sevastopol. Perhaps I could have done it if I had been able to carry out in time my first plan, but I have been master neither of myself nor of events.'[6] He died before he reached Constantinople.

The first decision that Canrobert had to take, in conjunction with Raglan, was vital for the conduct of any attack on Sevastopol. As the allied armies neared the southern coast of the Crimea they had to decide how to deploy. Logically, the British on the left of the allied line should have made a wide sweep to finish up on the left of the attack on the south side of Sevastopol. However, the British had the only cavalry units and these were best deployed on the right facing the interior of the Crimea and Menshikov's army. There was another problem. The allies had originally hoped that the port of Balaklava would be large enough to cope with the supplies for both armies. A preliminary reconnaissance showed this was not the case and that it could only be used for whichever army was on the right of the siege. Canrobert gave Raglan the choice of what to do. After a discussion with Admiral Lyons, Raglan opted for the right of the line and the use of Balaklava. The British fleet was instructed to sail round the coast to protect the new supply base. The French moved westwards and took over the much larger port of Kamiesh.

Balaklava was defended by just seventy militiamen and four brass mortars and, after a brief exchange of fire, it surrendered to the British. The tiny port was deep and well protected but the sharp curve at the mouth of the bay and the narrow approach were major problems. On a cliff near the village were the remains of a Genoese fort. *The Times* correspondent, William Russell, described Balaklava as 'a poor fishing village' and the bay as 'a little pond' and 'a highland tarn'.[7] The British decision to take Balaklava as their base was a major mistake. The port was small and hardly capable of handling the supplies needed for the army. It also involved a very long supply line – about nine miles in length and most of it uphill. The British found it almost impossible to obtain the resources to maintain this extended route. General Burgoyne immediately realised the mistake that had been made and wrote in early October:

> We are forced to take great precautions even to preserve Balaklava, which is full of our ships . . . and being so detached and at the foot of a mountain, I do not feel satisfied about its security, and have urged its being as much cleared as possible.[8]

Raglan ordered the port and village to be cleaned up, but no troops were available and so nothing was done. Overall, the British thought the 'flank march' had been, as Raglan described it, 'a perfect success' because 'the Enemy were by no means prepared'.[9] Russell's despatch to *The Times* described it as 'a brilliant and daring forced march' that had enabled the allied army to gain 'its magnificent position on the heights which envelop Sebastopol on the south'.[10] The key, however, was whether the allies were prepared to follow through any advantage they might have gained before the defences of Sevastopol were strengthened and before the onset of winter.

Hiatus

Although the allied armies needed a few days to organise themselves after the completion of the 'flank march' on 26 September, they took no action to attack Sevastopol for another three weeks. The delay was decisive in ensuring they did not capture the city. Almost immediately after arriving on the south side of Sevastopol, Canrobert and Raglan decided not to risk an immediate attack and to wait for reinforcements to arrive. It was not until the end of the first week of October that 4,000 British troops and the

French 5th Division arrived from Varna, producing a total allied strength of about 70,000 men. While they waited for these extra troops, guns from the Royal Navy ships were brought ashore and a naval brigade of about 1,000 sailors formed under Captain Lushington of the *Albion*. Supplies were slowly unloaded at Balaklava and by 3 October most of the British army had blankets and a rum issue twice a day. Balaklava harbour soon disintegrated into a collection of filth, rubbish and raw sewage. Raglan allowed Cardigan to spend every night outside the harbour on his private yacht *Dryad* with his friend Mr Hubert de Burgh and their French cook. Cardigan was always late for morning roll-call and any other early activities.

EYE-WITNESS
THE BRITISH ARMY CAMP

Captain L. G. Heath, HMS *Niger*

'The road is covered with conveyances of all sorts – Crimean bullock or camel waggons brought from Varna, Maltese mule carts from Malta, all with provisions, etc., and artillery waggons with shot, shell, or fascines and gabions; then comes an occasional aide-de-camp at a gallop, or an infantry officer, dusty and weary-looking, returning from Balaclava laden with whatever he has been able to buy – some preserved meats or a bottle of brandy, perhaps three or four ducks, or a pound of candles . . . You can have no idea of a campaigning soldier if you have only seen them in St James's Park or in a garrison ball-room. They live in their full dress coats, and the consequence is the scarlet has turned to port wine colour, and the gold lace and epaulettes to a dark coppery colour; the coat is generally full of holes, and the individual wears no shirt.'

The French army was reorganised into two corps. The 1st under General Forey, consisting of the 3rd and 4th Divisions, conducted the siege. The 2nd Corps under Bosquet, consisting of the 1st and 2nd Divisions, formed a 'corps of observation' to deal with Menshikov's army, which might attack the allies from the rear. The problem was that, as Raglan noted, 'we have no accurate information as to the strength of the Russians out of Sebastopol'.[11] By 4 October the French were ready to attack Sevastopol, but the British argued for more time to bring up artillery for a massive bombardment. The allies started digging trenches, indicating to the Russians that no immediate attack was likely. The first French trench was nearly a mile from the Russian defences at Bastion 5, and the British followed with theirs even further from the Malakhov and Bastion 3. Part of the problem was the rocky ground that made trenches difficult to dig, but these large gaps between the lines were to cause major problems – when they attacked, the infantry would have to cross a long, open space under fire.

The Russians were able to exploit the delay in the allied attack to strengthen their defences under the able direction of Totleben. The civilian population, sailors and soldiers worked almost continually digging earthworks and hauling guns into position. In early October, when the allies – if they had shown any initiative – might have attacked, the Russian defences were still in a very poor state. Bastions 5 and 6 remained badly exposed, Number 4 was an earthwork and Number 3 was just an entrenchment. Bastions 1 and 2 were almost non-existent – the Russians thought they could have been captured with cavalry. By mid-October more than 340 guns (one-third of them of heavy calibre) were in position. A pontoon bridge was built across the south bay of the harbour to shorten communications to the Inkerman bridge – the route through which supplies and reinforcements reached the city. The allies, as had been forecast before the invasion of the Crimea, did not have enough troops to cut off Sevastopol. There were still arguments within the Russian high command, especially with Kornilov's open contempt for Menshikov. Nevertheless more troops moved into the city and by 6 October the garrison was 27,000-strong and included some seasoned troops, unlike the situation at the end of September. By 3 October Menshikov's army was operating along the Chernaya River, threatening the rear of the allied position.

In London the news of the victory at the Alma arrived on 30 September, via Belgrade. Rumours spread that Sevastopol had fallen or was about to be captured. Politicians considered a quick election to cash in on popular enthusiasm. On the night the news of the Alma arrived, Graham wrote to Aberdeen, 'Do not lose sight of your great opportunity; take the tide at its rise, and let us have a new Parliament.'[12] Within five days it was clear that the rumours about Sevastopol were untrue and disillusionment set in. Ministers wanted a scapegoat and the unpopular Admiral Dundas was blamed for allowing the Russians to blockade Sevastopol harbour. Graham was prepared to let him stay to the end of the year because of his influence as an MP. However, Newcastle told Raglan that insubordination should be encouraged to get rid of Dundas: 'If Admiral Dundas gives orders which unnecessarily imperil your army, and you can induce Sir Edmund Lyons [Dundas's deputy] to do so gallant an act as to disobey orders, you and he shall have every support that I can give you.'[13]

EYE-WITNESS
WAITING TO ATTACK SEVASTOPOL

Sir John Hall, British army medical officer
30 September: 'Sickness continues to prevail in the whole army from exposure at night and cholera is particularly destructive among the newly arrived troops. I have urged the necessity of having tents and I believe they are to be found immediately. At present all attention is absorbed by the landing of material for the siege of Sebastopol which will commence in two or three days now and is not expected to last more than a week.'

George Lawson, doctor
7 October: 'Little in the way of taking Sebastopol has been done, that is to say the siege has not yet been commenced, but both sailors and soldiers are all busily engaged in landing the siege train which will be, when the guns are placed in position, the largest that has yet been ever brought against any town . . . When this is all to take place it is difficult to say. We have been here 8 or 9 days placed under fire of the Russians, and apparently doing nothing, wasting all the splendid weather . . . I hope this will not continue much longer, as all are not only getting tired of being in the Crimea, and existing in one suit of clothes and sleeping on the ground, but also are beginning to dislike being for so long targets for the enemy, allowing them quickly to build up batteries and try the ranges of the guns on us . . . Tents are now being issued to the men, so that it appears as if we are likely to remain here for some time yet.'

Frederick Dallas, officer
12 October: 'We are all the time preparing, & have not fired a shot yet. How ominous it must seem to them, seeing us quietly sitting down round their City . . . I expect that in a few days the whole town will be a heap of ruins, & that then we shall be sent to wherever we are intended to winter.'

George Lawson
12 October: 'We are still encamped in the same place as when I last wrote: Russians more annoying and troublesome with their round shot and shells than ever . . . for the last three nights and days they have kept up an incessant game, hardly ceasing during the whole time for half an hour . . . now working parties are out every night making the entrenchments, and all the necessary preparations for the guns which are being rapidly placed in

position . . . We are in good health compared with what we were in Varna, and during the whole time we have been on the hills above Sebastopol, only one or two cases of cholera have occurred.'

By 13 October the allies had not fired a single shell at Sevastopol. As the inaction continued, morale fell, not just in London and Paris, but also in the army. The decline from optimism to pessimism about the situation can be traced in the correspondence of the man primarily responsible for the decision not to attack Sevastopol immediately from the north, General Burgoyne. His doubts began the day after the allied armies arrived south of the city and soon grew:

27 September: They have an immense force of artillery mounted, and a large garrison, and it is not easy to get up all our means – it becomes impossible, therefore, to judge of the time we may be engaged in the operation; however, I hope not long.

29 September: I was in hopes that the Russians would not have made this effort at resistance at Sebastopol; but they seem determined to give us as much trouble as possible.

6 October: We are in difficulties that I do not see what prospect we have of getting out of.

7 October: The difficulties we have to face are far greater than I could have anticipated. It would have been unjustifiable to have stormed Sebastopol when we first arrived before it, and obstacles against our taking it increase every hour . . . I was much elated by the success at the Alma and its immediate results, and am grievously disappointed at this bad prospect after it. This is one of the contingencies which made the whole undertaking a desperate one from the commencement, although I did not anticipate the danger to be in this shape.

13 October: We are facing monstrous forces and difficulties – that is not *facing* them all, for we have them all round us.[14]

Nevertheless, the capture of Sevastopol was still expected before the winter. On 13 October Graham sent Burgoyne his instructions on what was to follow. Sevastopol harbour was to be cleared immediately to create a winter base for the fleet and the supply point for the allied armies. Then the Sea of Azov was to be brought under allied control so as to seriously disrupt the supply lines of the remaining Russian forces in the Crimea. All would now depend on the attack to be launched on Sevastopol.

The bombardment

On the evening of 16 October the allied war council decided that they were finally ready to launch a combined army and naval attack on Sevastopol which, it was hoped, would quickly lead to its capture. The bombardment, which would start at 6.30 a.m. the following morning, would, if successful, be followed by an infantry attack. However, the naval commanders, Admirals Dundas and Hamelin, had met on 15 October and were rightly sceptical about a naval attack on the stone forts of the harbour. The ships were low on ammunition and the Admirals were worried about the safety of their fleets, which were essential to maintain supplies to the allied armies. At the war council they did not tell their army colleagues that there would be no joint attack early in the morning.

The allied artillery bombardment opened on schedule on 17 October. It was hardly a surprise and the Russians immediately began counter-battery fire. The two sides had almost equal numbers of heavy artillery pieces. The significant moment came at 9.30 a.m., three hours after the start of the attack, when a Russian shell hit a French powder magazine, which exploded killing sixteen men and wounding thirty-seven. In the chaos French artillery fire slackened and shortly afterwards a second, smaller explosion put another battery out of action. At 10.30 a.m. the French artillery commander, General Thiry, ordered his batteries to cease fire. The British artillery was well dispersed, their guns were more effective and they maintained fire throughout the day. Fires were started in the city when red-hot shot was fired. Considerable damage was inflicted on the bastions opposite the British, especially the Malakhov and Number 3 (now called the 'Great Redan'). Huge damage was caused to the latter when a magazine exploded killing more than a hundred men. Raglan made no attempt to seize the Russian positions. Admiral Kornilov was badly wounded by a shell near the Malakhov. He lost a leg and died shortly afterwards in Sevastopol. By the evening it was clear that the artillery bombardment had achieved little.

EYE-WITNESS
THE BOMBARDMENT

Captain Reimers, commanding Bastion 4

'Finally, the awful day of the beginning of the bombardment came . . . What a frightening picture! Everywhere you could hear the moans and cries of the wounded. In a second everything was covered in smoke, and we thinking that the enemy is about to assault, opened fire from all our guns, firing, of course, heaven knows where!'

Colonel Charles Windham, British officer

'The pounding match went on as usual, without our gaining the slightest advantage, and I am more convinced than ever that we shall lose double the number of men in taking the place (if we do succeed) than we should have done had we attacked it twenty-four days ago. This long range firing is all nonsense; moreover the Russians are better at it than we are, and, from all I can see, our present attack is an absurdity.'

The naval attack was an even greater disaster. At 7 a.m. Hamelin boarded *Britannia* for a conference with Dundas. They agreed that the British would deploy to the north, with the French and Ottoman fleets on the south side of the harbour. Hamelin wanted the fleets to attack from a distance of well over a mile. A subsequent British conference agreed to operate at closer range. The operation was hazardous given the size of the stone forts and their batteries. On the south side of the harbour there was the Quarantine Fort, an open battery, and the two-decker casement, Fort Alexander. In total there were over a hundred guns. On the north side Fort Constantine had twenty guns that could fire on the ships below and there were a further ten guns in earthworks.

There was little wind and the battleships were slowly towed into position by steamers from 11.30 a.m. The French and Ottoman ships opened fire at 1.25 p.m. and their attack lasted for almost four hours. In that time just eleven Russians were killed and six guns put out of action. The British ships started firing just before 2 p.m., although the main body was not in position for another eighty minutes. They did manage to achieve some damage to Fort Constantine, but it was only out of action for six minutes. Because the British ships were closer to the forts, they suffered much greater damage than the French. Within two hours *Retribution*, *Albion*, *London* and *Arethusa* were out of action. Other ships took their place, but they too were badly damaged. *Agamemnon* was hit more than

200 times, every British ship suffered some damage and *Rodney* ran aground.

The allied fleets lost sixty-six men killed and nearly 450 wounded – the majority of the casualties were British because they were closer to the forts. The naval action achieved almost nothing. It merely confirmed what was already well known – wooden battleships could not attack stone forts successfully. If they closed in to a range to make their gunfire effective, they would suffer unsustainable damage. The day after the attack Dundas told Raglan that the action 'was a false one and one I decline to repeat'. He would do no more than create a diversion if a final attack was launched.[15]

Deadlock

The allies continued an artillery bombardment on the next two days, but its intensity rapidly declined and then petered out. British troops were reduced to throwing stones at the Russians.

EYE-WITNESS
THE AFTERMATH

Temple Godman, officer
'We do not seem to get on very fast, but the fact is when we landed we made too little of the great work before us, and everyone said we should be inside in about twenty-four hours. Confidence is all very well, but I think no one ought to boast too much before operations are commenced.'

Frederick Dallas
'The Siege is still going on tho' rather languidly. I can tell you no news about when we are likely to take the place . . . We keep on firing away constantly & the enemy at us, & if we do them no more harm than they do us, I don't see when it is going to end . . . We have not battered down the place at all in the way that our Engineers & Artillery led us to expect we should, & tho' I hear that the Authorities are quite satisfied with our progress, we who have hard work in the Trenches, & don't see much visible result, are getting rather tired of it. We are now firing our guns sparingly as we are afraid of running short of ammunition.'

George Lawson
'The diminution of our numbers every day is enough to cause anxiety. Out of 36,500 men borne on the strength of the army there are not now more than 16,500 rank and file fit for service . . . There is a steady drain of some forty or fifty men a-day going out from us . . . Even the twenty or thirty a day wounded and disabled, when multiplied by the number of days we have been here, becomes a serious item in the aggregate.'

General Sir John Burgoyne
'Events have turned out so different from all the bright anticipations of the speedy fall of Sebastopol.'

Frederick Dallas
'Altogether we are not in great force now. We shall have, we expect, to abandon Balaklava & our Authorities are blamed for having such extended lines in our rear, as we have not nearly men enough to keep them & carry on the Siege too.'

By 19 October it was clear that the aim of the Crimean landing had not been achieved. The enterprise had been risky from the start and required decisive and bold leadership to be successful. That was severely lacking among the allied commanders. The landing at Evpatoriya was successful because the Russians did not interfere. Everything had been staked on a victory at the Alma and that had been achieved, largely due to French military flair. Then crucial mistakes were made. With the Russians beaten, their army moving away from Sevastopol, and only a small, untrained, ill-equipped garrison left behind, an immediate attack from the north was the logical military choice. The allies had few supplies, no supply chain and no resources to fight a long campaign. They had to achieve a quick success before winter intervened. They rejected military logic and moved round to the south of the city in an action that could have been disastrous. The logic of that decision was to follow up with a quick attack. Instead everything was staked on a slow build-up to an assault, but this gave the Russians time to react and create a defensive system over a three-week period.

The failure of the attack on 17 October created a terrible situation for the allied armies. They were not strong enough to isolate Sevastopol and so supplies and reinforcements would continue to arrive, making any future assault even more difficult. In their rear they faced a Russian field army of unknown strength, which might attack at any time. Defeat here could cut allied supply lines. Even if the allied armies survived, they faced a long siege which would mean living in the open through the Crimean winter. Yet they had no supplies ready to meet this contingency. Everything had been staked on quick success. The allied failure produced a 300-day siege involving ever-expanding trench systems and vastly improved Russian defences that were very difficult to overcome. Some of the allied commanders were critical of the failures of the high command. General Sir George Cathcart wrote to his wife on 22 October:

> This siege is a long and tedious business . . . Had we attacked them as I wished . . . as soon as the whole army might have come up, they had not then recovered the defeat of the Alma and were not prepared for us. It was then an open town, but we have given them time to build up the most formidable entrenched positions possible, which I saw growing up for three weeks under my nose *without a shot being fired to disturb them*, and now we are surprised to find that our supposed superiority in artillery and engineering is all a mistake . . . God knows how it will all end . . . The weather is very fine, but about the 15th November they say intense cold commences and we could not live here.[16]

7

Balaklava

The Russian commanders in the Crimea were well aware of the allies' weak position after the failure of the assault on Sevastopol. They were also under pressure from the Tsar to take some action to try and relieve the besieged city. Information from within Sevastopol suggested that it might not be able to hold out under a sustained allied bombardment and that the centrepiece of the fortified position – the Malakhov – might fall. The problem that Menshikov faced was a lack of troops to carry out more than relatively minor operations. The 12th Infantry Division under General Liprandi arrived from Bessarabia shortly after the bombardment on 17 October following a series of forced marches, but further reinforcements – the 10th and 11th Divisions – would not arrive for another ten days or more. The Russians considered two possible operations. Colonel Popov argued for an attack on the centre of the British position in front of Sevastopol. If this were captured, artillery would be able to direct fire onto the remaining allied batteries and troops, almost certainly breaking the siege. Liprandi argued that not enough troops were available for such a major operation, and Menshikov decided not to wait for reinforcements. He therefore had little choice but to adopt Liprandi's plan for a raid on the long and exposed British lines of communication from Balaklava harbour. If these were broken, and Balaklava captured, then the British position on the heights in front of Sevastopol would become untenable.

The Balaklava defences

Most of the British troops (only about half the army was fit for service) were deployed for the siege of Sevastopol, leaving only thin forces to protect Balaklava. There were no defences in the harbour and the last line of defence was a series of batteries and earthworks in a semi-circle centred on the village of Kadikioi at the top of the valley leading down to the port. They were manned by a field battery and a battalion of Royal Marines. These defences were on the south side of the plain of Balaklava, which was about three miles long and two wide. The plain was bisected by the 'Causeway Heights' along which ran the Vorontsov road (Woronzoff to the British), the main route for supplies for the army in front of Sevastopol.

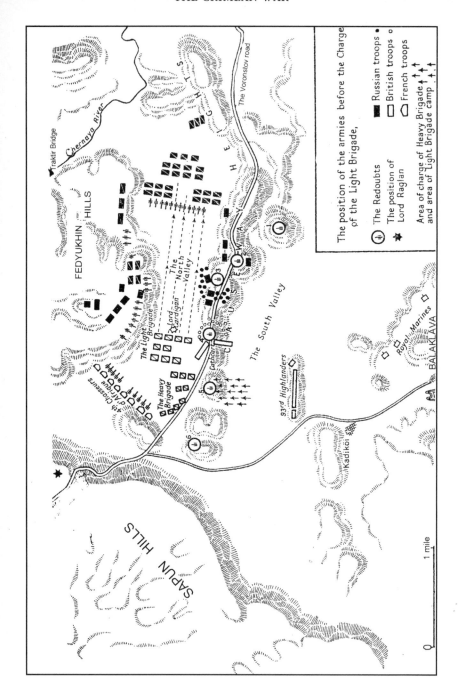

Map 6: The battle of Balaklava

On the far side of the heights was the North Valley with the Fedyukhin Hills to the north.

Along the Causeway Heights the British had built a series of 'redoubts' to defend their main line of communication. They were badly built (one of them had been put up in a day) and they were too far apart for mutual support and too far from the inner defence line of Balaklava. Four redoubts had been finished and two more were planned to the north-west towards the main camp. Three were equipped with two twelve-pounder guns and the main position (Number 1 to the north-east) had an extra gun. To man these flimsy defences the British had 2,800 troops available. Of these more than one-third were Ottoman forces, mainly poorly trained Tunisians – Omer Pasha kept his best troops at Evpatoriya. Apart from the Royal Marines, there were some 650 men of the 93rd Highlanders. Despite this weak position Raglan had done almost nothing to improve the situation. There was no systematic reconnaissance of the area at the rear of the British position or beyond the outer defences of Balaklava. This was exactly the work for which the Light Brigade (which had no role in the siege itself) was intended.

The British were, however, getting information that a Russian force was assembling for an attack. On 18 and 19 October the Russians conducted a reconnaissance of the outer defences. Raglan discounted these reports, telling London on 23 October that 'a considerable body of Russians' had appeared and disappeared two days earlier, but 'are no longer to be seen in our front'.[1] On 22 October Lord Dunkellin (a Captain in the Coldstream Guards) led a small party of men on reconnaissance. They saw a group of men ahead:

> 'There are Russians' exclaimed one of the men. 'Nonsense, they're our fellows' said his lordship, and off he went towards them, asking in a high tone as he got near, 'Who is in command of this party?' His men saw him no more.[2]

Dunkellin was later exchanged for a Russian artillery officer prisoner. On 24 October a spy employed by Brigadier Rustem Pasha of the Ottoman army reported that the Russians would attack the next morning from the direction of the Chernaya River where a large force was assembling. Raglan demonstrated the first signs of the incompetence that was to characterise his handling of the battle the next day. He failed to take any precautionary measures, merely asking to be kept informed of any other intelligence reports. The result of this failure to act was that the Russians achieved a large degree of surprise when they attacked early the next morning.

The Russian attack

The Russians had managed to assemble a considerable force for the attack on 25 October. Shortly before dawn 15,000 infantry, 4,000 cavalry and seventy-eight field guns began crossing the Chernaya River. The plan was to advance in a long line, taking the Fedyukhin Hills and the line of redoubts on the Causeway Heights. These would then be held as a smaller force moved towards Balaklava. Once captured, the harbour would be destroyed and then either held or abandoned depending on the position at the time. The Fedyukhin Hills were easily captured as they were undefended and artillery was moved up to dominate the North Valley. Lucan and his staff were, in accordance with their normal practice, out riding at daybreak (about 6 a.m.) when they saw flags flying from Redoubt No. 2 signalling a Russian attack. A messenger was sent to Raglan's headquarters but took over an hour to arrive.

What happened next is seriously misrepresented in most British accounts that tend to rely on Raglan's own despatch. This was deliberately misleading and designed to disguise the fact that he did not arrive on the battlefield for more than two hours after the fighting started.

EYE-WITNESS
THE RUSSIAN ATTACK ON THE REDOUBTS

Lieutenant Koribut-Kubitovich, Colonel Yeropkin's Combined Lancer Regiment
'At eight o'clock General Liprandi moved his infantry to the approaches to Redoubt No 1. Under the leadership of Colonel Krüdener, the Azov men went forward in company columns in a fine, orderly fashion. Accurate enemy artillery and rifle fire did not make them waiver . . . with each casualty they closed up as if on training manoeuvres. And now in a well-formed mass they reach the foot of the hill . . . A drawn-out shout of "Ura!" breaks forth and the steep slope is covered with a dense crowd of soldiers making their way up. With such a quick, brave attack, success cannot be long in doubt.'

The main Russian attack was centred on Redoubt No. 1 which was manned by about 500 Ottoman troops. They were outnumbered by about fifteen to one but resisted for two hours, a crucial point ignored by Raglan. Overall they suffered about 170 casualties (a higher percentage than the British cavalry in the 'Charge of the Light Brigade' a few hours later). Once the Russians had captured Redoubt No. 1 they were able to turn their artillery fire on the remaining positions and these were soon captured. The British took no action to help the Ottoman troops as they abandoned the redoubts. Troop Sergeant-Major Smith recorded:

> As they [Ottoman troops] gained the plain, a number of Cossacks swept round the foot of the hill, killing and wounding many of them. Some of them being unarmed raised their hands imploringly, but it was only to have them severed from their bodies . . . Had a dozen or two of us been sent out numbers of these poor fellows might have been saved.[3]

It was only at this point (shortly after 8 a.m.) that Raglan arrived at the scene of the battle and his account begins with the Ottoman troops fleeing from their positions, which – he implies – occurred without them offering any resistance. In fact the strong Ottoman resistance, which only ended under a full-scale Russian assault, was crucial to the outcome of the battle. It bought time for the British to begin to organise some sort of coherent defence. Raglan was not the only British commander to arrive late – Cardigan was, as usual, sleeping on his yacht outside Balaklava harbour and it took him over an hour more than Raglan to reach the battlefield and take command of the Light Brigade.

When Raglan took up his position on the Sapun Hills about 700 feet above the plain of Balaklava, the British position was precarious. Because he had taken no action the previous day there were almost no forces to defend the port on which the whole army depended. Raglan had available about 1,500 cavalry to the west of the Russian troops that now occupied the Causeway Heights and the redoubts, and about the same number of infantry in the earthworks at the top of the valley leading down to Balaklava. He decided, correctly, that he needed infantry. He ordered the 1st Division under the Duke of Cambridge and the 4th Division under General Cathcart to leave their positions in the siege lines in front of Sevastopol and march eastwards down to the plain. The only problem was that this manoeuvre would take several hours to complete and the British might not have this amount of time available. Even then Cathcart refused to move, telling Raglan's aide-de-camp, 'It is impossible for my division to move, as the greater proportion of the men have only just come from the trenches. The best thing you can do, sir, is sit down and have some breakfast.'[4]

Bosquet and later Canrobert joined Raglan on the top of the Sapun Hills, but they felt the Russian attack was merely a diversion designed to get the allies to move troops from the siege lines. They did no more than issue orders for two infantry brigades to move and two regiments of the

Chasseurs d'Afrique to move down to the plain to support the British cavalry.

Although Raglan was in a good position to view the whole battlefield, he failed to appreciate the different viewpoints of those several hundred feet below him. This was a contributing factor to the series of ill-judged orders he was to issue during the course of the battle. Far more important was his own limited ability – at the Alma he had done no more than order the infantry to advance, without giving them any objectives. The orders he issued at Balaklava were to be far more catastrophic in their consequences. The first order was to the cavalry. Lucan was instructed to withdraw to the west away from the left flank of the infantry defending the route to Balaklava. The order spoke of the 'second line of redoubts', even though there was only one. This movement exposed the flank of the 93rd Highlanders to a Russian cavalry attack. The order was so obviously wrong that it had to be countermanded almost immediately. However, in an attempt to cover his own incompetence, Raglan did not order all the cavalry to return – only eight of the ten squadrons of the Heavy Brigade. No doubt he hoped that this second order would appear to be a carefully judged response to a changing situation rather than a reversal of the first order.

The Russian attack halted

As Raglan began to make his initial deployments, the Russian units continued to advance after their capture of the redoubts on the Causeway Heights. Four squadrons of cavalry moved down into the South Valley towards Balaklava. The route was defended by the single artillery battery and about 1,000 infantry. Of this total about 500 (almost half) were Ottoman troops from the redoubts who did not, as Russell described in his report, flee to Balaklava. Although they formed a substantial part of the defences, they were ignored in British accounts, which immortalised the 'thin red line' (actually the 'thin red streak' in Russell's account). As the Russian cavalry advanced, the allied infantry held their fire until they were within rifle range. Once again it was allied technical superiority that was to prove decisive. The first volley, fired at about 700 yards, was ineffective, but the next two at 300 and 150 yards were enough to halt the advance even though Russian casualties were light.

EYE-WITNESS
THE RUSSIAN ATTACK ON THE 93RD HIGHLANDERS

Lieutenant Koribut-Kubitovich

'The cossacks headed for the Scots standing on the height's slope beside their camp, and moved round to engage them on both their flanks. The enemy's artillery met them with canister while the Scottish riflemen mounted the rise and coolly allowed them to approach to close range and only then did they open up a murderous fire. The stunned cossacks were bowled over but reformed and again threw themselves into the attack. This was again as unsuccessful as the first time . . . General Scarlett then reinforced his cavalry with two guards regiments. These fresh forces enveloped our hussars from both flanks. At the same time our cavalry was showered with canister and bullets. It did not withstand that treatment and quickly withdrew.'

The main body of the Russian cavalry – about 3,000 men under General Rykov – advanced westwards up the South Valley towards the British cavalry positions. The two cavalry units could not see each other because of the intervening high ground. The British and French commanders on the hills above could see what was happening and French artillery fire forced the Russians to veer to their left towards the British Heavy Brigade commanded by the fifty-five-year-old Brigadier James Yorke Scarlett who, like most British commanders, had never seen active service. The Heavy Brigade was outnumbered by about six to one and could not deploy to its left because of a vineyard, while the Russians also held the higher ground. Scarlett was already beginning to manoeuvre his forces to attack when Lucan's order to do so arrived. The British cavalry deployed just 350 yards from the Russians, but the latter made no attempt to interfere. They merely tried to form a semi-circle to envelop the British forces. The British charged at the centre of the Russian line in an attack that lasted no more than eight minutes. Casualties on both sides were surprisingly light in the hand-to-hand fighting. This was largely the result of the rusty and blunt swords used, the limited room in which to wield the weapons and the heavy Russian greatcoats that deflected the swords. The British suffered about eighty casualties, the Russians slightly less than three times that number. Nearly all the casualties on both sides were wounded, not killed.

EYE-WITNESS
THE CHARGE OF THE HEAVY BRIGADE

Major Forrest, 4th Dragoon Guards
'We had very bad ground to advance over, first thro' a vineyard, and over two fences, bank and ditch, then through the Camp of the 17th [Lancers], & we were scarcely formed when we attacked, & had but very little ground to charge over. Still we did not go in at so good a pace as we might have done. Once in, we did better, but the confusion was more than I had expected. The men of all regiments were mixed & we were a long time reforming . . . When once in amongst them I scarcely saw anybody – that is to recognise them. One could not look about much until the Russians began to run.'

Temple Godman, officer
'. . . the charge sounded and at them went the first line; Scarlett and his A. D. C. well in front. The enemy seemed quite astonished and drew into a walk and then a halt; as soon as they met, all I saw was swords in the air in every direction, the pistols going off, and everyone hacking away right and left . . . the 5th [Dragoon Guards] advanced and in they charged, yelling and shouting as hard as they could . . . for about five minutes neither would give way, and their column was so deep we could not cut through it. At length they turned . . . and the whole ran as hard as they could pelt back up the hill, our men after them all broken up, and cutting them down right and left. We pursued about 300 yards, and then called off with much difficulty . . . It took some little time to get the men to fall in again, they were all mixed up together of course, all the regiments in one mass . . . The enemy being gone, and we all right, had time to look round, the ground was covered with dead and dying men and horses. I am happy to say, our brigade lost but seven men dead, but had a considerable number wounded, some mortally. The ground was strewn with swords, broken and whole, trumpets, helmets, carbines etc., while a quantity of men were scattered all along as far as we pursued.

The Russians re-formed to attack the British units, but came under heavy artillery fire from the Sapun Hills. During the action the Light Brigade did not move and made no attempt to exploit the confusion in the Russian units. This was the result of Cardigan's rigid (and petulant) interpretation of Lucan's order (passing on one from Raglan) that the Light Brigade should hold its ground. The Russian cavalry retreated back to Causeway Heights and then eastwards to the end of the valley.

At this point the 'battle' of Balaklava (which was little more than a skirmish) appeared to be over. General Liprandi certainly thought it was and was content that his forces had obtained their immediate objective – the capture of the redoubts and the Causeway Heights. However, their position was not strong. They held both of the high points – the Causeway Heights and the Fedyukhin Hills – but these positions were isolated from each other by the North Valley, where there were no troops apart from the Russian artillery and cavalry at the far end. Raglan was also worried about the situation. The Russians held the outer defences of Balaklava (the redoubts) and could dominate the Vorontsov road, the key route for British supplies. He also believed that the French would regard the engagement as a defeat for the British because they had given up key ground. What took place next was a military disaster brought about by Raglan and the ambiguous orders that he issued.

The Charge of the Light Brigade: the orders

There was a lull in the fighting as the Russian cavalry retreated. There was still no sign of the infantry units that had been ordered from the siege lines around Sevastopol. Exactly what operation Raglan had in mind at this point will forever remain unclear because his orders were so badly drafted. However, one point is clear. Whatever attack was mounted, Raglan's orders would have produced a disaster. The countdown to that disaster began with the third order Raglan issued that day (the first two were the incompetent ones for the cavalry to withdraw and then for some of them to move forward). The order stated, 'Cavalry to advance & take advantage of any opportunity to recover heights, they will be supported by infantry which has been ordered advance on two fronts.'

If Raglan intended the cavalry to recapture the Causeway Heights, then any such attack would have been as great a disaster as – if not greater than – the eventual Charge of the Light Brigade. To carry out his order the cavalry would have had to attack uphill towards the Russian artillery units around the redoubts and then hold the area until the infantry arrived.

Down in the valley Lucan reasonably interpreted the order to mean that he should wait until the infantry arrived before launching a cavalry charge. He did, however, order the Heavy Brigade to move into a position from which an attack would be possible. The British cavalry held their positions for between thirty and forty minutes. There was still no sign of the infantry. To Raglan, with the French watching this British inactivity, the situation was acutely embarrassing even though the Russians were making no effort to remove the guns from the redoubts. It was at this point that

Raglan issued his fatal fourth order of the day. It was even more ambiguous than the third.

Raglan dictated his order to General Airey, his Quartermaster-General, under whose name orders were normally issued. Airey wrote it in pencil on a piece of light-blue paper torn from a notebook. On this occasion Airey, perhaps fearing the worst, made it explicitly clear that the order came from Raglan:

> Lord Raglan wishes the cavalry to advance rapidly to the front, follow the enemy, and try to prevent the enemy carrying away the guns – Troop Horse Artillery may accompany – French cavalry is on your left. Immediate.

It is difficult to see how any subordinate commander could have sensibly interpreted the intentions behind this order. The Light Brigade and the Heavy Brigade were not in the same place and so it was unclear what 'to the front' meant. From Lucan's position in the valley, neither the Russians nor the guns were visible. Furthermore it was unclear whether 'the guns' meant the Russian guns at the end of the valley or the British guns captured in the redoubts. Mention of the French cavalry was irrelevant because they received no orders. About the only point that was clear was that the cavalry should now attack without waiting for the infantry. Where they should attack was never stated. If Raglan intended an attack on the Causeway Heights, as his previous order seemed to imply, then the operation was suicidal.

Raglan's order was given not to Captain Thomas Leslie, the next aide-de-camp in line, but to Captain Lewis Edward Nolan, possibly because he was known as a fast rider. Nolan was given no explanation of the order, although Raglan may have shouted after him that Lucan was to order the cavalry to attack immediately. The thirty-five-year-old Nolan had served in the Habsburg cavalry and in India. He had written a short book, *Cavalry*, on his system for training cavalry horses. He was hot-headed and a strong believer, contrary to most evidence, in the power of the cavalry to determine the outcome of a battle. He was mortified by the failure of the cavalry to have any significant impact on the fighting so far in the war.

When Nolan handed Lucan the order, the latter found it incomprehensible. He was already in a bad mood following Raglan's first two contradictory orders and the unclear third order. Lucan disliked Nolan and a row rapidly developed between the two over the meaning of Raglan's order. Lucan, who could see neither the redoubts nor the guns, reasonably enquired, 'Attack, sir? Attack what? What guns, sir?' Nolan, in an arrogant and insolent mood, theatrically gestured at the heights at the end of the valley, which could be seen, and replied, '*There*, my Lord, is your enemy; *there* are your guns.'

Lucan ordered both the Heavy and Light Brigades to mount. There is some confusion about the exact sequence of events at this point. Cardigan seems to have questioned these orders and sent his ADC, Lieutenant Fitz Maxse, to confirm them from Lucan. The latter then moved across to the front of the 13th Light Dragoons to confer with Cardigan. Cardigan pointed out that any advance up the North Valley would be into the face of the Russian battery at the end of the valley, with the Russians having artillery and infantry on the heights on either side. What is clear is that Lucan did not show Cardigan Raglan's written order. He merely said that those were the orders and they had no choice but to obey. Cardigan is supposed to have said that he would therefore be the last of his family line, although Temple Godman of the Heavy Brigade commented that this supposed speech 'was I expect made for him in England, at least I have not heard that any of his brigade ever heard of this speech'.[5]

The scene had been set for the most tragic event of the Crimean War. What is extraordinary is the sang-froid with which the senseless orders were carried out. The discipline of the cavalry regiments held firm in the terrible situation they now had to face. The near suicidal orders were obeyed as though the charge into 'the valley of death' was no more than a fox-hunting gallop in the English shires. Most of the men involved had not even been under fire before.

The Charge of the Light Brigade

Cardigan now gave the deployment orders to the Light Brigade. The first line would consist of the 13th Light Dragoons and the 17th Lancers. The 11th Hussars would form the second line and the third would consist of the 4th Light Dragoons and the 8th Hussars. There were 658 men in the three lines, out of the 1,570 who had set out for the east six months earlier. Exactly how many took part in the charge is unclear – it may have been as high as 673 because of various extras such as two Sardinian officers – Gorone and Landrani. The 8th Hussars were also accompanied by their mascot, Jemmy, a rough-haired Irish terrier that ran with the cavalry and survived with only a small cut to its neck. At about 11.10 a.m. Cardigan gave the order: 'The brigade will advance. Walk. March. Trot.' Cardigan, in the uniform of the 11th Hussars, rode his chestnut, Ronald, and took up position about seven lengths in front of the first line. In the third line Lord George Paget of the 4th Light Dragoons was smoking a cigar. Once the advance was under way Cardigan gave no further orders and the charge was never sounded.

The Light Brigade had about one and a half miles to travel up the valley. On the north side of the valley along the Fedyukhin Hills the Russians had eight infantry battalions, four squadrons of cavalry and fourteen guns. To the south on the Causeway Heights there were eleven infantry battalions and thirty guns. At the end of the valley there were twelve guns and the main units of Russian cavalry. The Light Brigade had to advance into the bullets and shells from three sides and with no possibility of returning fire. The first part of the advance was downhill and it was essential to keep a slowish pace, with the horses in poor condition after their travels and inadequate diet.

After about fifty yards the first artillery salvo was fired. Shortly afterwards, Nolan, who had moved into the first line to join the charge, suddenly galloped obliquely from left to right in front of Cardigan, turned, pointed with his sword and shouted. Nobody heard his message above the noise. Then a shell exploded and part of it smashed into Nolan's chest, exposing his heart. He let out a terrifying scream and dropped his sword; at this point he was probably dead. His horse turned and passed through the advancing lines showing the rest of the cavalry his dreadful wounds until his body fell off into the dust. What Nolan was trying to do will never be known. It is possible that, in an act of gross insubordination, he was trying to urge the Light Brigade into the charge. Cardigan, who intended to have Nolan court-martialled, probably thought this was what happened. It seems more likely that Nolan realised his orders from Raglan had been misunderstood and that he was waving to try and direct the charge towards the Causeway Heights. The line of advance to the head of the valley and the Heights was the same for the first few hundred yards and the Russian infantry near Redoubts 2 and 3 did form into squares to repel a cavalry charge. After a couple of minutes of the advance, Nolan may have realised the terrible mistake that was being made and tried to avert disaster. He failed and the Light Brigade travelled straight on towards the end of the valley.

Raglan's order was for all the British cavalry to advance and the Heavy Brigade formed up to advance, but then it came under artillery fire. Lucan was wounded in the leg and his ADC was killed. Once Lucan realised what was happening to the Light Brigade, he cancelled the advance. The Heavy Brigade waited so as to give assistance to their colleagues when they began their return journey.

As the Light Brigade advanced up the valley, its pace steadily increased without any order to charge being given. There were heavy casualties from the start and, as the lines closed up, there was chaos as units became mixed together. The second and third lines were also disrupted as they rode over the dead and dying men and horses of the first line, which took the brunt of the fire from the twelve brass cannons at the end of the valley. Musket fire from the infantry was largely ineffective, but the artillery fire from each side of the valley was devastating. A charge in loose formation by the *Chasseurs d'Afrique* onto the Fedyukhin Hills did disrupt the fire on one side of the valley.

The slaughter continued for the eight minutes it took the Light Brigade to reach the Russian guns. The final salvo, fired at eighty yards' range, was disastrous – just fifty men of the first line survived. One of those who did was Cardigan, who travelled about 100 yards beyond the guns and narrowly avoided capture by the Russian cavalry. He then rode back through the guns and returned down the valley. He did not join in the fighting around the guns, believing that it was beneath his dignity to fight private soldiers. Nor did he make any effort to rally his troops, believing that his task was completed once he had led the men in the charge. The men in the second line saw Cardigan riding back before they had even reached the Russian guns. He was one of the first members of the Light Brigade to return; indeed, many thought that his rapid reappearance meant he had not taken part in the charge. Lord George Paget thought that Cardigan had deserted his men.

While Cardigan was back at the starting point of the charge, the remains of his troops were still fighting around the Russian guns. The second and third lines of the Light Brigade swept round the guns, some attacking the cavalry, others the gun crews. Many of the men were looking for Cardigan. It was left to Colonel Shewell to take command, rally the troops and lead about seventy men back through the guns and begin the retreat down the valley. No formal order to retreat was given. The journey back along the valley was chaotic as a mass of wounded men (most of them on foot) and horses (some carrying wounded men) staggered along, still under Russian fire. In a broken formation with smoke and dust everywhere they were a much more difficult target than they had been during the advance. The Heavy Brigade now advanced up the valley to support their colleagues, suffering greater casualties than during their own charge a couple of hours earlier.

The last survivor returned just twenty minutes after the start of the charge.

EYE-WITNESS
THE CHARGE OF THE LIGHT BRIGADE

Sergeant Mitchell, 13th Light Dragoons

'In a few minutes several casualties occurred, for by this time the guns on our front were playing on us with round-shot and shell, so the number of men and horses falling increased every moment. I rode near the right of the [first] line. A corporal who rode on the right was struck by a shot or shell full in the face, completely smashing it, his blood and brains bespattering us who rode near. His horse still went on with us. By this time the ranks being continually broken it caused some confusion. Oaths and imprecations might be heard between the report of the guns and the bursting of the shells as men crowded and jostled each other in their endeavour to close to the centre . . . We were now fully exposed to the fire from all three batteries, front, right and left, as also from the infantry on our right who were now able to reach us. As we drew nearer the guns from the front plied us liberally with grape and cannister, which brought down men and horses in heaps . . . We were now very close to the guns, for we were entering the smoke which hung in clouds in front. I could see some of the gunners running from the guns to the rear, when just at that moment a shell from the battery on the right struck my horse carrying away the shoulder and part of the chest, and exploding a few yards off. Fortunately I was on the ground when it exploded, or some of the fragments would most likely have reached me . . . I found my horse was lying on his near side, my left leg was beneath him . . . I tried to move, but just at that moment I heard the second line come galloping on to where I lay, and fully expecting to be trampled on I looked up and saw it was the 4th Light Dragoons [in the third line] quite close. I called out "For God's sake, don't ride over me" . . . After they had passed I . . . stood up . . . and soon found there were numberless bullets flying around me . . . our brigade had passed beyond the guns. The smoke had cleared, for the guns were silent enough now . . . so that we could see a number of men making their way back . . . The number of horses lying about was something fearful . . . By this time the mounted were making their way back, as fast as they could, some singly, and some in parties of two or three . . . There were several riderless horses galloping about the plain . . . I was getting tired, for we had been out since 4 a.m. and had nothing to eat since the day before.'

The aftermath

The survivors of the charge were not stood down for another five hours. During this time hardly anybody spoke and most of the men suffered from terrible hunger – they had not eaten for nearly twenty-four hours. That evening they were told not to light any fires in case the Russians renewed the attack. The soldiers had no hot food and had to manage on a diet of dry biscuits and a rum issue.

Cardigan left his men, rode back to Balaklava, returned to his yacht, had a bath, a bottle of champagne, dinner and retired to bed. Lucan was in his tent surrounded by mud.

After the Charge of the Light Brigade there was no further action that day. Overall casualties on both sides were low. The Russians and the allies each lost about 230 men killed. Without the Charge of the Light Brigade, the skirmish around the plain of Balaklava would be a little-remembered incident not worth the name of a battle.

Of those who took part in the charge, 118 were killed, 134 were wounded and fifty-seven were taken prisoner; 475 horses were killed or shot shortly afterwards. At the end of the day the Light Brigade had left just 195 men mounted and capable of action. It was no longer an effective military force.

The 'battle' of Balaklava was of little long-term importance. The Russians did not reach the port and, although they held on to the two easternmost redoubts, the other three were reoccupied by Ottoman troops. The Russians did hold the Fedyukhin Hills and this made British control of the Vorontsov road – and therefore communications to the main base in front of Sevastopol – more difficult. The British cavalry was rendered ineffective and played little further part in the war – but this would have been the case anyway during the protracted siege of Sevastopol. Russian morale improved after their limited success, but the attack merely alerted the allied commanders to the growing threat in their rear. Menshikov would probably have been wise to wait for a few more days for the 11th and 12th Divisions to arrive before launching a much stronger attack.

The Charge of the Light Brigade: the creation of the myth

The Charge of the Light Brigade was a military disaster caused by gross incompetence among the British commanders. General Bosquet, watching the charge from the Sapun Hills, rightly exclaimed, '*C'est magnifique mais ce n'est pas la guerre, C'est de la folie*', but a better explanation was required for the British public. In his longest despatch of the war William Russell provided the readers of *The Times* with a suitable story. The narrative was not one of the incompetence demonstrated by Raglan and Airey or the stupidity of Lucan and Cardigan. Nolan attracted some blame (he was conveniently dead), but Russell quickly added, 'God forbid I should cast a shade on the brightness of his honour.' The charge became a story of tragedy and heroism, but one without any convincing explanation of why it happened.

Russell admitted the result of the charge was a 'melancholy catastrophe which fills us all with sorrow'. This was because 'The whole brigade scarcely made an effective regiment, according to the numbers of continental armies; and yet it was more than we could spare.' But the men were all heroes. Russell described how, as the Russians opened fire, 'They swept proudly past, glittering in the morning sun in all the pride and splendour of war.' He added that 'their desperate valour knew no bounds'. Russell was watching from the Sapun Hills and wrote, 'A more fearful spectacle was never witnessed than by those who, without the power to aid, beheld their heroic countrymen rushing to the arms of death.' On their return he concluded, 'demi-gods could not have done what we had failed to do' and the 'band of heroes' had acted 'with courage too great almost for credence'.

Russell could also cast much of the blame on the Russians. Although they were perfectly entitled to attack the Light Brigade as they retreated down the valley, Russell portrayed this as a war crime, implying that this was where most of the casualties happened:

> There took place an act of atrocity without parallel in the modern warfare of civilized nations . . . to the eternal disgrace of the Russian name, the miscreants poured a murderous volley of grape and cannister on the mass of struggling men and horses.

Russell provided an account carefully judged to appeal to Victorian ideas of military heroism and a detestation of Russian barbarism. But there was no coherent explanation of why the Light Brigade had charged up the valley in defiance of military logic. He could only conclude that 'the Light Brigade was annihilated by their own rashness, and the brutality of a ferocious enemy'.[6]

The Charge of the Light Brigade: who was to blame?

British army officers in the Crimea were clear that explanations of the disaster were required. Frederick Dallas reported:

> A great gloom is cast over the Army from a most dreadful disaster
> that happened to our Light Cavalry . . . [that] in fact no longer exists
> . . . We all pray that whoever is to blame for this may be made to
> answer for it . . . As a French Colonel [de Noé] said to me yesterday
> (who saw it all), 'They might as well have been ordered to Charge the
> walls of Sebastopol'.[7]

Henry Clifford thought the charge was 'one of the greatest disasters, and
the most useless and shocking sacrifice of the lives of hundreds of brave
men that was ever witnessed'.[8]

Those involved in ordering the charge tried to allocate the blame to each
other as soon as it was over. Cardigan was in a strong position – he had
merely obeyed orders, even though they were catastrophic. Raglan was the
Commander-in-Chief and he was determined that the blame should not
fall on him, despite the fact that he had issued the incomprehensible orders.
Lucan sat uncomfortably in the middle. He had carried out the orders he
had been given, both in writing and verbally, but he had given the final
order to Cardigan. After the battle, when Cardigan rode up to Raglan, the
latter, shaking with rage, asked, 'What did you mean, Sir, by attacking a
battery in front, contrary to all the usages of war and the customs of
service?' Cardigan, was, as usual, more than ready to blame Lucan and
replied, with some justification, 'My lord, I hope you will not blame me,
for I received the order to attack from my superior in front of the troops.'
That evening Raglan told Lucan, 'You have lost the Light Brigade.' Lucan,
quite reasonably, replied that he was carrying out Raglan's own order,
which he then waved in front of him. Raglan could only respond with the
extraordinary argument that Lucan should have disobeyed orders: 'Lord
Lucan, you were a Lieutenant-General and should therefore have exercised
your discretion, and, not approving of the charge, should not have caused
it to be made.' Lucan argued that he could not disobey an order given by
Raglan's ADC – which, under Queen's Regulations, was equivalent to a
direct order from Raglan himself.

Raglan wanted to protect himself by keeping the question of the orders
that had been issued as quiet as possible. However, he had to send an
official despatch to London and the matter could not be entirely ignored.
His despatch (number 85) was sent on 28 October and was printed in *The
Times* on 13 November. The crucial passage was:

> It appearing that an attempt was making to remove the captured
> guns, the Earl of Lucan was desired to advance rapidly, follow the
> enemy in their retreat and try to prevent them from effecting their
> objects . . . From some misconception of the instruction to advance,

the Lieutenant-General considered that he was bound to attack at all hazards, and he accordingly ordered the major-general, the Earl of Cardigan, to move forward with the Light Brigade. This order was obeyed in a most spirited and gallant manner.

Raglan therefore praised Cardigan for his blind courage (he had always favoured him over Lucan) and subtly passed the blame to his subordinate. Lucan was not allocated direct responsibility for the disaster, but the meaning of 'from some misconception of the instruction to advance' was clear: Lucan was being blamed for making the crucial mistake.

Lucan did not see Raglan's despatch before the copies of The Times arrived in the Crimea on 28 November. He felt that he had been handed the role of scapegoat for Raglan's incompetence. He asked to see his commander, but Raglan rejected the request. Lucan therefore wrote to Raglan on 30 November. He argued that, 'After carefully reading the Order, I hesitated, and urged the Uselessness of such an attack and the Dangers attending it.' Nolan then told him that Raglan's orders were for the cavalry to attack. Lucan said that he asked where he was to attack, 'as neither Enemy nor Guns were within sight. He replied, in a most disrespectful but significant Manner, pointing to the further End of the Valley "There, my Lord is your Enemy; there are your Guns".' Lucan continued that he felt he had no alternative but to obey his superiors' orders and so told Cardigan he was to advance. He added that 'to the Objections he made, in which I entirely agreed, I replied that the Orders were from your Lordship'. Lucan told Raglan that he had no alternative:

> To take upon myself to disobey an Order written by my Commander in Chief within a few Minutes of its Delivery, and given from an elevated Position, commanding an entire View of all the Batteries and the Position of the Enemy, would have been nothing less than the direct Disobedience of Orders, without any other Reason than I preferred my own Opinion to that of my General . . . I did not dare disobey your Lordship.[9]

Lucan asked for his version of events to be circulated by Raglan. The latter, in an attempt to protect his own reputation, refused and sent Airey (who had written down the disastrous order) to persuade Lucan to withdraw his letter. He refused and Raglan eventually forwarded the letter to Newcastle in London.

This was a conflict Lucan could not win. Although Lucan was correct in his criticisms of Raglan's order and Nolan's interpretation of it, Raglan was not prepared to take any of the blame for the disaster and he was the

Commander-in-Chief. In his own letter forwarding Lucan's letter, Raglan told Newcastle that there could be no objection about the wording of his despatch and the phrase 'some misconception'. However, he then went on to place the blame for the disaster on Lucan, saying, 'not only did the Lieutenant-General misconceive the written instruction that was sent him, but that there was nothing in that instruction which called on him to attack at all hazards'. Raglan went on to argue that Lucan should have interpreted the order in the light of Raglan's own previous order (which was equally ambiguous and unclear) and should have known that the guns and the enemy were on the Causeway Heights (even though he couldn't see them there). He then stated that he did not want the cavalry to make an attack on the heights and 'there was nothing in the instruction to require it'. Raglan argued that any attack should have included the Heavy Brigade, Horse Artillery and the French – which would probably have done no more than increase the slaughter.

When Raglan's letter arrived in London, Newcastle consulted the Commander-in-Chief, Hardinge, who recommended Lucan's recall, not because of his conduct on 25 October, but because of his relations with Raglan. On 27 January 1855 Newcastle instructed Raglan that Lucan was to return to Britain. Shortly after his arrival in London Lucan demanded a court-martial. The army authorities could not grant such a request. Any such trial would require evidence from Raglan, Airey and Cardigan and, apart from the practical difficulties involved, would reveal with too much clarity a picture of general incompetence in the high command in the Crimea. Lucan used his membership of the House of Lords to initiate a debate on his actions on 2 March, 6 March, 9 March and again on 19 March after his second request for a court-martial was rejected. He achieved nothing. Cardigan, who had also returned to London, was basking in the glory of leading the charge. However, opinions about him in the Crimea were very different. The photographer Roger Fenton advised his publisher:

> If you have not got a portrait of him I should recommend you to take no trouble about it, as you will before long have a very different account of his conduct from that he has himself given. I have heard men and officers in the cavalry regiments discussing his conduct, and not one has a good word to say for him.[10]

Cardigan was telling everyone in London society that the disaster was the result of Lucan's arrogance and the quarrel between the two men that dated back decades.

The primary responsibility for the catastrophic charge of the Light

Brigade has to rest with Raglan. He was the man who issued the unclear and ambiguous orders, with no idea of the difference between his viewpoint on the hills and that of the cavalry in the valley. However Raglan's orders were interpreted, they would have led to disaster either from an attack on the Causeway Heights or, as happened, from the charge up the valley. His inability to issue clear and concise orders was compounded by the poor organisation of the British army. Untrained and inexperienced aristocrats were able to buy promotion over their social inferiors and experienced Indian army officers. They appointed staff officers from among their relatives who had no training in staff work. Cardigan, despite his arrogance and appalling behaviour towards his men, escapes much of the blame because he did no more than carry out orders. Lucan, despite his personal failings and inadequate military knowledge, was unfairly made to carry the blame for Raglan's mistakes. The latter's argument that Lucan should have disobeyed orders bears little scrutiny. What would have happened had Lucan, even if he was supported by Cardigan, decided to refuse to advance? Raglan's attempt to shift the blame only added to the numerous inadequacies he had already demonstrated during the campaign in the east. In the days before the battle he had ignored warnings of a Russian attack and he arrived on the scene two hours after the fighting started. His first order involved the cavalry retreating from a good position and exposing the flank of the infantry defending the route to Balaklava. The third and the fourth orders were so obscure that they were almost bound to lead to disaster. Nolan merely compounded these mistakes by his own arrogance.

8

Inkerman

On 26 October 1854, while the British army was still coming to terms with the disaster of the previous day, the Russians launched another attack. The skirmish involved only about 6,000 men and four guns, but Raglan panicked and ordered the partial withdrawal of ships and supplies from Balaklava. The attack was easily checked and Raglan's orders countermanded. The French and British commanders were now extremely worried about their situation. Their intelligence about the Russian army was very limited (it came from the odd deserter), but it seemed clear that reinforcements were arriving. The allied armies were in the open and exposed to an attack from the front (the troops in Sevastopol) and the rear (the field army under Menshikov). The weather was beginning to deteriorate (there was a severe frost on the night of 2 November) and the armies were ill-equipped to survive the winter in the open.

EYE-WITNESS
THE BRITISH ARMY AFTER BALAKLAVA

George Evelyn, militia officer
28 October: 'The weather has turned cold – so Deedes and myself have moved from our tent into our hut. Heavy rain during the night'
29 October: 'Still very cold. Officers endeavouring to hut themselves in some subterranean caverns – my horse terribly cut up by the weather.'
30 October: 'The first death from scurvy in our division happened this morning.'
31 October: 'I am building or rather digging a stable for 6 horses. The latter term is most applicable, as, for want of materials all huts, etc., must be made half-subterranean, so that the earth thrown up in digging serves to make a low wall . . . At the sale today a pair of warm gloves sold for 33/–. Horses went cheap.'

Temple Godman, officer
'They say we are to winter here. I hope not, it is wretched work, and the cold gives one diarrhoea. We are so far from water we seldom get a wash, and everyone is covered with lice which I pick out every morning regularly, but

---

they come again. We are often turned out in the night and often sleep in our clothes for fear of an attack. I never take off anything for weeks together but trousers and coat, it is too cold to take off more.'

George Lawson, doctor

'I am sorry to say that there is great talk of our wintering here . . . I sincerely hope not. The weather here is at times very warm at others very cold. We have had 3 intensely cold days with strong north-easterly winds in which we were all very miserable, cross and wish to be home again . . . Warm clothing, it is said, is to be sent out for the soldiers. I hope they will not forget the officers . . . As for myself I never was better, getting very fat, and feeling very jolly . . . during the cold weather bed is the most comfortable place, and as soon as it is dark we turn in, and have our grog in bed, and read the papers when we have any by candle light. We are never hardly later than 8 o'clock.'

Canrobert and Raglan agreed that a further effort had to be made to capture Sevastopol. Plans were drawn up for an attack on the night of 7 November commanded by General Forey, involving the French 4th Division and the elite Zouave units.

Russian plans

Menshikov was still under pressure from the Tsar to relieve the siege of Sevastopol. The pressure was increased when two of the Tsar's sons, Grand Dukes Nicholas and Michael, arrived at the commander's head-quarters. On 3 November the long-expected reinforcements from Bessarabia (the 10th and 11th Divisions under General Dannenberg) arrived. The Russians now had numerical superiority – their army in and around Sevastopol (excluding sailors) totalled about 107,000 men compared with a nominal allied strength of about 71,000.

Menshikov correctly identified the weakest part of the allied position – the Inkerman Ridge that formed the far right of the allied lines in front of Sevastopol. The ridge was about 400 feet high and ended at the eastern end of Sevastopol Bay with the Chernaya River at its base. To the west it was separated from the 'Victoria Ridge' (which overlooked the suburb of Korabelnaya) by the 'Careening Ravine' (*Kilen-balka* in Russian). There were other small ravines that led down to the bay. Here the engineer's road ran along the bay and crossed the Chernaya at Inkerman bridge – it provided the only route into the city. Inkerman Ridge was rocky and covered in scrub and was a no man's land in early November 1854. Raglan had, in yet another example of incompetence, failed – despite constant pressure from the French – to occupy this key position. The British did not have enough troops and Raglan was too proud to ask for French help. British forces merely formed a line of observation (unfortified) at the far south of Inkerman Ridge. The area was thinly manned by about 3,500 men of the 2nd Division under Sir George de Lacy Evans. Nearby were some 1,600 men of the Guards Brigade and 3,500 soldiers of the Light Division commanded by Sir George Brown.

Menshikov's plan was simple – to roll up the British line, occupy Inkerman Ridge and then move on towards the Sapun Hills and the centre of the allied position. The attack would take place on 5 November and in total just under 60,000 troops would be involved, of which about 35,000 would attack the ridge. To carry out this attack there would be four main movements. Some 19,000 men commanded by General F. I. Soimonov (commander of the 10th Infantry Division) would move from Sevastopol along the engineer's road, cross the 'Careening Ravine' and climb Inkerman Ridge. The second attack would be by some 16,000 men under General P. I. Pavlov, who would move from Inkerman village, cross the Chernaya and then fan out to climb the numerous small ravines to the top of the ridge. To aid this main attack there would be two diversionary movements. The most important would be led by General P. D. Gorchakov commanding 22,000 men, who would attack westwards from Chorgun village towards the Sapun Hills. They might capture the position, but if not, the attack ought to stop the French from moving reinforcements to aid the British. Finally there would be a small attack of 3,000 men from Bastion 6 in Sevastopol under General N. D. Timofeev. This would be aimed at the French left wing in the hope of pinning down more troops.

In theory this was an effective plan. There were, however, a number of weaknesses. The Russian high command was badly divided by personal disputes. Menshikov devised his plan without consulting any of his colleagues and then placed General Dannenberg in overall control. He had only just arrived with the troops from Bessarabia and was unfamiliar with the terrain. The other commanders had little faith in Dannenberg's abilities, and Gorchakov opposed anything that Menshikov proposed as a matter of principle. The Russian forces lacked any maps of the area to be attacked. There was an excellent map compiled by the 5th Corps when it was stationed in the Crimea a few years earlier, but it was now in the archives at Odessa and they would not release it to Menshikov. The sole copy was in St Petersburg, but could only be sent following a special order by the Tsar. This was eventually obtained, but the messenger carrying the map did not arrive at Menshikov's headquarters until the day after the battle. There were two other weaknesses. First, the Inkerman Ridge was simply too small an area in which to deploy a force of some 35,000 men, assuming that Soimonov's and Pavlov's troops were able to reach the top of the ridge. Second, the Inkerman bridge across the Chernaya was still under repair. Menshikov ordered the work to be completed by the night of 4 November (just before the attack), but the bridge was not ready on time.

The final problem was the weather. It rained all day on 4 November and through the night. By the morning of 5 November there was a steady drizzle mixed with a thick mist that cut visibility down to a few yards in most places. This gave the Russians the advantage of surprise in the initial attack, but then produced chaos, as units could not find each other. The damp also made the rifles and muskets very difficult to fire. Throughout the battle commanders, both Russian and British, could not exercise any control over units bigger than a few hundred men. It was impossible to get any overall picture of the progress of the fighting. The 'battle' was therefore a series of disconnected small attacks and counter-attacks (some against their own side) with hand-to-hand fighting and almost total confusion.

EYE-WITNESS
THE WEATHER

William Russell, *The Times* war correspondent
'The men in our camps had just begun a struggle with the rain in endeavouring to light their fires for breakfast when the alarm was given . . . The battle of Inkerman admits of no description . . . No one, however placed, could have witnessed even a small portion of the doings of this eventful day, for the vapours, fog and drizzling mist obscured the ground where the struggle took place to such an extent as to render it impossible to see what was going on at the distance of a few yards. Besides this the irregular nature of the ground . . . would have prevented anyone under the most favourable circumstances from seeing more than a very insignificant and detailed piece of the terrible work below . . . Our generals could not see where to go. They could not tell where the enemy were – from what side they were coming, nor where they were coming to. In darkness, gloom and rain they had to lead our lines through thick scrubby bushes and thorny brakes, which broke our ranks and irritated the men, while every pace was marked by a corpse or a man wounded by an enemy whose position was only indicated by the rattle of musketry and the rush of ball and shell.'

A coherent account of the 'battle' of Inkerman is therefore impossible, except at the most general level. The best description comes from the experiences of the men involved.

The Russian attack

EYE-WITNESS
THE RUSSIAN ATTACK

Pyotr Alabin, participated in the attack under General Pavlov from Inkerman bridge

'The night is dark. The rain, though it has completely abated, has made thick mud, which must inevitably make our ascent up the slope more difficult . . . But time does not wait. The regiments are beginning to move. Our horses are being saddled . . . We put the samovar on the embers of the fire and drink our fill of tea, perhaps for the last time? The regiments are standing at attention. Our horses are impatiently dancing. It's time to close my diary. Close it! . . . and will it be my fate once again to open these pages which are so close to my heart? . . . Soimonov attacked with his detachment at the point meant for our attack, and both detachments were forced into the space for one, having destroyed the English whom we met in our path there. Then, not seeing, not knowing and not receiving any orders from anyone as to what we were to do next, we stood and perished in our masses, until the battle turned into practically individual fist-fights . . . There are no general instructions . . . these advances are far from being the development of some unified thought process, far from being the carrying out of the ideas of one man, who with his bloody staff is draughting on the field of death signs incomprehensible to the majority, but the secret meaning of which is, all nevertheless one and the same – victory; no, all these disjointed actions are the children of chance – nobody knows what all this is leading to!'

Dannenberg had made a significant change in Menshikov's plan by moving forward by an hour to 5 a.m. the start of Soimonov's attack on the western side of the ridge. Soimonov then left most of his troops as reserves on the engineer's road and only used three regiments to climb to the top of the ridge. They did so undetected by the British, who could hear noises but assumed this was normal Russian movement along the road. When Soimonov's troops reached the summit they found no sign of Pavlov's

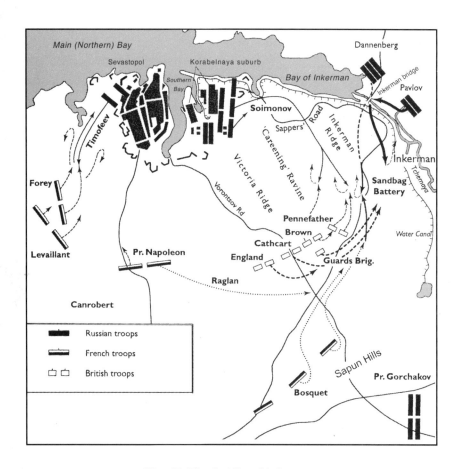

Map 7: The battle of Inkerman

forces. This was not just because they had started an hour early, but because Pavlov's 20,000 troops were held up at the Inkerman bridge which was still under repair. Soimonov's troops were soon engaged in fierce fighting with the small British forces on the ridge. Soimonov himself was killed at the start of the fighting and his second-in-command was badly wounded. The troops retreated back down the ravines to the road where the reserves were stationed. Their commander, General O. P. Zhabokritskii, took charge, but refused to move until he received further orders. None were forthcoming.

Pavlov's troops were finally able to cross the Inkerman bridge at 7 a.m., but it took another hour before they were ready to start climbing the ridge. They captured the 'Sandbag Battery' (an incomplete two-gun position that offered no real defensive standpoint) and this was to be the scene of the most intense fighting during the morning. Just over an hour later the small force under General Timofeev attacked the far left of the French line. They achieved tactical surprise in the mist and arrived unseen at the French lines. The French suffered heavy casualties (about 950 dead and wounded) and a number of guns were spiked. The Russians suffered a similar level of casualties (about one-third of those engaged). This action would probably have been decisive in tying down the French if Gorchakov had launched the main diversionary attack as planned. Possibly deliberately, he restricted the attack to a weak artillery bombardment, which did little damage because of the range at which the Russian guns were firing. The French quickly decided that this attack was no more than a diversion and were able to move reinforcements to help the British. Had Gorchakov carried out the planned attack, then the French, also fighting Timofeev's forces on their left, would probably have had to leave the British to fight on their own.

The main battle focused on the north-eastern end of the ridge and the 'Sandbag Battery'. The British knew they were under attack shortly after 6 a.m. Raglan arrived on the scene an hour later but, as normal, issued no effective orders at any stage. The early fighting involved the 2nd Division under General Pennefather (de Lacy Evans was unavailable after a fall from his horse). Reinforcements were moved in and slowed up the Russian advance. The Sandbag Battery was lost, but recaptured and held against Russian forces five times bigger. It was lost again and again and recaptured countless times during the morning as the battle ebbed and flowed. Further reinforcements from the Guards Brigade and the 4th Division were moved forward and fed into the battle piecemeal as they arrived. The Minié rifle of the British troops was particularly effective, but much of the fighting was hand-to-hand using whatever weapons were available. The British were slowly overrun and forced back by superior numbers, especially as the reserves under General Zhabokritskii finally climbed the ridge from the west and joined the fighting.

EYE-WITNESS
THE BATTLE

George Evelyn

'Our assembly sounded at 6, and the sound of musketry to our right explained the cause. We marched to . . . the top of the hill . . . [and] came into action. The enemy were in great force – our troops collected slowly and could hardly hold their ground. I saw a battery, the guns of which were silent for want of ammunition. Regiments were mixed. A party of men came towards me bearing Coote Buller shot through the thigh . . . Whilst binding up his leg, we were in a very advanced position, and our scattered line was passing us on both sides, in retiring before the rapidly approaching enemy . . . Two of our men got nervous and wanted to save themselves, and leave Coote to be bayoneted by our ruffianly foes; I was obliged to speak harshly to them of cowardice . . . My old comrade suffered very much during his transit to the rear. We were at first unable to get a stretcher, or even a blanket, with which to support his wounded limb. [Coote was eventually treated at the base hospital.]

'The fight was raging still, we merely held the ridge of the hill and the enemy was almost mixed with our men . . . I rode through the bush to the right . . . Kept along the ridge till I came into the fight again. I saw a dense column in the ravine down the road and, taking muskets from some Zouaves, fired from my horse into the mass below. I could not find my regiment . . . We were then rather advanced on the right of the ravine and almost alone, and the enemy's skirmishers were sneaking towards us through the bushes. I fired several times at them, but the colour of their clothes made it difficult to distinguish them . . . We were in danger of being made prisoners as they were advancing on all sides, so I drew my horse quickly back through the bushes and took advantage of the cover of the first brow to mount and gallop away . . . I went to the bivouack across the road, where I found most of the remaining men of my old regiment. There were men of all regiments there, sheltering themselves behind the low stonework . . . The fire was so heavy and so many of our small party were hit, that I could not get the men to keep up a fire . . . At last the enemy's batteries began to retire leaving many tumbrils and wounded horses. We advanced to the ground they had occupied. There were about a dozen horses killed . . . and as many more wounded by rifle bullets . . . I put some out of their pain with my revolver . . . We advanced to the top of the hill and saw Russian columns retreating along a ridge in our front. We remained hidden behind some stones and bush on the ridge till some men (not riflemen) foolishly opened with their rifles at an absurd range. This attracted the fire of a ship in the harbour hidden from us behind the hill, which gave us such a volley of shells that we were hardly able to stand our ground.'

Frederick Dallas, officer

'I can give you no general account of this battle which took place on a mountain, & in a valley called "Inkerman" . . . We were all alarmed about 6 A.M., by a good deal of Musketry on our right, where there has been an Army hovering about for some time. The "Assembly" sounded, and we all fell in . . . We marched as fast as we could to where the fighting evidently was . . . We found the Guards on the extreme right engaged with a large force of Russians on the brow of a hill . . . We immediately formed line, & set to work . . . the fire was very heavy. At last the enemy began to waver, & we took advantage of it & made a most splendid headlong Charge on them, pushing them down the steep side of the mountain, in utter confusion. The slaughter of them was here immense, for we charged right at them, & every man had shot away his 60 rounds (or nearly so) before we could get them to pull up. We then came leisurely back up the hill again, (of course scattered all over the side of it). When a few of us got nearly to the top from whence we had started, to our astonishment a most astounding fire opened upon us . . . We were placed, I should say 50 of us, with most of the Staff of the Division, on a small sort of natural platform, about 10 yds from the Russian Infantry Regiment which had outflanked us . . . How many of us escaped I can form no idea (few indeed did). We were so close to the Enemy that they threw stones, & clods of earth in our faces. Poor Sir George Cathcart fell there, shot, I believe, through the brain . . . We held our position till we had no more ammunition, & until few of us were left, & then retired a few paces down the Hill, just as a Cloud of Zouaves came dashing out of the right flank of the Russians . . . All that I had to do afterwards was to retire with what we could collect of our Division, & form again, get fresh ammunition & then lay ourselves down, as a sort of reserve or rather support to our Artillery – under the hottest cannonade for about 5 or 6 hours. We lost a good many men here for we were in very bad cover . . . Of my little Band we had 38 killed & wounded & 2 Officers wounded (not badly) out of 150 men & 6 Officers . . . I escaped unhurt except by a shot on a buckle that fastens my belt. A shot flattened against it & it saved myself. It was a great victory for our men & a great disgrace to our Leaders, that such a slaughter should have been necessary . . . we were attacked & altogether surprised, owing to the culpable carelessness & inefficiency of our Leaders . . . by an Army that partly came from the Town, & partly had been collecting under our very eyes for some time . . . A few hours work would have rendered our position unassailable, but they allowed us to be surprised, & nothing but our noble men saved our Camp & our Generals' reputation . . . The French by the bye, came up just in time, & helped much to pull us through. Our little Band, after Sir George fell, would certainly have been utterly annihilated. We had not a single round of ammunition left when the gallant Zouaves rushed up and attacked our foe in the Flank.'

At about 9 a.m. the rain stopped and the mist began to rise. This enabled the British to see the Russian positions, but it also enabled the latter's artillery to open fire. This consisted of twenty-four heavy, sixteen light and three field guns assisted by two frigates in the bay. British casualties rose rapidly. The commander of the 4th Division, General Sir George Cathcart, was killed, Raglan's position came under fire and Brigadier Thomas Fox-Strangways (commanding the artillery) lost a leg and died two hours later. The Duke of Cambridge's horse was killed and he left the battlefield. The British had run out of troops and were being forced back by superior Russian numbers. The main fighting was now concentrated around 'The Barrier', a road block on the Vorontsov road out of Sevastopol. By about 11 a.m. the British were on the point of defeat and finally asked for French help.

The decisive French intervention

At 6 a.m., just as the battle started, Bosquet visited Cathcart, Brown and the Duke of Cambridge and offered French help. The British rejected the offer. Bosquet returned to the French camp. Later in the morning French reinforcements were sent to their left to repel Timofeev's attack. Once it was clear that Gorchakov's 'attack' was no more than a very limited diversion, the French had a large number of reserves available. As soon as Raglan finally asked for French help, they moved in major reinforcements. These had an immediate and decisive impact, particularly on Russian morale. They were soon engaged in fierce hand-to-hand fighting and held the Sandbag Battery when the British Guards units were on the point of defeat. When he saw the position Bosquet remarked, '*Quel abattoir.*' After an hour of bitter fighting with the French, Dannenberg called off the attack. The Russian forces made an orderly retreat down the ridge and across the Chernaya. The allied forces made no attempt to interfere. Raglan asked the French to undertake the pursuit while British forces rested. Canrobert refused to do so unless the British participated in the action.

EYE-WITNESS
THE RUSSIAN RETREAT

Captain Hodasiewicz
'During the retreat, or rather flight . . . we lost a great many men from our ignorance of the ground; everyone ran according to his own judgement, and many found themselves at the top of high precipitous rocks or the quarries and such was the panic that had taken possession of the men that many of them, making the sign of the cross, threw themselves over and were dashed to pieces . . . numbers, especially wounded men crept into the caves that abound here and were never heard of more . . . Suddenly, as if he fell from heaven, appeared amongst us the General of our division, Kiriakoff [*sic*], whom we had not seen for some days. 'Halt, halt!' shouted he, frantically waving his Cossack whip, but the soldiers paid little attention to him, so, in order to gain proper respect from the men, he began to beat them with his whip, shouting that the officers did not attend to their duty, or the men would never have run. Some of the men who could not bear to see this, shouted "Go up there yourself." He has not been seen in the fight, but he makes himself felt now it's over.'

Leo Tolstoy
'It was treacherous, revolting business . . . we had to retreat, because half our troops had no artillery owing to the roads being impassable, and – God knows why – there were no rifle battalions. Terrible slaughter! It will lie heavy on the souls of many people! Lord forgive them . . . The news of this action has produced a sensation. I've seen old men who wept aloud and young men who swore to kill Dannenberg.'

Colonel P. K. Menkov
'It was the story of the Alma all over again, for no one knew the aim of the offensive, let alone how it was to be executed. Columns became confused, artillery got mixed up, and infantry, attacking without support of artillery, lost thousands of men. We did not make any use of our advantage in artillery or cavalry, none of which saw action that day. The artillery just crowded

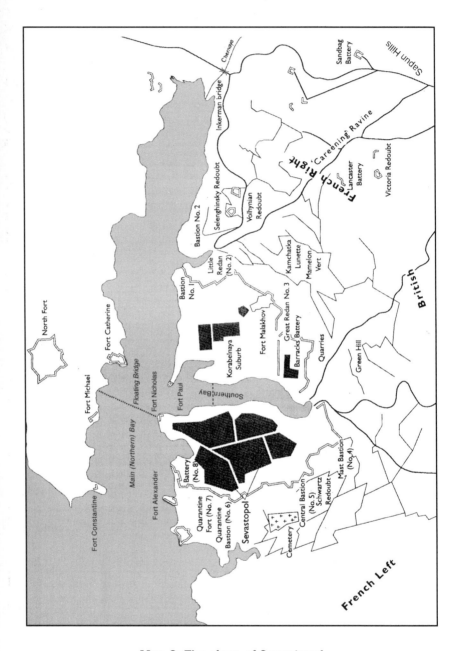

Map 8: The siege of Sevastopol

together, losing men and horses. We lost . . . 12,000 men nearly all our regimental and battalion commanders and senior officers. And all for nothing! Neither Dannenberg nor Menshikov did anything at all during the battle.'

Inkerman – the outcome

The six hours of fighting around the Inkerman Ridge on 5 November 1854 represented the most vicious of all the Crimean battles. The Russians lost about 12,000 men (about one-third of the forces that joined the battle) and casualties were particularly heavy among the officers and gunners who were the target of British rifle fire. The British lost 632 killed and just over 1,800 wounded (a very high proportion of whom died shortly afterwards). Total French casualties were about 1,700. Overall therefore the Russian losses outnumbered those of the allies by about three to one.

The Russians failed in all their objectives. Menshikov's plan was a reasonable one, but it was ineptly carried out by his subordinate commanders. His choice of Dannenberg to control the operation was disastrous. The Russians were unable to make their superior numbers count, partly because the attacks on the ridge were uncoordinated, but also because Gorchakov's major diversionary attack never took place. At a tactical level the Russian use of columns and their reliance on bayonet attacks was suicidal in the face of the superior firepower of the British with their Minié rifles. After this failure the Russians decided they would be unable to drive the allies out of the Crimea before the onset of winter.

Although the allies had been able to restore control of their positions and defeat the Russian attack, their situation was still precarious. For the British the victory was a pyrrhic one – their army was reduced to a strength of about 16,000 and there were no signs of any immediate reinforcements. As Clarendon, the Foreign Secretary, commented to Cowley, the Ambassador in Paris, 'Everyone is down hearted about the victory (if it was one) and feels that another such triumph, or another such attack, would finally smash us, and then will come the monster catastrophe.'[1] Nevertheless Raglan was promoted to Field Marshal and Bosquet was promoted within the Légion d'honneur.

EYE-WITNESS
THE AFTERMATH

William Russell
'The British and French, many of whom had been murdered by the Russians as they lay wounded, wore terrible frowns on their faces, with which the agonies of death had clad them. Some in their last throes had torn up the earth in their hands, and held the grass between their fingers up towards heaven. All the men who exhibited such signs of pain had been bayoneted; the dead men who lay with an eternal smile on their lips had been shot. But the wounded – for two days they had lain where the hand and the ball had felled them . . . The Russians groaning and palpitating as they lay around, were far more numerous. Some were placed together in heaps, that they might be more readily removed . . . The dead were generally stripped of all but their coats. The camp followers and blackguards from Balaklava, and the seamen from the ships, anxious for trophies, carried off all they could take from the field . . . Groups were digging away all along the hillside . . . a yawning trench, thirty feet in length by twenty feet in breadth and six feet in depth, at the bottom of which, in every conceivable attitude, lay packed together . . . some thirty or forty corpses . . . some of them had upraised arms, in the attitude of taking aim; their legs stick up through the mould as it was thrown upon them.'

Roger Fenton, war photographer, visiting the site of the battle in May 1855
'All over the steep sides of the Inkerman the grass and flowers are gradually budding; the pieces of torn cloth, ragged caps, shoes without soles, now form the principal indications of the struggle which took place there. I have been there now three times, and with people who were in the battle, and none of them can tell me where any of the principal incidents took place. Everybody was busy about what immediately concerned their own corps or department, and saw nothing of the general action.'

EYE-WITNESS
THE BRITISH PRISONERS

George Newman, foot soldier
'I found myself marching to the rear of the Russian army, most kindly

156

escorted by a bodyguard of three men, one having a tight hold on my right wrist, another my left, and one following behind me with his bayonet at the "charge", of which he would now and then give me a gentle prick about my great seat of honour, just to remind me, I suppose, that he was on the alert . . . I never expected to get out of the place alive, but by God's mercy I did, although I had five balls through my greatcoat . . . we now came into range of the Artillery and their shot and shell whistled and exploded about us very merrily . . . We descended a hill, when we came upon a circle of men of several regiments, seated on the ground . . . After two hours' rest we marched on again, and led along the bank of the harbour to the bridge that crosses the Chernaya river . . . We remained here about an hour . . . When we got over the bridge and plank road . . . we again sat down in a circle with the same amusement as before, smoking cigarettes and staring at the circle of Russians – and they at us . . . I looked round carefully for a chance to escape, but the bridge was blocked up with thousands of men descending from the hills on the far side . . . I saw several bodies of men on the crest of the hill . . . we could see the flash of the gun and the next instant a shell pitched right in among the crowd close to us. Another and another and many more followed in rapid succession.'

Newman was eventually taken to Sevastopol with the wounded, separated from the officers and spent two nights in one of the forts.

7 November: 'At about half past four we began our march away from the famed town of Sebastopol. We had not gone far before darkness fell, and I found that they were going to march us in the dark, to prevent us seeing too much. The soldiers were very civil, and struck lights for pipes as often as we wanted them. They would not allow us to wander or straggle outside the escort. We had two waggons to carry our baggage, which could easily have been put in a wheelbarrow, but the waggons were handy to take a rest on while we had a smoke . . . shortly afterwards came to the village [Belbec], and I saw the vineyards and orchards that I had such a lot of apples and grapes from when on the march from the Alma to Sebastopol . . . We were each served out with an old corn sack for a bed, and I got a large stone for a pillow. I pulled my old forage cap down over my ears and spread my old greatcoat over me and laid down. I lay for some time watching the stars shoot and thinking of the difference in my fate since I came over the same ground with my regiment.'

The British and French commanders now faced a difficult prospect. On 7 November they held a council of war to decide whether the planned assault on Sevastopol should take place. On the one hand, the Russians were likely to be demoralised after their failure and their heavy losses. On the other hand, were the allies strong enough to mount an attack with any chance of success, especially with a major Russian army still in their rear? The Duke of Cambridge suggested a withdrawal from the positions in front of Sevastopol to the heights around Balaklava, where stronger defensive lines were possible and the lines of communication would be shorter. General de Lacy Evans argued for evacuation because the allied plan for a quick capture of Sevastopol before the onset of winter had failed. He thought the current exposed positions could not be held during the long winter months. Raglan, probably wisely, rejected this proposal. There was not enough transport available to mount a full-scale evacuation and any attempt to start such an operation could be catastrophic if the Russians attacked. The allied commanders decided that they had little choice but to stay where they were throughout the winter and wait for reinforcements to arrive.

The morale of the army was, not surprisingly, low as the full enormity of their position became apparent. Even before the battle of Inkerman, General Burgoyne was worried about the strategic situation:

> As regards our relative state, between the Allied forces and the enemy, we do not progress at all: as we advance in front, they entrench in rear of their lines, and become relatively as strong. We receive a few occasional reinforcements; that is, the French do, not the British; so do the Russians, and as we believe (for we have no knowledge of particulars) in a far greater proportion.[2]

George Evelyn wrote in the days after the battle:

> It appears that the Army is to remain before Sebastopol, continuing the siege operations whilst the weather remains open, and then quietly to remain on the ground till the Spring without fighting unless attacked . . . The weather for some days has been wet and stormy . . . It is generally understood that our siege operations have turned out a failure, that the town cannot be taken until regularly invested.[3]

Henry Clifford was equally gloomy:

> Our position . . . is I must say a difficult and critical one; our force is now so much diminished. A large army quite at liberty and independent of the siege of Sebastopol has to be fought – winter is

coming on – and we are far from our resources . . . The siege is I fear only nominal; we are I believe, only keeping up appearances. Our force is much weakened by sickness and fighting, and can only hold the ground of our position and batteries till more *men* are sent out.[4]

The man largely responsible for the decision to move round Sevastopol and attack from the south, General Burgoyne, had been increasingly depressed about the prospects even before the failure of the assault on 17 October. Now he realised that the allies had badly misjudged the situation since the summer and that the invasion of the Crimea should not have been undertaken: 'we are clearly two months too late: if the expedition had started early in July, instead of September, we should now have had two good months before us'.[5] Instead the situation was grim:

The army is now, and is likely to continue in a terrible state of discomfort . . . The course of events here looks almost as gloomy as the weather; we have been brought to a standstill, but turn and show good fight against any that attack us . . . I think we have lost many advantages by over-caution, and not pressing harder upon the enemy, and that it could have been done without risk.'[6]

Burgoyne thought there was little chance that Sevastopol could be captured. Because the city was not fully besieged the Russians could move in reinforcements along the road from Inkerman bridge to maintain numerical superiority and the allies, even if they did attack, were unlikely to be able to use the harbour. Meanwhile the allies were getting weaker: 'our means are getting exhausted rapidly, while winter is not *coming* but *come* on'. He could only conclude that 'further attempts, at present, to take Sebastopol are hopeless . . . we have been engaged in an undertaking for which we had not sufficient means'.[7]

9

Crimean Winter

The position of the allied armies after Inkerman was grim. When they arrived in the Crimea they carried very few supplies and in the intervening period little had been done to improve the situation. The British and French navies guarded Sevastopol harbour, but spent most of their time ferrying supplies in order to keep the armies alive and operational. The military commanders, in particular Raglan, were reluctant to admit that their strategy had failed. They were optimistic that Sevastopol would fall and provide a base where the armies could spend the winter. Almost no preparations had been made to cope with the possibility of failure. (Raglan did not inform the head of the commissariat, Filder, that the army would winter in the Crimea until 8 November 1854 – far too late for him to make adequate preparations.) The road from Balaklava to the heights was not improved and rapidly turned into a morass of mud. Little was done to prepare winter quarters for the troops or the horses. Balaklava harbour was chaotic and overcrowded, with ships waiting for days to unload. However, the government in London had had greater foresight than its military commanders and, from late in August, had begun to make preparations for sustaining the army through the winter. Extra equipment and warm clothing was ordered and sent out to the east in October.

By the end of the first week of November, as the weather worsened, the situation of the cavalry was becoming difficult. The horses had no shelter and there was no transport to take fodder up to the camp. By 12 November the horses were surviving on a handful of barley a day. Cardigan, who was spending four to five days at a time on his yacht, refused to allow the Light Brigade to move to Balaklava where the horses could be fed. He also ordered that no horse was to be killed unless it had a broken leg or an incurable disease. The result was that the horses died slowly of starvation over several days, usually lying in the mud. Nevertheless William Russell reassured the readers of *The Times* that the condition of the troops was fine and that the army supply system was working well:

> Mr Commissary-General Filder deserves the greatest praise for his exertions in supplying our men with food. The stories which have been circulating respecting the insufficiency and irregularity of the supply of meat, biscuit and spirits, are base calumnies. No army was ever fed with more punctuality, and no army, I believe, was ever so

well fed under such very exceptional circumstances . . . no man in this army has ever been without his pound of good biscuit, his pound and a half or pound of good beef or mutton, his quota of coffee, tea, rice and sugar or his gill of excellent rum, for any one day, except it has been through his own neglect.[1]

Evidence from those in the army suggests that Russell was misleading his readers.

**EYE-WITNESS
THE BRITISH ARMY – EARLY NOVEMBER 1854**

George Lawson, doctor
'The poor fellows who suffer most are those men who are down in the trenches when it rains . . . when they are relieved and return to their tents, thoroughly drenched and tired, they have no change to put on, as clothes (altho' reported to have arrived) have not yet been issued out to the men . . . You cannot imagine anything more uncomfortable than wet and cold weather in camp. The ground here when it rains is in some places almost as bad as a marsh, and the wet tent does not form a cheerful place to go into, particularly as there are no chairs, or any fire, in fact nothing more than the canvas walls . . . all cooking is done in the open air, and the wind either almost scatters the fire or the rain puts it out . . . The men are now very badly and insufficiently clothed owing to their not having received any warm clothing since they have been in the Crimea. In this respect we are all badly off, officers as well as men . . . Latterly during the last two weeks, owing to the bad weather and state of the roads, the Commissariat have been unable to get up their full supplies, and the tea and sugar have not been issued; but we have supplied the deficiency by buying these in Balaclava . . . The French are very pleasant neighbours . . . they always have their band playing two or three times a day . . . They are now well provided with warm clothing; coats which they call "moutons", they are capital things, they are nothing more than sheep skins, dressed with the wool on, and they certainly are the proper clothing for out here, as they are very warm and strong. I wish our men had something of the sort . . . Many of them are almost shoeless and shirtless, their great coats worn to a thread and torn in all directions, having had not only to live in them during the day but sleep in them by night, covered only by the wet blanket which they have just brought up with them from the trenches.'

Temple Godman, officer

12 November: 'The winter is setting in and we have just had two days' rain, the misery of which you can hardly realize. The horses up to their fetlocks in mud and slush, through which one must paddle to get at them; the saddles soaked, the tents so crowded that the men have no room in them for their arms, which must therefore lie in the rain. In our tents everything is wet, except what one can wrap up in a waterproof; mud outside and mud within. The men of course are worse off, most having no change or only one of clothes – of course their clothes get wet in the daytime, and their cloaks, and these they must sleep in as also their boots, for if they pulled them off they would never get them on again, no wonder we had twenty-two cases of sickness this morning. Dysentery is on the increase. If we are left like this the horses must soon die, and the men be knocked up. I must say I do not see the use of our being kept here, for we are shut up inside a fortified line, out of which we must keep the enemy, and it is not likely we shall stir to attack them. Unless they make us and our horses huts soon we shall be quite useless by the spring, even if we get through the winter.'

The Great Storm

For five days after 9 November there was continuous heavy rain across the Crimea. This was followed by a natural disaster that was to affect the allied armies, in particular the British, for months to come. Shortly after 6 a.m. on 14 November storm-force south-westerly winds began to blow across the Crimean peninsula. Inside Sevastopol the Russians were reasonably well protected, but even here roofs were blown off houses and the main naval magazine was badly damaged. The allied armies encamped on the heights above Sevastopol suffered very badly. Tents pitched in the soft, muddy ground were torn down and blown away. Barracks were destroyed, makeshift hospital tents disappeared in the wind, exposing the patients to the elements. Trenches were flooded by the torrential rain that accompanied the winds. Only the Ottoman troops, who knew how to pitch their tents to cope with such conditions, survived reasonably well. After several hours of wind and rain the temperature dropped suddenly – much of the area was covered in several inches of snow and the troops were left in the open to cope as best they could.

However, the most important damage occurred at sea. Allied warships, especially the French, operated off the Crimean coast near the Kacha River (the only source of water for the allied armies) and the base at Evpatoriya.

Here the French lost the modern screw propeller-driven warship *Henri IV*, which was blown onshore, and the corvette *Pluton*. The French ships at their main base, Kamiesh Bay, were protected by a 2,000-year-old jetty built by the ancient Greeks and only three transports were lost. The overcrowding in Balaklava harbour, where thirty ships were already trying to unload, was the underlying cause of most of the British losses. Twenty-two vessels were waiting outside, half of which were sailing ships that could not put to sea in the storm. Even the steam-powered ships could not be manoeuvred in the storm-force winds and many were smashed up on the cliffs. Overall the British lost fifteen transports and five steam corvettes. The total allied losses on the day were about 500 men, nearly all of them sailors.

Of the ships outside Balaklava harbour, *Resolute,* carrying ammunition, sank, but the crucial loss was that of the steamship *Prince.* This was carrying nearly all the supplies that had been ordered by the War Office in August to provide the initial stocks of winter clothing for the army. In total the clothing losses were 25,000 fur caps, 8,000 sealskin coats, 15,000 pairs of leather boots, 40,000 fur coats, 40,000 pairs of leggings and 10,000 gloves. These stocks would have been enough to equip the small British army for the winter. The stores could be replaced, but it would take several months for the items to be made and shipped out to the Crimea. Equally important was the loss of more than twenty days' supply of hay for the horses. Without this fodder the horses would die and there would be no way of moving supplies (particularly food) from Balaklava to the troops several miles away on the heights before Sevastopol. When the horses died the troops would have to do this work themselves. The harbour master at Balaklava, Captain Christie, who had refused to let ships into the harbour, took most of the blame for the disaster. He was told that he would be court-martialled, but died and was posthumously awarded a CB.

EYE-WITNESS
THE GREAT STORM

William Russell, *The Times* war correspondent
'The sound of the rain, its heavy beating on the earth, had become gradually swallowed up by the noise of the rushing of the wind over the common, and by the flapping of the tents as they rocked more violently beneath its force . . . Mud – and nothing but mud – flying before the wind, and drifting as though it were rain, covered the face of the earth as far as it was visible . . . a harsh screaming sound, increasing in vehemence as it approached, struck us with

horror. As it passed along we heard the snapping of tent-poles and the sharp crack of timber and canvas . . . The whole headquarters camp was beaten flat to the earth, and the unhappy occupants were rushing through the mud in all directions in chase of their effects and clothes, as they strove to make their way to the roofless and windowless barns and stables for shelter . . . The air was filled with blankets, hats, greatcoats, little coats, and even tables and chairs. Mackintoshes, quilts, india-rubber tubs, bed-clothes, sheets of tent-canvas went whirling like leaves in the gale towards Sebastopol. The shingle roofs of the outhouses were torn away and scattered over the camp, and a portion of the roof of Lord Raglan's house was carried off to join them . . . men and horses were knocked down and rolled over and over; the ambulance wagons were turned topsy-turvy . . . Nearly one-half of our cavalry horses broke loose . . . In every direction fresh scenes of wretchedness met the eye . . . The officers of the guard had fled to the commissariat stores and there found partial shelter. Inside the commissariat yard, overturned carts, dead horses and groups of shivering men were seen – not a tent was left standing . . . Lord Lucan was seen for hours sitting up to his knees in sludge . . . Lord Cardigan was sick on board his yacht . . . Towards twelve o'clock the wind . . . chopped round more to the west, and became much colder. Sleet fell first, and then came a snow-storm, which clothed the desolate landscape in white, till the tramp of men seamed it with trails of black mud . . . Towards evening there were many tents re-pitched along the lines of our camps, though they were but sorry resting-places. They flapped about so much and admitted such quantities of snow, rain, and filth from outside that it was quite out of the question to sleep in them. What was to be done? Suddenly it occurred to us that there might be room in the barn used as a stable for the horses of Lord Raglan's escort . . . we at once waded across the sea of nastiness . . . tacked against several gusts . . . nearly floundered in big horse holes . . . What a scene it was! . . . The wind blew savagely through the roof, and through the chinks in the mud walls and window holes. The building was a mere shell, as dark as pitch, and smelt as it ought to do – an honest and unmistakable stable – improved by a dense pack of moist and mouldy soldiers . . . Nothing could be heard but the howling of the wind, the yelping of wild dogs driven into the enclosures and the shrill neighing of terrified horses.'

George Evelyn, militia officer
'A tremendous storm of wind and rain . . . lasted all day. The amount of damage suffered by the troops and shipping may prove sufficient to be fatal to the expedition. Almost all the tents in this division . . . were blown down

and partially destroyed; their wretched occupants having to stand shivering and exposed to the wintry storm. Immense hailstones, mixed with sleet and rain, fell and covered the ground – never was such a picture of desolation and misery. Four officers and two servants huddled together in my hut . . . It was impossible to light a fire on account of the wind, as the sparks would probably have ignited the roof of the hut. We took off our wet boots and huddled together for warmth, but our limbs were cramped and numb from cold and want of room . . . At night one or two of our tents were re-pitched, and officers and servants huddled up together as best they could. We had nothing to eat, except a few crumbs of biscuit till evening, when the wind moderated a little, enabling us to light a fire and boil some bits of mouldy ham. But our sufferings were nothing compared to those which the wretched parties in the trenches had to endure. It was necessary to send a fatigue party to help them up on their return, they being quite unable to carry their rifles and water bottles.'

George Lawson

'At about 6 o'clock . . . we were all awoken by a tremendous slapping of the tent in which we were sleeping, caused by the wind having suddenly risen, and in a short time were all obliged to leave it, as it was evident it was falling . . . Every tent was blown down, all the hospital marquees level with the ground and the unfortunate sick lying exposed to wind and wet. To attempt to put them up again was impossible, as the wind was so high that no one was able to keep his legs, even the horses could not hold themselves up, and all the arabas and means of transport we had were turned over on their sides. Camp kettles, soldiers' clothes and saddles were all to be seen flying before the wind . . . it rained and hailed hard at intervals, the weather all day being excessively cold, the thermometer not standing higher than 40. We were more fortunate than our neighbours, as by hanging on to the curtains of the tent, and continually pegging the ropes down we succeeded in keeping ourselves under cover . . . At about 1 o'clock things began to assume a more moderate aspect, and then it commenced snowing, the wind however still remaining very high.'

Pyotr Alabin, Russian soldier

'What a sight! Even in my dreams I have never seen the like! The sea, this time Black not only in name, but in colour, had merged with the black sky. It was as though some unfathomable huge monster had opened its bottomless jaw and had flicked into it a multitude of ships of the enemy squadron. Several vessels are already lying on the shore like corpses; amongst the squadron, are beating without masts.'

EYE-WITNESS
THE BRITISH PRISONERS LEAVE SIMFEROPOL IN THE GREAT STORM

George Newman, foot soldier

'On rising this morning we found the wind blowing a hurricane, accompanied by heavy rain . . . About ten o'clock we were fell in and marched outside the gates [of the local jail]. By and by the gates opened and out came a host of convicts, all heavily ironed and chained together by cross chains, in fours. Their irons made a great noise and the street was soon crowded with spectators to see the procession move off, although the rain came down very heavily and tiles and chimneys were flying about rather wildly . . . We were taken to another prison on the outside of the town, and, after waiting for a long time, we were served out with a new sheepskin coat each and a pair of new long boots that reached to our knees, and a pair of leather gloves with a piece of cloth inside . . . The storm grew worse and worse and the tiles were flying off the houses . . . and some of the glass was blown in and the rain and sleet came down very heavily, and the poor, miserable convicts were left in the whole of it . . . When the gates were opened for us to pass out I saw a crowd of miserable-looking women and children round the entrance, and, though nearly drowned and wet through, I wondered what they wanted; but I soon found out, for as soon as the troop of convicts came in sight they set up an awful cry . . . These were the wives, children, mothers and sisters of those poor wretches who were being dragged away to the mines of Siberia . . . The storm still continued and our sergeant made signs to us of going to sleep . . . We had to wade through a river and soon found ourselves in a village where we were billeted by fours and fives on the different peasants' houses . . . They put us in to a room and made a fire of straw in a kind of earthen oven, which soon warmed the room . . . I threw my old greatcoat on top of the oven to dry for it was wet through, and I shortly became aware that there was something burning. I looked at my coat and, to my horror, found that the whole of the shoulder and part of one sleeve was scorched into tinder. This was a bad job for me. In about an hour the mistress brought in the iron pot and placed it in the middle of the floor . . . We seated ourselves as do the Turks round the pot . . . It was a kind of macaronney soup – not bad to the taste, and being hot, went down very well. After we had done we lighted our pipes and the old man brought some dry straw and we laid down to sleep.'

EYE-WITNESS
BALAKLAVA AFTER THE GREAT STORM

George Evelyn
'. . . large trees, apparently in sheltered positions, have been torn up . . . The unfortunate ships driven on the rocks went to fragments in a few minutes – many men were saved, when clinging to the rocks in a half-dying state . . . The poor *Prince*, having lost all her anchors, endeavoured to keep her place by steaming into the teeth of the gale . . . Her crew had recourse to cutting away her masts, when the falling rigging got foul of her screw and stopped her way – in an instant she was on the rocks. The first bump carried away her rudder, the second, her entire stern; the third broke her up completely and she entirely disappeared . . . All the ships outside the harbour which succeeded in weathering the storm have done so at the expense of their spars – not a mast is now to be seen among them! A parcel of miserable hulks, deprived of all motive power, are still clinging to their anchors in the heavy sea, and with the exception of the wreckwood floating up the harbour, are all that remains of the splendid fleet of steamers and merchantmen lately riding proudly outside the port.'

William Russell
'The roads were mere quagmires. Dead horses and cattle were scattered all over the country . . . At the narrow neck of the harbour two or three large boats were lying, driven inland several yards from the water; the shores were lined with trusses of hay which had floated out of the wrecks outside the harbour, and masts and spars of all sizes were stranded on the beach or floated about among the shipping . . . The narrow main street was a channel of mud, through which the horses, wagons, camels, mules and soldiers and sailors . . . scrambled, and plunged, and jostled and squatted along.'

The British army

After the Great Storm the British army faced problems on a number of fronts. Once the wreckage from the storm was cleared from Balaklava harbour, it could operate. A reasonably efficient system was instituted for unloading, and waiting times were reduced. Ships were only allowed a limited period alongside so as to stop the selling of goods to the soldiers. Wharves and docks were allocated for specific cargoes – the first dock on the eastern side was for cattle so that they could walk ashore. Cinders were unloaded to help make roads. Most of the Royal Navy steamships were now engaged in ferrying supplies from Constantinople – at times only one ship was left off Sevastopol to enforce the nominal blockade.

The first crucial area was the state of the road from Balaklava. Raglan had failed to take any action to ensure that it remained usable. He seems to have regarded such problems as beneath his notice. In October the ground was still firm and goods could be brought up with ease, even off the road. Once the heavy rains started in early November the road disintegrated into an almost unusable rutted quagmire. Now it was too late to make improvements – a desultory attempt to lay a proper road, which should have been done in October, failed. The British decided they could not spare any men to work on the road and hired Ottoman troops to do the menial work. They were so badly treated that many died and in the end their conditions and treatment were so poor that the British could not even hire labourers.

EYE-WITNESS
WINTER 1854: THE SIEGE OF SEVASTOPOL

William Russell

25 November: 'The siege has been for many days practically suspended, our batteries are used up and silent, our army are much exhausted by the effects of excessive labour and watching, and by the wet and storm to which they have been so incessantly exposed.'

29 November: 'I suppose one must still head one's letters "Siege of Sebastopol" but really and truly, there is no siege of the place whatever, and all this delay increases the difficulty which was caused by our original neglect and indifference towards the formidable works which we permitted the Russians to throw up with impunity.'

Temple Godman

27 November: 'No news about the siege, if such it may be called. I was up at the front to-day, the French seem very near the town, but hardly any firing is going on, and what there is, is all from the enemy.'

3 December: 'I can't tell when the town is likely to be taken. Some say it will fall before Christmas, though why it should I can't see at the present rate of proceeding, for we never fire a gun hardly now. Others say that the place must be entirely invested first.'

The second major problem area for the British army was the lack of fodder for the horses. Under pressure from Cardigan, Raglan moved the cavalry to a weak sector of the British front on the far right in a desperate attempt to demonstrate to the Russians that the cavalry was still operational. However, as Lucan pointed out, this area had no forage and it was also very difficult to supply. The cavalry horses starved, became mad and dashed through the main camp in a frenzy as they tried to get at the forage of the artillery horses. On 1 December Lucan reported that the cavalry were incapable of action. Raglan removed them to Kadikioi where they were stabled in holes in the ground. The holes were soon infested with rats and the remaining horses died at a rapid rate. The artillery horses were overworked on their frequent trips to Balaklava and they too began dying.

EYE-WITNESS
THE CAVALRY AND THE ANIMALS

Henry Clifford
27 November: 'the weather has been very bad, rain day and night, the oxen and horses for transport of forage and provisions . . . overworked, badly looked after and not being able to live without food more than a certain time, are either dead or too weak to work and order came to the staff to inform them that they must depend upon their own resources to get hay and corn for their charges from Balaklava.'

Temple Godman
7 December: 'the state of the cavalry is melancholy; the Light Dragoons *led* their horses here [near Balaklava], and I don't think there are six horses in the brigade that could trot for a quarter of a mile, the most miserable starved horse you ever saw on an English common, is nothing to the horses here . . . I don't suppose they will save ten horses out of each regiment by spring at this rate. They are starved: an officer told me he saw two troop-horses eating a dead one the other day. Lord Lucan has reported the Division ineffective, and I think Lord Raglan must be to blame, he never seems to stir out of his house, nor to care how things go.'

Frederick Dallas
11 December: 'We see spectral Artillery horses dragging up immense guns every day. You will laugh at what I am going to tell you, but it is perfectly true. The horses have all been so starving that they have eaten each other's tails! & it is a fact that not one horse in ten of the Artillery has any hair at

---

all left on that ornamental part of their persons, which adds considerably to their ghastly appearance.'

The army was now in a vicious circle. Its main supply line was almost impassable and, as the horses died from lack of food, the men were left to try and bring up their own food as winter deepened. Each trip from the camp to the harbour took twelve hours without shelter, food or rest. Not enough food could be supplied and rations deteriorated. For more than six weeks the troops had no rice or vegetables; on two days they had to survive on a quarter of normal rations, and for one day there was none at all. Firewood to cook the food was almost unattainable. The soldiers were in flooded trenches for days at a time and then had to sleep in the open and survive on an inadequate and often uncooked diet.

EYE-WITNESS
THE BRITISH SOLDIERS

Frederick Dallas

26 November: 'The greatest trial here is seeing the sufferings of our men, without being in any way able to alleviate them. They are positively worked to death. If they were well fed (instead of being half starved), & if the weather was fine and warm (instead of constant rain and wind), & if they had a change of clothes in their camp; if they had all these benefits I don't think any but the very strongest could stand it. As it is they die miserably, not singly but in tens! Our officers are all pretty well . . . We are pretty well fed (by ourselves & pockets), not so hardly worked & have a dry wrap or two to get into when we come home from the trenches.'

6 December: 'It is a great sight for a reflecting man on a pouring day, or rather night, at 4½ A.M. with a wind that cuts you in two, to see 1000 men . . . parade to march down some distance to do duty in the Trenches for 12 hours, many very ill, all wan and haggard looking wretches, who had been told the day previous that "there would be no meat for that day" & given a handful of biscuit & a glass of rum. It is a curious sight to see these men half clad march off without a murmur . . . We are *now* commencing to get warm Clothing . . . I am writing this in bed . . . Mine is now a great fact & I get into it (whenever I am not in the Trenches) . . . I bought an immense blanket the other day & with a quantity of Plaids and Turkish great coats . . . I pass many pleasant hours.'

Private Harry Blishen
'I am happy to state that I am in good health, in spite of being up to my neck in mud in all weathers, and doing my natural sleep every night in a puddle of water. The weather here of late has been very wet; nothing but incessant rain, day and night; for my own part, I have given up all hopes of ever getting dry again. We cannot live in tents, in fact, the tent I used to live in, has long since become non-effective. We awoke one morning and found that the wind had made a large back door into it; so we are obliged to take in our canvas, and dig a large hole into the ground to live in; but before we could finish it, the wet weather commenced, so we are living in a well almost.'

Frederick Dallas
22 December: 'One of their [the soldiers] greatest hardships now is having to fetch everything, rations &c from Balaclava themselves, in addition to the constant Trenches, for the Commissariat has altogether broken down. All the mules and horses are dead . . . My servant went yesterday to Balaclava, on a ghost of a Pony he had found, or stolen, to get me stores, & came back pretty successful.'

Some of the problems were the consequence of army regulations. Soldiers were not supplied with vegetables as part of their ration – they were expected to buy them on the open market. In the Crimea there was no such market. No fuel was issued to the troops because regulations stipulated that this was done only when they were in barracks. Greatcoats could only be issued once every three years. Not surprisingly, sickness increased rapidly. The 46th regiment had 708 men when it landed in the Crimea in early September. By the second week of December 108 men were dead and 270 were sick. At the same time the 7th Regiment had only one-third of its strength available for duty. There were 3,500 men sick in the camp at Balaklava and their numbers were increasing at a rate of about a hundred a day. By the end of 1854 the 63rd Regiment had just seven men fit for duty. In early December the British army strength in the Crimea was already down to 20,000, but within a month this had dropped to 13,000.

The government in London was unaware that Raglan rarely visited the troops and took almost no interest in their welfare. He remained largely cut off in his own comfortable quarters, seemingly uninterested in the fact that his army was disintegrating around him, and he failed to devise any policy to deal with the problems. His fellow officers began to look on the army leadership with disgust.

EYE-WITNESS
VIEWS ABOUT THE GENERALS

Frederick Dallas

16 November: 'All this time we never see Lord Raglan, who is either unmoved by all this, or unable to find any relief for it. There is one general outcry against him. We are told that those about him don't like "talking shop" (to use the slang of the day). We all feel that something must be done, and that soon, or there will be no Army left . . . Lord Raglan has a dreadful amount of death and misery to answer for when called upon to do so . . . We have not seen his face since "Inkerman". I believe he does not go out in bad weather.'

Temple Godman

10 December: 'I attribute to Lord Lucan chiefly the blame for our not being housed, he is in a house, and does not seem to take any trouble about us. I wish we could get rid of him, he is not fit for the command he holds, besides which he has a most horrible temper, and is often most abusive, which I call anything but gentlemanly for a man in his position. Everyone hates him who has anything to do with him.'

21 December: 'People express much discontent at our Field Marshal [Raglan] – who is never seen and seems to take things precious easy. He got his promotion for nothing but his negligence, he did not turn out at Inkerman till long after the battle began . . . and as to commands not one was given.'

29 December: 'Certainly the army Staff could not be worse. We might as well have an old woman to command us as Lord Raglan, then our commissariat is nearly useless. Our ambulance totally useless, and our medical department very bad . . . *We* are now totally useless as cavalry.'

Officers did not suffer in the same way as the troops. Although they served in the trenches, they returned to heated tents or buildings where they could eat hot food and change their clothes. They had the money to buy food at Balaklava and had servants to collect it for them. Officers suffered some discomfort (compared with their usual standards), but little more than that. The Saxon minister in London, Count Vitzthum von Eckstaedt, reported that 'Several English officers, who went through that rigorous winter, have since told me with a smile that they first learned of their suffering from the newspapers.'[2] The senior medical officer, Sir John Hall, recorded at the end of November, 'About a quarter of the army is sick already, applications from officers to get away numerous.'[3] Of the senior officers who survived the fighting in the autumn, the Duke of Cambridge returned home, as did General Burgoyne; the latter claimed he was needed as Inspector-General of Fortifications. Lord George Paget of the 4th Dragoons returned after two months in the Crimea, on the grounds that he had only just married and that, since the cavalry would not be operational during the winter, he preferred to settle down at home. Lucan and Raglan were quite happy with this decision and gave Paget a luxurious farewell dinner. Although Cardigan was sleeping on his yacht and enjoying French cuisine, he asked Raglan on 19 November to be allowed to return home on medical grounds, although he thought it beneath his dignity to be subjected to a formal medical board. Raglan decided that the formal procedures should be followed, and on 3 December a medical board conveniently declared Cardigan unfit for military service. He left five days later with his friend Mr de Burgh, stopped at Constantinople and Marseilles and arrived back in England on 13 January 1855.

These senior officers (most junior officers stayed) left behind an army that was hardly functioning. Troops were in the trenches, but were in no fit state to fight. Food supplies were very poor, shelter often non-existent and sickness rising rapidly.

**EYE-WITNESS
CHRISTMAS IN THE CRIMEA**

George Lawson
'Christmas Eve was rather a miserable day, hard rain and cold winds, and towards the afternoon some sleet and snow. The roads of course were in a very bad state, so bad as to render it impossible to bring up the full allowance of rations for the men on the following day. We celebrated the evening of that day in our tent with the usual glass of grog . . . On the following morning . . . we found the ground covered with a thin layer of snow, and that there had been a hard frost during the night. Our little mess had taken good care to secure a good dinner for the day, and we had a plum pudding made as good as our material would allow, and a piece of roast beef, washed down with port wine and ration rum.'

George Newman
Newman had marched some 350 miles in seven weeks and was now north of Nova Moscow. 'There was only one Walki [Vodka] shop on all our road that day, but we pulled up for it at night and astonished the Russian peasants with our singing and dancing. The next day our heads were rather

---

queer, but we had done a long day's march not withstanding, and went to our litter of straw sober alright.'

The British army would probably have collapsed totally, had it not been for the help of the French and Ottoman armies.

The French army

The French army survived the winter reasonably well, partly because its logistic back-up had been developed over years of fighting in Algeria. Its supply ports – Kamiesh and Kazach bays – were much better than Balaklava. They were efficiently organised and large warehouses were built, together with a major slaughterhouse. There was also a bakery that baked fresh bread every day, often giving as many as 30,000 loaves to the British. The French diet was also much healthier than that of the British army which was over-reliant on meat and biscuit. French soldiers only ate about one-third of the meat of the British ration, but this was supplemented by dried vegetables that only had to be boiled in water. Food was cooked collectively in the French army, a much more efficient system than in the British army where each soldier had to cook his own food. When, in early 1855, the British adopted the French system, the health and morale of their soldiers rapidly improved.

The senior commanders in the French army were also far more efficient than their British counterparts. In mid-October the French army had food reserves for only three days (and just one day's meat). Reinforcements from Varna brought more food, and Canrobert introduced a system to monitor and report every day on the level of food available. Paved roads were built in good time from both harbours to the main French camp, and from there to the siege lines and along the rear of the camps. Over the winter of 1854–55 the French were able to sustain an army almost four times the size of its ally, even though they had far less shipping available. Conditions remained harsh, but the French army never suffered the privations and horrors inflicted on the British army.

For most of the winter the French army was the main effective allied army in the Crimea. They were not only able to sustain themselves, but also provided vital assistance to their ally. Parts of the French ambulance system were allocated to the British to help evacuate the sick from the trenches to Balaklava. More than 700 men tried to improve the mud track from the port to the main British camp. The British took no part in this work, leaving the rest of the task to Ottoman troops (as 'Orientals', they could be treated as coolies) and Russian prisoners. The French also provided 800 men to carry ammunition from Balaklava to the British batteries. As the British army declined in size, the French also had to take over more of the siege lines so that by January 1855 British troops were only staying in the trenches for twelve hours at a time – French troops stayed for twice as long. Relations between the ordinary soldiers were generally good, but at a senior level the French resented British arrogance. Raglan accepted French help as something to which the British were entitled and merely asked for more – he wanted the French to take over all the British trenches every third night.

The Russian army

Despite the fact that the Russians were fighting on home soil, the infrastructure to maintain an army in the Crimea was lacking and conditions deteriorated badly over the winter. Overall the Russian army was in a worse state than the French, though nowhere near as bad as that of the British. The normal peacetime garrison of the area was less than 50,000, but a much larger army now had to be supported in the Crimea. Because no invasion had been expected, no supplies had been stockpiled and no transport organised. Regiments had only a small number of carts for their own immediate needs.

A major problem facing the Russians was that the Crimea produced little of value for an army. Its main agricultural output was grapes and cattle and there was almost no hay available. The last, as the British discovered, was essential to keep horse-drawn supply lines open. During the winter it was very difficult to move supplies because the carts had to be loaded with so much fodder to keep the horses alive on the journey that hardly anything else could be carried. In early November the army along the Danube front transferred almost 6,000 carts (two-thirds of which were ox-drawn) to the Crimea and they arrived with biscuits and basic rations. However, it was very difficult to keep the animals alive and most rapidly starved to death. By late December the army in the Crimea had just 2,000 operational supply carts. Another convoy of biscuits arrived, but they were so mouldy that they had to be destroyed. Horses were fed on ship's biscuits and oak leaves. The Russian supply system could not find hay, and so officers were simply given money and instructed to feed the horses themselves. Most pocketed the money and the animals starved. In total about 125,000 peasant wagons and animals were requisitioned, mainly from the adjoining provinces, in order to keep the Crimean army alive, if not fully operational. This caused severe problems through the loss of animals and peasant drivers, many of whom died of disease.

Not only was food in short supply, but so too was ammunition. From October the garrison in Sevastopol was severely rationed until supplies arrived in the spring of 1855. Reinforcements had to walk for months in the depths of the Russian winter to reach the Crimea. In early December the Tarutinski Regiment left Nizhni-Novgorod, but it took five months of hard marching before it joined the Crimean army. Water was also in short supply, partly because the water table was more than 300 feet below the surface across much of the Crimean peninsula. The Russians had to dig out more than 250 wells to keep the troops supplied. Although the Russian army could be kept in existence, little could be done to improve the situation until the spring of 1855. Only then, as grass began to grow and provide fodder en route, could horse- and ox-drawn carts bring in supplies.

EYE-WITNESS
THE RUSSIAN ARMY

Pyotr Alabin

Describing the conditions along the main Sevastopol–Simferopol supply road: 'Rain, mud, slush. The roads . . . are an amazing sight. The mud comes up to the horses bellies; the road is narrow; huge furrows have been formed in it; at night there are frosts, congealing the mud, which, thanks to the clayey soil, makes the road quite impassable. Anyone travelling there has to ride literally over the carcasses of the horses and bullocks who drowned in the mud, and over the debris of carriages which it is impossible to pull out of the mud.'

Dr N. I. Pogorov, Russian surgeon

'. . . the whole road . . . was crowded with transports of wounded, guns and forage. Rain was pouring down as if from a pail, the sick, and among them amputation cases, lay two or three in a wagon, groaned and shivered from the cold; and men and animals scarcely moved in mud to the knee; dead animals lay at every step; out of deep pools protruded the swollen bodies of dead oxen, which burst with a crash; and at the same time one heard the cries of the wounded, and the cawing of predatory birds, flying down in whole flocks to their prey, and the shouts of tormented drivers and the distant roar of the cannon of Sevastopol.'

Marshal Saint Arnaud – French commander in the east until September 1854.

Lord Lucan – scapegoat for the Charge of the Light Brigade.

Lord Cardigan – the 'hero' of the Charge of the Light Brigade.

Florence Nightingale – a suitable heroine.

Mortar battery in the allied siege of Sevastopol.

Ordnance Wharf, Balaklava Harbour, Spring 1855.

Allied commanders confer before the attacks on Sevastopol in early June 1855.
Lord Raglan (*left*), Omer Pasha (*centre*) and General Pelissier (*right*).

Allied camp, early summer 1855.

Cookhouse of the 8th Hussars.

French Zouaves.

Leo Tolstoy, battery commander

At the town of Sevastopol in late 1854: 'The quayside contains a noisy jostle of soldiers in grey, sailors in black, and women in all sorts of colours. Peasant women are selling rolls, Russian mushiks with samovars are shouting "Hot *sbitén*" [a honey and spice drink], and right here, lying about on the very first steps of the landing, are rusty cannonballs, shells, grapeshot and cast-iron cannon of various calibres. A little further off there is a large, open area strewn with enormous squared beams, gun carriages and the forms of sleeping soldiers; there are horses, waggons, green field guns and ammunition boxes, infantry muskets stacked in criss-cross piles; a constant movement persists of soldiers, sailors, officers, merchants, women and children; carts laden with hay, sacks and barrels come and go; and here and there a Cossack or an officer is passing by on horseback, or a general in his droshky. To the right the street is blocked by a barricade, the embrasures of which are mounted with small cannon; beside them sits a sailor, puffing at his pipe . . . Your first impression is bound to be a most disagreeable one: the strange intermingling of camp and town life, of handsome town and dirty bivouac is not merely unsightly but gives the sense of an abominable state of chaos . . . Not on a single face will you read the signs of flurry or dismay, nor even those of enthusiasm, readiness to die, resolve – of that there is none: you will see ordinary, everyday people, going about their ordinary, everyday business.'

On the Russian defences at Sevastopol: 'After you have gone a distance of some two hundred yards or so, you will enter a muddy, churned-up area, surrounded on all sides by gabions, earthworks, magazines, dugouts and platforms on which large cast-iron cannon stand beside neat piles of roundshot. It all looks as though it had been thrown together at random, without the slightest purpose, coherence or sense of order . . . here, right in the middle of the open area, sunk half in slime, lies a fractured cannon; here an infantryman, musket in hand, is making his way across the battery, dragging his feet with difficulty through the clinging mud. Wherever you look, in every conceivable corner, there seem to be shell-splinters, unexploded bombs, cannonballs and camp remains, all of them half submerged in watery ooze . . . Here, perhaps, in the mud, you will see the wires of mines, dugouts so small that only two men can squeeze into them, and even then only if they bend almost double; and here too you will see the Cossack scouts of the Black Sea battalions eating, smoking, changing their boots and in general carrying on with their everyday lives, everywhere you will see the same stinking mud, camp remains and bits of scrap iron of all shapes and sizes.'

January 1855

In the first month of 1855, as the Russian winter reached its height, the fighting in the Crimea was in abeyance. None of the armies could do more than exist in the lines they had held since early November. The Russian garrison in Sevastopol was reasonably well housed, but was short of food and ammunition. The Russian army in the centre of the Crimea was able to do little more than survive and it was hardly an effective military force. The French army was in a reasonable condition, but had to undertake nearly all the military tasks of the allies in maintaining at least a nominal siege of Sevastopol. The British army was no longer capable of undertaking any operations. Indeed, it could hardly survive. Its logistical support had collapsed through lack of foresight and gross incompetence. There was just enough food to keep the soldiers alive but they still lacked suitable clothing and decent accommodation. They were falling ill and dying at an increasing rate. Without reinforcements the British army was diminishing in size (it was less than one-seventh of the size of the French army) and unable to do more than stay in its positions. Luckily the Russians were unable to mount an attack – if they had, it is doubtful whether the British army would have been able to put up any effective resistance.

EYE-WITNESS
JANUARY 1855: THE WEATHER

Dr Brush, British surgeon
'January was ushered in by storms of wind and snow, and the cold was also most intense during this month; towards the end of the first week the thermometer in my bell tent, which was lined, stood at 8 a.m. as low as 18F, and in the single tents it fell as low as 15 . . . on the heights before Sebastopol . . . the thermometer on one occasion fell to 12F. I never experienced anything so trying as the north-easterly winds which prevailed during the month – the cold blast seemed to search the very marrow – no woollen clothing could keep it out, unless rendered waterproof. Mackintoshes and sheepskins were alone proof against it.'

Temple Godman

6 January: 'There are now five or six inches of snow on the ground and a cutting wind from the north-east . . . Last night was the most severe we have had yet; our tents frozen stiff as boards, so that this morning the door flaps could hardly be undone. Everything was frozen, my boots and trousers quite stiff, and my waterproof bedcover, my cold pork for breakfast quite hard, and ink frozen up, even now it freezes in my pen . . . Our poor men suffer much, their blankets were frozen on them last night. I can't see how we can hold the trenches in this weather, and shall not be surprised if the siege is raised.'

Frederick Dallas

14 January: 'We have had great falls of snow the last 2 days & it is about a foot and a half deep on the plain . . . My feet are the only part of my person in grief, & they feel frozen from the time I get up till my return to my dearly beloved bed. The men suffer, of course, a good deal from frost bites, but on the whole I think their health is a good deal better than it was. We have got up this last day or two more warm coats for them . . . The Cavalry, to their great disgust, are turned to the only possible use that can be found for them, viz: to bring up our food, so that now we are pretty well off for food, tho' the cooking of it is a sad affair. There is hardly any wood left.'

George Lawson

'For two days . . . there was continued rain and sleet, varied now and then by a little hail. Last night this changed to snow . . . Imagine the condition of the poor fellows in the trenches, their clothing first getting wet thro' and then freezing on them, they have now to sit up to their knees in snow . . . So severe is the frost that, from your breath during the night, we find icicles all over our blankets in the morning, and many men who have long beards awake with them frozen. My boots and trowsers . . . have been for the last 4 or 5 mornings, in a perfectly rigid state.'

**EYE-WITNESS
JANUARY 1855: THE WOUNDED AND DYING**

William Russell

Describing the sick and dying being sent to Balaklava on French mule litters: 'Many of these men were all but dead. With closed eyes, open eyes and ghastly attenuated faces, they were borne along two and two, the thin stream of breath visible in the frosty air alone showing they were alive. One figure was a horror – a corpse, stone dead, strapped upright in its seat, its legs hanging stiffly down, the eyes staring wide open, the teeth set on the protruding tongue, the head and body nodding with frightful mockery of life at each stride of the mule over the broken road . . . Another man I saw with the raw flesh and skin hanging from his fingers, the naked bones of which protruded into the cold air, undressed and uncovered.'

Temple Godman

'It is dreadful to see the poor wretches brought from the front, they come down on horses wrapped in their blankets on the coldest days in all the snow; many have frostbitten feet and are otherwise ill . . . You see them with their feet, just with a bit of rag round them. Sometimes the horses fall in the snow and tumble on them, many seem almost senseless, too ill to hold the reins, and fall off insensible on the way, perhaps frostbitten, and require to be rubbed with snow, many cannot stand and are *held* in the saddle. A sergeant was found the other day still in the saddle, on his arrival at Balaclava, but quite dead.'

EYE-WITNESS
JANUARY 1855: DISORGANISATION

George Evelyn

13 January: 'No storehouses were established at Balaclava, though plenty of houses for the purpose might have been found. Stores were kept on board ship, where they could not be readily got at, or found, and troops were often in want of things which were secreted carelessly in the holds of vessels in the harbour . . . After the storm many ships were sent back to Constantinople for forage, some of which had forage on board at the time they left Balaclava – so much so, that on their arriving at Constantinople, all the forage on board them was collected and found sufficient to load two of their number.'

Frederick Dallas

1 January: 'What kills us out here is the utter want of system & arrangement in every department. Balaclava is strewed with wooden houses. The sailors make rafts of them; when nobody is looking they make firewood of them, but not a single Soldier has ever slept yet in anything but a tent. Hay, oats,

Biscuits, vegetables are rotting in the mud; yet the men until 3 or 4 days ago when they sent the Cavalry up with our rations, have been starving. It would be endless writing of all the mistakes & absurdities committed.'

5–6 January: 'It is the very outside of what the *whole of the remnant of the Cavalry* can do, to bring up food for the men. It is useless to talk of wooden huts at Balaclava, there is no means of getting them up here. There are no means of transport, the Commissariat up here has failed, the Ambulance, or the force that was called the Ambulance, no longer exists & when the food is brought up, there is no wood for them to cook with . . . Lord Raglan rode up on a sleek horse a day or two ago, & all he is reported to have remarked was that the "Artillery horses appeared insufficiently clad." God forgive him! . . . Government may be at home, & I believe have been, totally unprepared for so great a Campaign, & now are sending out, & will continue to send out, probably, reinforcements, but, as regards us who are here, they can do nothing. What *could* have been done could have been done by the Authorities here.'

EYE-WITNESS
JANUARY 1855: VIEWS ABOUT THE ARMY LEADERSHIP

George Lawson
To his brother on 15 January: 'As far as I have read of what you call the dismal news in *The Times*, there is not one syllable but what is perfectly true, and not in the least degree exaggerated. With regard to what *The Times* has stated about Lord Raglan, it is also true. Up to within the last week, or ten days he has been, as far as the troops are concerned, almost invisible, staying quietly at a very comfortable house at Headquarters about 2 miles from this camp and not knowing – and everyone here will go so far as to say – not caring as to what condition the troops are in. Latterly he has . . . made more frequent visits to camp, and did not relish the truth of the condition of the men being told him at first.'

Temple Godman
12 January: 'It is quite true that the most disgraceful mismanagement is destroying our army, but I don't think we shall ever do better with our present Commander-in-Chief. He rode through our camp the other day, the first time we have seen him since we came to the Crimea, except in the action at Balaclava.'

Frederick Dallas

19 January: 'Lord Raglan has been seen (somewhat) about lately, & is supposed to have read the *Times*. I am almost inclined to think, that the "faithful band" round him, have not allowed him to know the truth, not that I consider that any apology for him, as he ought to have found out, & looked about for himself.'

Henry Clifford

'The Officers are very much to blame for part of the misery of our men. I do not pretend to say that others are not in fault, who as their responsibility is greater and their power to remedy also greater, have much to answer for. But it makes me furious to see Regimental Officers crying out "Stinking fish" when they have helped to make it so.'

Frederick Dallas

'It is extraordinary how completely a long course of neglect & indifference in our welfare, & comfort, have utterly annihilated any enthusiasm in this poor army. I honestly think that there are not ten Officers in any Division that would not be delighted at any chance of getting away . . . Now he [Raglan] rides (rarely) through the middle of a camp, the soldiers don't know(!) who he is & the officers run away to avoid having to salute him!'

EYE-WITNESS
JANUARY 1855: THE BRITISH AND THE FRENCH

Temple Godman

'The French do everything for us, they make our roads, carry up our shot and shell, and bring down our sick, it is really sad to think that through mismanagement we should come to this . . . Our troops certainly are first-rate, but are useless, and become utterly destroyed for want of proper Staff and management.'

William Russell

'They are splendid fellows – our friends the Zouaves – always gay, healthy and well fed; they carry loads for us, drink for us, eat for us, bake for us, forage for us, and build our huts for us, and all on the cheapest and most economical terms.'

Frederick Dallas

'Altogether I don't think we bear our misfortunes with much dignity. The French manage these things, as they do everything connected with military matters, much better . . . They are getting, I should say, rather sick of us . . . they must be tired of carrying away our sick, guarding our Batteries, carrying up our shot and shell, & in addition to all, having to fight about three small battles every night with the Russians, waiting for our new batteries to be put up.'

Charles Addington, British cavalry officer

'The fact is the French understand this sort of work far better than we do, & know how to keep both themselves & their animals in first rate condition, whilst our men & horses are dying of cold and hunger . . . The French are doing everything for us; they carry our sick, they furnish horses to drag the guns up from Balaclava, for our horses are all dead or dying, they carry our shot & shell up to our siege-train depôt for us. In fact without them we should be quite at a standstill.'

Frederick Dallas

'Our part of the siege goes on very tranquilly. We just go down and sit in the Trenches & we don't shoot at the Russians (having no guns) & I am happy to say that they don't shoot at us [and] leave us comparatively quiet in our Trenches. The only times they have come (except once or twice) they have found all our men fast asleep . . . The French on their side have the most furious rows every night with the Enemy.'

EYE-WITNESS
JANUARY 1855: THE BRITISH PRISONERS

George Newman

In early January Newman was chased by wolves and then taken to a hospital in a town near Kharkov with a bad tooth.

'Our diet was: for breakfast, one pint of thin soup and about two ounces of boiled beef or mutton; for dinner, ditto and for supper, ditto; a loaf of white bread, very good and weighing about a pound and a half daily, but we used to send out for bread, butter, honey, milk and tobacco . . . After supper we used to commence card playing and generally kept it up until 12 o'clock; then we would go to bed and sleep until breakfast time, walk about the ward

– sleep, smoke and write through the day, and wind up playing cards at night.'

By 19 January Newman was on the march again.

'About 6 o'clock, while it was still dark, we commenced our journey. There were four women among the convicts, one of whom had a child in her arms. There was an officer in charge of the party, but he did not interfere with us walking on ahead, but we could not now as formerly get much in front, because the snow was so deep, and made walking very hard work, and we were also in danger of losing the road if we got too far in advance of our party, as the whole country is covered in snow, which was drifting greatly this day . . . The snow and my breath froze upon my beard and formed icicles three or four inches long and completely fastened up my mouth so right to, that I could not get the end of my pipe into my mouth without first thawing or breaking the icicles, and obliged to break them caused much pain.'

10

Crimean Winter: The Response

The failure of the Crimean expedition was apparent by early November. The inability of the allies to capture Sevastopol caused worries in London, as Newcastle reported to Raglan on 18 November 1854.

> I will not conceal from you that intense anxiety – I will not say as yet depression – prevails in all classes here, forming a strong contrast to the cheerful tone of all private letters received from your army . . . The follies of over-confidence in the beginning of October have given way to very different feelings.[1]

The deadlock over the winter, when fighting almost came to an end, created immense strain for all the combatants, but especially for the British, who lacked any system for coping with a war on this scale. They were forced to improvise a wide range of measures to provide for a prolonged war several thousand miles away. The failures of 1854 and the condition of the army in the Crimea began to raise serious doubts about the efficiency of the army and the government. The crisis led to the fall of the Aberdeen government, even though it had put in place most of the measures that would eventually remedy the situation. It was easy to blame the government for all the failings, though in fact many of the problems stemmed from the 'Great Storm' of 14 November and the inadequacies of the army leadership in the Crimea and its neglect of the men.

British manpower shortages

The central problem that the British faced was that the army sent east in the spring of 1854 had been produced by withdrawing troops from colonial garrisons and using soldiers from depots in Britain. No other troops were available to provide significant reinforcements and no system was set up to recruit more troops. In the autumn of 1854 the British sent about 11,000 extra troops to the Crimea, but this was far less than those lost as casualties and sick. The overall size of the army was increased, but this was only theoretical because the necessary men could not be recruited. Rates of pay were still poor (though they were increased in the spring of 1855), particularly in comparison with civilian wages, and the conditions were harsh. A new act allowing enlistment for a short period was passed in February 1855, but had little impact. Overall the strength of the army remained about a quarter below its authorised level. The poor state of recruiting can be judged from the fact that in March 1855 the army was short of 90,000 men, but only 4,500 could be recruited.

The first attempted solution was to use the militia to provide the necessary men. Under an Act passed only two years before the outbreak of war, the militia (which had long existed as a voluntary and primarily social organisation) could train for no more than three weeks a year and could be mobilised only if there was a threat of invasion. It could not be forced to serve outside Britain. On the outbreak of war, recruiting efforts were increased and the government changed the rules in May 1854 so that the militia could be mobilised when a state of war existed. The term for which men would serve was also extended – to twenty-eight days for married men and fifty-six days for unmarried. In July 1854 the militia took over garrison and guard duties in Britain as a way of releasing more regular soldiers for the army in the east. Pay in the militia was poor and nothing was given to the families of men who served – the government wanted to try and coerce men into volunteering for regular service. However, militia officers (who were usually landowners) discouraged volunteering because they did not want to lose the labourers on their estates and did not want to pay the extra poor rates for the families who would become dependent on relief. In practice the militia did provide a significant pool of recruits – some 33,000 during the course of the war. In late December 1854 the government forced through new legislation to allow the militia to serve outside Britain. The system was voluntary and each militia regiment was not allowed to send more than three-quarters of its strength. Only 5,000 men volunteered and in early 1855 they formed skeleton regiments that took over garrison duties in Malta and the Ionian Islands, thereby releasing some regulars for the Crimea.

The second expedient was to revert to a centuries-old British policy – recruiting foreign mercenaries. The idea was first raised by Prince Albert on 11 November, as it became clearer that a long war was now inevitable. The Cabinet discussed the issue four days later, but was divided. They discussed the possibility again ten days later after a despatch arrived from Lord Raglan asking for reinforcements. Palmerston was strongly in favour, telling Lord John Russell, 'Might we not get six thousand men from Portugal, ten thousand from Spain and then thousands from Piedmont?'[2] On 24 November the Cabinet agreed to introduce legislation to get such a scheme off the ground. The old eighteenth-century policy of buying regiments wholesale from the poorer European states (in 1701 such troops had made up more than half of the 'British' army) had to be abandoned –

it was clear no state would allow the British to do this. Instead the system was based on allowing foreign nationals to volunteer for service in special British-led units. Even this would have to be done surreptitiously to avoid breaching various pieces of legislation in foreign countries.

The British government was desperate for recruits and, with no idea how the scheme would work, or even where recruiting might be possible (the smaller German states seemed the best possibility), the Foreign Enlistment Bill was introduced in Parliament on 12 December. There was considerable opposition to the idea. General Burgoyne was particularly hostile and demonstrated common mid-Victorian prejudices:

> I deprecate strongly the foreign enlistment as likely to lower the reputation of the British army. A set of vagabonds of all countries serving for pay, and without any national feeling or prestige . . . They will never rise to our scale, but we may drop to theirs.[3]

Similar views in Parliament forced the government to change the legislation. No more than 10,000 men could be on British soil at any one time and officers were not, as had happened after the Napoleonic Wars, to be given half-pay once the war was over. The men could, however, be given free passage to any of the colonies. The government refused to state where the men might be recruited. The Bill was eventually passed, but without enthusiasm. The need for the men was desperate and it was also a way of avoiding reforming the British army so that more recruits might be encouraged.

From January 1855 preparations were begun to receive the recruits in Britain – 5,000 huts were built at Bexhill and Shorncliffe, although work slowed when the local clergy managed to get Sunday labour stopped. The first Swiss and German recruits arrived in May and June, although they had to be housed separately to stop outbreaks of fighting. Thirteen men died of cholera at Shorncliffe after waste was thrown into the drinking wells. The War Office refused to build a hospital for the foreign mercenaries. The German troops started training at Aldershot in July and were reviewed by the Queen and Prince Albert early the next month. They were reviewed again by the Duke of Cambridge (long returned from the Crimea) in late October just before they left Portsmouth. The Swiss left a month later. The local commanders asked for these troops not to go to the Crimea and they were held at Scutari and Smyrna. The scheme never provided a significant number of soldiers and none ever fought in the Crimea. However, it did, as we shall see in chapter 12, cause the British an enormous number of diplomatic problems and it almost led to war with the United States.

The Crimean railway

The fundamental problem faced by the British army was its lack of any logistic infrastructure. No European war had been fought for forty years and the army leadership was not interested in such mundane and boring matters. The crux of the supply problem in the Crimea – the inadequate road from Balaklava to the main camp on the heights near Sevastopol – was identified in London long before winter weather arrived and made the 'road' almost unusable. In late October the railway contractor, Samuel Peto of Peto, Brassey and Betts, saw the Duke of Newcastle and suggested that a railway should be built to move supplies from Balaklava. His firm would undertake the work under its own control and would do it without a contract, at cost price (with no profit). Speed of construction would be the main priority and the railway would not be built to British standards, nor would it be permanent. Newcastle accepted this extraordinary offer and the details were settled by early December. The total cost was estimated at about £100,000 (excluding wages) – about £5 million at current prices.

Peto immediately set about organising the project. An advance party of three surveyors led by Donald Campbell left in the first week of December and arrived in the Crimea at the end of the month. Meanwhile the thirty-four-year-old James Beatty was chosen as chief engineer at a salary of £1,500. Men were recruited at offices in Waterloo Road and were paid between five and eight shillings a day, together with a free outfit of clothes. (Four female nurses and a barber were also recruited.) A portable stove was provided for every ten men and a hut for every forty, together with coal, coke, firewood and two pounds of tobacco per man. The necessary materials were gathered from any available source – speed was the main requirement (usually they came from the stocks of Peto, Brassey and Betts contracts, but all the rails were supplied by the Great Western Railway). In total 1,800 tons of rails, sixty sets of points, 6,000 sleepers, 600 tons of timber, 2,000 tons of miscellaneous stores and thirty-five horses were ready within a few weeks. Peto chartered the necessary shipping and the first vessel (the 457-ton *Wildfire*) left Liverpool on 21 December, followed by eight other ships. Beatty left after Christmas using the faster overland route via Marseilles and arrived in the Crimea on 19 January 1855.

By the time Beatty arrived, the preliminary survey work was almost complete and the route of the line through Balaklava harbour and up the 1:14 gradient to the heights near Kadikioi was decided. About 200 soldiers were conscripted in late January to clear the area around the harbour where the railway yard would be established. The navvies arrived in early February and their huts were set up on the heights overlooking the harbour. On 8 February rails were laid out of the yard and down the main street of Balaklava. By 23 February the railway was open to Kadikioi and the first loads were taken up. Extra lines and storage space were then built in the harbour and at the initial terminus at the summit. The main problem was the lack of horses. The thirty-five sent out from Britain were adequate for construction, but another twenty had to be borrowed from the army before extras arrived. The railway was horse-drawn with a stationary engine to help the ascent of the steep incline up the valley. Almost immediately there was a significant improvement in the supply situation as up to twenty wagons at a time were brought up the line from the harbour.

From late February the railway was extended from Kadikioi towards the main camp, although the steep slopes involved meant that the stationary engine had to be moved here. The main horse track had to be fairly smooth so that the horses could walk easily, but the engine required a set of rollers for the rope and this was built alongside the track. By 23 March the railway was open to the main camp. Three days later the first load of ammunition was transported from the harbour to the main camp. The navvies had laid seven miles of track in seven weeks. The next stage was to double the line throughout, starting in the harbour where more buildings were knocked down.

The impact of the railway was immediate. Just over 100 tons of supplies were moved every day, and within two weeks each siege gun had a stock of 500 rounds of ammunition. The line was worked by about 100 horses and each of the thirty wagons made two trips a day. From early April the empty wagons brought the wounded down to Balaklava and they were also used to transport men to the front line. The navvies, who were on six-month contracts, stayed in the Crimea until June 1855, mainly engaged in maintenance work, which was heavy. In total forty-six of them died in the Crimea, and Beatty, who stayed on until November 1855, died less than six months after returning to Britain.

The line continued to be improved and it remained crucial to the maintenance of the British army throughout the remainder of the Crimean campaign. By the end of April 1855 about 180 tons a day of supplies were moved up the line; on some days the figure reached almost 250 tons. In the summer an extra 130 wagons, forty workers and ten men to shoe the horses were sent to the Crimea. In October and November 1855 four steam locomotives arrived, but they found it difficult to cope with the steep incline out of Balaklava. At its height in the winter of 1855–56, the Crimean railway had a staff of 330 with 215 horses, seventeen mules, four locomotives, three fixed engines and 190 wagons. It ensured that the terrible privations of the previous winter were not repeated. By February 1856 nearly 140 wagons a day were carrying loads of over 400 tons. At the end of the war much of the equipment was left behind, but the Russians had no use for it and the tracks were sold to the Ottomans.

Logistic support

During the winter of 1854–55 the British in the Crimea suffered far more than the French. This was the consequence of two factors. First, the choice of Balaklava as the supply port – it was simply too far from the main British camp. The French ports were much nearer their main base. Second, the French had a well-organised supply system, the *Intendance*, a corps of regular officers, which organised transport and had plenty of experience in supporting operations. The British had to devise a system from scratch.

In the summer of 1854 Lieutenant-Colonel McMurdo, an Indian army officer, suggested that a Corps of Muleteers or a Transport Corps should be formed. He thought about 10–15,000 men would be needed and that they could be recruited from India, Egypt and Africa. He was ignored for months. Only as the army in the Crimea disintegrated, and a major political crisis developed in London, was action taken. On 12 February McMurdo left for the Crimea to organise a Land Transport Corps, even though the formation of such an organisation was not formally agreed until the end of the month. McMurdo arrived in the Crimea four weeks after leaving London, but he then faced the problem of organising and recruiting the corps. This took months. Experienced officers and men could not be found and the base for the new corps, Horfield Barracks in Bristol, was inadequate and degenerated into chaos. An effective organisation in the Crimea was not created until the autumn of 1855 when 4,000 men had arrived, together with 10,000 mules and 3,000 wagons bought in Spain, the Balkans and the Ottoman empire. The military discipline of the corps was poor, but it was a key element in ensuring that the army survived the winter of 1855–56 in good condition. The British had finally learnt their lesson and the Land Transport Corps was retained after the war, although in peacetime it was reduced to a strength of just over 1,000 men.

The Land Transport Corps was supported by a civilian Works Corps. This idea was suggested by Sir Joseph Paxton during his election campaign in Coventry in May 1854, based on his experience in building the second Crystal Palace at Sydenham and as a railway contractor. It was almost a year before the Secretary of State for War, Panmure, invited Paxton to recruit about 1,000 navvies to help build fortifications and earth walls in the British lines around Sevastopol. Paxton agreed, but refused to take any formal position or accept any pay. Raglan and the Royal Engineers in the

Crimea objected to having civilians doing this work, but were overruled. In early June Paxton selected William Doyne to be Chief Superintendent of the Corps. He was paid a salary of £1,500 a year and the navvies were paid forty shillings a week (about the same as the railway workers), but were to be subjected to military discipline and army regulations. The first men began assembling at the Crystal Palace in June and left the next month. In early August the first units of the corps arrived in the Crimea. They eventually totalled 800 navvies, thirty-two gangers, sixty-five artificers and seventy carpenters and smiths. Almost immediately Paxton realised that more men would be needed for work over the winter. By early October about 1,700 more men had been sent out on two chartered steamships – *Pacific* and *Azoff*.

In the Crimea the Works Corps performed a vital role. During the autumn of 1855 just under 300 men were used to upgrade the railway to keep it operational over the winter. Doyne decided from the start that roads were the top priority to avoid a repetition of the disasters of the previous winter. He drafted in 6,500 soldiers to help in this work. The old road from Balaklava to the British camp was abandoned and a new one built. This metalled road, six and a half miles long, was finished before the onset of winter and involved constructing 150 culverts and ten miles of open ditches. Elsewhere platforms for the large siege guns were built, together with storehouses for ammunition and supplies. During the winter major works were undertaken on the Vorontsov road, which had deteriorated badly and was littered with abandoned artillery pieces. Much of this work had to be done under fire. The Works Corps, which overall cost £405,000, returned to Britain during the summer of 1856. The army remained unenthusiastic about the organisation, despite the fact that it had, together with the railway and the Land Transport Corps, played a key role in ensuring that the army in the Crimea was well supplied and in good condition over the winter of 1855–56.

Medical services

The Crimean War was to be typical of all wars fought before the twentieth century – far more men died of disease than died in combat. (Overall about one-fifth of the casualties were on the battlefield and the remaining four-fifths in hospital from diseases such as cholera, scurvy, typhus and typhoid – most of the wounded died before they reached hospital.)

This situation reflected the still primitive levels of medical treatment in civil as well as military life. Better health came from improvements in sanitation and water supplies, but 70,000 people had still died of cholera in London just six years before the outbreak of war. Finding clean water and providing adequate sanitation was a herculean task when tens of thousands of soldiers were encamped in a small area. The result was dysentery and cholera. Lack of washing facilities led to lice infestation and the risk of typhus and typhoid.

Medical treatment was still primitive. Ether and chloroform were first used in the 1840s, but many doctors remained suspicious of anaesthesia, believing that it weakened the patient during an operation. Anaesthetics were used in the Crimea, but had only a limited impact. Little was known about infection and the causes of disease: Joseph Lister's key work on antisepsis was still a decade away. The result was that amputations (the main form of 'treatment') had a 25 per cent death rate from shock and gangrene. Many of the subsequent criticisms of the medical services in the Crimea are unfair because they ignore the state of medical knowledge and treatment available at the time.

Until his death the Duke of Wellington remained unalterably opposed to any reform in the army's medical system. It was not, therefore, until February 1853 that a single organisation could be created by amalgamating the Army Medical Department and the Ordnance Medical Department (the latter had been run by the Marquis of Anglesey, who had no medical training). Dr Andrew Smith was put in charge of the new department, but he only had a staff of eight. In February 1854 he had to create a wartime organisation from scratch – he was also told that the expeditionary force would contain just 10,000 men. He had no wagons to transport the wounded, no stretcher-bearers, and doctors had to be recruited from volunteers over the next few months.

A Hospital Conveyance Corps was created under Colonel Tulloch made up of army pensioners, mainly from Chelsea Hospital, who were expected to act as stretcher-bearers, carry heavy loads around the battlefield and serve as officers' servants. Not surprisingly the experiment was a disaster. By the end of September 1854 the Constantinople correspondent of *The Times*, Thomas Chenery, reported:

> Whether it was a scheme for saving money by utilising the poor old men or shortening the duration of their lives and pensions, it is difficult to say, but they have been found in practice rather to require nurses themselves than to be able to nurse others. At Gallipoli and in Bulgaria they died in numbers, while the whole of them were so weak as to be unable to perform the most ordinary duties. The man who conceived the idea that the hard work of a military hospital could be performed by worn-out and aged cripples must have a slight knowledge of warfare or profited little by experience.[4]

Another problem was that Raglan ordered that only a small number of medical assistants should embark with the expedition to the Crimea – he thought the limited space was best used for soldiers. There were two designated hospital ships at Varna in August 1854 (*Andes* and *Cambria*), but they were taken over as troop transports. The captain of the *Andes* also offloaded all the medical supplies (without informing anybody) and they were not found until December.

The result of all these decisions was that after the Alma and other battles there were very few men to recover the wounded, almost no transport on which to move them and no hospital ships to convey them to the base hospitals around Constantinople. Some ships waited in Balaklava harbour for three weeks before they set sail and conditions on board rapidly deteriorated. In early December 1854, Dr Hall, the Inspector-General of Hospitals, described conditions on board the *Avon*:

> The ship is not in very good order and ports were all closed on account of the weather, which occasioned a bad smell in some of the small cabins where attention had not been paid to the emptying of the slop pails. There are 297 sick on board, 22 of whom are wounded and 275 cases of rheumatism, frost bite of the toes and bowel complaints. There are three medical officers on board.[5]

It was not until early 1855 that four hospital ships were in operation.

As criticism of the treatment of the sick and wounded mounted, Lord Raglan tried to escape his share of responsibility by placing all the onus on the Medical Department (which certainly was inadequate). Raglan issued an order placing the blame squarely on the medical authorities, and on Dr George Lawson (no relation to our eye-witness) in particular. He set up a disciplinary court of inquiry. Not surprisingly, this caused resentment among the army medical staff, as Lawson (our eye-witness) reported in mid-December:

> Lord Raglan . . . is anxious, I have no doubt, to throw on the Medical Department the blame due to the military authorities for not having those requisites placed on board ship which are essential for the comfort of the sick troops. The apathy which he complains of in Dr Lawson is the very complaint laid against him by all here, for looking after his own individual comforts and not caring much for the good of others in the Field. Very seldom do we see anything of him in or near camp, and I do not think anyone there will often catch him out in the wet.[6]

After Raglan formally censured the Medical Department, Sir John Hall wrote:

> His Lordship seems to have forgotten that the scant number of attendants [four per 100 men] was in strict conformity with his own orders . . . for it is quite evident he is preparing for enquiry and his intention is to throw as much discredit on the medical department as he can and so make that the scapegoat for all other mis-managements, both military and commissariat and so it will be I dare say as the weakest always goes to the wall and we have no friends to protect us.[7]

Hospitals and nurses

Although Raglan tried to pass off the blame for the way in which the sick and wounded were treated onto the medical department (with some justification) there was little that mid-nineteenth-century medical treatment could do in the face of the diseases affecting the army. Overall in the winter of 1854–55 more than one-third of the strength of the British army died of disease, most of them in hospitals. Of the almost 11,000 men who died, about half did so from cholera and bowel complaints (dysentery), with various forms of fever being the next biggest killer. Almost half of the deaths occurred in January and February 1855, with more than 3,000 deaths in the former month.

A major base hospital was established near Constantinople, at Scutari, where accommodation was provided for about 6,000 men, and in the Crimea four hospitals were set up. The General Hospital was open in September 1854, as soon as British troops arrived in the area, and the Castle Hospital (which had beds for 2,500 men) opened in April 1855. In addition to these two main facilities there was a convalescent hospital at the St George Monastery, and the Land Transport Corps had its own hospital at Karani.

In dealing with the operation of the hospitals and the nursing staff, one of the major problems of the historian is to assess accurately the role of Florence Nightingale. By the end of the war (and for decades afterwards) she had a saintly status. She was seen as a ray of light in a dreadful war, a person who single-handedly took on the military establishment in order to establish decent hospitals and professional nursing staff. In fact she was given the credit for the work of many other people. She did not institute many of the reforms ascribed to her, her area of responsibility was extremely limited and she spent much of her time fighting bureaucratic battles over discipline and her own status. At all times she was convinced of her own moral rectitude and the correctness of all her opinions. In medical terms she accomplished little (she never accepted the germ theory of disease) apart from providing basic comforts. Death rates in the hospital she controlled were higher than those in similar institutions.

Nightingale did not arrive at Scutari until 4 November 1854. By then the hospital was running well. At the end of September Thomas Chenery reported to *The Times* that 'the preparations for the reception of the sick and wounded have been as complete as those for the active business of the war'. The old Ottoman barracks had been 'cleaned and white-washed' and, although not 'sumptuous are sufficiently comfortable'. He added that 'the health of the men is wonderfully improved by the air of the Bosphorous'.[8] The junior minister at the War Office, Sidney Herbert, sent out – at the suggestion of Dr Andrew Smith, the head of the medical department – a commission to investigate the state of the hospitals. Nightingale travelled out with them in October and immediately after their arrival Dr Spence (who was to die a week later on the *Prince* outside Balaklava) reported to London: 'Just returned from Scutari, perfectly delighted to find things so well managed.'[9] A friend of Sidney Herbert, Mr Bracebridge, reported at the same time that the hospital was 'clean and airy' and that there were 'few bad smells'.[10] Although Florence Nightingale tried to portray the situation at Scutari as appalling before she arrived, this was not the case.

Florence Nightingale was chosen to head the nursing staff at Scutari through the influence of her well-connected friends. She was thirty-four when the war started and had spent most of her adult life trying to find some meaningful occupation within the very restricted sphere that upper-class Victorian women were allowed to occupy. Before 1850 she had not managed to find a suitable role, but during her return from a long holiday in Greece she spent three months at Kaiserwerth, a German Protestant institute for training female nursing staff. Much of their work was to report every week to the pastor (who headed the institute) on the spiritual state of the patients. On her return Nightingale wrote a three-volume book entitled *Suggestions for Thought to the Searchers After Truth Among the Artizans of England*. The lack of spiritual values among the working class was a common concern among evangelical groups, and she concluded that 'the world never makes much progress except by saviours' (among whom she placed herself). In late 1852 her wealthy, landed father provided her with an income of £500 a year so that she could live independently and leave home (a very unusual situation for a wealthy, young Victorian woman who was expected to make a good marriage and breed). In April

1853 Nightingale was (despite her almost total lack of experience) appointed Superintendent of the Institute for the Care of Sick Gentlewomen in Distressed Circumstances. This was achieved through the influence of two family friends, Lady Charlotte Canning and Elizabeth Herbert (the wife of Sidney Herbert), who were on the committee that ran the institute. The main recommendation of the post was, according to Nightingale, that 'there are no surgeon-students nor improper patients there at all'.[11] Nightingale had to undertake some basic training with the Sisters of Mercy in Paris before she could take up the post and within a year she was offered the position of Superintendent of Nurses at King's College Hospital.

Before she accepted this post she wrote to Elizabeth Herbert offering to take a small group of nurses to the Crimea and proposing to use her contacts with Lord Palmerston (a neighbour of the family in Hampshire) to achieve this. Dr Andrew Smith, the head of the Army Medical Department, supported the suggestion. The idea of female nurses in military hospitals was not new. It had first been suggested in 1847 by Sir Edward Parry, head of the Haslar naval hospital, who wanted to use Kaiserwerth as a model. The proposal had been considered at the start of the war in March, but rejected because military commanders did not want females at the front line. However, by the middle of October they were happy for such staff to operate at the base hospital at Scutari. Elizabeth Herbert persuaded her husband that Nightingale should be chosen and so, without any consultation or consideration of other suitable (or more suitable) candidates, Herbert invited her to lead the nursing party at Scutari. Her role was very carefully defined – she was only to be in charge of the nurses at the base hospital and she was to act under the authority of the medical officer, Dr Menzies. The team of nurses was selected by a committee including Elizabeth Herbert. A careful religious balance was struck. There were fourteen from various Anglican orders and ten from Catholic nursing orders; the remaining fourteen came from various unaffiliated English hospitals. Each of the nurses had to be given a certificate by Dr Smith and they were instructed to treat all patients, not to attempt to influence the religion of the patients, and only to go out in parties of three or more.

The nurses left Britain on 21 October, travelled overland to Marseilles and arrived in Constantinople on 4 November, five days before the wounded from Balaklava arrived. The head of the hospital reported, 'Miss Nightingale . . . stated on her arrival here that, after all she had heard, she was surprised at the regularity and comfort which appeared in every one of our wards.'[12]

She found that there were enough beds and supplies to deal with the

1,800 patients and the wounded who arrived in the next few days. The role of the nurses was restricted – they were not allowed to dress wounds, since that was a task for the doctors. The nurses provided other, equally essential, services, linen, food, clothes, supplies and the washing of the patients. Nightingale was a strict disciplinarian and alienated nearly all of the women under her. She was intolerant, would only accept her way of doing things and was determined to assert her position. She was soon complaining about her staff and some of the others involved in running the hospital: 'We are lucky in our Medical Heads – two of them are brutes, and four of them angels . . . the Devonport Sisters who ought to know what self-denial is, do nothing but complain.'[13]

Within a month she was writing home claiming, 'it appears to me certain that nothing would have been done if I had not acted in this way'. She went on to complain about some of the St John's Sisters. Two of them were acceptable, but 'with regard to the other four, I fear nothing can be made of them here . . . They do not keep the rules which I have made to ensure female decorum.' The four were reduced to needlework.[14] She later wrote to the directors of the order that 'the St John's Nurses are not well fitted for the work of this Hospital – nor have they improved by experience . . . I had hoped to have found some serious devotion to the cause we are engaged in.'[15]

The government decided to increase the number of nurses at Scutari and the other hospitals in the east. A number of nuns from the Sisters of Mercy and Sisters of Charity, under the control of their Mother Superior, travelled out. They were followed by thirty-three Protestant nurses under Mary Stanley, a friend of Elizabeth Herbert and a member of the selection committee that had chosen the nurses who accompanied Florence Nightingale. This decision produced an outburst from Nightingale to Sidney Herbert, whom she accused of undermining her position – the Catholic nuns would not be under her control and she refused to accept those led by Mary Stanley. When she heard the news about the extra nurses, Florence Nightingale wrote to Herbert that they were not required – indeed, there were too many already: 'About ten of us have done *the whole work*. The others have only run between our feet & hindered us.' If more arrived, 'good order' would break down because there was no room in the hospital for them and if they lodged elsewhere, 'regularity could not be preserved'. She would, however, continue with her duties: 'I am willing to bear the evil of governing (& preventing from doing mischief) the non-efficient or *scheming* majority . . . because I acknowledge the moral effect produced.'[16] Five days later she wrote another letter resigning her position. She refused to have the extra nurses, in particular the new nuns: 'The quartering them *here* is a physical impossibility – the employing them a moral impossibility.' It was impossible because:

> I have, by incessant vigilance, day and night, introduced something like system into the disorderly operations of these women . . . To have women scampering about the wards of a Military Hosp[l] all day long, which they would do, did an increased number relax their discipline & increase their leisure, would be as improper as absurd.[17]

Nightingale's letter was ignored.

When Mary Stanley arrived at Scutari, she reported, 'It is a *horrid* place – no one trusts another – no one speaks well of another . . . I am so shocked at the falseness of people. They abuse you behind your back & flatter you to your face.'[18] Many of Stanley's nurses went to Balaklava to assist the surgeons in the Crimean hospitals, undertaking much more difficult work than was being done in the base hospital at Scutari. Florence Nightingale, having rejected Mary Stanley and refused to go to the Crimea herself, now found Stanley's conduct 'inexplicable' and accused her of intriguing 'to set up an opposition'.[19] As the number of nurses increased, Florence Nightingale's position became much less important. By the spring and early summer of 1855 about 230 nurses were with the British army in the east. Nightingale was in charge of thirty-nine of them and this was not the largest group – that belonged to her rival Mary Stanley with a party of forty-seven.

Florence Nightingale continued her campaign against everybody else involved in medical care at Scutari. Lady Stratford, the wife of the British Ambassador, was 'in consequence of want of practical habits of business, nothing but good & bustling, & a time-waster & impediment'.[20] Yet it was Lady Stratford who had organised 125 workmen to renovate the new wards in the hospital. Her husband was an 'old man' not bothered by the sufferings of the army.[21] The officers who ran the support services in the hospital were equally bad. Wreyford, the head of the Purveyor's Department, was a 'vain, silly, swearing old man'.[22] Nightingale told Sidney Herbert that the hospital was a 'nest of official vice' and:

> The real humiliation, the real hardship of this place . . . is that we have to do with men who are neither gentlemen, nor men of education, nor even men of business, nor men of feeling, whose only object is to keep themselves out of blame.[23]

She flattered Herbert that they were the only two who really cared:

Among the men here, is there one really anxious for the good of the Hospitals, one who is not an insincere animal at bottom, who is not thinking of going in with the winning side which ever that is? I do believe that, of all those who have been concerned in the fate of these miserable sick, you & I are the only ones who really cared for them.[24]

Having dismissed everybody's efforts but her own, Florence Nightingale still had to impose the necessary discipline on her nurses. Two of them went out for a drink with a medical orderly and Nightingale wrote:

This was such a catastrophe that there was nothing to be done but to pack them off to England *directly* . . . Only one week's wages was due to them, which I have not given them, of course, as by rights they ought not to have a free passage home.[25]

She also found that her friends, Mr and Mrs Bracebridge (who had escorted her on her holiday in Egypt and Greece, while the latter had served on the original selection committee), were now 'deserting' her to go home. She decided, as she told her family, to stay in her lone mission to stop Scutari becoming like the other hospitals, 'where ladies come out to get married – where nurses come out to get drunk . . . but shall I be able to hold the reins single-handed?'[26]

Florence Nightingale certainly believed in her lone mission; and felt that she was right and everybody else was wrong, unfeeling and corrupt. What did she achieve? In terms of organising Scutari hospital, very little and certainly no more than the nurses in other hospitals. The nurses did provide basic care for the patients and improved the conditions under which they lived. Nevertheless under Nightingale the death rate at Scutari remained far higher than that of the front-line hospitals in Balaklava. The situation was improved when the Sanitary Commission arrived in early March.

The Commission consisted of Dr John Sutherland, one of the chief inspectors of the General Board of Health; Dr Hector Gavin, who had worked on controlling cholera in the West Indies; and Robert Rawlinson, an engineer. They put in hand a programme of basic sanitary improvements that, as elsewhere, produced a significant fall in the death rate. The hospital at Scutari was positioned above a huge cesspool. This was dug out and drained, floors were renewed, walls painted with disinfectant, double rows of mattresses changed to single ones and the wards and corridors were cleared of rubbish and waste every day. Their programme was an indictment of the previous management (including that of Florence Nightingale) and the death rate was subsequently reduced from forty-two per 1,000 in March 1855 to two per 1,000 by June. The conditions at

Scutari were also improved by reducing its size and setting up new establishments at Constantinople, Therapia, Kulali and Smyrna. The food at Scutari was improved by two initiatives. The Commissariat Commission (Sir John McNeill, a Poor Law Commissioner for Scotland, and Colonel Tulloch) organised the supply of food. Alexis Soyer, the chef at the Reform Club in London, travelled in the spring of 1855, at his own expense, to improve the kitchens, first at Scutari and then in the Crimea.

The nurses under Florence Nightingale did, like the other nurses elsewhere, improve the care given to the sick and wounded. Nightingale also undertook other tasks, such as arranging to send money back to the men's families in Britain, writing letters for them and setting up schools for the convalescent. Most important of all, she was taken up by the media as a symbol of light and decency in a terrible war. She was seen as fulfilling a number of key Victorian female roles. She was caring, devoted, a healer, a surrogate mother, a secular saint placed on a pedestal above the sordid world, a beacon of hope. She also came from a wealthy, respectable family and was therefore, by definition, suitable for these roles. *The Times* began the myth when it wrote:

> She is a 'ministering angel' . . . as her slender form glides quietly along each corridor, every poor fellow's face softens in gratitude at the sight of her . . . when all medical officers have retired for the night . . . she may be observed alone, with a little lamp in her hand, making her solitary rounds.[27]

Although other nurses were performing the same role, Florence Nightingale came to symbolise all their work and she came to be beyond criticism. Popular songs such as 'The Star of the East' and 'Angels with Sweet Approving Smiles' were written. *The Times* passage quoted above was transformed into the enduring myth of Florence Nightingale. It was Longfellow's poem 'Santa Filomena', published in 1857, that first used the phrase 'the lady with the lamp'. He wrote of her walking through the rooms at Scutari:

> And slow, as in a dream of bliss
> The speechless sufferer turns to kiss
> Her shadow, as it falls
> Upon the darkening walls.

During the spring of 1855, as others improved conditions at Scutari, Florence Nightingale looked for areas where she could extend her influence, which still did not stretch beyond the control of the forty or so nurses at that hospital. In early May she travelled with the members of the

Sanitary Commission and Alexis Soyer to the Crimea – it was the first time she had visited the scene of the fighting. She tried to extend her authority by 'inspecting' the nurses who were working in the hospitals, but Sir John Hall refused, pointing out that she had no authority to do so. Later in the month Nightingale fell ill with fever and returned to Constantinople to convalesce at the British Ambassador's residence. She did not return to work at Scutari until August. The doctors in the Crimea asked for the nuns under the Reverend Mother Mary Bridgeman (not those under Nightingale) to take control of nursing duties in the Crimea. Nightingale travelled again to the Crimea with Bridgeman, in another attempt to assert her influence. Again Hall and the medical authorities rejected her, pointing out (correctly) that her authority did not extend beyond the hospitals around Constantinople.

The situation was, however, changing. Florence Nightingale had now become the symbol of nursing care. Her public position was such that she could not be either criticised or replaced. In November 1855 the 'Nightingale Fund' was opened to public subscription to provide for the training of nurses – it would be run by Nightingale on her return. (A total of £44,000 was raised.) Nightingale, exploiting her position, lobbied her friend Sidney Herbert (now out of office) for control over all nurses in the east. A report by Colonel John Lefroy endorsed such a role. Lefroy was a strong anti-Catholic and sympathised with Nightingale's views when she wrote, 'I have always said that a R. C. can do everything which we cannot do, lie, steal, murder, slander because we are afraid of the Roman Catholics. What an advantage it must be!'[28]

Not surprisingly when Florence Nightingale travelled to the Crimea to assert her control (which was finally agreed in March 1856 as the war was ending), the Sisters of Mercy preferred to leave. They returned from the Crimea on 12 April and were given no award, recognition or even travelling expenses by the War Office. They were given £230 by the Sultan – they donated it to the poor.

Nightingale returned to Britain in July 1856. She was still bitter, writing to her aunt, 'Who has ever had a sadder experience? Christ was betrayed by one. But my cause has been betrayed by everyone – ruined, betrayed, destroyed by everyone alas!'[29]

On her return she visited the Queen and Prince Albert at Balmoral, wrote a report on her experiences and argued for reform in the medical services. Then in September 1857 she declared herself an invalid and largely kept to her bed for the next thirty-five years. Her illness may have been brucellosis, contracted in the Crimea in the spring of 1855, or it may have been psychosomatic, brought on by the realisation of her relative failure at Scutari with its high death rates.

Another woman who achieved as much, if not more, for the British soldiers was Mary Seacole, although she was given almost no recognition. Seacole was forty-nine when the war began and had been born in Jamaica, where her mother ran a boarding house for British soldiers. She had travelled across Central America acquiring a rudimentary medical knowledge and, knowing many of the regiments sent out to the Crimea, decided to offer her services. Unlike Florence Nightingale, Seacole was not well connected. In September 1854 she arrived in London and applied at the War Office to be a nurse, but was rejected. She applied to Elizabeth Herbert to work as a nurse with Nightingale – Mrs Herbert refused even to see her. One of the reasons was probably the fact that Mary Seacole was a mulatto.

The managers of the Crimean Fund refused her offer of help, and so Seacole travelled at her own expense in late January 1855. When she arrived at Balaklava she worked with an old acquaintance, Thomas Day, to set up stores for servicemen. She also worked among the sick who were lying along the quays waiting for the hospital ships. For a time she lived on board the ammunition ship *Medora*. By the late spring she set up a store (rapidly known as 'The British Hotel') about two miles inland from Balaklava by the side of the road to the main camp. It was protected by the troops of the local Ottoman commander who befriended Seacole. The store (a forerunner of the NAAFI) enabled servicemen to buy food and sit and talk in the warm. No gambling was allowed and the store closed at 8 p.m. Seacole organised her own supply chain from Constantinople and served local Turkish bread baked in Balaklava. She also provided various herbal remedies that she had developed over the years. She tended the wounded of all nationalities at most of the battles of 1855. She stayed in the Crimea until the final evacuation in the summer of 1856. Seacole was given the Crimean medal, but died in almost total obscurity in London in 1881.

Hospitals and nurses: France and Russia

The French army was from the start well organised and accompanied by nursing staff. Hospitals were established at Constantinople, Pera, Therapia, Gallipoli and Kalchi. There was also an effective system for collecting the wounded from the battlefield, transporting them to ships in specially converted wagons and then taking them back to the base hospitals.

The Russians were able to use existing hospitals in the towns of Sevastopol, Simferopol and Bakhchisarai and men could also be transferred to hospitals in Odessa and Nikolaev. However, the military and civilian hospitals in Sevastopol could only accommodate about 2,000 men and by late October 1854, even before the terrible battle of Inkerman, there were more than 18,000 patients needing treatment. Equipment was also short.

EYE-WITNESS
A RUSSIAN HOSPITAL IN THE CRIMEA

Pyotr Alabin, Russian soldier
'The sick and wounded were packed tight like herrings in a barrel. They were in their dirty clothes and linen, covered in blood, stained beyond measure; the men were unshaved, unwashed, many had not had their dressings changed more than once since the battle of Inkerman; lying on plank-beds with their uniform for a pillow and cloth trousers for bedding – for those who still had them – many had no bedding at all; the only coverlet for many of the wounded and sick was their immutable great-coat. Together with the lightly wounded lie many badly wounded, hopelessly ill and dying people.'

The situation was taken in hand by a military doctor, Professor Nikolai Pirogov, after his arrival in the city on 12 November. He had been a military doctor since the late 1840s and was one of the first to use ether and chloroform in field hospitals. He opposed early amputation (the main form of 'treatment' in other armies) and used a system of rigid dressing on bone fractures as a way of allowing healing to take place and avoiding amputation. Pirogov established a system for categorising the wounded according to their chances of survival and the treatment needed. He also established Simferopol as the major base hospital to ease the overcrowding in Sevastopol, although about one in ten of the patients died from the terrible conditions along the route between the two towns.

The Russians, like the British, organised their own system of nurses. After the battle of the Alma, Grand Duchess Elena Pavlona called on women to join the 'Order of the Exaltation of the Cross' as nurses in military hospitals for one year. Early in November 1854 (at the same time as Florence Nightingale arrived at Scutari) the first group of twenty-eight sisters led by Aleksandra Petrovna Stakhovich, the Directress of the order, left for the Crimea. They came from a variety of backgrounds. Some, such as Baroness Ekaterina Budberg, had court connections, but most came from much lower down the social hierarchy – they were the wives and widows of naval and military officers. Unlike British nurses, who were paid twice the amount they received in London as an inducement to volunteer, the Russian nurses were unpaid. They were maintained by money from the Grand Duchess.

There was less opposition to the nurses from Russian medical officers than from their British counterparts. Pirogov in particular was a strong supporter. The nurses faced the same arguments as their British equivalents about women not being able to stand the conditions; however, not only did they do so, but they also worked in much harsher conditions than the British nurses. In Sevastopol they were under artillery bombardment for much of the time; one of the nurses even worked in the Malakhov tower; and the Russian army allowed them to work in the field hospitals under fire. Apart from their medical duties, they undertook many of the same roles as Florence Nightingale and her colleagues. They issued many of the supplies (often from private sources), helped combat corruption and stealing from the wounded, and looked after the money given to soldiers who had suffered amputation. Altogether about 170 Russian nurses served in the Crimea, of whom seventeen died from various diseases, mainly typhus. Pirogov also contracted the disease and had to leave Sevastopol in May 1855, returning just as the city finally fell.

The strain of war

The cost of fighting a major war impinged on all of the belligerents. Military expenditure rose everywhere. Russia roughly doubled its spending between 1852 and 1854, but found it difficult to increase it further. France more than doubled its spending in the two years after 1853. Britain, by far the richest state in the world, was able to increase its military spending from £9 million in 1853 to £76 million a year later, before it fell back to around £35 million for the next two years.

The French were able to sustain their army by raising the annual rate of conscription from 80,000 to 140,000 men in 1854. They were also able to recall recently released reservists. We have already seen the problems that the British faced in trying to maintain their much smaller army. The Russians too could not produce more soldiers without seriously disrupting their social system and ruining agriculture, which depended on the labour of the serfs. The three levies of 1854 involved a total quota of thirty-one serfs per thousand and this was simply unsustainable. The Russians were also technologically far behind the allies. Not only did they rely on muskets rather than rifles, but they also had hardly any factories to make weapons. In 1854 there were just three weapons factories in the country and they could produce only 61,000 smooth-bore muskets a year. Since Russia began the war with just 533,000 muskets (half the required level), there was no way in which the army could be equipped even with these outdated weapons. In 1854 orders were placed in the United States for extra weapons, but they did not arrive until after the war was over. The Warsaw citadel armoury was able to make 1,500 rifles in 1854, but when they arrived in Sevastopol in the middle of 1855 it was found that 1,490 of them were defective and unusable.

Although the British had a strong economy they had to decide how to finance their first major war for forty years. On the outbreak of war the Chancellor of the Exchequer, Gladstone, took a strong moral stance on war finance. He, and many others, opposed the system of loans used to fund the Napoleonic Wars and the subsequent increase in the national debt. He wanted the war to be paid for by taxation and he doubled the rate of income tax to the equivalent of six pence in the pound (it was only paid by the wealthy), arguing, 'The expenses of war are the moral check which it has pleased the Almighty to impose upon the ambition and lust of conquest that are inherent in so many nations.'[30]

Gladstone found it impossible to sustain such a rigid moral position for more than a month. By the middle of April 1854 the Treasury began issuing Exchequer Bonds, theoretically repayable by 1860 (although in practice they were not redeemed, but added to the national debt). By early 1855 Gladstone was planning on taking a loan in the next financial year and he had also increased direct taxation on spirits, malt and sugar which fell disproportionately on the poor. The Chancellor of the Exchequer, Lewis, in the new government after February 1855 carried this policy further, and loans finished up financing about two-thirds of the cost of the war, just as in the past.

During the Napoleonic Wars the British had used large-scale subsidies to their allies, both to induce them to undertake the bulk of the land war and to keep them fighting. This policy was now regarded with less favour and no subsidies were actually provided, although one to Sweden to bribe them to enter the war was agreed in principle. The main question was therefore over loans. In early 1855 the Sardinian government was given a loan of £2 million as the price of entering the war. A possible loan to the Ottoman government, however, raised complex and difficult questions. In the autumn of 1853, once it was at war with Russia, the Ottoman government tried to raise a loan in the City of London. The government refused to use any influence. Gladstone took the view that 'the wishes of the Ministry weigh exactly nothing in regard to a question of lending money to a Foreign State'.[31] The British were, however, worried when the French government gave a loan of ten million francs. Their anxiety was increased in the summer of 1854 when the Ottoman government used

British bankers in Constantinople (Black and Durrand) to raise a loan of
£3 million secured on the annual Egyptian tribute to Constantinople. As
the war continued, the Ottoman government spent all the money from the
loan, but the British, knowing that they needed the Ottoman army, ignored
Gladstone's qualms about the role of government. In June 1855 the British
agreed with the French a guarantee of an Ottoman loan of £5 million
secured on the customs revenue of Smyrna and Syria. The loan was
obtained on favourable terms and the Bank of England agreed to manage
it as though it were a British government loan. The British and French
decided to use the loan as a lever to gain control over Ottoman finances.
A committee of three financial experts appointed by the allies had to agree
all contracts financed by the loan. The committee did not begin operating
until early in 1856, and by the end of the war only £1.8 million had
reached the Ottoman government. The financial controls were continued
after the war.

British administration under pressure

Involvement in a European war caused major problems for the confused
structure of British military government. At the beginning optimism
prevailed, as Newcastle claimed in April 1854. He argued that the army
had been sent to the east 'In more admirable order, and with greater
expedition than we had formerly any idea of, either in this or in any other
country . . . I believe that such careful preparations never were made
before.'[32] These words were to return to haunt the government before the
end of the year. In fact the system of military administration had long been
criticised. In 1851 a parliamentary select committee reported that 'effective
and economical conduct of military business is divided among too many
offices totally separate and independent of each other'.[33]

Defenders of the system could claim that there was a sound consti-
tutional logic behind the existing arrangements, although by the 1850s
these were largely theoretical. Nevertheless they were strongly defended by
the vested interests involved. The Secretary of State for War and the
Colonies was responsible for overseas defence and operations and issued
orders to the army in these areas. Since 1815 most of the work of this
minister had been taken up with colonial matters. There was also a
Secretary of State at War, who represented the army in the House of
Commons and was responsible for finance and military law. The Home
Secretary was responsible for the militia and home defence. On the military
side, the Commander-in-Chief controlled the army and appointments, but
he did not control the army in the Crimea – that was the responsibility of

Raglan. The Master-General of the Ordnance was a military officer, but the appointment was political (until 1828 this was a post in the Cabinet). The MGO was responsible for the Royal Artillery and the Royal Engineers and fortifications. He also controlled the civilian-staffed Ordnance Department, which supplied both the army and the navy with ammunition and some ordinary stores. The Commissariat was controlled by the Treasury and, when the army was in the field, provided land transport and non-military supplies. Not surprisingly this antiquated and overly complex system rapidly broke down under the strain of war.

The Commissariat was a small organisation – in February 1854 it had about 180 officers spread across the globe – but it now had to organise supplies for the army in the east. Sir James Filder was recalled from retirement to undertake the task and given just forty men to do the work – many were recruited in the spring of 1854 (mainly from the police) and had no experience of such work. Filder was not given any guidance by Raglan on the movements of the army. The organisation collapsed under the strain, but much of the problem stemmed not from Filder, whom the army blamed for everything that went wrong, but from the system itself. The Board of General Officers that investigated the deficiencies of the Crimean War in 1856–57 absolved Filder of responsibility and placed the blame on the Treasury, which controlled the Commissariat in 1854. For example, in early September Filder placed an order for 2,000 tons of hay, yet it took the authorities nine months to deliver the supplies.

Within a few months of the start of the war, ministers decided to reorganise military administration. On 9 June 1854 the office of Secretary of State for War and the Colonies was divided. Newcastle continued to control the War Office and Sir George Grey took over responsibility for the colonies. This was announced as a single political authority for all army matters, but in practice almost nothing changed. The Queen and Prince Albert were vehemently opposed to any alteration in the position of the Commander-in-Chief as the head of what was still regarded as the royal army. The militia was left under the control of the Home Office. The post of Secretary at War continued, and the Treasury did not transfer responsibility for the Commissariat until just before Christmas 1854. Newcastle did not even have a set of offices for the new ministry; he had to work out of a few rooms in Aberdeen's house. These cosmetic changes made no significant difference to the collapse of the army in the Crimea by the winter of 1854–55.

Crisis

The coalition government was under strain by early December 1854, largely as a result of Lord John Russell's manoeuvres – he still wanted to be Prime Minister. He suggested that the office of Secretary at War should be abolished and that Palmerston should take over a unified War Office. Aberdeen rejected the idea as no more than a dismissal of Newcastle. Palmerston was lukewarm and even Russell's Whig colleagues gave him little support. At a Cabinet dinner on 6 December Russell pressed his arguments, Palmerston refused to support him, Aberdeen said the proposal was merely an attack on him and Russell therefore threatened to resign. Clarendon described Russell as 'wrong in his facts, insolent in his assertions and most ill-tempered in his replies. No spoilt child could be more perverse . . . Everybody was dead against him.'[34]

Parliament met on 12 December, but was adjourned for a month after a sitting of ten days during which both the Foreign Enlistment and the Militia Acts were passed. During December criticism of the government over the state of the army in the Crimea was mounting, partly from Russell's reports in *The Times* and partly from private correspondence sent home from the east. On 12 December *The Times* was still enthusiastic about the situation: 'never was war prosecuted so vigorously and resolutely as at this moment'. Within ten days it made a complete volte-face and, seemingly unaware of its inconsistency, began attacking the conduct of the war and the aristocratic system that controlled the army and most of the government. On 23 December it reported:

> The noblest army England ever sent from these shores has been sacrificed to the grossest mismanagement. Incompetence, lethargy, aristocratic hauteur, official indifference, favour, routine, perverseness and stupidity reign.

On 30 December *The Times* argued, 'It can no longer be doubted, or even denied, that the expedition to the Crimea is in a state of entire disorganization.' Supporters of the existing system thought this state should continue rather than 'the equanimity of office and the good humour of society should be disturbed by a single recall, or a new appointment'. *The Times* thought the army and country could only be saved by 'throwing overboard without a day's delay, all scruples of personal friendship, of official punctilio, of aristocratic feeling and courtly subservience'.

As the state of the army in the Crimea grew worse and worse, those responsible – ministers in London and the army high command – began to blame each other in an attempt to escape responsibility. Palmerston thought Raglan was incompetent, but that it was impossible to remove him. He thought the blame should be placed on his immediate subordinates, Airey and Estcourt. Clarendon agreed, telling Lord John Russell:

> More than enough of everything required for the Army has been sent by the Govt yet the army has been in a state of miserable and disgraceful destitution . . . the orders of the Govt appear in several instances to have been disregarded.

He thought Raglan should be empowered to remove Airey and Estcourt, 'and if he does not do so he shd give his reasons for approving of their conduct'.[35] On 11 January the Cabinet agreed a despatch to be sent to Raglan. It argued that a 'want of foresight or of ability' of some officers under Raglan had 'led to an amount of suffering and sickness . . . which ought to have been avoided'. Some initial mistakes were allowable, but these ought to have been put right and the evidence of 'neglect and inefficiency' was overwhelming. Raglan was instructed to conduct an inquiry and recommend changes.[36] His reply was fatalistic and demonstrated his own lack of initiative and drive. He argued, correctly, that the British army was designed for colonial operations, but added that it was 'undoubtedly defective for operations in the field'. Raglan's excuse for his failure to point out the deficiencies or recommend remedial action was that 'it did not occur to me to suppose that Her Majesty's Government would be willing to form establishments upon a larger scale'.[37] By the time Raglan replied, the Aberdeen government had resigned.

The fall of the government

As the crisis in the Crimea deepened, *The Times* was becoming even more vehement. On 20 January it wrote, 'Affairs are left in the same incompetent hands . . . the Cabinet is engaged in endless discussions which lead to no result . . . A torpor and lethargy seem to have fallen on the spirit of our rulers.' Two days later it argued that the result of the current military system had been 'failure, failure, failure'. There had been continuous 'nonperformance, confusion, delay, perplexity, impotence and whatever ends in nothings'. It concluded, 'The deadlock is absolute, final, inevitable and desperate.' On 23 January the radical MP John Roebuck put down a motion for a committee of inquiry into the war. Later that evening Lord John Russell sent Aberdeen a letter of resignation. He had begun drafting the letter three weeks earlier over the Cabinet's refusal to accept his scheme to reorganise military administration, but felt this was now the opportune political moment to bring down the government and attempt to become Prime Minister himself.

The Cabinet met on 24 January when Newcastle offered to resign. Gladstone recorded him as saying, 'The country wanted a victim however, & he was most willing to be the victim & thought he ought to be so.' Newcastle suggested that Palmerston should take his place at the War Office, and the latter agreed, saying that any other government would be 'an evil to the country'. Clarendon suggested that Russell should return, but the rest of the Cabinet thought this was 'quite out of the question'.[38] At the end of the meeting the Cabinet decided to resign. Aberdeen travelled to Windsor to tell the Queen, but she refused to accept the resignations. The Cabinet met again the next day. It agreed to announce Russell's resignation and ask Parliament to adjourn for a day, after which there would be a vote on Roebuck's motion, which most members of the government thought they could not oppose. Russell was furious that none of his Whig colleagues followed his lead and resigned.

When his resignation became public, *The Times* described Russell's action in scathing terms. 'He must be something worse than a bad Minister who can choose such a moment of national calamity for personal resentment or party intrigue.' It thought his resignation was 'a wide and painful deviation from the rules of political conduct'. The Conservative, Lord Stanley, was more cynical and thought it 'a dextrous leap out of a sinking boat'.[39] The anti-war MP John Bright was even more abusive: 'Evidently he has deserted his colleagues in their hour of peril, after urging them to and joining them in all the acts which have ended so disastrously for the army and the country. There is much cowardice or treachery in this course.'[40]

The debate on Roebuck's motion was unexciting and it was passed by a vote of 305 to 148. The Cabinet met at midday on 30 January and agreed to resign. Aberdeen caught the 2 p.m. train to Windsor. This time the Queen had no choice but to accept the resignations and begin the process of forming a new government. It was far from clear what government could be formed, given the balance of parties in the Commons. After the Whigs, Liberals and Radicals, who numbered about 270–80 members, and the Peelites (the core of the Aberdeen government) who numbered about forty members, the only alternative was the Conservatives, who had 270 members. But they could never command a majority because their protectionist policies would unite all the opposition parties against them. The Tory leader, Lord Derby, was summoned to Windsor on 31 January. Disraeli (the effective Tory leader in the Commons) urged him to try and form a government. Derby wanted to recall Raglan – he was to become

Commander-in-Chief and be offered a seat in the Cabinet. Derby recognised that he would have to form a coalition and that this would certainly have to include Palmerston. The latter did not refuse the offer, but made the obviously impracticable suggestion that men like Clarendon, Herbert and Gladstone would also have to be included. They all declined (Gladstone insisted on remaining at the Treasury, something Disraeli could never accept). Palmerston therefore rejected Derby's offer. The latter told the Queen of his failure on 1 February and she consulted Lord Landsdowne on how to proceed. He refused to try and form a government himself, arguing that his health was too poor. He thought that Russell, who had precipitated the crisis, should be asked to try and form a government because 'the trial, the disappointment and mortification he would feel at being refused by his friends . . . would be a wholesome and necessary lesson'.[41] Russell did try and was, as expected, rejected by everybody – Clarendon told the Queen, 'The attempt of Lord John ought not to succeed if public morality were to be upheld in this country.'[42]

This left Lord Palmerston as the only option. He formally accepted the Queen's invitation on 5 February, although he had been discussing the distribution of officers with senior colleagues for some days. Many of the Peelites were reluctant to join – Gladstone thought Palmerston was 'not fit for the duties of the office of Prime Minister'.[43] However, Aberdeen thought Palmerston should succeed because there was no alternative. When he agreed to express 'confidence' in such a government, this was enough to ease the consciences of the Peelites and they agreed to join. The reconstruction of the government was therefore minimal. Gladstone stayed at the Treasury, Clarendon at the Foreign Office. Newcastle was replaced at the War Office by Lord Panmure, who had been Secretary of State for War and the Colonies in Russell's government of 1846–52. The post of Secretary at War was effectively abolished by being left unfilled – Panmure took on its duties as another small step in reforming military administration.

The new government was greeted with little enthusiasm and lasted for a fortnight. John Bright, who hated Palmerston, was understandably critical, but his comments had more than a grain of truth in them:

What a hoax! The aged charlatan has at length attained the great object of his long and unscrupulous ambition . . . it passes my comprehension how the country is to be saved from its disasters and disgrace by a man who is over 70 years of age, partly deaf and blind . . . and whose colleagues are, with one exception, the very men under whose Govt. everything has been mismanaged![44]

The first task of the new government was to decide how to respond to the vote in favour of the Roebuck motion. Was the committee to investigate the war to have wide-ranging powers, including investigating the army in the Crimea, or was its role to be restricted to the government in London? Now that he was Prime Minister, Palmerston modified his opposition to any investigation. At the Cabinet meeting on 20 February he argued that the Commons wanted a committee and 'if we opposed it we should be beaten by an overwhelming majority: to dissolve upon it would be ruinous: to resign a fortnight after taking office would make us the laughing stock of the country'.[45] Most of the Peelite ministers suddenly developed qualms over the issue and on 21 February, without consulting Aberdeen, many of them – including Gladstone and Graham, together with six ministers from outside the Cabinet – resigned. Most of the Peelites distrusted Palmerston, but to resign after less than three weeks in the new government achieved nothing except to weaken the group in the Cabinet that might have been prepared to accept a compromise peace. Palmerston took some time to reconstruct the government, but it emerged more homogeneous politically and closer in its composition to the Whig government under Lord John Russell from 1846 to 1852. In practice the government was much more successful than anticipated and Palmerston remained as Prime Minister until his death in 1865, except for a short interlude in 1858–59.

The demand for reform

The wave of criticism of Britain's institutions in early 1855 stemmed from the sufferings of the army in the Crimea and the perceived inability of the army leadership, dominated as it was by the aristocracy, to remedy the situation. Critics argued that the role of the aristocracy – especially the wave of promotions in 1854 when more experienced officers, who were less well-connected socially, were passed over – called into question aristocratic predominance in all fields. It was argued that the elite were simply unable to meet the challenges of modern warfare and society. Many of the critics came from a business background and their simplistic response was to demand that 'men of ability' (meaning those who had made money as entrepreneurs) should take over the running of the country. One of the reformers, A. H. Layard, asked, 'why does not the Government allow some great firm to contract for carrying on the war?'[46]

The new Palmerston government, which was merely a reshuffling of faces within the political elite, did not meet any of these demands, as they had been articulated by *The Times* in particular. Nor was there any significant change in the army leadership or its methods of administration. In early May 1855 the Administrative Reform Association was founded. Its aim was a wholesale reform of the system of government and the ending of the near-monopoly of power by the aristocracy. It was headed by a group of mainly second-rank politicians, figures from the City of London such as the Rothschilds and businessmen such as Samuel Courtauld. It was also supported by prominent literary figures including Dickens and Thackeray, and by papers such as *The Times*. It held two big meetings at the Drury Lane Theatre in June, but then went rapidly into decline. It had little backing and its programme was unclear – it made almost no concrete proposals.

EYE-WITNESS
REFORM OF THE BRITISH GOVERNMENT

The Times **leader, 5 May 1855 (the day the Administrative Reform Association was founded)**

'We have failed in everything because we have jobbed everything. In almost all our recent appointments, civil and military, we have promoted men without reference to merit, and refused to remove them without regard to failure. Our COMMANDER-IN-CHIEF missed the opportunity of taking Sebastopol when almost undefended, suffered himself to be surprised on a spot the weakness of which had been again pointed out to him; neglected his commissariat, disregarded his communications, and sat quietly at home while his army was perishing. But he was appointed by the Whigs and politically connected with the Tories, so he remains our Commander-in-Chief still. Our QUARTERMASTER-GENERAL has good interest at the Horse Guards, and so he receives and retains an appointment for which no one believes him to be qualified. Our cavalry is sacrificed to the discard of two noblemen, neither fitted for command, but both possessing influence. Our Transport Service is placed under an officer whom an extraordinary amount of concurring testimony convicts of being utterly incompetent for the duty. We make a man a War Minister because he is a Duke, and we make another a War Secretary because he is that Duke's cousin . . . we have learnt to acquiesce in seeing the government of England parcelled out more like an estate left to be equally divided among the relatives of half a dozen noble families than a great public trust to be exercised for the benefit of the people.'

Charles Dickens, *Little Dorrit*, chapter 10, 'Containing the Whole Science of Government' (written in September 1855 as part of his campaign with the Administrative Reform Association)

'It is true that How not to do it was the great study and object of all public departments and professional politicians all round the Circumlocution Office. It is true that every new premier and every new government, coming in because they upheld a certain thing as necessary to be done, were no sooner come in than they applied their utmost faculties to discovering, How not to do it . . . It is true that debates of both Houses of Parliament the whole session through, uniformly tended to the protracted deliberation, How not to do it. It is true that the royal speech at the opening of such session virtually said, My lords and gentlemen, you have a considerable stroke of work to do, and you will please to retire to your respective chambers, and discuss, How not to do it. It is true that the royal speech, at the close of such session, virtually said, My lords and gentlemen, you have through several laborious months been considering with great loyalty and patriotism, How not to do it, and you have found out . . . Sometimes, angry spirits attacked the Circumlocution Office. Sometimes, parliamentary questions were asked about it, and even parliamentary motions made or threatened about it, by demagogues so low and ignorant as to hold that the real recipe of government was, How to do it . . . And although one of two things always happened; namely, either that the Circumlocution Office had nothing to say and said it, or that it had something to say of which the noble lord, or right honourable gentleman, blundered one half and forgot the other; the Circumlocution Office was always voted immaculate, by an accommodating majority. Such a nursery of statesmen had the department become in virtue of a long career of this nature, that several solemn lords had attained the reputation of being quite unearthly prodigies of business.'

The wave of disgust with the system of British government that reached its peak in the first months of 1855 soon passed. The improvement in the conditions of the army, partly as a result of the decisions taken by the Aberdeen government in the autumn of 1854, but mainly as the weather improved in the spring, lessened the scope for criticism. A few military victories and the fall of Sevastopol in September seemed to justify the existing system. In the end the flurry of agitation and criticism produced no concrete results other than a reshuffle among the political elite, which made the strongly pro-war Palmerston Prime Minister.

Peace Rejected

In the summer of 1854, after the Austrians were successful in forcing the Russians to withdraw from the Principalities, the diplomacy of the war entered a new phase. It produced a reluctant definition of war aims by Britain and France, followed by an alliance of these two countries with Austria. The military stalemate over the winter of 1854–55 led eventually in March 1855 to a conference in Vienna that might have produced peace. It failed because neither side, and in particular the British, were prepared for compromise at this stage. Austria was able to continue with its complicated diplomatic manoeuvres and refused to join the war. Without Austria as an active ally, Britain and France stood little chance of inflicting a major strategic defeat on Russia.

The Four Points

In the summer of 1854 Austria told the allies that it could not enter the war without knowing allied war aims. The allies suspected, rightly, that Austria would use any clear statement of war aims to pressure Russia into negotiations so that the war would end quickly – a key Austrian aim. The outcome was an exchange of notes between the three powers on 8 August setting out the so-called 'Four Points' (there were actually five) as the allied conditions for peace. These were:

- Russia was to give up its treaty rights to protect the Orthodox population of the Principalities and Serbia. (The Ottoman government had already revoked these rights.)
- An international guarantee of unrestricted navigation of the Danube (this was overwhelmingly an Austrian interest).
- A revision of the 1841 Straits Convention on the passage of the Dardanelles by warships when the Ottoman empire was at peace.
- Russia to renounce all claims to a protectorate over the Orthodox population of the Ottoman empire. It was to be replaced by a collective European guarantee, in conjunction with the Ottoman government, of the Christian population throughout the Ottoman empire.

The crucial fifth point allowed Britain and France to raise further demands, depending on the outcome of the war. This made the Four Points into the minimum terms that Britain and France would accept and raised the possibility of a long war for still undefined aims.

Each of the Four Points required a substantial change in the Russian position over which they had gone to war and, taken together, would lead to a general weakening of the Russian position in the Black Sea area. The fifth point was so open-ended that it was impossible for the Russians to accept, particularly because by August 1854 they had not suffered any military defeat and their territory had not been invaded. Britain refused to promise to negotiate, even if the Russians accepted the Four Points. In practice they would have had little choice but to do so, but were saved from this unpalatable prospect by a Russian rejection of the terms. The Russians still felt strong enough not to seek peace and were prepared to leave Austria in limbo (without any gains in collusion with Britain and France) because they were fairly sure that the Austrians were unlikely to join the war.

The road to negotiation

During the autumn of 1854 the balance of interests between the European powers shifted enough to increase the pressure for talks about a possible peace. The Russians suffered some military defeats – Bomarsund was destroyed in the Baltic and the Crimea invaded. Even though Sevastopol had not fallen, the Russians had been unable to expel the allied armies. Austrian military preparations in Galicia seemed to be increasing, and neutral Prussia urged Russia to compromise before the war escalated into a full-scale European war. Although the allies had not achieved their military objectives and the campaign was now in stalemate over the winter, they – and in particular the British – were reluctant to accept peace before they had achieved some military success.

Austria continued to play a key role in the negotiations as it gradually moved closer to the allies. In early October it suggested a limited defensive alliance to Britain and France. The allies rejected the idea because it would do no more than protect Austrian interests, if Austria was attacked by Russia. Austria continued its policy of trying to tempt Britain and France into negotiations with the offer that, if Russia rejected reasonable terms, Austria might join the war. Its real aim was to end the war before the opening of the spring campaigning season. Britain and France finally agreed to an offensive-defensive alliance in which the three powers pledged themselves not to make a separate peace with Russia and that any peace was to be based on the Four Points. In a separate treaty, France pledged that the Austrian position in Italy would be guaranteed until the end of the war, but this was hardly very reassuring in the long term. Britain and France had also not made any commitment over what they might put in the crucial fifth point on wider war aims. The vital factor, though, was that Austria was no longer neutral. The post-1815 system designed to contain France through the grouping of Russia, Prussia and Austria had been broken – that had always been Napoleon's central aim.

Each of the powers was being less than frank about its own position. Austria did not tell its new allies that it had already obtained Russian agreement to negotiate unconditionally on the Four Points until after the alliance was signed. The British Cabinet pressurised the French into a two-faced approach over the third of the Four Points (the Straits Convention of 1841). Austria would be told that the allies merely intended to end Russian preponderance in the Black Sea (this would appeal to the government in Vienna). However, the allies agreed on much stiffer terms – the demolition of the Sevastopol base and all other fortresses along the Black Sea, together with a Russian guarantee not to rebuild them. Russia would also be limited to a fleet of four warships, the same as the Ottomans. There was no chance that Russia would accept such terms. In late December Britain, France and Austria agreed on the vague interpretation of the Black Sea clause. The Russians were hostile and only agreed to a conference after the Austrians gave an undertaking that they would not accept any interpretation of point three that impaired Russian sovereignty in the Crimea and the Black Sea.

The Vienna negotiations

The Vienna conference began on 15 March and continued until 4 June, although in practice it had collapsed by early May. The delegates were Buol (Austria), Gorchakov (Russia), Drouyn de Lhuys (France) and Lord John Russell (Britain). The last had been chosen as part of the political negotiations over the formation of a new government in early February. Palmerston did not want Russell as a free agent in the Commons and most of the Cabinet still hated him for his actions, which had precipitated the political crisis. Palmerston wanted Clarendon to stay in London and therefore sent Russell to Vienna, where he arrived accompanied by his wife, five children and two doctors. Palmerston told Clarendon that he was worried about:

> [Russell's] habits of acting upon sudden impulse, his rather dry and stiff habits, his aptitude to be swayed by others, and the

circumstances that if he came back with success he would be more inconvenient to the Government than he would otherwise be.[1]

Palmerston's concerns were to be borne out by events.

Within a few days of the start of the conference, agreement was reached over the less contentious points. On the Principalities (point one) there was to be a five-power guarantee of their traditional privileges. Free navigation of the Danube (point two) was agreed within a week. As expected (and as intended by Britain and France) there was a rapid deadlock over point three on the future Black Sea regime. Russia rejected any limitations imposed by treaty as a violation of its sovereignty and a threat to its strategic interests. The Austrians suggested the idea of voluntary limitations by Russia (which was compatible with their earlier assurances) and the British and French negotiators began to compromise. Russell wanted to accept voluntary limitations as a way of ensuring his personal success and that of the conference. Clarendon was unhappy, writing to Palmerston, 'It seems impossible to submit to [this] miserable proposal and we don't even know whether it would be accepted by Russia, yet we must weigh our chances of success in war before we take a final decision.'[2] The governments in Paris and London agreed on a joint response – there must be a direct and low limitation on the Russian navy in the Black Sea or, failing that, neutralisation of the area. If this could not be obtained, then the conference should be broken up. Neither expected Austria to join the war if this happened.

In Vienna the French put forward the neutralisation proposal, which Russia immediately rejected. This left voluntary limitation, which Clarendon was worried Russia might accept. If it did:

> We shall be accused of bad faith if we don't agree. Moreover the question will then be reduced to a difference of 3 or 4 ships and it will be difficult to defend the continuation of the war for such a cause. In short I see nothing but embarrassment ahead.[3]

Clarendon's assessment of the situation was shrewd, but Russia saved the British from such an embarrassing situation by rejecting any idea of voluntary limitation – all that St Petersburg would accept was a commitment not to exceed the size of the Black Sea fleet in 1853.

With the conference on the brink of failure, Austria made its 'final' proposal to Britain and France. Any formal limitation on the size of the Russian fleet was abandoned; instead there would be a series of agreed, graduated responses if it exceeded its 1853 size. The Ottoman government would be able to summon the British and French fleets to Constantinople before war began (a significant modification of the 1841 convention) and all the great powers would guarantee Ottoman integrity. There would be an Austrian-British-French treaty of alliance to support the Ottomans in a war with Russia, or if Russia did build a fleet bigger than it had in 1853. If Britain and France agreed to this proposal, then Austria was prepared to present the terms as an ultimatum to Russia and join the war if the terms were rejected. Both Russell and Drouyn supported the Austrian proposal. They returned to their capitals on 23 April. In Paris, Drouyn deliberately misrepresented the peace terms by claiming that Austria would go to war if the current Russian fleet size (rather than the much higher one of 1853) were to be exceeded.

Peace rejected

The first crucial discussions took place after Russell arrived in London on 29 April (a Sunday) and went to the Foreign Office the next day. Russell, determined to try and secure peace, misrepresented the peace terms in exactly the same way as Drouyn. Clarendon reported to Palmerston that Russell argued that 'if the Government refused to make a peace as was now within their reach they would commit the greatest blunder that any Government ever committed'. He supported this argument:

> By reference to our war prospects, the *cowed* state of the French army, the improbability of our taking Sebastopol or of getting away safely from the Crimea and the possibility of our having to get worse terms from Russia after another campaign.[4]

Clarendon thought that Russell's arguments for a very poor compromise peace, which would have achieved none of the allied aims at the beginning of the war, would not have much support in Cabinet. The Cabinet met on 2 May. Clarendon reported the outcome to Cowley in Paris:

> The affair is so grave and the consequences at home and abroad so momentous of giving up what we have been contending . . . that it is impossible to come to a hasty decision . . . I must tell you in confidence that the Cabinet is divided and Lord John would probably leave it on the question . . . the greatest evil of all [is that] we have Generals in the Crimea not worth their salt.[5]

Palmerston was not prepared to accept a compromise peace. He told Clarendon:

The evacuation of the Crimea by 180,000 allied troops with Sebastopol untaken and the Russian Army untouched would undoubtedly be a moral and military triumph for Russia which would raise, instead of making to cease her preponderance in the Black Sea.[6]

The British Cabinet faced a difficult dilemma. The Crimean campaign had been little short of a disaster, and after a year of war there had been no major military success. The politicians were reluctant to admit this failure and the strategic stalemate that had followed. The terms drawn up by Austria were hardly tempting – they made it rather too clear that the allies had been unsuccessful. Opinion was badly divided. Russell was supported by Prince Albert, and others were content to accept the peace terms as misrepresented by Drouyn and Russell. Palmerston was strongly opposed to peace, but Clarendon was wavering. When the Cabinet met again, Russell naturally favoured the proposals but, as Clarendon reported to Cowley, 'nobody liked it very much – some disliked it very much. Others thought it a penalty for our military failure and the price to pay for the escape of our armies.'[7] It was agreed to wait and see how the French reacted.

The British probably had little choice but to defer to their ally because the French were bearing the greatest burden in the fighting – their army was more than four times the size of Britain's. Nor could the British continue the war on their own if the French wanted peace. The key figure in the discussions in Paris was Lord Cowley, the British Ambassador, who was close to Napoleon III. He was strongly opposed to the Austrian plan and disliked Drouyn. He met the Emperor on the morning of 4 May and persuaded him that the Austrian proposal did not meet the fundamental allied demand for a strict limitation on the size of the Russian navy. The proposed alliance with Austria might well be ineffective if the diplomatic balance shifted. In the afternoon the Emperor met Drouyn together with Marshall Vaillant, the Minister of War who was also strongly opposed to the Austrian scheme. Cowley invited himself to the meeting and was able to expose Drouyn's duplicity, forcing him to admit that the Russian navy would be limited to its 1853 size, not its much smaller current level. Drouyn also had to acknowledge that this limitation would not be subject to a treaty with Russia, but merely an agreement with Austria on how the three powers might react if the voluntary limitations were exceeded. Vaillant and Cowley persuaded Napoleon to reject the Austrian proposal. The British followed suit.

The aftermath

After his duplicity had been exposed, Drouyn felt he had no option other than to resign. Russell said he wanted to follow suit because his 'honour' was at stake. Cowley sent a deliberately false account of the meeting to London, stating that Drouyn had resigned over a personal dispute with the Emperor, not over the peace terms. Russell probably suspected the truth. The problem for the French and British governments was how to bring the Vienna talks to a satisfactory close. The Austrian government was understandably angry, but decided it was too dangerous (and too late) to start supporting the Russians. It was, however, impossible for the British and French to stop the Austrians putting their proposal to the conference in a formal session. On 4 June the Russians accepted the Austrian terms, but declared the negotiations at an end because of the British and French rejection.

The breakdown of the peace talks meant that the allies were gambling on achieving some military success before returning to the negotiating table – without this it was difficult to see how they would get better terms. The allies declared that the agreements reached in Vienna on points one and two were null and void – this was an attempt (particularly on the part of the British) to move away from the Four Points. In mid-July they refused to tell the Austrians whether they still accepted the Four Points as a basis for peace. In response the Austrians told the Russians that they regarded themselves as released from the terms of the December 1854 treaty of alliance.

The Austrians published just enough of the diplomatic papers to reveal the peace terms and that they had been accepted by Drouyn and Russell. This placed Russell in a difficult position when questions were raised in Parliament about his behaviour. On 12 July Palmerston, who was still suppressing the true account of events in Paris on 4 May, insisted that Russell state publicly that he accepted the need to continue the war and that he now rejected the Austrian proposal as inadequate. The next day Russell resigned. Many of his colleagues thought that Russell had asked his supporters to plant the questions so as to force him to resign. They believed he was positioning himself to be the leader of a 'peace' government, should the war continue to go badly. Much, not just in domestic politics but also in the nature of any peace settlement, would now depend on whether the British and French armies could secure some success in the Crimea.

12

The Wider War

The 'Crimean War' is misnamed not just because the British regarded the Baltic as a crucial theatre of operations, particularly in 1854. The war was also fought in the Principalities and the Caucasus (a normal area for fighting in an Ottoman-Russian war) as well as across the globe from the Arctic to the Pacific. It also affected nearly all the states in Europe and not just the major neutrals such as Austria and Prussia. We have already seen the impact on Sweden in 1854. In early 1855 Piedmont joined the allies, and Spain was also important in the diplomacy of the war. The possibility of war spreading into Persia, Central Asia and perhaps even to the borders of India had to be taken into account by the British. The impact of the war also seriously affected relations between Britain and the United States and brought them within measurable distance of conflict. If the war had continued much longer it is more than likely that the United States would have sided with Russia against Britain and France.

Economic warfare

One of the policies that turned the war into a global conflict was British policy on trade with Russia. As a major trading and naval power, the British had always seen economic warfare as a central feature of their strategy. It had been applied on a large scale in the Napoleonic Wars, but there were real doubts about the wisdom of this policy in the war with Russia. Total prohibition of trade and the assertion of belligerent rights would be both ineffective and potentially very damaging. Most trade with Russia went by land through Prussia and Austria. A naval blockade could therefore have only a limited effect. An assertion of belligerent rights with the widespread interception and capture of neutral shipping would also be very likely to damage seriously relations with the United States (it had been one of the reasons behind the war of 1812–14). In addition the British had to take account of the susceptibilities of their ally – France had a long-term interest in restricting the effectiveness of British economic warfare.

The British decided their policy in February 1854, one month before war was declared. They accepted from the beginning that the blockade and belligerent rights would have to be modified from their traditional practice. The British therefore adopted what had, until then, been the

French and neutral policy of 'free ships made free goods' (i.e. neutral ships would not be subject to blockade unless they carried war contraband). This represented a reversal of the traditional aggressive British policy deriving from its position as the world's biggest naval power. Clarendon told Graham that it would be best not to 'disagree with France or get into war with America'.[1] In particular the idea of using privateers should be abandoned and 'left off with other barbarisms of the middle ages'.[2] The main reason for the latter change was the danger that Russia would issue letters of marque to privateers who would be mainly American citizens.

In addition to these changes the British did not ban trade with the enemy, or even provide for a prohibition on the export of arms. The latter course had been imposed in an Admiralty proclamation of 16 February 1854, which banned the export of arms, ammunition, military and naval stores and every component of an engine or boiler, together with all woodworking machinery. It rapidly proved to be unworkable. The government's chief adviser on international law, Sir John Harding, argued that 'if arms are allowed to be exported at all to places which trade with the enemy they will reach him'.[3] This may have seemed like a counsel of despair, but it probably reflected reality and the prevailing belief about the sanctity of free trade. The latter point was made by the President of the Board of Trade, Cardwell, who argued that if neutrals were not prohibited from trading with Russia, then 'the justification for prohibiting it to our own subjects is gone'.[4] He then persuaded Gladstone, Clarendon and the Admiralty legal advisers that he was right. The new British policy was implemented on 11 April 1854. The ban on the export of military materials now applied only to northern and eastern Europe, and a longer list of items such as iron, chemicals, coal and machinery was subject to a complex set of regulations. Exporters were also required to provide a bond against items being re-exported to Russia. All British trade was prohibited through blockaded ports.

The new policy, which lasted for the rest of the war, tried to get the best of both worlds. Russia was weakened through a blockade and limited export restrictions. But some trade, especially Russian exports via neutral states, continued. In the main the people who suffered were the merchants who dealt directly with Russia and those who drew their supplies from that country, although the latter could usually find alternative sources. There were also a number of loopholes that took time to close. The order of 11 April did not apply to the Isle of Man and the Channel Islands until early June 1854 and was not enforced in Canada and the West Indies until the end of 1855, too late to have any real impact on the war. The close blockade was only enforced intermittently. It never really applied in the

Black Sea, although in practice the Dardanelles was closed to Russian shipping. The blockade in the Baltic was of dubious legality and that in the White Sea was not effective before the beginning of August 1854. In addition the Russians were able to reflag many of their ships to neutral states such as Denmark and Tuscany. The British courts accepted these changes; the French did not.

The main problem facing British economic warfare was the extensive land trade, especially through Prussia. Arms supplies from Belgium to Russia travelled along this route and the British decided to do nothing other than protest. In the last resort Prussia was too important diplomatically to be threatened. That was not the case with the smaller German states. Within a couple of weeks of the outbreak of war the British were protesting to the trading cities of the Hanseatic League that they were dealing in contraband goods with Russia. The towns denied the claims, but the British still placed a warship at the mouth of the Elbe to intercept and search suspected ships. Hamburg was a small state that could be put under pressure, and the British hoped that their action would be a warning to Prussia that similar action might be taken at their ports, such as Stettin, Danzig and Königsberg. It seems to have made little difference. Denmark, Hanover, Hamburg and Lübeck did prohibit the arms trade, but Prussia did not do so until early March 1855. Even then the ban was largely symbolic because it exempted articles manufactured within the *Zollverein*, the German customs union.

Although the Russian economy was largely agricultural and therefore not easily susceptible to economic pressure, the British measures did have an impact, particularly on arms manufacture. Overall Russian imports kept up reasonably well – by 1855 they had only dropped to 80 per cent of their level in 1852. This was largely the result of a massive shift from maritime trade in the Baltic to the overland trade via Prussia. The latter increased from 10 per cent of the total in 1852 to more than 90 per cent three years later. Russian exports, however, collapsed badly. By 1855 they were at one-third of their level in 1852. This was partly because timber was simply too expensive to transport by land and Russia suffered a permanent loss of markets to Sweden. Overall the British measures certainly weakened Russia and were a factor in the latter's decision to accept peace talks in early 1856.

The war in the Caucasus

This area was a traditional theatre of operations in Russo-Ottoman wars, although the two powers had not fought each other there since the war of

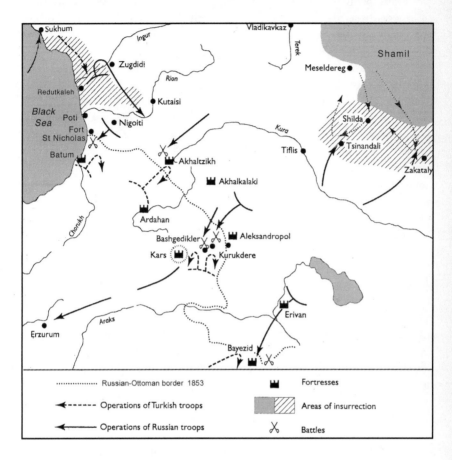

Map 9: The war in the Caucasus

the late 1820s. The Russians had also been trying to subdue the various mountain peoples for more than four decades as they expanded their empire southwards. The Caucasus was a difficult, remote area for military operations and it was almost impossible for either side to achieve a significant victory. For the Ottomans, the areas in the far east of Anatolia were not strategically significant. For the Russians, the main danger was that the Ottomans might be able to foment a revolt that would divert Russian forces and prove to be very difficult and costly to suppress. However, many groups, especially the Christian Georgians, Armenians and Kakhetians, would be very unlikely to support the Ottomans, and the Circassians distrusted both the Russians and the Ottomans. The main support for the Ottomans would come from the Chechens, who strongly opposed the Russian conquest and take-over of their lands, and from the peoples of the remoter parts of Daghestan who, under their leader Shamil, were still resisting Russian forces. To this group a Russo-Ottoman war would be a welcome bonus in diverting the growing Russian pressure on their remaining territories.

The Ottoman forces could rely on the strong fortresses of Trebizond on the Black Sea coast and those further east at Erzerum, Batum and Kars. The other forts at Ardahan and Bayezid were in a poor condition. Overall the Ottomans had about 60,000 troops in the Caucasus area in 1853, although this had doubled by the spring of 1854. On the Russian side the Governor-General and commander, Prince Michael Voroncov, was deeply pessimistic about the situation. His army was scattered over a wide area and faced a variety of threats. These included Persian intervention in the war and British and Ottoman landings along the coast, as well as the need to contain the various mountain groups. He felt he could not move many troops to the south-west frontier with the Ottomans. Voroncov claimed he only had four battalions along the Ottoman frontier. This was a gross underestimate designed to produce reinforcements. The ruse was successful and twenty-six extra battalions were sent, bringing Russian strength up to about 160,000 men by the spring of 1854.

The initial skirmishes in this area took place in 1853. In the summer, as the Russians were forced to move troops to deal with the Ottoman threat, Shamil was able to take offensive action by concentrating almost 15,000 troops for an attack on Zakataly. This was unsuccessful and Shamil then moved his forces nearly fifty miles to the north to attack the Russian post at Meseldereg (Mesed el-Kher). The Russians held out until reinforcements arrived and Shamil and his troops retreated back to the mountains for the winter. Once the war between the Ottomans and Russians started, the former were able to use their slight superiority to undertake a series of limited offensives. At the end of October 1853 an Ottoman unit from

Batum crossed the frontier and captured Fort St Nicholas. This loss forced the Russians to evacuate the port of Redutkaleh, thereby cutting sea links with the Crimea and allowing a revolt to spread in the mountains behind the port. On 10 November the Russians were defeated at Aleksandropol, where they lost one-fifth of their force. Three days later the Russians defeated the Ottomans in the area around Akhaltzikh. As Russian reinforcements arrived, the Ottomans withdrew to Bashgedikler. It was here that the main battle of 1853 was fought on 1 December. The Ottoman army of 36,000 was badly defeated, losing 6,000 dead and wounded and about 15,000 men from desertion. The remainder retreated to Kars. The Russians probably lost about 1,500 men and did not follow up their victory – the fighting ended for the year with both sides back inside their own frontiers.

There were no significant operations in 1854 until July. Then Shamil, with about 16,000 men, moved on Tiflis. His advance guard was defeated at the village of Shilda, north-east of the city, but his main units forced the Russians back to Tsinandali. Just as it seemed possible that he might achieve a major success, Shamil faced a Kakhetian revolt and had to divert some of his forces; the remainder were dispersed in the middle of August. Shamil moved his troops towards Chechnia, hoping to link up with the local resistance under Muhammed Amin, but the move was unsuccessful. Once again it had been shown that Shamil and his troops could hold their mountainous areas, but could achieve little further afield. Along the Ottoman border there was little action in 1854. In mid-July a small Ottoman raid was defeated, but the main battle was at Kurukdere on 5 August as Russian troops crossed the border. The Ottomans lost about 8,000 men, either as casualties or prisoners, and another 10,000 deserted after the battle. The Russians probably lost about 3,000 men. Both sides retreated to their respective fortresses, Kars and Aleksandropol, and this battle marked the end of the limited military action for that year.

The allies knew that the Caucasus was an area of potential Russian weakness, but they had little knowledge of the region and no capacity to exploit any opportunities that might arise. Although there was grandiose rhetoric in London, particularly from Palmerston, about encouraging a revolt and creating a series of independent states 'liberated' from the Russians, this was not practical politics or strategy. The Ottomans were hardly in touch with Shamil and the other mountain groups, and were very suspicious about any British and French attempts to interfere in the area. The allies shipped a few weapons from Constantinople in May 1854, and in the summer the French sent Captain Hippolyte Manduit to the area to investigate the possibilities of revolt.

It may have been this French action that prompted the British to do the same the next year. In April 1855 James Longworth, author of the book *A Year Among the Circassians* (published in 1840), was sent out east because Clarendon thought 'he is the only person to be sent . . . Better send someone acquainted with oriental customs or not at all.'[5] His mission was to discover 'whether those tribes are hopelessly divided among themselves or whether for a common object it would be possible to unite them'. [6] Longworth's instructions were clear:

> You will be careful not to give a political character to your visit to the country so as to raise expectations which may not be realized. The ostensible object of your visit should be to inquire as to the amount of cavalry which the Circassians could place at the disposal of the British government.

He could take gunpowder from Constantinople as a present and was also told, 'there will be no difficulty in adding a supply of rifles and mountain guns if the Circassians should stand in need of them'. Longworth was to find out about Shamil and his objectives, and what protection the tribes might want from a Russian revenge attack after the war. He was told, 'You will, however, be particularly careful to abstain from pledging H. M. G. to anything beyond present assistance in carrying on the war.'[7]

Given the limited scope of the Longworth mission, little was likely to be achieved. The British and French distrusted Shamil and did not think he was a suitable ally. They particularly disapproved of his taking two Georgian princesses and their French governess hostage during the fighting around Tsinandali in 1854. Longworth spent most of the summer of 1855 cruising around the Black Sea, but he did make one trip ashore. He found the situation very different from his visit in 1838 and his main contact, Sefer Bey, no longer wielded much influence. Longworth was unable to establish contact with Shamil. At the beginning of September 1855 he reported that there was 'no probability of Circassian action'.[8] It was, however, at this time that the Russians, worried by their weakness in the area, opened contacts with Shamil and suggested the possibility of a settlement. Nothing happened over the winter and by the spring of 1856, with the war coming to a close, the Russians decided to crush Shamil and his forces. It took a three-year campaign before he eventually surrendered in September 1859.

By the early summer of 1855 the Ottoman army in the Caucasus area was in a poor state. Its strength was down to fewer than 55,000 and the garrison at the key fortified city of Kars was below 15,000. Omer Pasha pressed the British and French to transfer the bulk of the Ottoman forces from the Crimea to this front – they refused to do so until August. The new

Russian commander was the more energetic General Nikolai Muraviev who, unlike his pessimistic predecessors, did not advocate withdrawal from the Caucasus. The main Russian aim for the 1855 campaign was to blockade Kars and cut its links with the main Ottoman supply base at Erzerum. Although the latter had a garrison of only 1,500 men, Muraviev decided against trying to eliminate it first, because it was too far inside Ottoman territory. The siege of Kars would, however, be a major operation. It was defended by a ring of eight forts together with a series of trenches and redoubts around the citadel. The main problem for the defenders was the lack of food – inadequate stockpiles had been set up in the months before the siege.

EYE-WITNESS
THE SIEGE OF KARS

General Williams

1 September: 'The most is made of our provisions; the soldiers are reduced to half allowances of bread and meat or rice-butter. Sometimes 100 drachmas of biscuit instead of bread; nothing besides. No money. Musselman population, 3,000 rifles, will soon be reduced to starvation. Armenians are ordered to quit the town to-morrow. No barley, scarcely any forage. Cavalry reduced to walking skeletons, and sent out of garrison; artillery horses soon the same.'

Dr Sandwith, British medical officer

Diary, 14 November: 'All the mosques, khans and large houses are full of invalids. The citizens nobly furnish us with beds, which, however, scarce suffice for our numbers. Women are seen gathering the dust from the flour-depôts to eat . . . I observe people lying at the corners of streets, groaning and crying out that they are dying of hunger.'

General Williams

19 November: 'We divide our bread with the starving townspeople. No animal food for seven weeks. I kill horses in my stable secretly and send the meat to the hospital, which is now very crowded.'

The siege began in the middle of the summer and proceeded in a desultory fashion. The Ottoman defences were directed by a number of British engineers under General Williams. It was only in mid-September, when Muraviev heard that Ottoman troops from the Crimea had landed at Batum, that decisive action was taken. He was worried that the Ottoman forces would move towards Kutaisi and then Tiflis – if they succeeded they would cut off the Russian forces besieging Kars. Muraviev decided to mount a rapid assault, even though he had no idea where the weak points of the fortifications were located and his troops were still unfamiliar with the terrain. The attack was launched on 29 September. It was meant to be a night assault, but one group got lost and attacked in the wrong sector. The main attack was postponed to the morning when the Russian troops moved forward in columns, making them easy targets for the defenders who were well equipped with rifles. The Russian assault was called off just before noon after they had suffered more than 7,500 casualties.

At this point the Ottomans made a crucial mistake. They did not follow up their success and attack the demoralised Russians. One of the reasons they did not do so was that they had no cavalry – General Williams had ordered that all the horses should have their throats cut to save on food and provide meat for the garrison. The Ottomans expected the Russians to abandon the siege and retreat back to their bases for the winter. Instead Muraviev acted decisively. The Russian troops built a new fortified camp and encircled the city. As food supplies dwindled, about a hundred Ottoman troops were dying every day from starvation. The 35,000 Ottoman troops on the coast used Sukhum as a base and marched south-eastwards towards the River Ingur. They were supported by some Georgian forces, although most stayed loyal to the Russians. On 7 November they fought about 20,000 Russian troops and, in the confused fighting, the Russians retreated away to the south-east. The Ottoman forces followed-up, but were unable to secure a decisive victory. By the third week of November the garrison and people of Kars had almost no food left. On 26 November General Williams surrendered to the Russians. About 18,000 Ottoman troops were taken prisoner; Williams and the other British officers were treated as honoured guests and travelled back to Russia. The capture of Kars was a key victory for the Russians – one of the few they obtained during the war – and it gave them an important bargaining counter in the peace negotiations.

War in Asia?

The 'jewel in the crown' of the British empire was India, but keeping it under control and its borders secure posed major problems to a power that had a very limited army. Russia was Britain's great rival throughout the vast area stretching from the Caspian across Central Asia to Afghanistan.

But the two powers were still too far apart to confront each other directly – that did not happen until after the Crimean War, following Russia's conquest of the Central Asian khanates and the building of railways in the area. In the 1850s the two empires were still trying to establish spheres of interest across the region. However, the outbreak of war with Russia was bound to increase tensions throughout the area from Persia to India.

The established British view was expressed by Lord Dalhousie, the Governor-General of India, on the outbreak of war:

> There is no ground left for believing that Russia, separated by enormous tracts and many wild tribes from the sources of her military power, could by any possibility succeed against the British power in the East.[9]

However, the Russian threat could not be ignored and in any war they would be bound to try and create problems for the British. Seymour, the Ambassador in St Petersburg, had forecast in March 1853 that 'Russia might be expected to revert with increased eagerness to her designs upon the Indian possessions of Great Britain and she would do so under infinitely more favouring [sic] circumstances than at any preceding period.'[10]

One of the key areas where the two states did clash was Persia, which for 400 years had been anti-Ottoman. It was bound therefore to be sympathetic to the Russians, and its relations with Britain had been bad for years. Britain sent steam-powered warships from Bombay into the Gulf to threaten Persia, but doubted whether they would ever be able to counter Russian military power in the Caspian area and the influence this gave them. Ultimately the British could not provide an army to defend Persia and therefore felt they could not push her into open conflict with Russia. Sir Charles Wood, head of the Board of Control responsible for Indian affairs, wrote to Clarendon just after the outbreak of war:

> Can we fairly urge Persia into hostilities with her powerful neighbour without being prepared to support her through all the consequences immediate and future? Are we prepared to guarantee her that support?[11]

Ministers discussed the issue and agreed that Wood was right – Persia should be advised to remain neutral. A Russo-Persian treaty of September 1854 also provided for neutrality in return for Russian financial concessions. (Relations between Britain and Persia deteriorated so rapidly that they were at war by late 1856 when a military expedition was sent from India.)

The British government decided that the best way of containing any threat from Russia (and possibly Persia) was to seek an agreement with the rulers in Afghanistan and at Kalat further south. A treaty and subsidy to the ruler of Kalat was agreed in May 1854 (extending an earlier treaty signed in 1841). London was not keen on the idea of a subsidy – Wood argued, 'I see no reason for paying him annually to do what it is so clearly for his own interest to do for himself.'[12] In September 1854 the Indian government heard from envoys sent by the Khan of Kokand that Russian troops were moving east of the Aral Sea and had captured Ak-Mechet, 300 miles up the River Jaxartes. Dalhousie told London that if Russia continued to push into Central Asia, 'she will be in a position to work infinite evil to the British power in the East'.[13] He argued that any peace treaty with Russia ought to contain limitations on Russian territorial expansion into this area. The government discussed this possibility, but concluded that any such proposal would be opposed by the French because it would merely confirm their suspicions that Britain was only fighting the war for its wider imperial interests.

The war in the Pacific

Russia had been expanding its power into the Pacific area since the seventeenth century (it had settlements on the Pacific before it had territory on the Baltic). It also, under the Russian-American Company, controlled Alaska. In the early 1850s, exploiting Chinese weakness during the widespread T'ai Ping rebellion, it pushed into the Amur River area to take the area from China. In 1852 it sent a mission under Rear-Admiral Efim Putiatin to the still semi-isolated Japan. The main British aim during the war was to limit and reduce Russian power in the area. The only region excluded from the fighting was the Canadian Arctic and Alaska, where the two rival commercial enterprises, the Hudson's Bay Company and the Russian-American Company, signed an agreement just before the outbreak of war. The deal was confirmed by the governments in London and St Petersburg.

The Russian commander in the Pacific, Count Nikolai Muraviev (not the same person as the commander in the Caucasus), told St Petersburg in December 1853 that he would probably be unable to defend the Kamchatka Peninsula – he simply did not have enough resources. His aim was to concentrate his forces and defend the Amur River area. However, reinforcements did arrive and he was able to garrison Mariinsk and Nikolaevsk (the key towns on the Amur River) as well as Petropavlovsk on Kamchatka. News of the outbreak of war did not reach the far east of

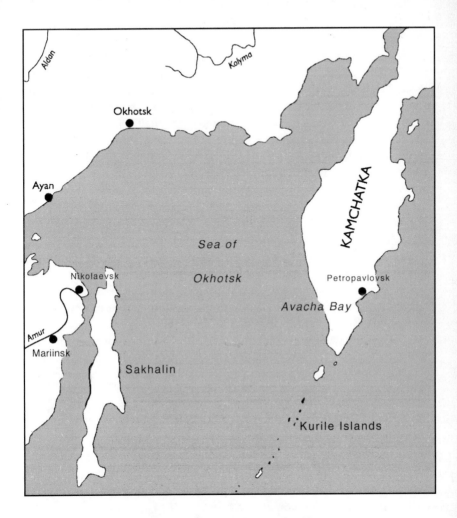

Map 10: The war in the Pacific

Siberia until June 1854 – when Muraviev immediately ordered the evacuation of the island of Sakhalin.

In East Asia the British and French fleets had an overwhelming superiority over the Russian fleet. They had twenty-six warships, including six steamers, compared with a Russian fleet of six, quickly reduced to four after the *Diana* was destroyed by a tidal wave and it was decided that the flagship *Pallada* was too old to be used in operations. However, the incompetence of the local British and French commanders more than offset any numerical advantage. They had almost no intelligence on the area – even its basic geography remained a mystery. In mid-April 1854 the retiring Commander-in-Chief of the China Station, Vice-Admiral Sir Fleetwood Pellew, informed London that the Russian ships under Putiatin had wintered at Manila and would now sail south for Batavia: 'It is certain that he cannot return to the northward towards China or Japan.'[14] The Admiral's assurances were wrong – the Russian ships sailed north to Nagasaki and then Sakhalin, while the British fleet under its new commander, Rear Admiral Sir James Stirling, spent months fruitlessly searching for them across the South China Sea and the East Indies.

While the British China squadron tried to find the Russian fleet, the British and French Pacific fleets were at Callao in Peru under their commanders Rear Admirals David Price and Auguste Fébvrier-Despointes. On 15 April, six days after the British and French ships arrived at the port, the Russian frigate *Aurora* sailed into the harbour. She had left Kronstadt in September 1853 and was sailing via Rio de Janeiro to reinforce the ships in the north Pacific. *Aurora* left on 26 April and news of the outbreak of war arrived on 7 May. It was another ten days before the allied warships sailed and travelled via the Marquesas Islands before reaching Honolulu on 17 July. Here they discovered that the *Aurora* had left a month earlier. Demonstrating no sense of urgency, the fleet stayed for more than a week, enjoying a series of receptions and dinners with the local ruler. On 25 July an allied force of nine warships finally left, sailing north-west towards Alaska before changing course for Kamchatka. They arrived at Avacha Bay on 28 August before moving towards Petropavlovsk.

Here the allied commanders found that their prolonged voyage across the Pacific had given the Russians time to prepare their defences. *Aurora* had arrived on 14 July (before the allied ships had even reached Honolulu) and half of its guns had been unloaded and placed in six shore batteries. An armed transport was blocking the passage into the harbour and reinforcements, which arrived on 8 August, had increased the garrison to about 1,000 men. On 29 August there was a desultory exchange of gunfire before the allied ships retreated out of range. The allied commanders decided on a major bombardment of Petropavlovsk the next day, aimed at knocking out two-thirds of the shore batteries. The attack began at 6 a.m. but achieved little. The British commander, Rear Admiral Price, took lunch at 11 a.m. and retired to his cabin on the *President*. Shortly after noon he shot himself and died about five hours later. Fébvrier-Despointes took command, stopped the bombardment and decided to try a landing the next day. On 31 August a party of British and French marines and sailors landed and captured one of the batteries. The Russians successfully counter-attacked and the troops were forced to re-embark. A major assault was launched on 4 September when 700 men landed in two separate parties. They climbed a hill, where they were ambushed and driven back by the Russians. As they retreated many fell over the cliffs in their panic and others were drowned as they tried to clamber onto the small boats moored just offshore. Overall the Russians lost 115 men (just forty died on 4 September) whereas the allies lost 209 killed and more than 150 wounded (over half the force) during the disastrous operation. After this fiasco the attack on Petropavlovsk was abandoned and the allied ships set sail back across the Pacific. The French wintered at San Francisco, the British at Vancouver.

Although it is difficult to believe, the allied campaign in 1855 turned out to be even more ineffective than that of the previous year. The Pacific squadrons had been reinforced and the British now had ten ships under Rear Admiral Henry Bruce, and the French six commanded by Rear Admiral Martin Fourichon. They decided to begin the campaign earlier and arrived off Petropavlovsk in late May and early June. They were already too late. In December 1854 Muraviev had decided to evacuate the town because he expected a more powerful allied fleet to return in the spring. Ships had been sent as soon as the ice broke up and the troops, inhabitants and stores had been evacuated from Petropavlovsk on 17 April. Admiral Putiatin, who had been in Japan since signing a treaty of peace and friendship in early February, arrived off the town on 22 May, but left immediately and avoided the allied fleets. The allies found they could do nothing but destroy what remained of the town and set it on fire.

Three warships under Commodore Charles Elliot then found the *Aurora* trapped by ice in a mainland bay opposite Sakhalin island. It was crowded with the stores from Petropavlovsk and had only sixteen guns operational. The British ships approached the trapped vessel and shots were exchanged. Elliot decided to retreat, arguing, 'After mature deliberation I deemed it to be imprudent to attack this superior force [sic].'[15] He decided to move south and blockade the ship, believing Sakhalin to be a peninsula attached to the mainland rather than an island. When the ice broke up the *Aurora* sailed north on 27 May and reached the Amur River ten days later. The Russians under Captain Nevelskoi had already shown Sakhalin to be an island six years earlier and this fact was known to the British diplomatic staff in the area. The Royal Navy had not bothered to consult them and Admiral Stirling tried to blame the fiasco on the perfidy of the Russians: 'It is worthy of notice how adroitly the Russians have managed to keep this fact [Sakhalin being an island] so well concealed from the world, for it has never appeared on any of their charts.'[16]

The allied ships set off to sail around the north Pacific from Japan to Alaska looking for Russian ships. They found none because there were none in the area. The allied ships had no charts and only the most basic understanding of the geography of the region and in these circumstances they were unlikely to achieve much. The Russian settlement at Ayan was stormed. However, it turned out to be undefended and occupied only by the Archbishop of Siberia. In early September the allies occupied Uruppu in the Kurile Islands. They thought they were capturing a Russian colony, but the only inhabitants were the local Ainu. Uruppu was grandly renamed *L'Isle de l'Alliance* and the Kuriles retitled 'Fog Archipelago'. The fleets departed for Hong Kong, never to be seen again in the area. On 15 October Commander Elliot landed on the mainland opposite Sakhalin but was ambushed and driven off by the local militia. When he returned ten days later under a flag of truce the local Russian commander finally revealed the great 'secret' – and Elliot's earlier incompetence – by telling him that Sakhalin was an island.

The war in the Pacific was over. Luckily for the allies there was no time for any operations in 1856. In his report to London on the campaign Rear Admiral Stirling, with commendable understatement, tried to turn the 'operations' into a geographical expedition: 'In the course of the preceding operations no brilliant success has been achieved, but the Seas of Kamchatka, Japan and Okhotsk have been traversed in almost every direction.'[17]

The war in the Arctic

The smallest of the campaigns in the war of 1854–56 was in the Arctic. The port of Archangel at the mouth of the Dvina River had been founded by English merchants, but by the mid-nineteenth century most of the trade was purely local and in the hands of the merchants of Finnmark, the northernmost part of Norway (which was still part of Sweden). The Swedish government asked the British and French not to interfere with this trade. Any campaigning season in the region was also bound to be very short – Archangel was only ice-free from late April until early October.

In 1854 a small allied force was sent to the Arctic. The British fleet consisted of three ships (a sailing frigate and two corvettes, with auxiliary steam power) commanded by Captain Erasmus Ommaney. The French sent two ships (a sailing frigate and a corvette) under Captain Pierre Guilbert. They stopped at the Norwegian port of Hammerfest en route and formally established the blockade of the White Sea on 23 July. Archangel was well defended by a garrison of about 6,000 troops and so the allied ships attacked the armed monastery on the Solovetskie Islands (it had been attacked numerous times before by Swedish forces). After a bombardment the allies demanded unconditional surrender. The Russians rejected the call and the allied ships sailed away. The Russians had not suffered any casualties; the British lost one dead and five wounded. On 22 August one British ship (the French were present but took no part in the operation) sailed into the mouth of the Kola River, destroyed a battery and anchored near the small fishing port of Kola (near modern Murmansk). Kola was bombarded from 3 a.m. the next day. The attack achieved little apart from setting fire to the wooden houses – 110 out of a total of 128 were burnt down. That was the end of any military action for the year, and the allied ships left for home at the end of September.

The 1855 campaign in the Arctic was even more insignificant. The British sent three ships under Captain Thomas Baillie and the French increased their contribution to three ships, again under the command of Captain Guilbert. The blockade was declared in the middle of June and this year, despite the pleas of the Swedish government, local trade was not allowed. The allies, in their only military actions, seized about sixty small vessels, but since they could not be towed to Britain and France as prizes they were either sunk or set on fire. The small allied fleet returned home slightly later than the previous year, leaving the area on 9 October.

Sardinian entry into the war

The kingdom of Sardinia (which had its capital at Turin) was a minor European power, but saw itself as the leading independent Italian state and was therefore strongly opposed to Austria, which still ruled Lombardy and Venetia. It posed a threat to Austria, especially if it was supported by Napoleon III in a 'war of national liberation'. The leading politician in Sardinia was Count Cavour, who later came to be seen as one of the leaders of the *Risorgimento* that unified Italy. In 1854–56 his main aim was to improve Sardinia's position in European diplomacy. Although Napoleon was more sympathetic to Italian aims than most of the British government, he was cautious – in the last resort Austria, particularly if it could be encouraged to enter the war, was far more important to the allies.

At the beginning of the war Sardinia was warned to keep out of the conflict. The British minister in Turin, Sir James Hudson, a close confidant of Cavour and a supporter of Italian unification, was instructed to tell the government that it should not attempt to 'take advantage of the war for selfish purposes'.[18] The Sardinian government took the view that as long as Austria did not fight alongside Russia, there was very little it could do. It was more worried by the possibility that any Franco-British-Austrian alliance might involve a deal at the expense of Italy and Sardinia. In the end the Franco-Austrian convention of 22 December 1854 did no more than preserve the status quo in Italy for the duration of the war. By the time it was signed, Sardinia was on the brink of joining the allies.

The pressure to enter the war did not come from Cavour as part of a grandiose plan to ensure the future unification of Italy. In the autumn of 1854, as the situation in the Crimea deteriorated into deadlock, Britain and France were looking for all the help they could get. The French minister in Turin, the Duc de Guiche, put pressure on King Victor Emmanuel to enter the war. The latter gave an ultimatum to Cavour to join Britain and France or be replaced by the much more conservative politician, Count Thaon di Revel. On 29 November Clarendon instructed Hudson to find out, informally, how a request for troops would be regarded by the Sardinian government. Hudson had in fact raised this question on his own initiative in April when he had suggested a force of about 15,000 troops. The subject was raised again in late November, when Cavour argued that before Sardinia could participate, a long-standing dispute with Austria over the sequestration of the assets of Italian 'revolutionaries' should be settled on Sardinia's terms. He also demanded that Sardinia should be guaranteed a place at the peace conference (thus confirming its status as a 'great power'). The British Cabinet met on 19 December and rejected these terms, although Gladstone and Palmerston would have gone some way towards Cavour's position. The French rejected them too. Although Cavour had not achieved his aims, he decided to go ahead anyway. The Sardinian government split over the issue and when the Foreign Minister, Dabormida, resigned, Cavour combined the office with that of Prime Minister. On 7 January 1855 the allies presented what was effectively an ultimatum to the government in Turin – it was to join the alliance unconditionally or give up any hope of uniting with Britain and France. Three days later Sardinia joined the Anglo-French alliance.

On 26 January a military convention was concluded. The Sardinian government would provide a contingent of 15,000 troops, which would be commanded by a Sardinian (General Alfonso Lamarmora was chosen). In return Britain and France would guarantee Sardinian territorial integrity (it would be very vulnerable to an Austrian attack with almost one-third of its army overseas). At the same time the British provided a loan of £1 million (it was to be a loan not a subsidy, to meet Sardinian sensitivities). Half the loan was given immediately, the rest in July. The British also provided transport to move the Sardinian troops to the east, and paid all of the costs. Sardinia formally declared war on Russia on 4 March.

The Sardinians provided not just infantry, but also six squadrons of cavalry and six artillery batteries. British transports arrived at La Spezia in early April and left just before the end of the month. The British and French argued over how the extra troops should be used. Napoleon wanted them kept at Constantinople as a reserve alongside French army units. As far as the British were concerned, they were paying for the Sardinian troops, which made up a force more than three-quarters of the size of the British field army in the early months of 1855. They saw this as an opportunity to increase their bargaining power with the French. As soon as the military convention was signed, Clarendon told the Secretary of State for War, Panmure: 'the sooner it is made clear that the Sardinians don't belong to the French and are not to be ordered about by them, the better'.[19] Panmure sent instructions to Raglan 'not to let the French dispose' of the Sardinian troops, because Napoleon 'has a design to lay his hands on them, but this must never be allowed'.[20] In practice the Sardinians were under a joint Anglo-French command when they arrived at Balaklava on 8 May. They were stationed on 'Gasfort Hill' near the scene of the Charge of the Light Brigade. The troops rapidly came down with cholera – some 3,000 were affected, of whom more than one-third died.

Spain

Like Sardinia, Spain had no direct interest in the conflict that led to the war. In April 1854 it declared its neutrality, although this was always interpreted in a pro-French way, especially after the revolution of June 1854, which brought the *Progresistas* to power. Pro-British sentiment was much weaker. Spain supported the 'Catholic' cause and was strongly anti-Orthodox – it had had no diplomatic relations with Russia since 1833. Internally it was weak economically and militarily and still fractured by the civil wars of the 1830s.

In early 1855, with the allies in difficulties in the Crimea, and with Sardinia joining the alliance, the French government explored whether it might be able to tempt the Spanish into the war. On 30 January the Spanish Chargé d'Affaires in Paris saw Drouyn, the Foreign Minister, who asked whether Spain would follow the example of Sardinia and hinted that if it did so, the allies might guarantee their overseas possessions. This was bound to be the main Spanish requirement – they were under pressure from the United States, which wanted their colony of Cuba. Relations between Britain and the United States were deteriorating rapidly (as we will see later in the chapter) and it was possible that the United States would join the war on the Russian side. Spain took its time considering the French offer, but on 22 June the Foreign Minister, General Juan de Zabala (who was strongly pro-allied), saw the British minister in Madrid. The Spanish offered 20,000 troops for the Crimea as long as Britain paid for their transport and upkeep. The British decided that Spanish help was not worth much and took a tougher line than they had with Sardinia, telling Spain to declare war without any conditions and to send the troops at its own expense. In July the Spanish renewed their offer in talks with the French, but Napoleon left the decision to the British since they would be bearing the cost. The Spanish government now made it clear that its price for help would be a clear guarantee of its colonies. The British did not bother to reply until 17 September (after the fall of Sevastopol) when Spanish help was no longer of any great consequence. They once again made it clear that any Spanish offer should be unconditional (as, in theory, the Sardinian offer had been). In early October Spain accepted this condition and offered 30,000 troops. With the Crimean campaign drawing to a close, these troops were no longer required and the British never replied to the Spanish offer.

British mercenaries – Switzerland

Switzerland, with its poor peasant agriculture and lack of land, had long been a traditional recruiting ground for mercenaries. However, under the 1848 constitution and the 1851 military code, it was illegal for foreign states to recruit in the country. Britain, which, as we have seen, was desperate for extra troops, decided to ignore this prohibition. In early February 1855 the British minister in Berne saw the Swiss President, Dr Furrer, and explained that recruitment would take place, though to meet Swiss sensibilities enlistment would actually occur at a British depot in France (Schlettstadt in Alsace). Furrer made it clear that the less the federal government knew about what was going on, the better and that law enforcement was a matter for the individual cantons. On this basis the British went ahead and set up a committee to organise recruitment. The chief figure was Colonel Johann Baumgartner, a highly corrupt member of the federal General Staff. He was important because he had the right political contacts. The other members were Colonel Johann Sulzberger, an instructor in the Thurgau militia, and Lieutenant-Colonel Eduard Funk, an artillery expert in the Berne militia.

The British operation was headed by Colonel Charles Sheffield Dickson, who began work in May 1855. From the beginning there were major problems. The conditions being promised by the Swiss committee were not those authorised by the Foreign Enlistment Act. Baumgartner drew up his own articles of enlistment promising fifteen months' pay on disbandment (the British only allowed three) and also forged the signatures of the other two members of the committee. Sulzberger was promising potential recruits an annual pension of £200, something specifically prohibited by British legislation. The British also had to raise the fee paid for each recruit to more than £5 in order to compete with the French who were recruiting for their *Seconde légion étrangère* under Colonel Ulrich Ochsenbein. They had depots along the Swiss border at Saarlouis, Colmar, Gex and Besançon – French border guards were instructed to let the Swiss recruits for both the French and British units through unhindered.

Recruiting for the British units went very slowly – by the end of 1855 only 1,600 men had enlisted. They were formed into two regiments commanded by Jacob Blarer and Balthazar Bundi. The latter was a seventy-two-year-old veteran of the French army who had taken part in Napoleon's invasion of Russia and had served in Charles X's Swiss Guard until it was disbanded after the 1830 revolution. Dickson was placed in overall command of the two regiments, even though the agreement with the Swiss recruits stated that all officers would be Swiss. The first units completed training and left for the east in late December 1855. They only got as far as Smyrna before it became obvious that the war would soon end. Recruiting stopped in mid-March 1856 and the Swiss units arrived back at Dover in July. They were taken by train across France and allowed back into Switzerland because they had not broken Swiss law – they had enlisted outside the country. Overall the British recruited just over 3,000 troops at a total cost of £235,000. None took part in combat.

British mercenaries – Germany

As the Foreign Enlistment legislation was being passed through Parliament, the British minister in Frankfurt, Malet, advised that the German confederation would almost certainly oppose open British recruiting. However, a few of the smaller states might tolerate it, as long as no direct request was made. In early 1855 the British persuaded Baron

Richard von Stutterheim to act as their chief recruiting agent. He had considerable experience as a mercenary – he had served in the British Legion in the Spanish civil wars of the 1830s under de Lacy Evans and had also recruited troops in Paris to serve in Mexico. Von Stutterheim was made a Lieutenant-Colonel in the British army in April 1855.

As predicted, the German states, led by Prussia, opposed British recruiting. Hamburg and Lübeck issued proclamations banning recruitment and the British Consul in Cologne (part of Prussia) was imprisoned for his activities, but subsequently pardoned by the King. Von Stutterheim concentrated his activities in the north German towns where there were plenty of unemployed veterans from the *Freikorps* who had fought in the Schleswig-Holstein wars of 1848–51. These provided high-quality recruits – more than four out of ten of the recruits from Germany had already had military training and fewer than 5 per cent were illiterate, compared with well over half of the British army. The British paid £10 a head for recruits (twice the rate in Switzerland) and more than 5,000 men were recruited very quickly. However, the local police intercepted many and also arrested some of the recruiting agents – it was an offence to recruit anybody who had not yet done their military service. In May 1855 the British gave von Stutterheim authority to recruit another 5,000 men.

Once the recruits had avoided the local police, they sailed from the small fishing villages along the north German coast to the British colony of Heligoland, where a large training base was constructed. There was no water on the island in summer apart from rainwater, and so stills capable of distilling 3,000 gallons of seawater into drinking water were built. Large huts and a hospital were put up in the winter of 1855–56. Overall three regiments were formed and they reached Constantinople and Scutari by early 1856. Like the Swiss units, they did not see combat.

After the war the men in these units faced major problems – most could not return home after illegally joining a foreign army. Like the Swiss units, they had been misled about their terms of service and thought they had enlisted for up to five years, rather than for the duration of the war. The 3rd Jägers, who protested most strongly about the disbandment terms, were the first to be dissolved in May 1856. When the other troops returned to Britain in July 1856 there was a series of incidents. At Aldershot fighting between British and German soldiers reached the point where the military police attacked the German units. A large number of huts were destroyed and six British soldiers killed. In Portsmouth marines and navvies attacked the Germans and drove them out of the town. In the end some of the German soldiers enlisted in various Latin American armies and 500 went out to Canada. The largest single group – 2,361 men together with 378 women and 178 children – were sent as settlers to Cape Colony in

November 1856, where they formed a settler/frontier police unit. The remainder of the men were able to return to Germany because they had not broken local laws.

British mercenaries – Sardinia

Although Sardinia was an allied state and part of its army was in the Crimea, the British approached the Turin government in May 1855 about recruiting a 'foreign legion' in the same way as it had units from Switzerland and Germany. Cavour agreed immediately – he was keen to rid the country of the exiles and deserters from Lombardy and Venetia who represented a major political problem in the delicate relations with Austria. London authorised the formation of the legion on 10 June and a depot was set up at Novara near the Austrian border, despite strong Austrian objections.

The British took a month to select a commander for the unit. They chose the socially acceptable Lieutenant-Colonel Lord Henry Percy, the son of the Duke of Northumberland. The choice was a poor one. Percy was in the Crimea and it was several weeks before he arrived in northern Italy, where he quarrelled almost immediately with the British minister, Hudson. Recruitment went very slowly because Percy would not take any man unless he could produce his Sardinian army-release papers. The conditions in the barracks were poor and the food was dreadful. A large number of men deserted because of the floggings. (Five deserters were court-martialled and shot.) By October only 350 men had joined and Percy's resignation was gratefully accepted by the government in London. Colonel Constantine Read was chosen as his successor, but he did not arrive in Italy until January 1856. By then the number of recruits had risen to about 2,000. They were given deceptive assurances that they would be kept on after the war – hints were dropped about service with the British in India.

Most of the men were drawn from the Austrian-controlled areas of Italy and they saw that country – and not Russia – as their enemy. On 22 February 1856 a conspiracy to cross into Lombardy and spark an anti-Austrian revolt was discovered in the legion. It followed the British decision to move the unit to Malta. Sardinian police were brought in and arrested twenty-six 'ringleaders'. Cavour asked for the unit to leave Italy although he hoped, with British consent, to use it later to invade and annex Sicily. The legion was taken to Malta (the nearest it ever got to the fighting in the east) in April. A series of disturbances and near mutiny were quelled when the British brought up the warships *Hannibal* and *Spiteful*, which trained their guns on Fort Manoel where the legion had its quarters.

After the war ended the British decided that the legion had to leave Malta. The Sardinian government agreed to take back 1,700 of the men who were Sardinian citizens, as long as the British transported them to Genoa. This left another 1,200 exiles and deserters to deal with. They left Malta on 19 August, en route to England. Two days into the voyage they took over the ships and held the British officers prisoner. Their aim was to divert the convoy to Calabria and start a revolt against the King of Naples. The leader of the 'mutiny', Lieutenant Francesco Angherà, was captured and detained at Plymouth. (Four years later he was one of the 'thousand' who landed in Sicily with Garibaldi.) The other troops were put in barracks at York and Portsmouth where more disturbances broke out. Eventually the British government persuaded the Argentine government to accept the men as military colonists. They left Britain in December 1856 but most deserted and took up civilian occupations in Argentina.

The United States and the Crimean War

The country where the British faced the greatest problem over the recruitment of mercenaries was the United States. This reflected the general state of relations between the two countries. Britain and the United States were rivals across the western hemisphere from Canada to the Caribbean and Central America, and in the Pacific and the Far East. There were long-running disputes over the border and fishing rights with Canada and over a possible canal linking the Atlantic with the Pacific. In these circumstances it was extremely unwise of the British even to consider a recruiting campaign.

The Democrat Franklin Pierce became President in 1853. He, like so many US Presidents, was a former General. He had fought in the aggressive and unprovoked war to seize territory from Mexico in 1848. He was close to the expansionist southern slave owners who wanted to take over Spanish-held Cuba, and he relied on the growing Irish vote in the northern cities, which was strongly anti-British after the scale of suffering in the recent famine. As a neutral, the United States was bound to be affected by British blockade policy – during the Napoleonic Wars the British assertion of belligerent rights had been a major factor behind the 1812–14 war between the two countries.

From the American point of view, the outbreak of the Crimean War produced both problems and opportunities. The conflict between neutral and belligerent rights at sea might provoke numerous disputes in which the United States could threaten the widespread use of privateers acting on behalf of the Russians. The existing very friendly relations between the

United States and Russia (they saw Britain as their mutual enemy) might produce an alliance – it was certainly inconceivable that the United States would enter the war on the allied side. The Anglo-French alliance was also seen as posing a long-term threat to the United States – if it was extended to the western hemisphere, the allies might act together to restrict the expansion of American power.

The Russians hoped to exploit their friendship with the Americans. In early 1854, before the new British blockade policy was known, the Russians instructed their minister in Washington, Eduard von Stoeckl, to try and embroil the United States in maritime disputes with Britain. A number of Americans approached the Russian legation volunteering to act as privateers under the Russian flag. The American government was sympathetic, but could not openly support such moves and Stoeckl dropped the idea as too dangerous. In late July 1854 the two countries signed a bilateral convention on neutral rights at sea (the Russians accepted the American position), but it had almost no impact because of the British change of policy away from a harsh interpretation of belligerent rights. In February 1855 Stoeckl revived the idea of recruiting American privateers and discussed it with the Secretary of State, Marcy, who thought that such action was no different from the British recruitment of mercenaries. Stoeckl also spoke to Senator William Gwyn, who proposed using San Francisco as a base for such operations in the Pacific. The idea was eventually vetoed in St Petersburg by Nesselrode, but only on the grounds that it might endanger relations with the United States.

Other Americans volunteered to help the Russians. In Kentucky 300 riflemen did so, but they never reached the Crimea. Thirty-five American doctors did travel to Russia and twenty-four of them served in the Crimea (eleven died of typhoid). The Americans also sent a military delegation to Russia to study the war. It was headed by Captain George B. McLellan, later an important Union General in the civil war. The United States government also turned a blind eye to a number of technical breaches of their neutrality by Russia. It allowed Russia to sell merchant ships that had been interned in American ports at the start of war. A far more significant breach involved construction of the steamship *America* in New York. Although American cover names were used, the government was well aware of what was happening. The ship sailed for the Pacific in the autumn of 1855 and when a British warship tried to seize it off Rio de Janeiro, an American naval officer intervened to prevent the British from taking control. The ship arrived off the Amur River in early 1856.

Even after the agreement with the Hudson's Bay Company to exclude the area from the war, the Russians were worried about the vulnerability of Alaska. The British had naval supremacy in the Pacific and might be tempted to seize the territory. The United States enquired whether the Russians wanted to sell Alaska (they eventually did so in 1867) and the Russians considered making a fictitious sale to an American company. The Russian Consul in San Francisco, P. S. Kostromitinov, organised the American-Russian Commercial Company and drew up a pre-dated contract for the purchase of the Russian company that owned Alaska. The contract was sent to Washington at the end of January 1854. Stoeckl discussed it with Marcy. Even though President Pierce favoured the idea, Marcy decided not to proceed because the British would see through the arrangement. He was right to be cautious: the British knew what was happening and Palmerston, for one, wanted to seize Alaska 'to forestall the Bargain between Nicholas and the Yankees'.[21]

Most Americans were pro-Russian. Pierce told Stoeckl in April 1854 that the United States wanted to be neutral, but 'God knows if this is possible' because British attitudes had 'considerably Russified us'.[22] The American minister in London, James Buchanan (who became President in 1857), told Clarendon just before the outbreak of war, 'it might be necessary for us to ally ourselves with Russia for the purpose of counter-acting [British] designs'.[23] Much of the press in the United States took a more extreme position. The spring 1854 issue of *De Bow's Review* contained an article on 'The Russo-Turkish Question' by William Henry Trescot. He argued:

> England has already touched that point beyond which any *increase* of her power is dangerous to the world, while Russia has not yet developed the matured proportions of that influence which she can fairly use for the world's benefit.

In April 1855 the *United States Review* carried a much more emotional piece comparing Britain and Russia:

> It is true that the government of Russia is a despotism . . . but the despotism of the present day is not so bad and outrageous . . . as the reign of Henry VIII in England. It bears no comparison with that of Charles I . . . We can see little or no difference between Botany Bay, and St Helena of England; and the Kamtschatka and Siberia of Russia – between crushing the body and soul in the factories of Manchester . . . and performing the same labor of love in the serfdoms and saltmines of Russia.

(American slavery was conveniently excluded from the comparison.)

From the winter of 1854–55 until the end of the war the United States tried to take advantage of British and French preoccupations to make gains around the globe. In the Pacific, after having obtained Russian consent, it tried to purchase Hawaii. The American agent, David Gregg, was given authority to annex regardless of any British and French protests. The allies objected strongly to such a move (one of the reasons their Pacific fleets called at the islands in the summer of 1854). However, it was only the demands of King Kamehameha (he wanted a subsidy of $300,000 a year and immediate statehood) that torpedoed the idea. He may have been put up to these demands by the British and French but, more likely, he simply preferred to remain independent. The British, after trying to delay negotiations for as long as possible, felt that it was prudent to solve a long-running dispute over Canadian fisheries, largely on American terms. In October 1854 the American representatives in Europe met at Ostend at the request of Marcy to discuss the European attitude to Cuba (i.e. whether Britain and France would back Spain in resisting an American take-over). The public 'Ostend Manifesto' made the remarkable argument that:

> If Spain, actuated by stubborn pride and a false sense of honour, should refuse to sell Cuba to the United States, then, by every law, human and divine, we should be justified in wresting it from Spain if we possess the power.

In private the American minister in Madrid, Soulé, told Washington that 'neither England nor France would be likely to interfere with us'.[24] The British and French governments urged Spain to be cautious and not expel Soulé. The US government also decided to be cautious – it expected to gain Cuba anyway and did not want another war so soon after the one with Mexico.

The major dispute between Britain and the United States was over the recruitment of American mercenaries. Under the 1818 Neutrality Act it was an offence for any power to hire or retain recruits in the United States or for them to proceed outside the United States to be enlisted. On 16 February 1854 the British minister in Washington, John Crampton, was instructed by London to begin recruiting. He took informal legal advice and reported back that all such recruitment would be illegal under American law. The government in London rejected that advice and once again ordered him to start recruiting.

In late March Crampton issued instructions on recruitment. The scheme had to be based on the right of people to leave the country freely. No written agreements could, therefore, be made in the United States and the men would travel to Halifax in Nova Scotia before they were formally recruited. The men were, however, given travel vouchers to get to Halifax and this was probably an illegal inducement in American law. It was also unclear whether advertising for recruits would be legal. In order to distance the British government from these dubious activities, a number of agents were employed. Joseph Howe, a well-known Canadian political figure, spent more than £5,000 establishing a network of local agents. Crampton also enlisted two main agents. The first, Henry Hertz, a Dane, worked in Philadelphia with the British Consul, George Matthews. The second, Max Ströbel, a former Bavarian army officer, worked with the British Consul in New York, Anthony Barclay. Offices were set up in these two cities together with Boston, Baltimore and Cincinatti, a network that was expanded in May 1854 to include Buffalo, Detroit, Chicago and Cleveland.

The American government immediately took action to stop the flow of recruits. Harbours were placed under surveillance and ships leaving for Nova Scotia were searched. The scheme was also unpopular. Sixty Irishmen were signed up on the pretext that they were travelling to Canada to work on railroad construction. On arriving at the base at Halifax, they refused to enlist and were left there, penniless, by the British authorities. The story was well publicised by the Irish newspapers in New York. Overall only 700 men were recruited (none was ever recruited from the offices in Buffalo, Detroit, Cleveland and Chicago) and of these just 135 reached Halifax. Many of the local agents were corrupt and pocketed the enlistment fees or produced fictitious recruits. On 22 June Crampton formally ended the recruitment project. None of the men ever reached Europe.

Even before Crampton ended it, the British scheme was in severe trouble. A number of the agents were arrested by the American authorities, beginning with Hertz on 22 May. The British Consul in Cincinatti, Charles Rowcroft, was arrested. On 15 July Marcy sent instructions to Buchanan in London that he was to demand the closure of the Halifax base, the discharge of all the men who had been enlisted and the punishment of those responsible. For some reason Buchanan did not deliver this message until 2 November. By then the situation had escalated. On 2 September Marcy saw Crampton and told him that he thought British government money was behind the recruitment campaign and that, if this were the case, it would be a serious violation of American neutrality. That Marcy's suspicions were correct was confirmed when the trial of Hertz and Ströbel began on 22 September in Philadelphia. The two men gave plenty of evidence about Crampton's involvement in the scheme and the judge ruled that the provision of travel vouchers was an illegal inducement. Immediately after the end of the trial Marcy sent Buchanan the details of the evidence against Crampton and the others involved, and instructed him to ask the British government to state its position.

The American government was also increasing the diplomatic pressure by allowing groups of freebooters to bombard and then land on the coast of Central America near the site of the proposed canal. In August the government reopened negotiations with Britain over the canal and sought a revision in its favour of the 1850 treaty. The British tried to stall. At the end of 1855, in his annual state-of-the-union message Pierce said, 'this international difficulty can not long remain undetermined without involving in serious danger the friendly relations which it is the interest as well as the duty of both countries to cherish and preserve'. In the face of these threats the British reinforced their naval squadron in the West Indies.

The British did not respond to the American protests over recruiting and on 28 December 1855 Buchanan was instructed by Washington to demand the recall of Crampton and the three Consuls most heavily involved in the scheme – Matthew, Barclay and Rowcroft. In late January 1856 (shortly before leaving to start his campaign for the presidency) Buchanan reported to Washington that, with peace in Europe now imminent, there were real dangers facing the United States:

> The pride of the British people recoils from the idea of terminating the war without having acquired equal glory with the French . . . in this state of affairs, the British people being sore and disappointed and being better prepared for war than they have ever been, Lord Palmerston, whose character is reckless and his hostility to our country well known, will most probably assume a high and defiant attitude on questions pending between the two countries.[25]

In his last message Buchanan reported that relations with Britain 'seem to be approaching a diplomatic if not belligerent rupture'.[26] He expected that if Crampton was expelled from Washington, then he would be asked to leave London and diplomatic relations would be broken off.

In Washington President Pierce asked Congress for extra military spending of $3 million. With the British still refusing to take any action over the recruiting scandal, the American government felt it had no alternative but to act. On 27 May 1856 Crampton was declared *persona non grata* and the three Consuls had their letters of recognition revoked. The British were as cautious as ever about provoking a conflict with the United States – Canada was almost impossible to defend. They decided, now that the war was over, to draw back. In mid-June they told the Americans that they would not break off relations over the expulsion of Crampton. It was a tacit acceptance that they had acted very unwisely and probably illegally.

13

The Baltic: 1855

The naval expedition to the Baltic in 1854 had been despatched in a mood of great optimism. The British hoped that this might prove to be the decisive theatre where the war could be won. The results were disappointing in the extreme – almost nothing was achieved, apart from demonstrating the limitations of naval power. However, some lessons were learnt. It was clear that wooden ships could not attack coastal fortifications successfully. The only possible option was to construct a fleet of small, shallow-draught, armoured gunboats that could operate close to the fortifications and withstand artillery fire.

Preparations for the new campaign

The initial work on these new types of ship was undertaken by the French in July 1854. They carried out trials by covering a wooden vessel with armour plating. These were successful and the Ministry of Marine placed an order for ten shallow-draught, 1,400-ton vessels built (because speed of construction was vital) with green timber. They were steam-powered, had no masts or spars and had to be towed to the point of action. However, there was only enough four-inch-thick armour to equip five ships. The French called these vessels 'floating batteries' and their armour was strong enough to withstand cannon shot. Although based on experience gained in the Baltic, they were intended for use in the Crimea. Three were ready by the autumn of 1855 and saw action during the last stages of the war in the east. The French gave the plans for these ships to the British in return for plans of their mortar ships and gunboats. The British constructed five ships to the French design, but they were under-powered and poorly built. Two ships were towed out to the Crimea in the summer of 1855 but never saw action. A third was destroyed by fire and the other two never left Sheerness Dockyard.

The British gunboats and mortar ships were significantly different from those of the French. The aim was to provide a mass of small armoured ships, each with only one or two heavy guns, so that there would be too many targets for the forts to attack. The first orders for six of these armoured gunboats were placed in June 1854. Twenty more of a slightly improved design were ordered in October and another ninety-eight in early

1855 (this last batch was not finished before the war ended). Some of the ships could operate in as little as four feet of water. The wooden hulls were built in sixteen different yards across the country and then sent to a special dockyard at Haslar near Portsmouth, which had been designed by Isambard Kingdom Brunel, where they were completed. The ships used interchangeable parts, but the main problem was building enough engines. In addition twenty dockyard lighters were converted into mortar ships for bombardment of coastal defences.

The fleet that was sent to the Baltic in the spring of 1855 was better equipped for the conditions than its predecessor. In particular, all ships were steam-powered and there were some fifty gunboats and mortar vessels so that some attack could be mounted on the Russian fortifications. The British sent 105 ships, including eleven battleships and thirty cruisers, under the command of Rear Admiral Sir Richard Dundas. He had been promoted through political patronage (he was son of Lord Melville) and turned out to be as indecisive as his predecessor, Admiral Napier. The French fleet was commanded by Rear Admiral André Penaud, who at least had some experience of conditions in the Baltic – he had been second-in-command of the French fleet in 1854. However, unlike the previous year's campaign, no troops were sent with the fleet and both governments accepted that little would, therefore, be achieved. Operations in the Baltic would be no more than diversionary, designed to tie down Russian forces and give the illusion of activity.

The Russians had also had time to improve their defences. The army in the area had been increased to just over 300,000 men, of whom about one-third were in Finland and another third acted as a 'mobile' reserve. The Russians decided it was impossible to guard the whole of the Finnish coastline and therefore concentrated their forces in the key towns where effective defence was possible – Helsinki, Sveaborg (modern Suomen-linna), Viborg (modern Viipuri) and Turku (modern Åbo). Small forts were simply abandoned as being too weak. Elsewhere the Finnish militia and light cavalry were the only defences. The Russians also employed the German firm of Siemens and Halske to build a telegraph line from Helsinki to St Petersburg, and were able to develop and lay more mines – more than 300 were placed around Kronstadt, with others at Sveaborg.

The early stages of the campaign

The first elements of the fleet did not leave Britain until 28 March, later than the previous year because the exceptionally severe winter in the Baltic meant that the ice was very late in breaking up. The main part of the British fleet left on 4 April and almost immediately the flagship, *Duke of Wellington*, collided with an American merchant ship off Beachy Head and had to return to Portsmouth. Dundas took over the *Nile* as his flagship. The fleet arrived at Kiel on 18 April, visited Copenhagen and finally left for the Baltic on 3 May. It entered the Gulf of Finland just over three weeks later. The French ships left Brest on 26 April and joined up with the British at the beginning of June.

The British ships sailed around the smaller Finnish ports destroying ships, but the level of resistance from the militia was much greater than in 1854. The towns of Kotka and Lovisa were burnt to the ground, but the large-scale destruction of the previous year was not repeated. The blockade was imposed again and was more effective because the new shallow-draught vessels could operate in coastal waters. The allied ships carried out a reconnaissance of the various ports and fortifications of the area, including Reval (Tallinn) and Kronstadt, but found the defences much strengthened. At Kronstadt the British landed briefly on Tolbukin Island, about two miles from the outer defences, and sailed around – the Russian court held a ball on one of their ships to watch the British offshore. On 9 June *Merlin* became the first ship to be damaged by a mine when it was sailing close to the shore investigating the defences of Kronstadt. The allied ships started picking up mines and Captain Sulivan reported what happened when Admiral Sir George Seymour took one to Dundas's flagship:

> They all played with it; and Admiral Seymour took it to his ship, and on the poop had the officers round examining it . . . Some of the officers remarked of the danger of it going off, and Admiral Seymour said 'O no. This is the way it would go off', and shoved the slide in with his finger . . . It instantly exploded, knocking down everyone around it.[1]

The mine contained more than eight pounds of explosive and a number of people were badly injured. Seymour, whose stupidity had caused the incident, lost an eye in the explosion.

The attack on Sveaborg

Having achieved nothing at Kronstadt (it was too well defended), Dundas and Penaud discussed what to do next. They decided to attack Sveaborg (the 'fortress of Sweden') on the islands off Helsinki. The fortifications had been begun in the late 1740s by the Swedes as a direct rival to Kronstadt, but were handed over to the Russians, along with the rest of Finland, in 1809. The Russians had done little new work on the seven islands before 1854. The fortifications were weak – a test firing of a battery in 1854 caused the walls of one fort to collapse. The main defences now were sunken ships that blocked the passages round the islands and the large number of mines – the Russians laid forty-four electrical mines and 950 chemical ones. Dundas and Penaud decided not to risk their main ships. Instead twenty-one gunboats and a similar number of mortar ships were used. The French also erected a small battery on the unoccupied island of Abraham. The allied Admirals did not expect to achieve significant results. The bombardment was designed partly for home consumption and partly as a warning to the Russians about the effectiveness of this new form of naval warfare.

The attack began at 7 a.m. on 9 August and lasted, with interruptions, for three days. Some 6,000 shells were fired. Many fell short, but a number of forts and installations and a large number of wooden houses were destroyed. The Russians fired back, but mainly to improve morale. The only casualty in Helsinki was a nine-year-old girl. A large number of people watched the attack from Observatory Hill in the southern part of the town. The British mortar ships quickly developed serious problems. Most of the new mortars were unable to fire more than thirty rounds and eight of them burst. They had been made by Grissell & Co. at the Regent's Canal Ironworks and the holes that had developed during manufacture had been plugged up with soft lead. By the afternoon of 9 August nearly all the new British ships were out of action, although those with the older 1813 mortars and the French ships were still able to fire.

On 12 August the allies stopped the bombardment and waited to see if the Russian forts were able to fire. The population of Helsinki expected the pause to be a preliminary to an allied landing. Long queues of people formed as they fled to the countryside. But the allies did not even have enough troops to land and destroy the forts, and on 13 August their ships steamed away. Although they made inflated claims about the effectiveness of the attack, it had in practice achieved little. Russian casualties were about fifty killed and roughly three times that number wounded. There were no British deaths, just some sailors wounded. Much of Sveaborg had been destroyed, but it had not been an important Russian naval base even before the attack.

The end of the campaign

In view of the limited success at Sveaborg, Dundas and Penaud abandoned any idea of attacking the more important base of Reval. The British mortar ships were in a bad shape and were towed back to Britain on 17 August. There were a few small operations, ships were intercepted and some undefended towns and forts were attacked, without any significant results. Ships were sent to Bomarsund, the scene of the main engagement in 1854, but it had not been reoccupied by the Russians.

The ships spent the rest of the summer in what was almost a pleasant cruise around the Baltic. The main fleet anchored at Nargen, where the *Duke of Wellington* was damaged yet again when it was hit by a French ship. The British officers spent much of the time on the island playing cricket. In Estonia one of the British commanders, Captain Sulivan, and a few other officers landed to explore the local countryside. They met the local landowner, visited his castle, met his wife who spoke excellent English and had dinner followed by coffee on a terrace in the grounds. At dusk, about 10 p.m., they drove back the three miles to the coast and rejoined their ship. From the middle of September the allied ships began to leave the Baltic, the last departing at the end of October. Dundas was back in Kiel by the middle of November and, after a pleasant three-week stay, left for Spithead where he arrived just before Christmas. The blockade was formally lifted, but a small force of paddle steamers attempted to keep station off the Kattegat to stop any Russian ships entering the North Sea. They normally retired to Hull during the worst of the winter weather. However, on 29 January 1856 *Polyphemus* was driven ashore near the Hansholm lighthouse on the coast of Jutland and twenty-eight men were drowned. This was the only British ship lost during the two Baltic campaigns, even though it had never entered the Baltic.

14

Crimean Spring

During the winter of 1854–55 there was very little military action in the Crimea. The Russians made seven limited sorties out of their defences around Sevastopol and their artillery kept up a steady fire, but the intention was only to wear down the allies. Menshikov did not take any decisive action even against the British, who throughout December and January would have been incapable of offering effective resistance.

Much of the Russian effort was concentrated on building up the defences of the key Malakhov fort that dominated the other defensive positions and the harbour. It was steadily converted into a full bastion with walls, ditches, dugouts, proper powder magazines and large artillery emplacements. It was to become the centrepiece of the fighting around Sevastopol for the next nine months. The Russians and French were also engaged in another standard feature of siege warfare – mining and counter-mining. The Russians did not have any trained mining engineers (the men were trained as they worked) and lacked ventilation equipment and compasses. The men worked in three shifts, but the conditions were dreadful – the head of the mining operations, Captain A. V. Melnikov, had to be sent home on extended sick leave after spending too long underground. By late January 1855 the Russians had dug twenty-two shafts and nearly a mile of tunnels around the Malakhov. They used electricity to detonate their mines (the French fuses were much more unreliable). After packing the tunnels with powder and sandbags, the Russians exploded them on 21 January causing huge flames and smoke in the French trenches. The explosion was backed up by heavy artillery fire. A few days later the French too set off an explosion, but it was only to destroy their own shafts – they felt they could not defeat the Russian miners. Throughout the rest of the siege mining continued on a limited scale, but it did not have a decisive impact.

February 1855

As the worst of the winter weather in the Crimea passed, military operations became feasible. The condition of the British army improved with the better weather and as the supplies, ordered after the disaster of the 'Great Storm' in mid-November, began to arrive. Food was plentiful, winter clothing abundant and the supply lines worked effectively as the railway from Balaklava began to operate.

EYE-WITNESS
THE BRITISH ARMY IMPROVES

William Russell, *The Times* war correspondent

22 January: 'I rejoice heartily to think that before severe cold sets in again the army will be prepared to meet it with better chance of success than before. Warm clothing is arriving in great quantities, and the remnant of our army will soon be all comfortably clad, or it will be their own faults. The great-coats, boots, jerseys, and mits furnished by the Government to officers and men, are of excellent quality, and the distribution, though late, is most liberal. A fur cloak, a pea-jacket, a fur cap, a pair of boots, two jerseys, two pairs of drawers, and two pairs of socks, are to be given to each officer.'

19 February: 'The drying winds continue, and the plateau to the south of Sebastopol can be traversed easily on horse or foot, even at the bottom of the ravines. With this fine weather the good spirits and energies of our men have returned . . . the men get all they want; provisions are abundant; hay has arrived and fresh vegetables have been sent up to the front to check the scurvy. The progress of the railroad is extraordinary.'

2/6 March: 'We had had only a few warm days, and yet the soil, wherever a flower had a chance of springing up, poured forth multitudes of snowdrops, crocuses and hyacinths . . . The aspect of Balaklava was greatly altered for the better . . . the cesspools and collections of utter abomination in the streets were filled up; and quicklime was laid down in the streets and lanes, and around the houses . . . the dead horses were collected and buried beneath lime and earth . . . The railway, which swept right through the main street . . . extended its lines by night and by day. The harbour, crowded as it was, had assumed a certain appearance of order . . . Fresh provisions were becoming abundant . . . A great quantity of mules and ponies, with a staff of drivers from all parts of the world was collected together and lightened the toils of the troops . . . The public and private stores of warm clothing exceeded the demand.'

Temple Godman, officer

2 February: 'I do not think I shall want a box every fortnight, we are living in comparative luxury, being so near the ships, and with so many parcels.'

26 March: 'Some keep chicken for fresh eggs and have regular hen roosts.

Round our huts and tents many have small gardens, with juniper trees, snowdrops and crocuses.'

George Lawson, doctor
'I am in right good health, living on the fat of the land . . . Shiploads of good things are continually arriving, and from them we are able to buy all we can desire; and although our servant is unable to make fine dishes, yet we can buy them already cooked and only to be warmed before eating. Sherry, very decent, can be had at about 3s a doz. I am daily expecting the arrival of a goat which I have ordered to be purchased for me, for the purpose of supplying me with fresh milk every morning . . . I saw a fine fat pig about to be killed on board one of the transports, and in a luxurious mood I purchased one half of the animal.'

Roger Fenton, war photographer
On 28 March he dined with Captain Holder at the Guards Camp. 'We had gravy soup, fresh fish caught in the bay, liver and bacon fried, a shoulder of mutton, pancakes with quince preserve, cheese, stout, sherry and cigars.'

However, the British army was small and unable to take part in operations – the fighting was undertaken by the Russian, French and Ottoman armies. Around Sevastopol the Russians were able to hold their own in the low-level fighting – the French attack on 24 February was repulsed, with the French suffering more than 200 casualties.

The most significant encounter took place near the spot where the allied armies had landed in mid-September – Evpatoriya. During the winter it was held by only about 300 French troops, with the ships wrecked during the 'Great Storm' (*Henri IV* and *Pluton*) acting as defensive batteries. In early 1855 the allies realised that the Russians had removed nearly all of their troops from the Principalities and therefore decided that the Ottoman army under Omer Pasha should be moved from Varna using British transports. During January nearly 40,000 troops, 11,000 horses and 111 guns were taken across the Black Sea to Evpatoriya with the loss of just one horse. This major redeployment caused the Russians real anxiety. They thought that the Ottoman army would move inland to cut the Simferopol–Perekop road – the main supply route for the army in the Crimea. Menshikov moved about 19,000 troops (including 600 Greek volunteers) under General S. A. Khrulev into the area by the middle of February.

On 15 February a Polish deserter told Omer Pasha about Russian plans and the Ottoman army was put on the alert. The Russian attack two days later was a disaster. After a preliminary bombardment the Russian field artillery was overpowered and knocked out by the French naval guns. When the Russian infantry attacked, they found it almost impossible to cross a deep water-filled ditch and could not climb the defensive wall around the Ottoman positions. The attack was called off and the Russian troops retreated back into the interior of the Crimea. The Russians suffered about 750 casualties, the Ottomans about half that number. However, the Ottomans found it difficult to exploit their success and advance out of Evpatoriya because they lacked sufficient cavalry to deal with the Russian Cossacks.

Russian and allied reorganisation

The Russian failure at Evpatoriya was the last straw as far as the Russian government was concerned. Menshikov was recalled after the long series of disasters he had overseen and was replaced by Gorchakov, who arrived from Bessarabia in early March. Immediately on his arrival he wrote to the Minister of War. He tried to protect his position by saying that he was unimpressed by what he had seen and that victory in the Crimea was not possible: 'It is a deadly heritage that I have received . . . I am exposed to being turned, cut off, and perhaps broken, if the enemy has a little good sense and decision.'[1]

Luckily for the Russians, the allies demonstrated their continuing inability to plan or conduct successful operations. In early February Canrobert and Raglan agreed that they could do nothing other than continue the siege (except that it was not a siege, because the allies could not fully invest and isolate Sevastopol). Napoleon's confidence in Canrobert was beginning to evaporate rapidly, and on 10 February General Pélissier was moved from Algeria with the intention that he should supplant Canrobert at some point. Napoleon also sent out the engineer General Adolphe Niel, an expert in siege warfare, to direct some of the operations. Under his influence it was decided that the British army was now so reduced in numbers, and its effectiveness so low, that even more of the line would have to be taken over by the French. The French army was reorganised into two Corps. The 1st, under Pélissier, held the left sector of the siege line, which had always been a French responsibility. The 2nd, under Bosquet, was responsible for the observation line into the interior and for the right sector of the siege line opposite the key fortresses of the Malakhov and the Little Redan. The British were left with the small central sector in front of the Great Redan. On 12 March an allied war council agreed that 12,000 Egyptian troops would be moved from

Constantinople to Evpatoriya where they would act as a garrison. This would release 20,000 troops under Omer Pasha to join up with the French at Kamiesh.

Despite (or perhaps because of) their inferior position among the armies conducting the siege, the British continued to demonstrate their hostility to their allies. Raglan objected to Ottoman troops moving into the siege lines because he thought they were dirty. In London the new Secretary of State for War, Panmure, thought – despite all the evidence to the contrary – that the French were poor troops who did not yet 'possess that moral superiority over the Russians which our troops have established'.[2] In late March Panmure told Raglan of his views about the French:

> I have my suspicions of them, and I only hope you will not be induced to give way to them one inch more than you consider right. It is all very well to talk of the necessity of keeping a good understanding with the French, but I have no notion of doing so to our own risk.[3]

In the Crimea there was dissension between the commanders. Canrobert was ready to order a major attack on the Russian defences on 12, 20 and 23 March, but Raglan refused to agree, claiming that his forces were not ready. Despite their reluctance to attack, the British for some reason thought Canrobert was indecisive. They also felt that the French were incompetent, not as brave as the British and jealous of British military success (just what success they had in mind is unclear).

Meanwhile the British and French were trying to agree on strategy at a higher level. On 22 January Napoleon wrote to Cowley, once again suggesting a rationalisation of military effort and command structure. The British contributed about four-fifths of allied sea power and therefore should have command of the allied navies. The French contributed about the same proportion of the allied armies and therefore should take over command of land operations. The British once again refused – they could never accept a French command over their small army. They were also worried about rumours that Napoleon would go out to the Crimea to take command of the French armies in person. This too was seen as very damaging to British prestige.

Some of the strategic questions were settled during the four-day state visit to Britain by Napoleon and the Empress Eugénie in mid-April. Queen Victoria, who had originally regarded the couple as terrible social upstarts, was captivated by them both. Napoleon was invested with the Order of the Garter and there was a military review, a ball at Windsor Castle, a lunch at the Guildhall, a visit to the opera to see *Fidelio* and a trip to the Crystal

Palace on its new site in south London. In this crowded social programme it proved possible to fit in a War Council at Windsor on 18 April. On the British side it was attended by Palmerston, Prince Albert, Clarendon, Panmure, Cowley, Burgoyne and Hardinge. Napoleon was accompanied by Vaillant and Walewski. The British and French leaders agreed that it was necessary to fight a mobile campaign in the Crimea. The siege was to be maintained by about 60,000 troops while a three-pronged attack would be made on the interior. About 30,000 Ottoman troops would move from Evpatoriya to threaten the Russian right flank; 50,000 troops (about half of which would be British) would be commanded by Raglan and would take the Mackenzie Heights on the route to Simferopol. Meanwhile a major French army would move by sea and land to Alusha in the east of the Crimea, attack Simferopol and join up with the British forces. Once this was completed and the Russian field army defeated, the supply routes into Sevastopol could be closed off and the city captured. This was a bold plan, but it was never carried out. The Ottoman troops were already being redeployed from Evpatoriya and both Canrobert and Raglan objected and refused to carry out orders. They preferred to carry on with the siege. Even the opening of the telegraph line from Varna to Balaklava on 25 April, bringing London and Paris into direct touch with the Crimea for the first time, could not help impose the agreed strategy on the allied commanders on the spot.

The attack on Sevastopol

While the Russians were turning the Malakhov into the centrepiece of their defences in front of Sevastopol, they did not have either the time or the available effort to take over the small 'Green Hill' (*Mamelon Vert* to the French) that lay between it and the French lines. It remained in 'no man's land' in mid-February when Bosquet decided to capture it. The night before the attack the Russians built the Selenghinsky Redoubt on the north slope of the Inkerman Ridge. It provided excellent cover for both the Malakhov and the *Mamelon Vert*. A French attack on the new redoubt was repulsed on 24 February. Four nights later the Russians built another redoubt, the Volhynian near the Selenghinsky. On the night of 10–11 March they built the Kamchatka Lunette on the top of the *Mamelon Vert*. The Russians had acted far more decisively in building a set of impressive defensive works that made the capture of the Malakhov much more difficult. For the rest of March there was a series of attacks and counter-attacks between the French and the Russians in which neither side was able to secure a decisive advantage. On 17 March the French captured five pits in front of the *Mamelon Vert*. Five nights later a Russian attack with fifteen battalions penetrated the allied lines because the British provided inadequate protection to the French flank, even though both Canrobert and Bosquet had warned them of the forthcoming attack. The Russians suffered about 1,300 casualties, the French 642 and the British eighty-five.

It was clear by early April that the allies were still a very long way from capturing Sevastopol. However, over the last couple of months the allied artillery had been significantly strengthened. They now had more than 500 guns (including 130 large siege mortars) which was four times greater than in October 1854 when the bombardment had been such a dismal failure. Large stocks of ammunition had also been accumulated. However, the Russians had also had time to strengthen their defences, but although they had some 1,000 guns, these were of limited firepower and ammunition stocks were low. On 2 April at a council of war the allied commanders decided to launch yet another unimaginative bombardment of the Sevastopol defences. They were confident that they now had enough strength to succeed. The last phase of the operation would be an infantry attack to capture the city.

The artillery bombardment began early on the morning of 9 April and continued for nine days until it was called off. Every night the Russians repaired the damage sustained during the day, and no significant effect was achieved by the long bombardment. During the attack the allies fired 168,700 shells into Sevastopol and the Russians replied with just under half that number. Throughout the attack the Russians were extremely short of ammunition and had to shift stockpiles from one fort to another as necessary. Their biggest guns were limited to fifteen rounds a day and the fifty smallest to just five rounds. By 14 April each battery was ordered to keep a 'final reserve' of fifty rounds for each gun for use during the expected allied assault. Overall the casualties during the nine-day attack were surprisingly small. The Russians lost 6,000 men, mainly from repairing the damage each night and from keeping reserves near the front line in case of attack. The French suffered 1,500 casualties, the British 260. The second allied assault on Sevastopol was as great a failure as the first in October. The only argument in its favour was that, in a war of attrition, the allies were more likely to win than the Russians.

EYE-WITNESS
REACTION TO THE APRIL BOMBARDMENT OF SEVASTOPOL

Temple Godman

12 April: 'This is the fourth day of the second bombardment, and we seem to be doing *no good*. The enemy keeps up his fire well, no one is in the least sanguine as to the result. Some talk of storming, but I hardly think this likely . . . If the bombardment fails, which there is every reason to suppose it will . . . I fear we shall never do anything so long as Sebastopol can communicate with the country.'

Colonel Charles Windham

'How true it is that "War" is usually a series of mistakes. The conduct of the Allies, since we arrived in this country, has been one continued piece of blundering stupidity . . . We have now fired upon the place for several days, have lost many hundreds of men, and, unless we follow it up with bloody assaults at different places, we shall never take it; and, should we lose a large amount of men in doing so (which is more than probable), we shall have thrown away more life and more money, for a useless object, than was ever done before.'

George Lawson

15–16 April: 'It is now almost a week since we opened fire with all our guns . . . and not withstanding that the cannonading has not ceased . . . Sebastopol remains untaken . . . the town . . . appears but little damaged . . . From all the works of the Russians there is a continuous line of smoke; one can hardly imagine so much ammunition being consumed and yet no decided effect produced . . . Everyone here is amazed at the little damage we are doing, and disgusted at seeing the termination of the siege almost as far off as ever.'

Frederick Dallas, officer

13–15 April: 'I am sorry to say that upon carefully looking over the town & its Batteries & works, that I never saw them look better in my life & to this day I see no alteration in the place, nor is there any material injury done to their works though we have thrown in an almost fabulous number of shots and shells . . . The Russians have fired well and steadily (very few shells) but have knocked about our batteries considerably . . . What we are going to do I cannot conceive. I have no doubt but that this attempt will be as fruitless as the last & I can hardly believe that we shall begin again . . . the town is just as near being ours as it was 6 months ago.'

20 April: 'Our second siege must now be numbered among the things that have been. It is over & has been a more ridiculous & disgusting farce than the first. The Russian Batteries & works are as good & strong as ever . . . We are no nearer our end than we were months ago. There is one universal feeling of disgust and humiliation amongst us at this second ridiculous exhibition . . . We are now, as we have been for months, ourselves the besieged in our corner of the Crimea. We have a most splendid army thrown away by our chiefs, either by their dissensions or their incompetency.'

Lieutenant William Young

'I do not know when we are to get out of this place or take Sebastopol. I am heartily sick of the trenches, new batteries, new mortars and I don't know what else, and the Russians as bad if not worse than ever. There is no honour or glory to be got in the trenches . . . I would ten thousand times sooner take the field and march about with my knapsack on my back, and fight a couple of decent battles in the field . . . I say Sebastopol never will be taken until invested, and where are the men to do that?'

Captain Pyotr Lesli, with the Russian army in Sevastopol

'No one can understand what their aim was in opening up another bombardment; it seems that experience has shown that it is not all that easy to make our batteries fall silent, and if they want, having knocked out our batteries, to go for a storming, then they've a long wait ahead.'

Roger Fenton

29 April: 'As for taking the town on the present system, it is a perfect farce. The Mamelon, the most advanced of the Russian earthworks, is as neat in its external finish as if a ball or shell had never touched it. The French make much fuss and seem to attack every night, but one generally finds each morning that the Russians have made some slight advance towards them.'

The first expedition to Kerch

The stalemate in the Crimea caused a number of reactions among the British leadership. The Royal Navy disliked its inferior position and being reduced to ferrying troops and supplies around the Black Sea. With the small Russian fleet either sunk or in port, there was no prospect of a decisive naval encounter. It reverted to the traditional British policy of advocating amphibious operations away from the main theatre of operations. Many in the army and the political leadership in London resented playing second fiddle to the French – an inevitable result of the fact that the French had four times as many troops in the Crimea as the British. These harsh facts had been made very apparent at the War Council meeting at Windsor. The President of the Board of Control, Sir Charles Wood, told a Cabinet colleague in early May:

> All that can be done now is to aid and assist in the greater operations which I suppose they [the French] will conduct with their con-centrated force. I cannot help wishing that we had a distinct operation in which we (the English I mean) could take our own part and responsibility.[4]

In the Crimea the local commanders had devised just such an operation: an attack on the town of Kerch on the eastern tip of the Crimea near the Sea of Azov.

Much of the preliminary work for this operation was undertaken by a civilian, Charles Cattley, who had been acting since the summer of 1854 as a sort of intelligence officer to Raglan. Cattley was born in St Petersburg in 1817 into a family of British timber merchants. From 1841 until the outbreak of war he was Vice-Consul at Kerch and travelled widely across the Crimea. He was expelled by the Russians in April 1854, but was forced to travel overland to St Petersburg and did not arrive in London until mid-July. Newcastle sent him out to Raglan in Varna at the beginning of August – Cattley kept his salary as a Consul (£200 a year) and the War Office paid him a guinea a day plus expenses. He acted as an interpreter and also interrogated prisoners and deserters and gradually built up quite an accurate picture of Russian army strengths and dispositions in the Principalities and the Crimea. Cattley, who obviously knew the area well, argued for the importance of Kerch from an early stage. On 20 January he sent Raglan a paper on the 'Sea of Azof' (sic). It argued that this was the key area for Russian supplies from Rostov and the Don area, which had to cross the Sea of Azov to reach the Crimea. Cattley asserted that if Kerch were captured, then the Russians would have to rely on very inferior roads, 'being merely tracks across the steppe', and that this would badly affect supplies, both food and ammunition, reaching Sevastopol.[5] Cattley's assessment was reasonably accurate, but it neglected other routes in the area, in particular the Changiar bridge across the Putrid Sea, which was sixty miles closer to Sevastopol. Failure to attack here would seriously reduce the effectiveness of any operation against Kerch.

No operation at Kerch was possible until the spring because of the weather, but a reconnaissance expedition was sent out under Major Gordon and Lieutenant-Colonel Désant. They made hydrographic soundings and produced drawings of the fortifications and the coastal defence batteries. They noted that the area was blocked by about thirty or forty sunken ships, but that this barrier had been badly disrupted by the winter storms. They thought that a force of about 9,000 troops ought to be sufficient to capture the town. Canrobert was unenthusiastic, believing that available forces should be concentrated against Sevastopol. After the failure of the April bombardment he reluctantly agreed to the attack and provided three times as many troops as the British.

The expedition to attack Kerch set sail from Balaklava and Kamiesh just after 6.30 p.m. on 3 May. It consisted of a flotilla of fifty-six ships (mainly British) carrying 7,500 French and 2,500 British troops. Three hours after the ships left a telegram arrived at Canrobert's headquarters from Paris, using the newly opened route via Varna. It contained the instructions for the strategy agreed at the Windsor conference. Canrobert was to take the offensive as soon as reinforcements arrived from Constantinople; meanwhile his forces were to remain concentrated and were not to be dissipated elsewhere. (Paris did not know about the plan for the attack on Kerch.) Canrobert and Raglan met for three hours that night to discuss what to do. Raglan convinced Canrobert to carry on with the Kerch expedition. After their meeting a second telegram arrived from Paris. At 2.15 a.m. Canrobert changed his mind and a fast boat was sent after the flotilla. The French commander was ordered to return and the British had no alternative but to do the same.

In the aftermath of this fiasco relations between the French and the British disintegrated badly. Raglan received no orders from London – they were not sent by telegram and the letter from the War Office took several weeks to arrive. Because he had no instructions, Raglan refused to prepare any orders for the joint operation agreed at Windsor – the three-pronged attack aimed at Simferopol. As the tension mounted, Canrobert asked to be relieved of his command on 17 May. Napoleon accepted the resignation immediately and Pélissier took over two days later. He was well regarded in the army and had a deserved reputation for being blunt, aggressive and determined. He was far less worried than Canrobert about obeying Napoleon's instructions from Paris. Pélissier immediately reorganised the French command structure. A corps of reserve was created – it was mainly made up of the Imperial Guard, which had been arriving a brigade at a time since early in 1855. The corps was commanded by General Regnault de Saint-Jean d'Angely. Canrobert refused to take over the 1st Corps, which would have been a straight swap with Pélissier, and opted instead to return to his old division (the 1st), which was part of Bosquet's 2nd Corps.

The second expedition to Kerch

Pélissier was bound to be the dominant force in creating allied strategy because he commanded 120,000 troops and the next-biggest army was that of the Ottomans under Omer Pasha, with a strength of about 55,000 men. The British army under Raglan consisted of 32,000 troops and the Sardinian army was 17,000 strong. The day after his appointment Pélissier held an allied war council. Raglan still had no orders about the Simferopol operation (more than a month after the Windsor conference) and so it was agreed that the siege should continue. This was Pélissier's view, too – he was not keen on mobile operations in the centre of the Crimea. He decided to placate Raglan by agreeing to revive the Kerch expedition. Omer Pasha wanted an all-Ottoman force for the attack, but the Ottomans were only allowed to provide the garrison that would remain behind after the capture of the town.

The second expedition was larger than the first – there were 7,000 French troops, 5,000 from the Ottoman army and 3,000 British troops. The British provided the majority of the sixty ships involved. The ships sailed on 22 May and, after a diversion off Kaffa (to try and deceive the Russians into believing they were about to land), arrived near Kerch on 24 May. The troops landed on a beach about five miles from the town, and Kerch and Yenikale were captured without resistance as the small Russian garrisons retreated. The Russians destroyed the main fortifications and the allied troops the rest of the batteries. Both towns were sacked by allied troops.

EYE-WITNESS
THE EXPEDITION TO KERCH

Roger Fenton

Civilians were not allowed on the expedition, but Fenton went, on Raglan's express orders, as an 'engineer officer'.

'Got on board the "Bahiana", a steamer on which officers of the staff were to embark, and then set myself to watch what was going on. Immense excitement and confusion: people getting into the wrong ship and being knocked out, horses being hoisted on board and stowed in the hold; and on deck officers' servants arranging their masters' luggage, commissariat mule-drivers, soldiers and sailors tumbling over one another . . . Next morning we got out of the harbour, waited outside for a ship we were to tow, and then set off with it along the south coast of the Crimea. The following

---

morning we were off Cape Takli . . . [after the troops landed, Fenton and others followed in the late afternoon] . . . What a sight! In the morning, a beautiful beach covered with long rough grass and wild flowers . . . Now the beach was strewn with baggage of every description, horses were splashing through the water to the shore, men dressed in every kind of garment that was ever worn, were walking about, scrambling, swearing, shouting and laughing – a vast deal of the latter. Servants were keeping guard over their masters' baggage horses. [Fenton camped for the night and advanced the next day with the French troops.] . . . In about four miles we came to Kertch, a very pretty town beautifully situated along the bay. All the authorities were gone and the best houses had their shutters closed, but groups of Tartars were standing by the side of the streets, taking off their hats and smiling most obsequiously . . . sentries were placed at the doors of the principal houses and public buildings and the army marched through the town without stopping. [On the far side of the town] the country was covered with stragglers. Turkish and French, but principally the latter, intent on plunder. We could see the French rushing through the plantations into the houses and coming out again laden with fowls, geese, looking-glasses, chairs, ladies dresses and everything useful or useless that they could lay their hands on. As they got to the contents of wine casks they got more outrageous discharging their muskets right and left at fowls, pigs and birds. [Fenton and a British doctor saved an old peasant's only cow.] . . . As we got on, the disorder became greater, the stragglers were more drunk, the cries and shouts more savage, the firing of muskets and the whizzing of shot past our ears more continual, and it was evident that all control over the French army was gone. [At Yenikale] . . . There was a terrible scene: French, Turks, and I am sorry to say a few Highlanders, were breaking into the houses, smashing the windows, dragging out everything portable and breaking what they could not carry away. The inhabitants had all fled with the exception of the Tartars and a few Russians, amongst whom was the priest; from the treatment of those that were left, it was lucky they had . . . During the night the French set some houses in the town on fire and a fatigue party of English had to go down and put it out, which they did by pulling the houses down on each side of them.'

William Russell
Describing the destruction by British and French troops of the museum at Kerch: 'The floor of the museum is covered for several inches in depth with the débris of broken glass, of vases, urns, statuary, the precious dust of their contents, and charred bits of wood and bone, mingled with the fresh

splinters of the shelves, desks, and cases in which they had been
preserved. Not a single bit of anything that could be broken or burnt any
smaller had been exempt from reduction by hammer or fire.'

Once Kerch had been captured, allied ships operated in the Sea of Azov
and bombarded Taganrog and Yeisk. Storehouses and port installations
were burnt down, 246 merchant vessels were destroyed, together with
about £150,000 worth of flour and grain. Allied ships also sailed to the
Circassian coast to attack several ports, but found the main town of Anapa
deserted – it had been evacuated by the Russians on 5 May. The French
began withdrawing their troops from Kerch on 13 June (three weeks after
the attack) and two days later the main force departed. The allies left
behind a garrison of just over 10,000 troops (mainly Ottoman) in the
towns of Kerch and Yenikale. Nothing of significance happened in the area
for the rest of the war.

Allied control of the Sea of Azov was important, but not decisive. It
certainly made the movement of supplies by the Russians into the Crimea
much more difficult, but the overall impact was limited. Sevastopol was
well supplied with food after the 1854 harvest and there were no shortages
before the city fell in September 1855. Indeed, allied troops found vast
stores still in the city – 330,000 pounds of flour, 300,000 pounds of wheat,
one million pounds of black bread and 132,000 pounds of salted meat.
There were some other shortages in the summer of 1855, in particular of
nails and timber for fortifications, but the main problem was the lack of
ammunition and gunpowder, and the Kerch expedition had no impact in
this area. The main instigator of the expedition, Cattley, had to admit, in
early July, that the attack had not had the impact he expected:

> There does not appear to be any want of provision so far among the
> troops in the Crimea. A regular train of transports has been formed
> from Simpheropol to Perekop & further north, by which a regular
> supply of provisions & ammunition & etc. are brought up, the same
> arrangements are made as to the road by Tchangiar.[6]

Where the attack was important was in tying down Russian troops. The
garrisons at Kerch and Yenikale meant that the Russians used about
34,000 men as covering troops and in protecting their supply routes
through Perekop and Changiar from attack. This was almost a quarter of
their army in the Crimea.

Napoleon III was less than impressed with this unauthorised operation.

He told Pélissier on 30 May, 'I am glad that it was successful; but nevertheless I can't help regarding as *fatal* anything which today tends to scatter your forces.' He made it clear that he wanted a defeat of the Russian field army in the centre of the Crimea, followed by the full investment of Sevastopol, its capture and destruction and an evacuation of the Crimea. 'I leave you master of the choice of methods; but as for the general course, you must follow the explicit orders which I give you.' He concluded, 'You must reassemble all your forces and lose no time in striking a decisive blow.'[7] On 3 June Napoleon sent a crystal-clear set of instructions to Pélissier:

> I order you positively not to persist at all with the siege without having completely invested the place. You are then to consult Lord Raglan and Omar Pasha to insure the most effective offensive, be it by the Tchernaya or against Simpheropol. In laying out the course to follow, we leave both of you the widest latitude on the means that you employ.[8]

Pélissier ignored the order, claiming that the telegraph from Paris was not working properly. He was determined to continue the siege and capture Sevastopol without defeating the Russian field army.

EYE-WITNESS
THE BRITISH PRISONERS AT VORONEZH PLAN TO ESCAPE

George Newman, foot soldier

Newman was being held at Voronezh, where he was teaching English to some local ladies. He knew of the expedition to Kerch and of allied control of the Sea of Azov from English papers that the ladies took. He was also able to look at some of their maps to plan his escape – his friend Thomas King of the 4th Light Dragoons intended to join him.

'My plan was to steal as much black bread as possible and conceal it in a wood about 4 versts from the town and on the banks of the river. I chose black bread because of its durability and cheapness. I also intended to have bought a small keg, of which there were plenty in the town, to keep water in, should I be fortunate enough to reach the sea. I intended also to have bought some old Russian clothing and to have left the house privately about 1 o'clock and gone to the river and stole one of the skiffs, then row to the wood and take my provisions, and then made the best way onwards, travelling at night only and hiding myself and boat during the day in the long

---

rushes in the stream; or if there should be none, I could sink the little boat in the shallow water close to the shore and hide myself and the oars in some place on shore. I knew I could not take the wrong route as the stream always flows the one way – to the Sea of Asoff, there being no tide. After reaching the sea I intended to trust to providence to fall in with some English or French ship or gunboat. As there was no such thing now as calling the roll of prisoners in the house, I was sure of having two or three days start before I was missed, and I thought they would not think of the river. The only difficulties I could see were the chance of discovery when passing those large towns on the banks of the Don.'

The renewed attack on Sevastopol

By early June 1855 the allies held a decisive numerical superiority. In total they had about 225,000 troops in the Crimea compared with a garrison of about 50,000 in Sevastopol. The Russians had another 21,000 men in the field army in the rear of the allied positions and more troops in other areas of the Crimea. The problem was whether the allies could deploy their much greater strength effectively.

While the attack on Kerch was under way there was a series of small-scale battles around the siege lines in front of Sevastopol. French troops attacked Russian outposts at Chorgun village and occupied the Fedyukhin Hills. The Russians also evacuated the redoubts they had captured at the beginning of the battle of Balaklava some six months earlier. Sardinian troops reinforced the positions on the French right around Gasfort Hill. These operations did much to secure the rear of the allied armies from immediate attack. In the siege lines themselves French attacks on their far left on 22–23 May captured the Russian trenches in front of the Quarantine and Central Bastions. The fighting in the area was very tough and the French captured and lost the trenches five times before they secured full control. Casualties were heavy – the French lost 1,500 men and the Russians twice that number.

EYE-WITNESS
INSIDE SEVASTOPOL

Captain Ershov, Russian artillery officer

Allied cannon balls and unexploded shells were collected, often by children, and handed in for money. 'I was struck by the grateful appearance of one boy aged about twelve, who had dragged in four pounds of bullets he had collected in a sack. I began to question him and found out that he was the son of a night-watchman who had been killed by a cannon-ball in the first bombardment on 17 October, that his mother was ill and bed-ridden, and his ten-year old sister was badly injured by a rock, when a bomb exploded a week ago and was now bed-ridden too.'

Captain Pyotr Lesli

'The saddest thing of all was that to every one of our shots, they would answer with ten. Our factories could not keep up with manufacturing the amount of ammunition that we required in order to do at least some harm to the enemy; and moreover, transport on carts was much more cumbersome than by steamship which is the method the Allies used to bring them everything.'

Leo Tolstoy, battery commander

'The large, high-ceilinged chamber, lit only by the four or five candles the surgeons used on their rounds of inspection, was literally full. Stretcher parties were constantly arriving with casualties, setting them down one beside the other on the floor – which was already so closely packed that the wretched men were jostling one another and smearing one another with their blood – and then leaving to fetch more. The pools of blood that were visible wherever there was a vacant space, the fevered breathing of the several hundreds of men and the sweating of the stretcher-bearers combined to produce a characteristic thick, heavy, stinking fetor, in which the surgeons' candles bleakly glimmered from various corners of the room. A murmur of groans, sighs and crepitations, broken now and again by a bloodcurdling scream, ran throughout the entire area. The Sisters, with their calm faces that expressed not the futile, morbidly tearful kind of sympathy that might have been expected of women, but an active, no-nonsense and practical concern, strode to and fro among the wounded men, bearing medicine, water, bandages and lint, their uniforms flashing white against the blood-stained shirts and greatcoats. Gloomy-faced surgeons in their rolled-up shirtsleeves knelt beside wounded men while an apothecary assistant held up the candle, pushing their fingers into bullet wounds and searching them, or turning over severed limbs that still hung by a thread, in spite of the terrible groans and entreaties of the sufferer . . . A crowd of some forty soldiers who were acting as stretcher-bearers and were waiting for patched up casualties to take to hospital or corpses to take to the chapel, stood at the doorway observing this scene in silence; now and then one or other of them would heave a deep sigh.

Pélissier decided in early June that the main attack should be aimed at the Malakhov – the key position in the Russian defences. However, before this could be done it would be necessary to capture the new forts that the Russians had constructed earlier in the year. A plan was drawn up by Bosquet and agreed by Pélissier and Raglan. The aim was to batter down the defences and then capture the Kamchatka and Volhynian Redoubts and the *Mamelon Vert*. The attack began with a sustained artillery barrage directed at the three positions, which lasted for almost twenty-four hours. This stopped the Russians from repairing the defences overnight. By late in the afternoon of 6 June most of the Russian defences were in ruins – the walls had collapsed and the guns were out of action. The Russians moved up eight infantry battalions as reinforcements before the expected attack, but they were spread too thinly to have any real impact.

At 6 p.m. the signal was given for the infantry to attack. The French had about 400 yards of open ground to cross under heavy fire, but did so successfully. They captured the two redoubts (Kamchatka and Volhynian) and the *Mamelon Vert*. From the last position the Zouaves pursued the fleeing Russians towards the Malakhov. Under very heavy fire they jumped into a seven-foot-deep moat in front of the bastion and could not get out. A Russian counter-attack, including the detonation of a mine inside the Kamchatka position, drove the French back. The Russians briefly regained this redoubt, but another French attack retook it. In their sector British troops occupied the Quarries.

EYE-WITNESS
THE ATTACK ON SEVASTOPOL: EARLY JUNE 1855

Roger Fenton
8 June: 'The bombardment of Sebastopol recommenced the day before yesterday at three in the afternoon . . . all the batteries on our side began

to send forth puffs of white smoke, and soon the air was ringing with the increasing din. It was seven minutes before the Russian guns replied. The fire was far more rapid than the last time and the guns heavier and nearer the town, so that before evening it was very plain that many of the enemy's guns were silenced and their works much knocked about . . . [The next day] I went down to the edge of the ravine down which the troops were to march to the trenches before the attack. The French columns were approaching, Zouaves leading; as they drew near, our soldiers not on duty stood as a hedge on either side and cheered each regiment as they passed. Most of the French seemed wild with excitement, though some looked very anxious, and well they might, for it was certain that many of those voices cheering so loudly would be still in death before the sun had set . . . There was no place where the English attack in the quarries could be seen, so I went up to the look-out of our three-mortar battery to watch the French assault on the Mamelon . . . At last with our glasses we could see the French troops creeping along the inside of their advanced trenches . . . A rocket went up from the Victoria Redoubt on our right, and immediately every gun in our trenches and in the French lines began to vomit out a stream of shot and shell . . . This fire lasted, as far as I can remember, ten minutes or a quarter of an hour . . . Then the French began to swarm across their own trenches and rush up the hillside to the Mamelon. There was a sharp musketry fire for a few minutes and then I saw first one or two, then half a dozen, and then scores on the top of the parapet and leaping into the interior . . . Soon we saw them engaging on the other side and rushing up to the Malakoff: well done the French! Then, however, we saw that there was a check: instead of climbing the parapet as at the Mamelon, they spread themselves out in the front and kept firing away without advancing. From the interior, globes of fire, bursting with a thousand sparkles, were constantly hurled amongst them, rifles spat out their fire, and one or two guns still fit for use ploughed their ranks. Their line got thinner, I saw fellows stealing away back to the Mamelon, and in a few minutes the attacking force seemed to have melted away to nothing. There was a slight pause, but while congratulating each other that at least the Mamelon was taken, musketry was heard on the other side of it and I saw something like a dark serpent coming up the hill leaving the Russian trenches. While we were trying to believe this was a French reinforcement, the stragglers began coming out of the Mamelon, then a crowd and then the whole body were hurrying down the hill. The breastwork of the Mamelon was crowded with Russians firing into their retreating enemy . . . After a pause of half an hour during which we were all exceedingly distressed at the defeat the French had sustained, a trumpet

> sounded the *pas de charge*. Again a swarm of men issued from the lines
> and advanced to the attack, there was a short but firm fire at the edge of
> the parapet, and then we thought we could see one of the figures on the
> parapet against a blue sky waving a flag and beckoning the assailants on,
> and soon a few men were seen jumping into the inside. By degrees the
> parapet was clear but the fire inside seemed gradually to retreat; it was
> evident the French had retaken the fort.'

Overall the allied attack on the evening of 6 June was very successful. All three of the key positions around the Malakhov were captured and were rapidly turned into batteries – the Russians did not have enough ammunition to stop the allies doing this. The allies were now in a very good position from which to launch an attack on the key points of the Russian defences – the Malakhov itself and the Great Redan. However, the casualties in the operation were high. The French lost 5,500 men, the Russians roughly the same number. British losses were relatively small, at just under 700 men. After the attack Napoleon refused to send congratulations to the troops involved until Pélissier asked him to do so. Napoleon replied on 14 June, making clear his continuing dissatisfaction at the refusal to carry out his instructions:

> I wished before sending congratulations on the brilliant success to
> learn how great the losses were. I am informed of the figure by Saint-
> Petersburg. I admire the courage of the troops, but I would observe
> to you that a battle fought to decide the entire fate of the Crimea
> would not have cost you more. I persist in the order . . . to make all
> your efforts to enter resolutely into a field campaign.[9]

Pélissier replied, making it clear that he would quit if the criticism continued. 'Your Majesty must free me from the narrow limits to which you have assigned me or else allow me to resign a command impossible to exercise in co-operation with our loyal allies at the somewhat paralysing end of an electric wire.'[10] Pélissier would not be the last commander to complain about the effects of that new invention, the telegraph.

The great allied attack – 18 June 1855

After the success of the operations on 6 June Pélissier decided to make the decisive attack on the Malakhov. On 16 June a meeting of allied commanders decided to go ahead – Raglan was seriously ill with cholera and made no objection. The attack was fixed for 18 June, the anniversary of the battle of Waterloo. The date was intended to be symbolic of the new alliance between the two countries and of a revival of French military prowess that would to some extent erase the memory of the earlier defeat. The plan was for an initial bombardment followed by an attack at 3 a.m. involving three French divisions. On the right the aim was to capture Point Battery and the Little Redan. In the centre two divisions would attack each side of the Malakhov and the British would advance on the Great Redan, but only after the French had captured the Malakhov (the operation would be impossible otherwise).

Although the plan seemed, on the surface, to be a fairly straightforward repetition of the successful tactics employed on 6 June, there were serious problems. It was drawn up too quickly and, as was pointed out at the conference on 16 June, the distances that the infantry had to cover in the open were too great. Around the Malakhov and Great Redan it was about 250 yards, but on the right at the Little Redan it was more than 600 yards. Bosquet opposed the attack for exactly this reason. Pélissier removed him to the corps of observation in the rear and replaced him with Saint-Jean d'Angely. He was a poor leader, unfamiliar with the ground and was given just thirty-six hours in which to prepare the attack.

The initial bombardment on 17 June appeared to be very successful. The Russian guns were gradually silenced and around the Malakhov sixteen guns were destroyed, many of the walls were severely damaged and more than 1,600 defenders badly wounded. However, unlike the earlier bombardment this one stopped during the evening. This gave the Russians, ably directed by Totleben, time to repair some of the damage and prepare for the assault. The Russians had also learnt to keep their reinforcements out of range of the bombardment and did not move them forward until the firing stopped. At the same time they moved up their remaining field guns, which had a wider arc of fire than the guns inside the bastions. The allies did not have the essential element of surprise in the infantry attack.

The allied assault went wrong from the start. It was due to begin at 3 a.m. when Pélissier would personally give the signal. A quarter of an hour before the appointed time General Mayran, commander of the troops on the French right, mistook a rocket for Pélissier's signal and began the attack. The infantry were able to advance just under 200 yards before they came under heavy fire from the Russian guns, including from warships in the harbour. They retreated and Mayran was killed. In the centre the troops under General Brunet got lost in the dark and were not in the forward trenches in time to begin the attack at 3 a.m. When they did advance, the Russians were ready and opened fire immediately. Brunet was killed and the troops retreated. On the left side of the Malakhov the French were more successful and did capture the Gervais Battery. However, Russian reinforcements attacked and the French troops retreated to their starting trenches. The British advanced when they saw that the French were in trouble and some troops did get near the Great Redan before retreating. The next day Raglan explained to Panmure why he had ordered the attack: 'Of this I am quite certain, that, if the troops had remained in our trenches, the French would have attributed their non-success to our refusal to participate in the operation.'[11]

EYE-WITNESS
THE ALLIED ATTACK: 18 JUNE 1855

Roger Fenton

18 June: 'We have just passed through what seems to be a hideous dream. Last night after a continuous and apparently successful bombardment of twenty-four hours it was resolved that the assault on the Malakoff should be made by the French and on the Redan by the English, early in the morning. Everyone seemed to be certain of success . . . We had a merry evening, everyone anticipating a short though perhaps sharp struggle and a triumphant close to this terrible siege . . . Few of us went to bed. I slept for a couple of hours but rose at half past one, got a cup of tea . . . We went down the hill towards the batteries and found a few more spectators sitting on the grass looking through the mist . . . The batteries were firing hard, the town was on fire in three places, a lurid smoke rose curling above the white cloud that enveloped all the batteries . . . Before sunrise a rocket rose perpendicularly from Fort Victoria and instantly there began a rattle of musketry which rolled round the base of the Malakoff . . . We could only judge of the progress of the conflict by the sound of the musketry . . . The sun rose and began to dissipate the mist . . . every eye was strained to catch a glimpse of them [the French] swarming up the steep sides of the Malakoff. When they did succeed in getting high enough up for us to see them we could see Russian officers standing on a parapet braving the fire and pointing to their men where to aim their guns. After a while, in front of us rose another rattle of musketry, indicating that our troops were attacking the Redan . . . but still we could see flashes from both the forts, showing that the Russians were still in possession. The first onset of the French evidently failed, for their fire diminished, then it renewed again and through the smoke a flag was unfurled on the top of the Malakoff and we all cried out, "They're in at last; now for the Redan!" but we were soon undeceived:

the flag was hoisted by the Russians . . . By this time it was eight o'clock . . . I could see with my glass our storming party clustering like bees in the quarries and lying in long black lines under the shelter of the trenches taken from the Russians last week. Nearer behind our batteries, lay a double line of redcoats ready to go in as a reserve, and when it was evident that both we and the French had been beaten back, the Guards and Highlanders were marched in to act as a reserve for a final attack. While waiting to see the result of this, sad rumours began to spread . . . Soon the rumours became a certainty, and gloom was seen on every face . . . Bye and bye slightly wounded men came up supported by other soldiers and the tale they told confirmed all our fears. Our men had attacked twice and been driven back each time by a frightful fire of grape . . . Litter after litter came pouring in, bringing wounded men to the hospital . . . returning to breakfast – and it is an odd thing that in the midst of all these horrors no one loses his appetite.'

Frederick Dallas

18 June: Yesterday we got orders that today we were to assault the two principal works of Sebastopol the 'Redan' and the 'Malakoff Tower', the former our share, the latter that of the French . . . We all paraded and marched down, at 1 A.M., full of hopes and almost certain of success. Instead of the result we so fondly anticipated there ensued nothing but mismanagement and frightful carnage. As we were . . . merely lying in one of the trenches and enveloped in smoke I can tell but little of what occurred. We remained there with a tremendous cannonade going on . . . where the proposed assault took place the result was that the French failed at the Malakoff, and by some misunderstanding, our Stormers (whose attack on the Redan was supposed to depend on the success of the French at the Malakoff) went on to the Redan under the most terrific fire of every description of missile. It was utterly impossible for them to get on as they were literally mowed down. It was almost a good thing that comparatively few faced it, or the slaughter would have been only more horrid . . . The whole affair was hideously mismanaged . . . Some of the Regiments, I fear, did not behave very splendidly, and could not be brought to follow their officers into the fire. The whole affair is a very sad thing. It is the first time our troops have been beaten . . . I had . . . nothing to do as it turned out, but to lie in a crowded sort of trench from 2 A.M. until 10 A.M. and straight in the road of all the poor wounded who were carried past us in troops, and a very sad sight it was . . . We came home about 11 A.M. very tired and roasted by such a sun, having to lie quite still in it for some hours.'

Captain Pyotr Lesli, in a battery on the forward face of the Malakhov
On the night of 17/18 June: 'Our work was terrible. At least 2,000 men crowded into that small space to dig up earth to remake what had been destroyed by the bombardment during the day, and throughout this time, there was literally not a minute when a shot was not being fired . . . I don't remember any of the preceding bombardments having been even a little like this one. This time it was pure hell. It was clear that they had prepared themselves for something out of the ordinary . . . Finally before dawn, from our former Kamchatsky Redoubt, one after another three rockets were launched like a cascade – a spectacular sight – and then a few moments later rifle crossfire belted out on the left flank of our tower. At first you could not see a thing, but then, as the smoke cleared, we saw large enemy columns advancing on the first and second bastions. But our men did not miss a trick over there and opened fire on the enemy with bullets and grape-shot, and forced their retreat . . . more than once we all burst into laughter when a column of French, cheerfully advancing, suddenly turned around like rabbits and made a run for the ravine.'

Nikolai Berg, on board a frigate in Sevastopol harbour
'The fires on the southern side went out. There was only one place where smoke was still burning, rising in a thin streak . . . A fresh wind blew away the cloud of smoke, and we saw the retreating, disorderly columns of the enemy . . . We were joyful for a long time. The June days could be counted as the best days of the whole siege. It seemed that we had repulsed all future assaults.'

Pélissier called off the attack at 8.30 a.m. He blamed Mayran and Brunet (both conveniently dead) for the failure and the heavy casualties. The French lost 1,600 men killed and probably about 3,000 wounded. Russian casualties were about 1,500 and the British roughly the same.

EYE-WITNESS
18 JUNE: THE AFTERMATH

Henry Clifford, officer
19 June (there was a truce for burying the dead that day): 'The sun was so hot that it was impossible to recognise the dead, their bodies were swollen to an enormous size and their faces and hands quite black, and so dreadful

was the stench that the men who were taking them off the field often vomited. Some, Sir John Campbell amongst others, had already begun to decompose and worms and maggots were eating away the flesh. I saw as I thought a dead rifleman on the ground partly hid by the grass. I went to the spot. It was the backbone of one with part of his bowels and a lump or two of flesh with part of his jacket and head by it; all the rest had been blown away by a shell.'

Napoleon was probably right in arguing that a major attack to destroy the Russian field army would not have been more costly than the two attacks in June 1855. Although important gains were made earlier in the month, the major assault on 18 June was a disastrous failure and achieved nothing. Morale in the allied armies slumped. They had now been encamped in front of Sevastopol for nine months and seemed to be no nearer capturing the city.

15

The Fall of Sevastopol

Although the Russians had defeated the allied attack on 18 June 1855, their situation was grim. On the day before the assault the allies had fired more than three times as many rounds as the Russians. They now had 800 guns (the biggest concentration of firepower in history so far) and could, at times, fire 75,000 rounds a day. By August the Russians were lucky if they could fire one-sixth of that number. Slowly they were being worn down in this battle of attrition and the damage they suffered was greater than they could repair. In late July reinforcements arrived (the 4th and 5th Divisions), but they were debilitated by their long march across southern Russia. An extra 13,000 militia made the overall increase in the garrison about 35,000 troops. The problem was that the French were bringing in reinforcements, too – about 2,000 men a day from late June. In addition the Russians were losing about 400 men a day (and twice that number by August) and the French fewer than 200. The Russian commanders were convinced that it was only a matter of time before Sevastopol fell. In early July Gorchakov wrote to the Minister of War in St Petersburg:

> If I were to attack the enemy . . . I would be smashed by the third day with the loss of between 10,000–15,000 men. On the fourth day Sevastopol would be lost. But, if I do not attack, the enemy will take Sevastopol anyway in the course of the next few months.[1]

Gorchakov held a conference with his chief commanders. The overwhelming majority thought the situation was hopeless. They were outnumbered and outgunned, and the majority favoured evacuating the south side of the city while continuing to hold the forts in the north. Gorchakov and his Chief of Staff, Kotsebu, rejected this idea, but they could not offer any long-term hope for the defence of the city.

The French leadership

After the failure of the attack on 18 June Napoleon III, not surprisingly, felt that his views about strategy had been vindicated. Pélissier argued that continuing the siege was the only viable option. He told Napoleon, 'The Turks can only be counted on as a symbol . . . Our allies, the English, have trouble getting started and are unimaginative.'[2] However, Pélissier's position in Paris was being undermined by reports sent by Generals Bosquet and Niel about the very poor direction of the attack on 18 June. On 3 July Napoleon sent a message to Pélissier that he was no longer to disobey orders and sacrifice units in useless assaults. He was to set out his future plans and to do nothing without prior approval from Paris – if he could not accept these conditions, he was to hand over command to Niel. However, the Minister of War, Vaillant, who was a supporter of Pélissier, sent Napoleon's message by ordinary mail. It was stopped at Marseilles after it became clear that Pélissier's subordinates were only complaining in order to boost their own careers and that morale among the troops was still high.

On 6 July Vaillant sent a private message to Pélissier telling him just how insecure his position had become and to deal carefully with Niel, who was acting as Napoleon's main source of information. Pélissier decided to reverse the command changes of mid-June that had helped create the disaster on 18 June. Bosquet was restored to his command and Saint-Jean d'Angely was sent back to the Imperial Guard. In the last week of July Napoleon 'invited' Canrobert to return to France on grounds of ill health. He did so once he had been promised a position in Napoleon's personal entourage. In mid-August General MacMahon arrived in the Crimea and took over command of the 1st Division from Canrobert. He was held in high esteem in the French army for his work in Algeria.

The British command

On 26 June Lord Raglan died of cholera – he had been suffering from the disease for ten days. His body, accompanied by his retinue of staff officers, was returned to Britain for burial. He was decent and gentlemanly and kind to his personal staff, but utterly out of his depth in commanding a field army in mid-nineteenth-century warfare. He was responsible for many of the failures in the Crimean campaign and had shown a lamentable lack of leadership qualities. The major problem was who should succeed him. The only choice seemed to be the sixty-three-year-old General Simpson. However, he was widely, and correctly, regarded as gloomy and despondent. Both Clarendon and Palmerston had grave doubts about the choice, but Panmure, an old friend of Simpson, argued in his favour. There was no obvious alternative available and so he was appointed.

Simpson did not feel up to the job and on 30 June asked Panmure to send out a replacement: 'my health is sure to give way as I have constant threatenings of gout . . . and therefore hope soon to be relieved from work that is too much for me'. In addition he did not like working with the French – 'I feel it very irksome and embarrassing to have to do with these Allies' – and wanted the best soldier available to replace him, since 'with the Allies we have to deal with, this is of vital consequence'.[3] These problems with the French stemmed from the fact that Pélissier would not tell Simpson about his future plans, and from Simpson's recognition that the British army was 'too weak to form any plan of [its] own', although he thought it might 'give valuable aid in a general attack'.[4]

Ministers in London quickly realised that they had made a mistake in ever appointing Simpson. Panmure, despite his earlier support, rapidly developed doubts and Palmerston held a meeting with the Commander-in-Chief, Lord Hardinge, about possible successors. The options were hardly enticing. Hardinge, who was seventy years old, ruled himself out – his legs tended to swell and he could hardly walk, let alone ride a horse. It was thought that the seventy-six-year-old Lord Seaton would not survive the Crimean climate. General Ferguson was a possibility, but he had only just been appointed Governor-General of Gibraltar. The Duke of Cambridge would have royal support, but he was judged to have failed at Inkerman. Panmure was being tactful in stating that the Duke had 'hereditary courage', but he was damning when he argued that 'he might fail in self-control in situations where the safety of the Army might depend on coolness and self-possession'.[5] It was agreed that Codrington was by far the best General available, but it was thought that the Queen would resent having to promote the fifty-one-year-old over the heads of four more senior Generals in the Crimea. Palmerston and Hardinge reluctantly decided that Simpson should stay, but that Codrington would be nominated as his successor.

On 14 July Simpson sent another gloomy message to London:

> I am struck with the conviction that these four armies never can carry on any joint and united operations in their present condition . . . I am an unworthy successor to Lord Raglan . . . of course I continue to do the work as well as I can until you decide what is to be done. I have been ill this past week with gout in my ankle and foot . . . The correspondence here is sufficient to break down any man. I labour at it from four in the morning until six in the evening . . . My outdoor military duties are therefore much neglected.[6]

An increasingly irritated Panmure told Simpson that he should either do the job or admit his inadequacies and resign: 'Either buckle up your reins vigorously for the work or at once claim the consideration which your long and honourable services entitle you to receive.'[7] The rest of the Cabinet had also lost what little patience they had with Simpson. Clarendon told Palmerston that Simpson was planning for failure and withdrawal: 'there appears to be no energy, no directing mind, nothing like united action and above all no plan except to wait for the winter and for that no preparation seems to be making'. Palmerston agreed, but thought that it was perhaps now too late to take action and that there was no alternative but to wait for the winter. 'I fear we made a mistake in not at once appointing Codrington as we have lost six precious weeks under the command of an old woman but as the campaign is to all practical purposes *over* the most important thing now is to secure our communications with the sea by the railroad.'[8]

Panmure sent a blunt message to Simpson at the end of July:

> Your letters have certainly been most disheartening . . . It is impossible for a man feeling as you do to face the difficulties of any position, or to cheer on others in the arduous task before them. If you are so weighed down by a sense of your own inability to bear the burden of the command, you *must* write to me so officially and request to be relieved. It is neither fair to me nor to yourself to do otherwise.[9]

Panmure also sounded out Simpson about the possibility of Codrington as his successor. In his reply in mid-August Simpson argued that he should stay, partly because there would be a revolt in the army if Codrington was chosen:

> He is, in my belief, the best General here; but I am in full hopes not to be compelled by illness to act on your instructions at the present time of very imminent chance of our being attacked; for you must be aware of the very great disgust that will be occasioned to Bentinck, Campbell, Barnard and Rokeby, if Codrington is called to the chief command. They will, of course, take the most immediate measures to quit the army.[10]

Nothing was therefore done about the command of British forces in the Crimea before the final assault on Sevastopol. However, the threats made about the promotion of Codrington did not apply in the case of other officers. Even though the army could not properly man the existing five divisions in the Crimea, Panmure gave in to Queen Victoria's insistence that a sixth division should be created solely to enable Lord Rokeby, a well-connected Guards officer, to receive a divisional command before the campaign ended.

EYE-WITNESS
VIEWS ABOUT THE BRITISH MILITARY LEADERSHIP

Frederick Dallas, officer

22–25 June: 'We have a poor account to give of our Generals . . . Pennefather is going home I hear . . . Codrington is ill on board ship. The former is I think no loss to us, for he is a most excitable man under fire, or when anything is doing . . . The latter is one of the best Generals we have . . . We are sick and weary of our Generals, one seems as perfectly incompetent as another. Sir George Brown I firmly believe to be the head and origin of our disaster the other day [18 June], having given the signal for the attack, which he ought never to have done . . . [he] is ill on board ship, and altogether we have but few Generals left. If I might say it respectfully, I shouldn't wonder if we got on better without them.'

2 July, on the death of Raglan: 'All those good qualities he possessed, his charming manners, his kindness, and his long reign in the hearts of all those who personally knew him, have made him as much and as sincerely regretted as if we had lost a great General. All his staff are broken up and most of them go home with him I believe – if fame speaks truly of them, a more perfectly gentlemanly, useless crew never burdened an army.'

5 July: General Simpson is 'like a dear old English General somewhat scared at being made Commander-in-Chief . . . I fancy neither he himself nor anybody out here seems to think him much fitted for such an appointment.'

Temple Godman, officer

Simpson 'gives what orders he likes, one is that we shall all wear swords, and he is said to threaten the use of the razor again. It is evident he has not spent either last summer or winter exposed to this climate, or these absurd orders would not have appeared, if this is all he came out for he had better have been kept at home.'

Henry Clifford, officer

'A very great number of Officers have left, some from ill health, *many from pretended ill health* who are as well as I am, and others from disgust and tired of the long dreary siege. A very great number will throw up their commissions before the winter sets in again.'

EYE-WITNESS
THE BRITISH ARMY: SUMMER 1855

Frederick Dallas

28 June: 'I am afraid there is but small chance of our "taking the field", and the summer is slipping by so rapidly that we are all somewhat gloomily looking forward to another winter in these our dreary Quarters . . . We hear constantly of new "Siege Trains" and big guns & mortars that we are going to put to somewhere or other to destroy the Russians . . . I believe we are going soon to recommence the old story, and now we are getting so skilful at dragging up shot and guns that we can have a Siege about once a fortnight.'

12 July: 'This prolonged siege, the most harassing of a soldier's duties, has only the gloom and none of the excitement of a Campaign for us out here.'

16 July: 'I do not think we have ever been so completely without a rumour of any change, any expedition, any attack, any sort of movement in fact. The wise ones are beginning to dig holes and make huts for the Winter.'

23 July: 'I find here a more hopeless oppressive life of idleness than that I thought to escape from at home. I can assure you that the most remote outquarters in England or Ireland offer a much more exciting life than we lead here. Day after day, we get up and sit perspiring in our reeking tents with no chance or hope of any change, or doing anything, and if an opportunity does come of any active measure, we all have the most perfect confidence in its being badly done.'

30 July: 'I believe that we are getting up some Batteries, & shot & shell into them, but nobody seems to take much interest, and I really think that under the new "Régime" we have less purpose, energy or plan than ever.'

10 August: 'We are rapidly approaching the end of Summer, & unless our Leaders feel perfectly certain of our being in the Town by the Autumn, nothing can excuse their want of preparation & miserable supineness. We have made and are making no sort of road to Balaklava, no intermediate stations or Depots for provisions . . . McMurdo's Transport Corps is the most costly failure ever undertaken. We are still in the same sieves of tents that we lived & died in last Winter . . . With such a prospect as this, in addition to the utter & complete want of confidence on all our sides in our Chiefs . . . can you wonder at me, or anyone else, wishing to get out?'

Temple Godman

31 August: 'We get very good dinners, soup and turbot (the Black Sea turbot are very good), a joint, generally mutton, some fowl and hash, and a tart of

preserved fruit or rice pudding. Claret cup (not quite so good as in England) and often ice . . . I generally stay in all day till about four, and then ride to bathe, or to the front, or round the outposts, and home to dinner at seven, to bed about ten, and we parade every morning at four.'

EYE-WITNESS
THE BRITISH PRISONERS MOVE TO ODESSA

George Newman, foot soldier

'One day we had the Adjutant General of the Russian forces come to inspect us by the order of the Emperor preparatory to our departure. We (the proper prisoners) were fell in in one part of the yard and the deserters in another. He only looked at the prisoners and did not go near the deserters. He again offered the same conditions to those who liked to stop and gave orders for us to be clothed before starting. In a few days after we were all marched to a place where a great many tailors were at work making clothing such as we had often seen the Russian recruits wear. We were all clad in long grey overcoats, and a pair of rough black trowsers. They also gave us caps and stocks but we soon threw them away. The next day we each had a pair of boots and a rough Russian shirt . . . [The police chief] came to our house the next morning to see us start and were fell in in the yard with our bags and bundles. He told us . . . that the officer had orders not to wait on the road and, if any man got drunk and missed his passage he would be marched back again to wait for the next exchange . . . There was a tremendous string of waggons waiting for us, each with two horses. They were brought to the gate one at a time and two men mounted each . . . We soon left the town behind us. We found the roads very dusty and the wind was high and blew it in our faces, and we were like so many chimney sweeps at the end of the day's journey, through the black dust settling on us . . . We travelled at a good speed, having fresh horses and waggons waiting for us in different villages . . . We had some fine sport in crossing those large, level plains . . . for we would take the whip and reins from the driver and race each other for miles, very often ending by breaking a wheel or axle and sending the passengers flying out of the vehicles . . . our route from this place very slow and tedious, for we could get no more horses . . . we now looked for a good long waggon with plenty of hay or straw in it, so that we could lie down and sleep if we liked. I generally walked on ahead of the caravan and when I got tired I would sit down and wait until they came up

. . . In the next large town . . . I was billeted at a Jew's house and, because they would not oblige us with utensils and fire for cooking . . . we rubbed their pots and other utensils with pieces of bacon fat and left pieces of the same in them, and next morning saw them taken out and broken up as being defiled. While we were in the town an old German Jew told, in a whisper and with great caution, that he knew for certain that Sebastopol had been taken, but we did not believe him.' [They were right not to do so – it was another month before the town fell.]

The battle of the Chernaya

Throughout July and the first two weeks of August the siege of Sevastopol continued in the usual way. The allies seemed to be making little, if any, progress and most of the troops were bored with an interminable siege that seemed likely to continue into a second winter. That it did not was largely the result of Russian decisions. The Tsar (Nicholas I had died in early 1855 and been succeeded by his son Alexander) wanted decisive action. Although Alexander II held no responsibility for the outbreak of war, he was acutely conscious of his prestige. Understandably he did not want to begin his reign with a military failure. He felt, with some justification, that simply moving more reinforcements to Sevastopol achieved little. At the end of July he sent his Adjutant-General, Baron Pavel Vrevsky, to Gorchakov's headquarters bearing a simple message:

> I am convinced of the necessity that we should attack; otherwise all the reinforcements recently sent you, as has happened in the past, will be sucked into Sevastopol, that bottomless pit . . . You cannot avoid significant losses, but, with God's help, you may achieve a momentous result.[11]

Gorchakov was reluctant to accept such a gamble and in his reply pointed out that failure in any set-piece battle would inevitably lead to the fall of Sevastopol. The Tsar did not shift from his position, urging 'the necessity to do something decisive in order to bring this frightful massacre to a close'.[12]

On 10 August Gorchakov held a military council to discuss the options – the Tsar had not actually ordered an attack, but his views were clear. A majority of seven Generals, led by Liprandi, favoured an attack. There was some logic in their position. Sevastopol would probably be lost in the next few months and a battle, if successful, might at least gain better peace terms. Even if the battle were lost, the Russians would not be much worse off. Four Generals, led by Osten-Sacken, were strongly opposed, arguing that the Russians had lost 65,000 men in the last year (excluding those who had died of various diseases) and were simply too weak to attack. Khrulev made a far more radical proposal – the south side of Sevastopol should be destroyed and the allies attacked from two sides simultaneously. At the end of the meeting Gorchakov agreed with the majority – he was far from convinced by the arguments for an attack, but at least he was doing what the Tsar wanted.

Over the next few days the Russians drew up their plans. They would attack the Fedyukhin Hills that they had given up in May. These were now held by 18,000 French troops supported by 9,000 Sardinian troops on Gasfort Hill. (These allied forces could be reinforced very quickly.) The initial Russian attack would be made by 30,000 men divided into two equal wings. The right (7th and 12th Infantry Divisions) would be under General N. A. Read and the left (17th and 6th Infantry Divisions) would be commanded by Liprandi. The right wing would cross the Chernaya and storm the heights, while the left wing would gain control of Telegraph and Gasfort Hills. It was at this point that the central weakness of the Russian plan was demonstrated. Gorchakov would control the reserve of 20,000 troops and he would decide where to deploy it once the initial stage of the battle was completed. The commanders on the spot would have to wait for his orders.

The Russian plan was straightforward, unimaginative and roughly what the allies expected them to do. They had observed reinforcements arriving and their reconnaissance was, on this occasion, good. They also had some information from diplomats in Berlin that Gorchakov had been ordered to attack at all costs. Simpson reported to London just before the attack:

> I could not go on board the Royal Albert last Saturday [11 August], as medically ordered, because we had reason to expect a general attack. It did not take place but there seems every probability of the enemy attempting to force the Tchernaya, and he will probably make a sortie from Sebastopol at the same time. Fresh troops have evidently arrived, and a large portion relieved the garrison, or part of it, yesterday.[13]

The lack of tactical surprise made the weaknesses in the Russian plan even more apparent. The battle of the Chernaya was, after the Alma, the most important of the Crimean battles and Russian failure ensured that Sevastopol would fall. However, it is usually given little importance in

British accounts of the war because British troops were hardly involved – just one artillery battery and some cavalry held in reserve that did not take part in the fighting. On the allied side the battle was fought by the French and the Sardinians.

On the night of 15–16 August Russian troops descended from the Mackenzie Heights and took up their positions along the Chernaya River and in front of Telegraph Hill near the village of Chorgun. French and Sardinian troops discovered the Russian movement and, fully prepared, took up their positions. The Russians attacked just before dawn and the troops under Liprandi easily captured Telegraph Hill. After this initial success Gorchakov, who was with Liprandi, sent orders to Read to start. Read naturally understood this to mean that he should begin the assault. In fact Gorchakov meant an intensification of the artillery bombardment, which in this sector had been feeble because the Russian guns were almost out of range of the allied positions. Read sent his two divisions across the Chernaya River, but both came under heavy fire and suffered major losses as they tried to climb to the Fedyukhin Heights. Liprandi, hearing heavy firing on his flank, shifted his troops along the Chernaya River to give support in the attack on the Fedyukhin Hills. These troops too came under very heavy fire from the French artillery on the heights above them.

By about 7.30 a.m. both of Read's divisions leading the attack in this area had retreated under the intense French fire. At this point elements of the 5th Division, which had been held in reserve, began to arrive. Read then made the fatal mistake of not waiting for the whole of the division to be ready to attack. He chose to feed the reinforcements into the battle a battalion at a time. The inevitable result was that they were cut to pieces without achieving anything of significance. Some Russian troops did manage to brave the intense artillery fire and get to the top of the hill, where there was hand-to-hand fighting with the French troops, but before 10 a.m. the bulk of the Russian army was in retreat back to the far side of the Chernaya. Read and Vrevsky were killed by artillery fire during this phase of the fighting. Gorchakov regrouped his troops on the far side of the river and retreated back to the Mackenzie Heights. The French and Sardinians made no attempt to pursue the defeated Russian army.

EYE-WITNESS
THE BATTLE OF THE CHERNAYA

Lieutenant Ricci, Sardinian army
'Everyone was asleep in the Allied camps when a burst of shooting surprised us about an hour before dawn. It was the Russians who, having marched and manoeuvred for a good part of the night, were starting battle with a furious attack on the Piedmont advance guard. The combat was short, but very lively: we fought with bayonets, with the stocks of our guns, finally even with stones. This was enough to alert those in the camps behind us, and they got into a defensive position in good time.'

Anonymous soldier in the French Third Zouaves
'The Russians had crossed en masse by way of flying footbridges and yoked beams. But we bore down on them at an athletic pace and By God! From that moment on I couldn't quite say what happened. Just like at Inkerman and at the Mamelon Vert we had to dig in, advancing and retreating in turns, climbing over the wounded and dead bodies, closing our eyes sometimes, so as not to see what we were striking . . . How anyone got out of there safe and sound is impossible to explain. We can only thank God . . . Finally however we managed to push the Russian columns back down to the river, where many unfortunates, tied up in their long cloaks, drowned.'

Frederick Dallas
'The Russians had the temerity, poor creatures, to come on against our lines in the Valley of the Tchernaya, where the French and Sardinians are camped, and got so tremendous a beating that I don't think they will attempt anything more for some time . . . We [the British] had nothing engaged but 1 or 2 Batteries of Artillery . . . We have known for some little time of the arrival of large reinforcements in the Enemy's Camp, & have been on the look-out for some attack on our trenches for the last few days . . . I went down to the field of battle this morning early . . . They (the wounded) said that they had come from Moscow, poor creatures. They looked very sad, and wretched as they always do, more like the Peasantry of a Country than Soldiers.'

Overall the fighting lasted for about four hours and ended, as Gorchakov had predicted, in a severe Russian defeat. They had achieved none of their objectives and their casualties were heavy. They lost about

10,000 men compared with about 1,500 French troops and 250 from the Sardinian army.

Russian and allied preparations

Gorchakov had begun planning for the evacuation of the main town of Sevastopol on the south side of the harbour immediately after the allied attack on 18 June. In order to evacuate the troops and civilian population to the north side it was necessary to build a bridge across the 1,800-foot-wide harbour. The suggestion for how this major engineering feat could be done came from Lieutenant-General Aleksandr Bukhmeier. He was an engineer officer who had constructed the large bridge across the Danube at Izmail during the 1854 campaign. Materials were gradually assembled on the beach (much of the timber was brought in on wagons from across southern Russia) and more than 200 men began work on 26 July. It took a month to construct eighty-six separate rafts, each about twenty feet wide. The rafts were free floating, but had two anchors (mainly damaged guns) to keep them in place. They were lashed to their neighbours and a rail was built along the side once all the rafts were in place. The bridge was ready for use by 27 August.

EYE-WITNESS
SEVASTOPOL: LATE AUGUST 1855

Captain Pyotr Lesli
'A kind of apathy has set in with all our commanders and seeing this all your energy disappears too. In general it's time to finish this terrible blood-letting war . . . with every hour that passes it gets harder and harder. Everything has become so loathsome that, oh, oh, – there's no strength left! And I would be prepared to leave for Siberia at once to do hard labour, even for a lifetime, if only it meant I could get out of Sevastopol.'

Nikolai Berg
'On 27 August, after the mass to mark the Feast of the Dormition, the bridge was opened and blessed – and whole crowds of people walked and rode along it. It was strange to hear the clatter of horses' hoofs and the thunder of carts in the middle of the harbour, over the ripple of the waves . . . The huge logs, sticking out from under the rafts, were soon covered in long, pale strands of underwater grasses and in these strands . . . parted

---

on two sides, tiny fish swam in and out . . . playing in the sunshine like flashing blades.'

The Tsar now changed his mind. Having argued for a decisive battle, he balked at the consequences of the defeat which the Russians had sustained. He told Gorchakov: 'Our glorious troops have had enormous losses without any gain.' He wanted Sevastopol to be held and the allied attacks to be beaten off, as in the past. He opposed retreat to the north side of the harbour: 'The evacuation of the south bank would in any event be a grave undertaking.'[14]

Even after the overwhelming success at the Chernaya, the allies remained uncertain about Russian intentions. Simpson reported to London on 25 August that he expected:

An attack every day, as our information all confirms the design of the enemy to attempt to raise the siege . . . We may expect a sortie, especially when attacked on the Balaclava side. The enemy has very nearly completed his bridge across the harbour – a splendid work – portending mischief.[15]

The Russians continued to make diversionary movements near the Chernaya to which the allies responded by moving troops, away from Sevastopol. In early September Simpson still thought that another Russian attack would take place: 'we expect to be attacked every morning and are disappointed day after day. There can be no doubt of the enemy's intention, however.'[16]

After the Chernaya battle, the allies continued to bombard Sevastopol. At the same time trenches were extended towards the Russian fortifications in order to reduce the amount of open space that the infantry would have to cross when they attacked. By early September they were between thirty and ninety yards from the Russian positions. The allies also brought in heavier artillery, including thirteen-inch mortars, which could be dug in and fired throughout the night because they did not need to be aimed. On 3 September the allied commanders held a war council to agree the plans for what they hoped would be the final assault on Sevastopol. The bombardment, which had almost ceased after 27 August, would restart on 5 September and would be continuous until the infantry attack was launched at around noon on 8 September. The French would, necessarily, take the leading role. Their main objective would be the Malakhov (the key to the defences in front of Sevastopol), but they would also attack the Korabelnaya suburb. The sole British objective would be the Great Redan, which they would attack once French troops had captured the Malakhov.

The final assault on Sevastopol

The allied bombardment began on schedule on 5 September. It was continuous for more than three days, apart from occasional breaks to tempt the Russians out of their shelters in the expectation of an infantry attack. The allies fired just under 100,000 artillery rounds during this period. The Russians sustained about 7,500 casualties and their defensive works were badly damaged. The Malakhov was in too bad a state to repair and only eight of its sixty-three guns were operational. The dugouts were full of wounded and they could only be evacuated at night. In Sevastopol itself there were widespread fires, but none of the fire-fighting equipment was operational. Only fourteen houses in the city remained undamaged. Ships in the harbour were attacked and one ammunition ship blew up.

EYE-WITNESS
SEVASTOPOL: THE FINAL BOMBARDMENT

Nikolai Berg
'On the morning of 5 September, the last, terrible bombardment began, the like of which there had never been before. The whole of Sevastopol (the southern side and the Karabelnaya) was drowned in smoke, which at the beginning rose up in sparse white columns, but then merged into one grey, dense cloud, and for three days in a row, this cloud hung over the town. You couldn't see the sun.'

Yanuari Kobylynski, company commander, Zhitomir Chasseurs
'Bombs, shot, shells, various kinds of grape-shot and bullets poured as though through a sieve and fell, exploding as they hit the ground . . . Before noon and in the evening the firing stopped for fifteen or twenty minutes . . . on our side there was an extraordinary flurry of domestic activity: everyone was clearing away the rocks, pieces of wood and gun-carriage strewn all over by the enemy's shells, levelling out the pits made by the bombs . . . The work was not yet completed . . . and a whole mass of iron was flying at us again, tearing up the ground, scattering masses of stones, hitting people, guns . . .'

On the morning of 8 September the allies outnumbered the Russian defenders by about two to one, although in the key central sector the advantage was somewhat greater. The French attack on the Malakhov was fixed for noon – not the usual time for an attack, but it was when the Russian gun crews were changing over. The Russians had also got used to short pauses in the allied bombardment over the previous seventy-two hours and did not suspect that an attack was imminent. When the signal was given, the Zouaves quickly covered the short distance to the fort from the forward trenches and vicious hand-to-hand fighting ensued inside the fort. Most of the Russian troops, a reserve division of aged veterans, were killed and the tricolour was raised over the Malakhov. Inside French troops found the mines that the Russians were in the process of laying, but the powder was not in position. Once the French had captured the Malakhov, it proved almost impossible to dislodge them despite numerous Russian counter-attacks. The tower was fortified to the rear as well as to the front and the Russians had almost no artillery that could be trained on the fort.

EYE-WITNESS
THE FRENCH ATTACK ON THE MALAKHOV

Vladimir Kolchak, a Russian naval officer who was second-in-command of the Glasis battery at the Malakhov

'A shout rang out, "The French!" Rear-Admiral Karpov . . . ordered the alarm to be sounded; but the drummer had been killed and the alarm was sounded by the bugler standing by. Rapid crossfire could be heard, like dried peas poured from a sack . . . Naturally a few shots could not hold back the advance of an animated mass. The French just kept on advancing and advancing towards the Tower . . . The guns were already covered in earth, or put out of action; they stood on broken platforms. The French, having jumped the ditch, were swiftly clambering across the embrasures and parapets with the help of ladders, and onto the battery. Hand-to-hand fighting began . . . our soldiers were fighting in separate groups with the overwhelming mass of the French. They fought with bitterness – using anything that came to hand: bayonets, the butts of their fire-arms, cleaning rods, pick-axes, spades, even stones.'

The raising of the tricolour over the Malakhov was the signal for the other attacks to begin. Overall the allies attacked another twelve Russian defensive bastions and did not capture a single one. The French did briefly control Number 2, but lost 150 men as prisoners when it was recaptured. They attacked again and were successful, only to be driven off by yet another Russian counter-attack. The British attack on the Great Redan was a disaster. The British infantry had to cross about 250 yards in the open because the rocky ground made it impossible to bring the trenches any closer to the Russian positions. Many were cut down before they reached the fort and large numbers refused to obey orders to attack. Three assaults were mounted by 11,000 men against a Russian garrison of about 7,000. All were beaten off.

EYE-WITNESS
THE BRITISH ATTACK ON THE GREAT REDAN

Edmund Maynard, Roger Fenton's brother-in-law

'Our storming party . . . got orders to move on against the Redan . . . the scaling ladders were soon fixed . . . we were brought up at the double, having an open space of 5 or 600 yards from our trenches to the ditch of the Redan to run across; but before we could accomplish this, many of our fellows were swept down by the raking fire which was poured in amongst us . . . those . . . who were remaining went straight at the ditch, but here were unavoidably mixed up with other regiments when we came to mount the different ladders . . . the first I came at I went at waving my sword and shouting, I believe, like a madman to urge my company to follow, which they did, but some of the poor fellows were knocked over before they reached the parapet. Many were obstructed by the crowds of men on the bank side. I was scarcely mounted on the top of the parapet myself, before my face was covered with blood and brains spurting from a poor fellow of another regiment who was shot close to me. Such a sight as I must have been for the 2½ hours we remained up there, men falling in every direction . . . then the moans of the poor fellows as they lay at one's feet dying and crying for assistance . . . dead and dying were alike forgotten and trampled under foot. Still the enemy could not be driven in. They assailed us with all sorts of missiles and showered us with big stones, bayonets . . . We could not bring our men to face it and make a charge over the parapet and jump in amongst the enemy. At one time I endeavoured to get volunteers, determined to lead the way in myself if they would only follow, but this proved a failure; no more than six or eight would enlist for the work . . . Officers did their utmost to get the men in, but without effect. At last, in spite of every endeavour, the men became panic struck and made a rush to retire, and it was most fearful to see the way in which they upset and tumbled upon each other in the ditch. I kept my hold on the ladder as long as I could, cheering and trying to keep them up, till at last I was sent head foremost.'

Henry Clifford
'What almost breaks my heart and nearly drove me mad, was to see our soldiers, our English soldiers that I was so proud of, run away . . . was it right to send any men two hundred yards in the open against a place like the Redan, with guns vomiting forth grape? . . . the French, with older and more tried troops, would not assault the Malakoff again till they had silenced the fire of the guns and brought their trenches within twenty yards of the Ditch from which the sharpshooters could keep down the fire from the parapet . . . as it was certain that the Malakoff would command the Redan, when the former was in the hands of the French, was it right to sacrifice thousands of lives in attacking the Redan, only because the French went at the Malakoff?

William Russell, *The Times* war correspondent
'There was a feeling of deep depression in camp all night. We were painfully aware that our attack had failed. The camp was full of wounded men; the hospitals were crowded; and sad stories ran from mouth to mouth respecting the losses of the officers and the behaviour of the men.'

By the evening of 8 September the allies had captured the key position of the Malakhov, from which they would be able to dominate the other Russian forts and the town of Sevastopol. Losses had been heavy on both sides during a day of vicious fighting. The Russians suffered about 13,000 casualties and the allies only slightly fewer. The French lost 7,500 men, the British 2,500 and the Sardinians forty.

The Russian evacuation

At about 4 p.m. Gorchakov inspected the Russian positions. He decided that the Malakhov could not be recaptured and in these circumstances there was little alternative but to retreat from the whole of the south side of Sevastopol. He decided to do so immediately while the allies were still disorganised after the attack. The allied commanders did not believe they had achieved a decisive success. They expected further Russian counter-attacks on the Malakhov and were uncertain whether it could be held. Pélissier ordered his troops to consolidate their positions and resume the attack on the adjacent forts early the next morning.

The allies spotted the first movement of Russian troops across the bay to the north side of the harbour at about 7 p.m. They thought it was probably exhausted units moving to the rear and that they would be replaced by fresh troops. The Russians had long planned how to conduct the withdrawal operation and it went remarkably smoothly over the night of 8–9 September. Five infantry regiments held barricades in the town and acted as the rearguard while volunteers continued to man the forts and kept up some artillery fire. Troops and civilians crossed the bridge in a reasonably orderly manner and all the wounded, except about 500 men who were too ill to move, were evacuated to the north. It was decided that it was too difficult to move large numbers of wagons and artillery across the bridge, especially with so many people crossing. Most of the wagons were burnt and the guns dumped in the bay. The allies fired a few artillery rounds at the bridge, but they all missed. Once the main garrison and the civilian population had crossed, a rocket was fired as a signal to the rearguard that they should now start their evacuation. Thirty-seven powder magazines were blown up and the fires started in Sevastopol burnt for two days. By shortly after 8 a.m. on 9 September the last elements of the rearguard had crossed the bridge to the north side of the harbour. The remaining ships were sunk in the bay and the bridge was destroyed. The Russians had successfully completed one of the most difficult operations of the whole war.

Later on 9 September the first allied troops moved into the deserted Russian defences and then into the city. Fires were burning everywhere and ammunition dumps were continuing to explode. The siege that had begun almost a year earlier was finally over.

EYE-WITNESS
THE FALL OF SEVASTOPOL

Nikolai Berg

'It is impossible to describe what was happening on the bridge. A wave of carts, horses, people flooded over it for six or seven hours in a row, sometimes it seemed to those crossing that the bridge had collapsed and was sinking to the bottom. Crowds, shouting and screaming, ran back; the crossing was held up . . . in the meantime, the sky flared with shots and bomb after bomb burst over those retreating. Then the town burst into flames.'

William Russell

'About twelve o'clock, the silence having attracted the attention of our men, some volunteers crept up an embrasure of the Redan, and found the place deserted by all save the dead and dying. Soon afterwards, wandering fires gleamed through the streets and outskirts of the town . . . and before daybreak the town of Sebastopol . . . was on fire from the sea to the Dockyard Creek. Fort Alexander was blown up early in the night . . . At sunrise, four large explosions on the left followed in quick succession, and announced the destruction of the Quarantine Fort, and of the magazines of the batteries of the Central Bastion and Flagstaff Fort . . . At 5.30 there were two of the largest and grandest explosions . . . that ever shook the earth – most probably from Fort Alexander and the Grand magazine. The rush of black smoke, grey and white vapour, masses of stone, beams of timber, and masonry into the air was appalling . . . All this time the Russians were marching with sullen tramp across the bridge and boats were busy carrying off *matériel* from the town, or bearing men to the south side, to complete the work of destruction . . . As soon as it was dawn, the French began to steal from the trenches into the burning town.

Frederick Dallas

'On Sunday morning, the 9th., there was not a Russian to be seen, & frightful explosions at intervals taking place in their Batteries &c, & the whole town in flames. There are occasional explosions even now . . . The Russes have sunk their remaining ships all except the Steamers & have of course destroyed their bridge across. They have made, I imagine, the most glorious defence in the history of war, & their end was worthy of it, for knowing that the loss of the Malakoff must lead sooner or later to the capture of the whole place, they went away, having repulsed us at two, out of three, of the points of attack, & having fought at the other for nearly 5 hours, leaving us the smoking ruins of the Town.'

Henry Clifford

'If a few days before I had been told "on the morning of the 9th September at five o'clock Sebastopol will be in the hands of the Allies and you will stand in the Redan held by the English", I should have said, "Oh!, that will be a proud and happy moment, that will repay us for all we have gone through, even the loss of so many lives, so much suffering and hardship will not have been thrown away in vain!" But no, I stood in the Redan more humble, more dejected and with a heavier heart than I have yet felt since I left home.'

Frederick Dallas

'I hope you will now make Peace for us at home. Of war I am quite sick. This last "Butcher's Bill" [of dead] has very nearly finished my list of old friends and acquaintances, & now it is all over I may confess to you that nothing could exceed the horror of our Duties during the Siege . . . Thank God, it is all now over, & I only pray I may never see another Siege.'

News of the fall of Sevastopol reached Paris the next day when the guns at the Invalides were fired to announce the success. On 14 September Napoleon III attended a celebratory *Te Deum* in Notre Dame, all the Parisian theatres were opened for free and crowds celebrated in the streets. Pélissier was promoted to the rank of Marshal.

EYE-WITNESS
THE CAPTURED CITY

William Russell

On 9 September Russell got into Sevastopol late in the afternoon and visited the hospital in the dockyard, which had been badly shelled by the allies, especially by shots that had travelled over the Redan.

'Of all the pictures of the horrors of war which have ever been presented to the world, the hospital at Sebastopol offered the most heartrending and revolting . . . I beheld such a sight as few men, thank God, have ever witnessed. In a long, low room . . . dimly lighted through shattered and unglazed window-frames lay the wounded Russians. The wounded, did I say? No, but the dead – the rotten and festering corpses of the soldiers, who were left to die in their extreme agony, untended, uncared for, packed as close as they could be stowed, some on the floor, others on wretched trestles and bedsteads or pallets of straw, sopped and saturated with blood which oozed and trickled through upon the floor, mingling with the droppings of corruption. With the roar of exploding fortresses in their ears – with shells and shot pouring through the roof and sides of the rooms in which they lay – with the crackling and hissing of fire around them, these poor fellows . . . were consigned to their terrible fate. Many might have been saved by ordinary care. Many lay, yet alive, with maggots crawling about in their wounds. Many, nearly mad by the scene around them . . . had rolled away under the beds . . . Many, with legs and arms broken and twisted, the jagged splinters sticking through the raw flesh, implored aid . . . The attitudes of some were so hideously fantastic as to root one to the ground by a sort of dreadful fascination. The bodies of numbers of men were swollen and bloated to an incredible degree; and the features distended to gigantic size, with eyes protruding from the sockets and the blackened tongue lolling out of the mouth, compressed tightly by the teeth which had set upon it in the death-rattle, made one shudder and reel round.'

Frederick Dallas

21 September: 'I took advantage of a glimpse of sun a few days ago, to go down on a pony to the town and as you might suppose found it the most interesting sight . . . It is utterly knocked to pieces by our shot & I can't conceive how "Ruski" ever managed to live at all in it . . . I certainly could hardly find a space of 1 yard square, without one of our shot & a lot of shells on it, the houses either utterly knocked to pieces, or riddled with holes, guns in position & Batteries in every street nearly, and preparations made for defending the place inch by inch . . . everywhere there are signs of the most hasty flight: long galleries of Barracks with all their knapsacks and possessions lying about . . . It must have been a most lovely town: such quantities of magnificent houses, and such beautifully built Public Buildings. The Docks are splendid & will take, odd to say, 2 months' hard work to destroy them.'

16

Stalemate

Although the allies had captured the south of Sevastopol, the end of the siege brought few tangible gains. The Russians still held the north side of the harbour from where they were able to shell the devastated southern side. It could not therefore be used as a base for allied troops and the harbour was still blocked by sunken ships that were impossible to remove because of Russian artillery fire. The allied troops were worn out after a year of trench and siege warfare. The capture of Sevastopol had come late in the campaigning season and, given the experience of the 1854–55 winter, the best policy seemed to be to prepare for another winter in camp. The commanders on the spot decided that it was too difficult to drive the Russians out of the north side of Sevastopol and that they were too strong in the rear of the allied armies to risk a set-piece battle.

The allied armies spent the weeks after the fall of Sevastopol in almost total inactivity. In the only action of note, three French cavalry regiments and some Ottoman troops, under the command of General d'Allonville, routed eighteen Russian cavalry squadrons and Cossack units near Evpatoriya in late September. However, it was impossible to exploit this success since a large garrison could not be sustained at Evpatoriya – there was almost no drinking water available and the Russians had destroyed all the wells in the surrounding area.

EYE-WITNESS
THE BRITISH ARMY AFTER THE FALL OF SEVASTOPOL

William Russell, *The Times* war correspondent
12 September: 'It is delightful to abandon the old heading "The Siege of Sebastopol" . . . but it is not clear what is to be put in its place, for the enemy having abandoned the south side, seems prepared to defend the north.'
14 September: 'The silence in camp is almost alarming; were it not for a gun now and then between the north side, and across the Tchernaya, it would be appalling.'

Frederick Dallas, officer

12 September: 'I have no idea what our further intentions may be. I am so sick and weary of war & sickness, and all one's friends being killed and mutilated, that I should prefer resting after our success. I think we are certain to make a mess of any more that we attempt . . . I am very tired of the whole business . . . I suppose I ought to be grateful for being alive at all.'

21 September: 'There are constant rumours of some or all of us moving to take the field before the Winter comes on. I don't & have never believed in it. It is too late in the year & our Transport is so insufficient. The honest truth is, and a very melancholy truth it is, (that with all our exultation at the fall of Sebastopol & our success generally) we have completely used up our Army. The miserable mobs of Recruits that we now have in all Regiments are a very sad lot compared to the Army that we landed with, (wasted as those men were by disease) . . . The general run of our men now are almost children in years & barely know how to load their guns . . . Between you and me, the sooner, as far as our fame is concerned, you make peace the better, for little as we have done, we shall never do anything as good again.'

Henry Clifford, officer

25 September: 'Today our troops, the few that had been sent into Sebastopol to be quartered there, have been obliged to return to Camp, as the fire from the North side has driven them out, and as long as the Russians hold the North side, we cannot live in the South. Nevertheless the blessing of this part of the town having fallen, is felt more and more every day; *no more Trenches!!* This alone is a hatful of bliss, and then the firewood! and the tables! and the chairs! and the banishment of those sad stretchers! and no wounded! no dead men! quiet nights! etc. etc.'

A frustrated Napoleon sent Pélissier a set of options. He could attack the Russians around the Mackenzie Heights, land at Evpatoriya or Kaffa for attacks into the interior of the Crimea, land in the Caucasus area, move 100,000 troops across the Black Sea into Bessarabia or attack Kherson on the Dnieper River.

Ministers in London despaired about the performance of the military. Clarendon thought Simpson should be court-martialled for the disgraceful failure at the Redan (particularly because the French had been successful). Panmure told Simpson on 15 September that he should give the Russians no rest after their defeat at Sevastopol 'till his overthrow or expulsion from the Crimea' and that 'you must not suffer your mind to rest upon any expectation of peace'.[1] Two days later he followed up this message with an even sterner one: 'We cannot tell why you are resting on your oars. You neither fire nor lay plans for attack, nor tell us what you are doing with what you have got. Don't waste your time in idleness.' [2] After nine days of further inactivity Panmure sent another telegram complaining about the lack of initiative in the Crimea. He told Simpson: 'nearly 3 weeks have elapsed in absolute idleness, this cannot go on and in justice to yourself and your army you must prevent it'.[3] Queen Victoria thought Simpson's despatches showed 'a total want of energy of mind on his part'.[4] Two days after Panmure's message Simpson finally took the hint and resigned (though he remained in formal command until early November). He told Panmure he 'could not continue in command while the Government considers that I and my Army are passing our time in absolute idleness'.[5] He argued that the army was not idle, but was fully occupied in repairing roads before the onset of winter. Prince Albert commented, '*How* can a Commander-in-Chief believe that 200,000 men are sent to Sebastopol to make roads?'[6]

Ministers agreed that Simpson should be allowed to resign on grounds of ill health (his health had been bad for months, as he had pointed out when he was appointed in late June). In the summer the government had agreed that Codrington was the obvious successor. Now they had doubts. Newcastle, who was in the Crimea, wrote to Clarendon that Codrington 'showed sad lack of the necessary qualities of a General on the attack on the Redan'.[7] Palmerston was unimpressed, but thought, 'if our Codrington is only a good officer he will be an improvement upon what we now have'.[8] Codrington was duly appointed but he, like Simpson, could achieve little if Pélissier, who commanded by far the largest allied contingent in the Crimea, was reluctant to take action. Ministers in London remained deeply unhappy with the leadership of the army, as Clarendon told Palmerston in mid-October:

> Everything connected with our military system is inferior to the French . . . the war has not brought to light any military talent and the best proof of that is that in replacing that poor old woman Simpson who succeeded Raglan of whom we had so much reason to complain we have only been able to select among the different grades of incompetency.[9]

The attack on Kinburn

On 29 September Pélissier chaired an allied war council to consider Napoleon's suggestions about operations. They decided to attack not

Kherson, as Napoleon wanted, but Kinburn, the small fort at the mouth of the Dnieper River. Together with Ochakov on the opposite side of the river, Kinburn protected the route to Kherson and Nikolaev (the main construction base for the Black Sea fleet). It was a poorly constructed fort (only part of it was stone) with a small garrison, and its capture would achieve little except blocking the river and possibly providing a base for operations if the war continued into 1856. The expedition was on a small scale and designed primarily to provide the illusion of military activity before winter set in.

The plan for the attack was drawn up by the French and they commanded the expeditionary force. Admiral Bruat was in charge of ten major battleships (four of them French) and seventeen frigates (six French), plus a collection of corvettes, mortar boats and auxiliary vessels. Most important of all was the inclusion of the three French ironclads – *Devastation, Lave* and *Tonnante*. They had been intended for the bombardment of Sevastopol, but arrived just after the fall of the city. The attack on Kinburn was the first use of ironclads in war. In total there were about 9,000 troops with the expedition. The French contingent was commanded by General Achille Bazaine. (He was chosen by Pélissier because he wanted Bazaine out of the way so that he could continue his affair with Madame Bazaine, who had accompanied her husband to the Crimea.)

The naval units arrived off Odessa on the afternoon of 8 October and were joined by the transports six days later. They sailed for Kinburn in the afternoon of 14 October. Early the next morning the troops landed on the sandy spit in the mouth of the river about four miles from the fort, cut off its communications and dug in about 400 yards away. The ships then moved into position in front of the fort, with the three ironclads closest in, at a distance of about half a mile. On 16 October there was too much wind and the swell was too strong for a naval bombardment and the operation was postponed. The attack began at 9 a.m. on 17 October and the ironclads were a huge success. They fired about 3,000 shells and, although they sustained about seventy hits, these had no impact. Within an hour and a half the fort was on fire and the walls were crumbling. The battery on the spit was abandoned at 3 p.m. and the Russians surrendered. The troops under Major-General Kokonovitch marched out and threw their weapons on a huge pile in front of the ruined fort. They had lost forty-five killed, 130 wounded and 1,500 men were taken prisoner. The allies lost two dead and thirty-two wounded.

The day after the surrender the Russians blew up Fort Ochakov. The allies made no real attempt to move ships up the rivers and, although a small detachment of troops moved inland without encountering any resistance, there was no attempt to attack Kherson or Nikolaev. A small garrison was left at Kinburn (which was held until the end of the war) and kept the two towns cut off from the Black Sea. The naval force was now withdrawn.

EYE-WITNESS
THE BRITISH PRISONERS ARE EXCHANGED

George Newman, foot soldier

After his march to Odessa, Newman spent about a month in the city while the formalities of the prisoner exchange were settled.

'We were soon ready and some waggons arrived loaded with packing cases and, on being opened, was found to contain shirts and boots; one pair of boots and one shirt were given to each of us . . . They distributed some money among some of the men as being the balance of their pay after paying for rations . . . we were marched through the town to the dockyard on the shores of the bay. Here we were joined by the Turks but they had to wait until we had embarked. We were put in a large boat and pulled off to a small steamer that lay off the shore . . . There was a white flag of truce flying on the flagstaff in the dockyard, another on the small steamer and one in the bows of each of the boats employed in embarking us . . . There was no time lost, but as soon as we were all on board the steamer started . . . We were soon changed from the little steamer to the English boats and then to the English steamer . . . We gave the Russians three cheers; and as soon as the little steamer returned to the shore all the white flags were lowered and the truce was ended . . . the next day, about 12 o'clock, an order came for us to be sent on board the Agamemnon . . . The pea soup and plum duff went down very nicely after so long an absence and the crew took care we should have plenty of it . . . On 26th [October] Capt. Torrens of my own regiment came for us . . . We had a bad march up to headquarters, for our new wellington boots drew our feet greatly and many of the men were crippled through them . . . The place was much altered since I left and had I been left to myself I should never have found my way to the Light Division, but we reached our regiment about half past eight – the bugles had just finished sounding the Last Post – and we were given over to the adjutant. The news soon spread through the regiment of our return and they cheered us. I was soon surrounded by old comrades and dragged off to the canteen.' Newman had been a Russian prisoner for almost a year.

Stalemate

By mid-October it was clear that nothing of any significance would be achieved in the Crimea before the spring. The allies had captured Sevastopol but that did not defeat the Russian army or bring any major strategic gains apart from the morale boost following the successful end of the long siege. The commitment in the Crimea, so thoughtlessly embarked upon in the late summer of 1854, had taken up far more resources than anticipated, but it was unclear how it could be exploited to bring any major gains.

In the middle of October Napoleon told the British about Pélissier's views on future strategy. The French commander thought that Sevastopol should be totally destroyed and that the allied troops should then retire to Kamiesh, from where many could be evacuated while the remainder held key points until the end of the war. Ten days later Cowley, the Ambassador in Paris, managed to obtain sight of some of the key points in Pélissier's despatch:

> What conquests can we make in the Crimea or even in Southern Russia? Sterile plains which the Russians will abandon after some battles in which they will lose a few thousand men, a loss which causes them no decisive damage, whilst at every step the Allies with a great sacrifice of men and money and with nothing to gain will risk each day the destinies of Europe. [10]

The British were even more worried when Vaillant, the Minister of War, sent them proposals to reduce the allied armies in the Crimea to about one-third of their current strength of more than 200,000.

The British Cabinet discussed future strategy at a series of meetings in late October. It rejected the French idea of withdrawal as too humiliating (especially after the failure at the Redan) and queried where the armies could go – if they came home, the war would effectively be over. Instead the British argued that decisive orders should be given 'to drive the Russians out of the Crimea before the season closes – if that is impossible to harass them in every way during the winter'.[11] Worried about French attitudes, Lord Lansdowne was sent to Paris for two discussions with Napoleon. He told the Emperor, 'no government in England could withstand any withdrawal of forces from the Crimea'.[12] Napoleon agreed that it might be unwise to try an evacuation during the winter, but told the Duke of Cambridge, who was in Paris in mid-November, that he was 'determined not to have a third fruitless campaign in the Crimea'.[13] The British, who provided less than one-fifth of the allied forces in the Crimea, were in a weak position and could not enforce their demands. They agreed that Britain and France would hold a major war council early in 1856 to decide strategy – assuming that the war continued into 1856.

Winter 1855–56

During the winter of 1855–56 campaigning in the Crimea came to an end. The allied armies remained in their camps (they could only loot Sevastopol, not occupy it). With no enemy to face in the southern side of the city, they could easily contain the considerably weakened Russian forces that remained in the centre of the Crimea. By early December Russian forces were withdrawing from the area around Kerch, and in early January 1856 allied intelligence officers thought they detected signs that much of the Russian army was moving out of the Crimea. The Russian army was now weak and its supplies were low – it could do no more than fight the odd skirmish with allied troops.

During the winter the British army was well supplied and its conditions were far better than they had been in the terrible winter of 1854–55. Food and forage were plentiful, warm clothing was abundant and the main problem was boredom. The officers passed the time with an endless round of dinners, amateur theatricals, horse races and military reviews. The men largely ate, drank and slept.

EYE-WITNESS
THE BRITISH ARMY: WINTER 1855–56

Frederick Dallas

In early October Dallas was made ADC to Major-General Robert Garrett who commanded the 4th Division. Having spent much of the previous year criticising staff officers, Dallas now found the extra pay and comforts very agreeable.

19 October: 'I lead a very comfortable life now . . . I have no tiresome Regimental Duty, & nothing can be more jolly and kind than the Old Chief. We generally have somebody to Dinner every day. Altogether, I think I have found the employment suited to my energetic disposition, good pay, good food, & good company & no walking, & lots of forage for one's horses.

24 October: 'Our roads are getting on wonderfully, & I really think that with ordinary foresight & care there ought to be no difficulty about feeding the army this winter. What we should have done if the siege had not ended, I

---

can't conceive. It is only by having the whole of the army released from all military duties, that we are able to make our preparations.'

1 November: 'In the course of making these roads a certain Colonel Munro . . . who happens to be a great antiquarian & Geologist . . . was in charge of a number of men who were digging up stones to lay down in the road, & he came across a most curious Greek Temple full of urns, Amphorai, coins etc. and now about 100 men are employed under him making further excavations & clearings.'

3 December: 'Our people are now really pretty comfortable. Heaps of little private huts to be seen all about our Camps and in each, perhaps the last animal you would expect to see, the cat!! The town was full of jolly tame cats & all our men have their cats in their huts & very useful they are as the amounts of rats and mice is something awful.'

9 December: 'The weather is so dreary, rain, rain, rain, & one great scene of mud all round us; no want & no suffering as in the last wretched winter, but oh, such a dullness . . . The truth is we live here a sort of exceedingly stupid & muddy garrison life.'

4 February: 'We are now again in the midst of snow and frost, tho' I must own that today was a perfect day for doing what I unfortunately don't enjoy, walking. However, I did walk down to Sebastopol and saw a splendid sight: the destruction of Fort Nicholas by our Allies. It was done at 1.00 P.M. and very well done too. There was one great cloud of dense smoke, then a roar, repeated I think, 8 times in about one minute, and where an immense casemented fort stood before, as the smoke cleared away, there was nothing but a long ridge of stones by the water side.'

This winter it was the French troops who faced the real problems, largely as the result of the huge increase in numbers during the summer. Unlike the British in the previous winter, they could be supplied with sufficient food, clothing and shelter. The problems came from the breakdown of the sanitation system and the outbreak of disease – mainly cholera and typhoid. Between January and March 1856 the fourteen French base hospitals around the Bosphorous treated 53,000 patients, of whom about 10,000 died. In addition about 20–25,000 men died in the field hospitals of the Crimea and another 5,000 on the transport ships. In total about 35–40,000 French soldiers died from disease. Medical facilities were simply overwhelmed by the sheer scale of the epidemic. In Pera hospital there were 2,400 beds, but there were only six surgeons and four assistants to treat the patients. There was no time and no staff to change the bedding between patients. Given the primitive medical treatment available, the severe shortage of doctors probably contributed little to the death rate. The problems stemmed from overcrowding, lice and poor sanitation – all of which were common in all nineteenth-century armies when they were in the field.

The Allied War Council, Paris, January 1856

In a letter to Queen Victoria on 22 November 1855, Napoleon set out three possible ways of continuing the war. First, the naval blockades of the Black and Baltic Seas could be enforced in the hope that an exhausted Russia would sue for peace. Second, a wider 'nationalist' war could be instigated by promising independence for Poland, Finland, Hungary, Circassia and Italy. This would start a war to revolutionise Europe and would involve Austria as well as Russia. Third, an alliance with Austria (which would probably be followed by one with Prussia) would enable a major land war to be fought with Russia. Such a war should lead to a decisive victory. Napoleon thought the third option was the best, but made it clear he would be happy with the second. Palmerston personally favoured the second option, though most of his Cabinet colleagues did not – they thought it was far too revolutionary. The general consensus in London was that the third option was probably the best, but that plans should be laid for continuing the war without Austria.

The discussions about strategy for 1856 were overshadowed, as we will see in the next chapter, by the increasing likelihood that peace would be signed before the new campaigning season opened. The discussions therefore had a slightly unreal air because most of the protagonists knew that they were only going through the motions. The Council of War, presided over by Napoleon, met in the middle of January. It was not attended by the commanders in the Crimea, but senior military officers from both sides were present (the Duke of Cambridge led the British delegation) and there was a strong political representation, too – Cowley, the Ambassador, headed the British diplomatic team. The Council met four times as a full group, beginning at 9.30 a.m. on 10 January in the Tuileries. Napoleon kept close control of the proceedings and at the first meeting read out a series of questions – fourteen on operations in the east and five on the Baltic. The council then split into two groups (Baltic and Black Sea) to consider these questions.

The Baltic operations for 1856 proved to be the least contentious. The strategic situation in this area had changed in the months before the Council of War met. During the limited allied operations in the Baltic in 1855 little attention was paid to bringing Sweden into the war. However, in late May the British Consul in Christiania (Oslo), John Crowe, reported on Russian claims to Finnmark (the northernmost province of Norway). Nominally they were asking for pasturage rights for the reindeer herds of the Lapps of northern Finland, but in practice Crowe thought they wanted an ice-free port in Varangerfjord. Palmerston took the issue seriously and wrote to the Swedish government asking them not to make any concessions to the Russians and promising British support if the Russians attacked them over the issue. Sweden agreed, but asked for a British and French guarantee of all of its territory, not just Finnmark. The allies accepted this demand in late August and Canrobert was sent to Stockholm to negotiate the details of a treaty. A defensive alliance between the three countries was signed on 21 November and made public on 17 December. It contained secret clauses about how it could be converted into an offensive alliance for the 1856 campaign. Canrobert also held discussions in Stockholm and Copenhagen about military plans for the new campaign.

The Baltic sub-group in Paris was chaired by Canrobert and included the commanders of the 1855 expedition – Dundas and Penaud. It met over three days (17–19 January) at the Ministry of Marine. The British were keen that this should be the major theatre of operations for 1856 and believed that they now had the right equipment – large numbers of shallow-draught gunboats – to attack the forts, and argued that Kronstadt near St Petersburg should be the main target. Canrobert had worked out plans for a major army operation in the Baltic. A Swedish army of 20–30,000 troops, protected by the Royal Navy, would occupy the Åland Islands and 40,000 British and French troops (together with 16,000 from Denmark) would land in Estonia. Swedish troops would also invade Finland. The group rejected these ideas in favour of a mainly naval operation backed up by a large force of marines. The British fleet would consist of sixteen battleships, nine blockships, sixteen frigates and corvettes, eight large floating batteries, 164 gunboats and 104 mortar vessels. The French would provide four battleships, six floating batteries and sixty-five mortar vessels. The primary aim would be the destruction of Kronstadt. Once that had been achieved, decisions would be made on how to exploit the situation. This proposal was agreed by Napoleon and then by the government in London in early February.

The Black Sea sub-group, chaired by Admiral Lyons, was composed of five Generals and reached some basic conclusions fairly quickly. Evacuation of the Crimea was rejected as both impossible and humiliating. This meant that about 70,000 troops would be needed to hold the area currently controlled by the allies around Sevastopol. This left about 150,000 troops for other operations, although there was only enough shipping capacity to move about 60,000 men by sea. However, the group could not agree on any operations for 1856 – it rejected attacks around Kerch, in Bessarabia (because there was no suitable base), at Kherson and Nikolaev (to follow up the attack on Kinburn), in the Caucasus and even an assault on the Mackenzie Heights. To try and get round this deadlock General Martimprey drafted a plan for Napoleon. It was little more than a slight modification of his April 1855 proposal that Pélissier had refused to carry out. The aim was to clear the Crimea of Russian troops. Ottoman troops would continue to hold Kerch and Yenikale, while an army of 65,000 commanded by Codrington would move north from Sevastopol. It would join up with a French army of 125,000 operating from Evpatoriya.

The British did not like the French plan. They preferred a holding operation in the Crimea while an Anglo-Ottoman army (with a French contingent) drove the Russians out of Georgia and the Caucasus area. Panmure told the Queen on 2 February that 'if no operations were undertaken in Asia, the Campaign would turn out certainly a disappointment to Your Majesty's people, and any credit gained would be more likely to accrue to the Army commanded by the French General than to that under the English'.[14] Two days later Napoleon rejected the British plan for simultaneous operations in the Crimea and the Caucasus. The British Cabinet discussed the situation on 7 February. Given the size of the British army (even including the foreign legions), they were in no position to insist on the adoption of their views. They agreed to drop the idea of operations in parallel. They accepted that the first priority was to clear the Crimea of Russian troops which, rather optimistically, they thought should take no longer than a month. Codrington was instructed that an invasion of Georgia and the Caucasus would therefore start in early May and that he should begin preparing for the operation immediately.

The problem the British and French had not been able to resolve was that the 1856 campaign, if it took place, would not provide a solution to their fundamental dilemma, which had been present since the start of the war. Operations in the Crimea, even if they were extended to the Caucasus, could not inflict a major strategic defeat on Russia. The attack on Kronstadt, if it were successful, would have much greater impact. Even so, a substantial strategic victory over Russia would only be achieved through a huge land campaign in eastern Europe and that would require Austrian (and probably Prussian) involvement. Without help on this scale Britain and France would have to settle for limited gains. Was it worth continuing the war to gain only limited objectives?

17

The Road to Peace

The capture of the south side of Sevastopol by the allies marked a decisive moment in the war. After almost a year of fighting, the main aim of the British and French landing in the Crimea had finally been achieved. The fundamental problem was what could and should be done next (or rather when the 1856 campaigning season opened). The only way in which a major defeat could be inflicted on Russia would be through a full-scale European war involving Austria and Prussia (and probably Sweden and Denmark too) and war on this scale might also drag in the United States on the side of Russia.

A number of powers, in particular Austria, had very strong interests in avoiding such a war, which could easily run out of control, transform the map of Europe and possibly bring about revolution. In the winter of 1854–55 Austria had tried to secure peace, but had failed for two reasons. Britain and France felt that they had not secured any significant military victory to appease public opinion and the terms Russia would accept were not close enough to the minimum allied demands. The winter of 1855–56, when fighting in the Crimea and the Baltic would be in abeyance, would provide perhaps the last chance for diplomacy to take centre stage. This time the balance of factors would be very different from the previous winter. The allies had achieved some military success and faced a real dilemma about how to continue the war. Russia was also coming under greater strain both economically and socially as the war, which for it had begun in 1853, moved towards its fourth campaigning season. Could Russia risk continuing the war? Austria (and Prussia too) were becoming increasingly alarmed about the possibility of the war expanding if it was not brought to an end quickly.

The key decisions on the allied side would be made by France. It provided almost two-thirds of the allied armies and, if it favoured peace, then the British would not be able to continue the war on their own. By the autumn of 1855 Napoleon had achieved two of his key aims. First, the capture of Sevastopol provided a military victory sufficient to appease public opinion. This aura of success might be undermined if the war in 1856 was primarily in the Baltic, where the British would win the plaudits. Second, and in many ways more important, the old 'Concert of Europe' had been broken up by the diplomatic crisis that led to war and by the war itself. In particular the rift between Austria and Russia ended the policy that had existed since 1815 of 'containing' France. Napoleon considered continuing the war on a more 'revolutionary' and 'nationalistic' basis by demanding the 'restoration' of the Kingdom of Poland (as had been intended in 1815), but the British (apart from Palmerston) were unenthusiastic and he dropped the idea. Napoleon was also getting reports from the prefects across France of increasing war-weariness. A poor harvest in 1855 led to rising grain prices (there were riots in Angers) and the French economy was also showing signs of strain. Inflation was a growing problem and between August and October French gold reserves fell by one-third.

If the French favoured peace, then the British knew that they would have no option but to go along with their stronger ally. There was also a growing rift between the two powers over war aims. The British favoured fighting in the Caucasus – which would serve their wider imperial interests. The French had no incentive to help in this cause. Similarly, the British took little interest in Napoleon's grand ideas about remaking the map of Europe, which would only increase French power. The British hoped that Austria (which was bound to be the intermediary with Russia) would become entangled in any peace negotiations and, when they failed, would join the allies. To some extent the government in Vienna had an interest in a continuation of the war without Austrian participation. As Franz Josef told the ruler of Saxony in August 1855, 'it may sound inhuman, but the longer they go on killing each other in the Crimea, the more we may count on having peace'.[1] However, the danger of a wider European conflagration outweighed this narrow consideration. In late August 1855 Buol, the Austrian Foreign Minister, told a diplomat in Vienna that once Sevastopol had fallen he would have to secure peace before a wider European war began in the spring of 1856.

The Buol–Bourqueney negotiations

From early September 1855 there were a number of diplomatic initiatives under way. Count Pfordten, the chief minister of Bavaria, and his counterpart Count Beust in Saxony acted as intermediaries between Paris and St Petersburg. In Paris itself the French Foreign Minister, Walewski, talked with Baron Seebach, the Saxon minister to France who was also Nesselrode's son-in-law. Walewski made it clear that Russia had to come up with some clear proposals, which reflected the fact that Sevastopol had fallen and which would be sufficient for the French to overcome British reluctance to agree to peace. The main negotiations, however, took place in Vienna between Buol and the French Ambassador, Adolphe de

Bourqueney. It is unclear how far Bourqueney was acting on his own initiative (he had long been pro-Austrian) and how far he was acting with the tacit approval of Paris.

On 8 September (just as Sevastopol was about to be captured) Bourqueney met Buol secretly in Styria, where the latter was on holiday. Bourqueney returned to Vienna where he saw Gorchakov, the Russian Ambassador. During the talk it became clear that Russia was weakening, but Gorchakov insisted that Russia could not, for reasons of prestige, ask for peace terms, but that it was certainly very willing to listen to any reasonable offer. This was enough for Buol and Bourqueney to start their talks about possible peace terms on 29 September. They agreed that the Four Points of the spring negotiations would form the basis, although both men recognised that they would have to be interpreted in a more pro-allied manner after the fall of Sevastopol. They decided that Bourqueney would first gain his government's agreement to negotiations with Austria and that only then would the project be put to the British. The two diplomats agreed that Austria would submit the terms agreed by Austria, France and Britain as an ultimatum to Russia and would break off diplomatic relations if they were rejected. However, there was to be no Austrian commitment to join the war – it was hoped that the mere threat that they might do so would be sufficient to persuade the Russians to agree to a peace conference. The process was little different from previous Austrian attempts to secure peace, but now the French were engaged in a joint effort.

In early October Bourqueney returned to Paris on the pretext that he had family business to resolve. He discussed progress with Walewski and on 17 October Napoleon and the council of ministers agreed to negotiations continuing. The British knew of the Buol–Bourqueney talks, but almost nothing of their content. They were suspicious about their French allies, but Cowley tried to reassure London that Bourqueney 'will not betray the Allied interests on his return to Vienna'.[2] The British government preferred to put their own stiff peace proposals to Russia so that they would be rejected. However, they knew that neither the French nor the Austrians would accept this. They therefore allowed the talks in Vienna to continue – in practice they had no choice in the matter.

Before Bourqueney returned to Vienna, Walewski saw the Austrian Ambassador, Hübner, and made it clear that France had its own modifications to the Four Points to demand. First, the Principalities would be united under a single ruler, while remaining under nominal Ottoman sovereignty. This would be the first step towards the creation of a Romanian state. Second, Russia would have to cede territory at the mouth of the Danube that would go to the Principalities. This ought to open up the Danube to international shipping – the Russians had allowed the Danube delta to silt up over the previous decades in an attempt to divert trade to Odessa. Austria objected to both these points. It saw a unification of the Principalities not just as a threat to its own influence in the area, but as a long-term danger because it would increase the pressure from nationalism across the Balkans. It also wanted Russia to make a larger cession of territory, including land in Bessarabia. The French made it clear that they would consider these objections only as long as Austria accepted – as in the previous negotiations – a fifth point allowing the allies to raise any issue they wished during the peace talks. The French knew that they could use this point in two ways. The British could be reassured that the French would support them in anything they cared to raise, while Russia could be told that the point was meaningless. Once the British were brought to the negotiating table, they would not be able to insist on any extreme demands under this heading.

Bourqueney returned to Vienna on 1 November and immediately after his arrival Buol saw the Emperor. Buol argued that it was worth taking a few risks in order to gain control over the Danube and that the plan did not require Austria to go to war, even if Russia rejected the ultimatum, which, he believed, it almost certainly would not do. It took just a few days to agree the details of the new proposals, which Buol and Bourqueney initialled as *Projet de préliminaires de paix* on 14 November. The new terms were more pro-allied than the Four Points agreed in August 1854. As in the earlier proposals, the protection of the entire Christian population of the Ottoman empire was to be a pan-European responsibility – there was to be no special Russian protectorate over the Orthodox population. Now Russia was to lose control over the Danube and there was to be a 'rectification' of the Ottoman-Russian border in Bessarabia. Freedom of navigation along the Danube was to be ensured and regulated by European institutions. The key new demand was on exactly the point on which the Vienna conference in the spring had broken down: the neutralisation of the Black Sea. In the spring Russia had rejected any treaty limitations on its defences and its fleet. Now all military and naval installations along the shores of the Black Sea were to be abolished (effectively a neutralisation of the Black Sea) and there would be a separate Ottoman-Russian treaty on the number of small vessels allowed for customs and coastguard work. The final (fifth) point allowed the belligerent powers to add special conditions (*conditions particulières*) that were in the European interest (*dans un intérêt Européen*). In addition to these peace proposals there was a separate agreement on how Austria would act. It would present the demands to Russia and require that they be accepted unconditionally. If Russia rejected this ultimatum, Austria would break off diplomatic relations and consult France and Britain about future action. Buol made it clear that there was no Austrian commitment to go to war and that this would only ever happen after all other expedients had been exhausted.

Britain and the peace negotiations

The French government accepted the Buol–Bourqueney proposals immediately – that was not surprising because they were to a large extent their own work. They sent the details to London on 18 November, explaining that they were Austrian proposals with which they agreed. The British government had very strong suspicions about what the French had been doing, but had no choice but to consider the plan, knowing that it had already been accepted by their stronger ally. In transmitting the proposals to London, Cowley, who was beginning to lose influence with Napoleon, argued that the Emperor was preoccupied with the problem of 'leaving 150,000 men locked up in a corner when all the Generals said they could do nothing more'.[3] Cowley also told Palmerston, 'If Louis Napoleon for his own interest really wants to slip out of the war then these propositions may be a godsend.'[4] He obviously still did not suspect that the French had largely devised the plan for exactly this purpose. Clarendon replied to Cowley, 'I cannot divest myself of suspicions wherever Austria is concerned', but hoped that Russia would not accept these terms. He concluded, 'I am favourably disposed to the terms tho' I would have preferred no such propositions had been made to us provided we were *quite sure* of France.'[5] Clarendon set out the British dilemma very clearly when he wrote to Lord Lansdowne on the day the proposals were received in London:

> We may not like the terms nor think them as much as we are entitled to demand or perhaps such as we *hope to be in a position to demand* . . . but I think the rejection of them would be difficult as regards the professed objects of the war, dangerous as regards the alliance with France where. . . [conditions] render the continuance of steady vigorous cooperation with France doubtful.[6]

The British might dream about inflicting a major defeat on Russia, but they did not have the military means to secure such a success. France was the dominant military power and if it wanted peace on terms that were slightly better than those rejected earlier in the year, it was almost impossible for the British to oppose them.

The Cabinet met for six hours on 20 November to discuss the Buol–Bourqueney proposals. There was no fundamental objection to offering peace (even from Palmerston). The discussion was about what terms should be included and whether those terms could be stiffened up so that Russia would reject them and Austria might be dragged into the war. At the end of the meeting the Cabinet agreed what Clarendon described, with considerable understatement, as some 'trifling alterations'.[7] The neutralisation of the Black Sea was to be extended to the Sea of Azov and the number of warships was to be regulated by the main peace treaty and not by a separate Ottoman-Russian treaty. British consulates were to be set up in the Black Sea ports so that the Russian navy could be monitored. For the first time a demand about the Baltic was made – the Åland Islands were to be demilitarised. Finally the peace conference was to discuss the status of the peoples along the eastern coast of the Black Sea, which would enable the British to raise one of Palmerston's pet projects – Caucasian independence. This demand was included because the British were sure the Russians would reject it and, with it, the Austrian ultimatum.

In transmitting the British conditions to the embassy in Paris, Clarendon made it clear to Cowley that the ultimatum had to be an Austrian ultimatum, but they could indicate that if Russia accepted the terms, then so would the allies. He continued:

> I think you will consider we have been very moderate considering that we have no confidence in Austria and feel sure she will play us a trick . . . make the Emperor understand how much we have deferred to his wishes . . . we incur very great risk.[8]

A few days later Clarendon explained to Stratford in Constantinople the dilemma that the government faced:

> We can't carry on the war alone with all Europe against us, and France having made peace without us, and the certainty that the [United] States will declare against us the moment we were without allies and it will be most difficult, perhaps impossible to avoid being hustled into a peace we disapprove.[9]

The British government disliked the Austrians for, as Clarendon put it, 'cramming her ultimatum down our throats rather than that of Russia'.[10]

By late November the British thought, with justification, that they had just as much reason to distrust the French as the Austrians. They discovered that the French had not been transmitting an Austrian plan, but had been involved in drafting it, behind their backs, for more than two months. Cowley told Clarendon, 'we have to deal with a set of men to whom national honour is of no value'.[11] As his influence with Napoleon rapidly declined, Cowley became even more disillusioned. He reverted to the normal British prejudices about French politicians. He described Napoleon as surrounded by 'the sinister counsels of dishonest men' and said that the Emperor was 'doomed to consort with liars and rogues'.[12]

It was in this atmosphere that Britain and France had to negotiate over the proposed British amendments to the Buol–Bourqueney memorandum. Under French pressure, the British dropped the demand about widening neutralisation to include the Sea of Azov (it was hardly needed anyway because the area was too shallow for major warships). Britain also dropped its demand about the establishment of consulates, provided the French agreed to help secure it in the final peace treaty. And Britain accepted a separate Ottoman-Russian treaty to regulate small warship numbers, provided its terms could only be modified with the agreement of the major powers. The French said they would tell the Austrians of the other British terms, but did not in fact do so. The British, suspecting the French, approached the Austrians direct, but it made no difference because Buol refused to include the British terms in any Austrian ultimatum. The British had little choice but to accept – they were keen to keep the Austrian ultimatum and still hoped the Russians might reject it. The British hoped they might be able to impose their terms as the price of agreeing to an armistice. They did not, however, tell Austria and France that this was their position. It was unrealistic anyway – if Russia accepted the ultimatum and the proposed peace terms, stiffer armistice terms could not then be imposed.

The Austrian ultimatum

Once the disputes between London, Paris and Vienna were ended, if not resolved, the ultimatum to Russia could be drawn up. It was ready on 16 December and that evening the Austrian Ambassador to St Petersburg, Count Valentin Esterházy, left Vienna and travelled to the Russian capital. He delivered the ultimatum on 28 December and demanded unconditional acceptance within eight days. If it were accepted, there would be an armistice and peace negotiations. If it were rejected, Austria would break off diplomatic relations on 18 January. Esterházy explained that Austria had not agreed to any conditions in the fifth point (thereby making it clear that Austria would not go to war over any demands the allies made under it). He added that the fifth point would not include any cession of territory (that in Bessarabia came under another point) and that there would be no indemnity. Esterházy did not communicate any of the British demands.

The Russian Crown Council, chaired by the Tsar, met at the Winter Palace on 1 January 1856 to decide their response. There was general agreement that the outlook, if war continued into 1856, was not good and that renewed fighting would probably result in even worse peace terms. However, there were strong objections to the Austrian terms on two points. The council would not accept point five, because it was potentially so open-ended – if Britain and France were determined to raise an issue at any peace conference, it might be very difficult to reject it. There were even greater objections to the ceding of territory in Bessarabia. Russia was an expansionist power and had not had to give up any territory since before the reign of Peter the Great in the early eighteenth century. The cession would also represent the first time territory had been given to the Ottoman empire – something that was seen as particularly degrading. The territory that would be lost included the highly symbolic fortress of Ismail, which had been captured by the legendary Suvorov during the reign of Catherine the Great. Russia therefore decided to accept the ultimatum, but to negotiate on point five and the loss of territory.

On 7 January Esterházy saw Nesselrode and informed him that the counter-proposal and modification of the ultimatum were the equivalent of rejection. Four days later Buol formally told St Petersburg that the Austrians regarded the Russian reply as a rejection and therefore diplomatic relations would be broken off on 18 January, as set out in the original timetable.

Russia accepts peace

The Crown Council reconvened on 15 January to discuss the situation. Before the meeting General Miliutin circulated a paper headed 'The Dangers of Continuing the War in the Year 1856'. (He would not have circulated it unless he had known which way opinion was moving.) Miliutin argued that about 800,000 serfs had been conscripted since the start of war, but the economy could not withstand the loss of any more agricultural labourers. In addition there were not enough officers for the larger army. Arms supplies were also running out. One million infantry weapons had been stockpiled in 1853, but there were just 90,000 left. The munitions industry could not cope with any major orders and almost no weapons could be imported through the blockade. Gunpowder stocks were low – production had increased fivefold in 1855, but all of this had been used up in Sevastopol and there was nothing left for other fronts. In addition stocks of the saltpetre and sulphur needed to make more gunpowder were very low. The army currently in the Crimea could not be supplied – local agriculture could not cope and it was impossible to move in supplies from the rest of Russia. There were no railways, and draught animals ate almost as much on the journey as they could carry. Miliutin concluded that there was no alternative but to accept the ultimatum. Kiselev, the Minister for State Property, argued that Russia's resources were inferior to those of Britain and France and that there was a very real prospect of internal disintegration if the war continued. The amount of money in circulation had doubled since 1853 and inflation was rampant. Exports had fallen by 80 per cent as the blockade began to bite. The level of military expenditure could not be sustained. The number of peasant revolts in 1855 was double that of the previous year and they had only been suppressed by using the army. A long war could, he argued, wreck Russia for generations.

Nesselrode was worried about the diplomatic situation. There was no prospect of gaining any allies and the neutrals were becoming increasingly hostile. He was particularly worried about the position of Sweden – its defensive alliance with Britain and France had been made public just before Christmas. He thought it was quite possible that Austria would join the war if the ultimatum was rejected, and Prussia would then be tempted to join the allies too. In these circumstances Russia's position would be impossible. Nesselrode had some information about likely allied plans for 1856 (they had probably been leaked by the French to try to concentrate Russian minds). He forecast the loss of the Crimea, a possible invasion of Bessarabia (this had been rejected as an option) and a major campaign in the Baltic with the possibility of a Swedish attack. Nesselrode argued that the Austrian peace terms were probably the best they could get – if the war continued, they would certainly be worse. During the negotiations it ought to be possible to exploit the very obvious differences between the allies – the French were already making it clear informally that they would welcome a closer relationship with Russia once peace was agreed.

The council finally decided that there was nothing in the Austrian ultimatum that was fundamentally damaging. It could be accepted and Russia would recover. The alternative was to continue the war in the expectation of worse terms and the risk of social, economic and perhaps even political collapse. On 16 January the Russian formal acceptance of the Austrian ultimatum was conveyed to Vienna.

The British accept peace negotiations

Even as the Russians were considering the Austrian ultimatum, the British were still trying to wriggle out of the idea of peace on these terms. Palmerston argued, unconvincingly, that the ultimatum represented merely the terms on which Austria would break off relations with Russia – Britain had different terms that would have to be met before an armistice could be granted. Palmerston was on stronger ground when he argued that Austria had refused to pass on the stiffer British terms. However, Britain had accepted the terms of the ultimatum because it could not afford to alienate France. It seemed now that the British were trying to change the terms once Austria was committed. On 8 January a message was sent to Vienna demanding that the British terms be sent to St Petersburg – Buol, knowing that Britain could not back out now, refused.

In parallel the British raised the issue with the French. Cowley was instructed to tell Napoleon (the British no longer trusting the Foreign Minister Walewski) that the Buol–Bourqueney memorandum:

> Might have been all very well at the time it was agreed to, and we might upon the acceptation pure et simple of the conditions by Russia have signed preliminaries of peace, *if* we had reserved to ourselves the right of not only proposing further conditions but of *keeping them in reserve* until negotiations had commenced.[13]

Cowley was to point out that the British had stated their more detailed conditions (demilitarisation of the Åland Islands, Consuls in all Black Sea ports and discussion of the future of the Caucasus area) and that Austria had refused to forward them to St Petersburg. Napoleon was to be told that the war would have to continue until Russia did accept these conditions. There was never any chance that Napoleon would agree to this course of action, and he made this clear to Cowley when they met on 12 January. However, there was agreement that neither Britain nor France would support Austria at any peace conference. Why should they make gains from a war in which they had not participated?

The government in London was also moving to this view and blamed Austria for the weakness of its position. Clarendon told Cowley:

> I heartily wish we could wash our hands of Austria and have only to do with Russia for I believe it would facilitate every arrangement, as Russia must hate the idea of concessions that Austria would benefit from more than the true belligerents.

He went on that if Austria '*frees herself* from her engagements because we have the presumption to want our own terms of peace', then he would be happy to negotiate direct with Russia.[14] The Austrian view of the British was no better. On 18 January Buol thought their tactics 'can only inspire a profound disgust'.[15]

After a long and inconclusive correspondence with Paris, the British were unable to insist on acceptance of their terms before an armistice was signed. The French would do no more than reassure the British that they would support them at the peace conference. Russia had agreed to the Austrian ultimatum and the outline of peace terms contained in it, and there was no realistic prospect that this could or would be unscrambled at such a late stage. Palmerston finally gave way and on 29 January the British accepted the outline protocol for the peace conference. They resented not just the Austrians but also the French, who they thought had forced them into an unsatisfactory peace. However, the British did not have the military power to continue the war on their own and the political leadership had no faith in the military, as Clarendon explained to Palmerston:

> If I should feel the least secure that we should be more successful this
> year than the last I should have been even more averse to peace . . .
> but I have no such feeling for I think that our military administration
> is not such as can render our army efficient and moveable.[16]

On 1 February 1856 the protocol on the preliminaries of peace was signed in Vienna by all the belligerents (except Sardinia), together with Austria.

18

The Peace of Paris

Once the preliminaries of peace were signed at the beginning of February 1856, the belligerents agreed that they all disliked the Austrians more than each other. As punishment for Austrian behaviour, they agreed that Vienna should not host the peace conference. The British suggested a neutral venue (Brussels, Frankfurt or Mainz), but they lost the argument when the Russians adroitly suggested Paris in order to curry favour with the French. Napoleon was delighted at the decision – it emphasised the increasing status of the French. He hoped the conference would become a general European Congress that would settle the future shape of the continent in the way that the Vienna Congress had done in 1815.

All the belligerents would be present (Britain, France, Russia, the Ottoman empire and Sardinia), together with Austria. This left the question of whether Prussia should attend. Buol had promised them that they would do so, as one of the recognised great powers in Europe. However, the other powers were not bound by this promise. On 14 November 1855 the French had agreed with the Austrians that when they presented their ultimatum to Russia, Prussia would be invited to support it and 'the degree of support which the court at Berlin would lend it might merit a role in the general negotiations'.[1] In early January 1856 the Prussian government was also warned by the British that if the war continued into 1856, there would be a major campaign in the Baltic and the Prussians would not be able to maintain their neutrality. As a result they did intervene in St Petersburg and recommend acceptance of the Austrian ultimatum, but their efforts were half-hearted. As a result France was lukewarm about Prussian participation and the British remained strongly opposed. Prussia was therefore excluded until all the major questions had been settled. It was then invited to discuss the revision of the Straits Convention – it could hardly be excluded from this since it was a signatory of the original 1841 agreement.

The Paris conference

The peace conference formally convened in the Salon des Ambassadeurs at the Quai d'Orsay. On the walls were life-sized portraits of Napoleon III and the Empress Eugénie and on a shelf there was a marble bust of

Napoleon I. The twelve negotiators sat at a round table in French alphabetical order – the Austrians had insisted on this arrangement so that the two sides did not confront each other. The French Foreign Minister, Walewski, was chosen as the President of the conference and Benedetti, the Director of the political section of the Foreign Ministry, took the minutes. The British were represented by Clarendon, the Foreign Secretary, and Cowley, the Ambassador in Paris. The Russian representatives were Count Orlov from St Petersburg and Brunnow, the ex-Ambassador in London. The delegates from the Ottoman empire were Ali Pasha, the Grand Vizier, and Mohammed Djemil Bey, their Ambassador to Paris and Turin. Sardinia was represented by Cavour and Villa-Marina, the minister in Paris. The Austrian representatives were Buol and Hübner, the Ambassador in Paris. When Prussia was finally admitted, the negotiators were joined by Manteuffel, the Prussian Prime Minister, and Hatzfeldt, the Ambassador in Paris.

The sessions usually began at 1 p.m. and finished by 5 p.m. at the latest. At the first meeting the outline preliminaries were agreed and on 29 February hostilities were declared at an end. (The formal armistice was signed at the Traktir bridge over the Chernaya on 14 March. Britain maintained its blockade, but the Royal Navy was instructed not to commit any hostile act.)

**EYE-WITNESS
ARMISTICE IN THE CRIMEA**

Frederick Dallas, officer
29 February: 'Today is a rather memorable day to this Army as the Armistice was settled and arranged this morning by the various "Chiefs of Staff" . . . I don't quite see the use of it, as it interrupts nothing except active hostilities which in all probability could not take place until April, & all preparations and movements of troops, reinforcements arriving, even the completion of our work of destroying the South Side [of Sevastopol], go on as usual. On the whole we have somewhat the best of it as they sometimes killed one of us & we never fired at all at them.'
9 March: 'Nothing has yet been settled about the armistice but, through a sort of understanding, there is no shooting.'

The armistice would only last until 31 March – the British wanted a short period, in the hope that the negotiations might break down, and the French agreed, hoping that a limited armistice would increase the pressure to reach a quick settlement. In practice the French were proved right – most of the main issues were either settled by 10 March or the outlines of an acceptable compromise were already apparent. The preliminary negotiations since October 1855 had, in practice, already settled the main issues and only the details needed to be resolved. The conference saw few real arguments and heated disputes. In most respects it was undramatic. The negotiations took place in the various committees established to settle individual problems, and it is easiest to follow the work of the conference topic by topic rather than chronologically.

Bessarabia and the Principalities

This proved to be the most difficult dispute to resolve because all of the main participants had very different objectives. Russia wanted to keep the humiliating loss of territory in Bessarabia to an absolute minimum and hoped to gain as much as it could from its possession of Kars. Austria wanted the maximum possible loss of Russian territory, so as to secure its own control over the mouth of the Danube and give the Ottomans (and by implication the Austrians too) the best possible defensive line against another Russian attack. Russia accepted that its exclusive control over the Principalities would end, but its main objective was to limit Austrian influence as much as possible. In this it had the support of the French and the British. Napoleon was happy to restrict the Russian loss of territory in Bessarabia, which he thought would only benefit Austria, and trade this for the return of Kars to the Ottomans. Napoleon, however, was isolated in arguing for a unification of the Principalities (he suggested a complex and very anti-Austrian deal, making the Archduke of Modena the new ruler, with Modena going to the Duchess of Parma who would, in return, cede Parma to Sardinia). The British, like the Austrians, opposed unification, but for different reasons. The Austrians disliked the national principle being established in the Balkans because it would threaten their multi-national empire, and the British were worried that a unified Principalities would drift away from the Ottomans towards Russia.

All of these complex issues were eventually settled because of Franco–Russian co-operation. As Orlov reported to St Petersburg, 'Napoleon's direct intervention, I might say, decided the question in our favour. We had an opportunity to find out how weak, even humiliating, our adversaries' position has become.'[2] The outcome was that Russia only had to give up two-thirds of the territory in Bessarabia that it had agreed to cede when it accepted the Austrian ultimatum. This was a major defeat for Austrian ambitions. France, however, did not succeed in its plans for the

Principalities. All the participants (except Russia) were agreed that the exclusive Russian rights in the area (and in Serbia) should be abolished. They would remain autonomous areas within the Ottoman empire and their privileges and immunities would be guaranteed by all the parties to the peace treaty. Ottoman authority was restored and they continued to have effective control over foreign relations, as the British wanted. The territory ceded by Russia would go to Moldavia, but the two principalities were not to be unified – their rulers would continue to be chosen as they had been before the outbreak of war.

Danubian navigation

Although the Austrians did not secure their objectives in Bessarabia and the Principalities, they did slightly better in their other main objective – securing freedom of navigation along the Danube. The river was to be placed under international supervision to ensure that it was not blocked. The question was whether this new international regime should apply to the whole length of the river and whether states that did not border the river should be involved. Austria did not want outside interference in those parts of the Danube that ran through its territory.

Eventually two bodies were set up. The Danubian European Commission was established immediately and was composed of representatives of all the powers who signed the peace treaty. Its activities were confined to the area around the mouth of the river and its task was to open up navigation through the area. When this task was over (after about two years), it would be replaced by the Danube River Commission. This would take over the work of the first body, but would also regulate shipping along the entire length of the river. Only states that bordered the river would be members: Austria, Bavaria, Württemberg, the Ottoman empire and Serbia, Moldavia and Wallachia (the commissioners from the last three would have to be approved by the Ottoman government). It was also agreed that all of the signatories of the peace treaty could station two light warships at the mouth of the Danube.

The neutralisation of the Black Sea

In the Vienna negotiations in the spring of 1855 it was this subject that caused the breakdown of the talks – Russia refused to accept anything more than voluntary restrictions on its power in the Black Sea area. The fall of Sevastopol and the destruction of the naval base over the succeeding months had altered the situation fundamentally. It was in this area that the allies secured their most substantial victory over the Russians in the peace negotiations.

The final treaty provided for the neutralisation of the Black Sea. All ports would be open to the merchant vessels of all states (an important gain for the British), and there would be no fortifications and no major warships. This met the fundamental allied demands. The details proved a little more complex to settle. The Russians refused to include the Sea of Azov in this agreement, and the British, lacking support from any of their allies, had to give way. The Russians also refused to give up their shipyards and fortifications in cities such as Nikolaev and Kherson situated on the rivers that led into the Black Sea. However, they did agree that these shipyards would not build warships other than very small vessels. The British secured another of their objectives when both the Russians and the Ottomans agreed to admit foreign Consuls to all the Black Sea ports.

A more difficult question was the regulation of warship numbers and tonnage under the new Black Sea regime. Russia refused to have this as part of the peace treaty as the British wanted. Instead a special convention was annexed to the treaty – it therefore appeared to be freely negotiated rather than imposed. However, this convention could not be modified without the consent of all the powers signing the peace treaty, which was the British fall-back position. The convention allowed the Russians to maintain, for customs and coastguard duties, six steamships with a maximum displacement of 800 tons and four light steamships (or sailing ships) up to 200 tons.

The treaty also (with Prussia as a signatory) reaffirmed the 1841 Straits Convention that closed the Dardanelles to foreign warships while the Ottoman empire was at peace. The Sultan could, however, permit light vessels in the service of the embassies at Constantinople, together with those that would be stationed at the mouth of the Danube, to pass through.

The Ottoman empire and its Christian population

The ostensible cause of the war proved to be one of the easiest issues to resolve and most of the work was done before the Paris conference met. The Ottoman government was, rightly, suspicious of all the other European powers, not just the Russians. It therefore decided to take the initiative before a settlement was imposed at Paris. On 18 February the Sultan issued a *hat-I humayun* (a decree) guaranteeing all previous privileges and special immunities of the Christian and other non-Muslim communities. It also went much further than the Ottoman government had previously been prepared to accept. It guaranteed freedom of religion and instituted a series of administrative reforms. This decree was referred to in the treaty of Paris, but – and this was the important point from the Ottoman perspective – it stated that the decree was a sovereign grant of the Sultan. It did not, therefore, give the European powers the right to interfere either individually or collectively in the affairs of the Ottoman empire.

Under article seven of the peace treaty the European powers, individually and jointly, guaranteed the independence and territorial integrity of the Ottoman empire. This, together with recognition of the Sultan's decree, invalidated the Russian (and French) claims that they had rights to some form of protectorate over either the Orthodox or Catholic populations of the empire. In this sense the Ottomans had secured substantial gains from the war and they were also recognised as a constituent part of the European system of great powers. The downside of the deal was that the Ottomans had recognised religious equality and started a series of reforms that would eventually undermine and weaken the Ottoman state.

The Caucasus

The British were the only participants interested in this area and they were unable to make their views prevail in the face of hostility and indifference. Indeed, their position was fatally undermined before the conference even began. At a preliminary meeting on 21 February with Walewski and Clarendon, Buol raised the issue of the Caucasus. He knew that Britain and France differed fundamentally on the issue and was worried that the British might try to use it to wreck the conference. He asked Clarendon to define British objectives. The Foreign Secretary, caught unawares and without having read up on the subject, replied that the Kuban River should be the southern frontier of Russia. This would have returned Georgia, Circassia and other frontier areas to Ottoman control, and Russia would have lost gains that it had taken decades to accumulate. This could not be achieved without a major and successful war. By overplaying his hand Clarendon merely demonstrated the unrealistic nature of British demands. He then had little alternative but to concede the point. On 4 March it was agreed that pre-war boundaries in the area would be restored (this meant that Kars was restored to the Ottomans). A four-power (Russian, Ottoman, British and French) commission would fix the frontier and resolve any disputes.

The Åland Islands

This was the only area of the peace discussions that did not involve some aspect of what became known as the 'Eastern Question'. In order to spare Russian susceptibilities, the provision was not included in the main treaty but formed a separate convention negotiated and signed by Britain, France and Russia. The Russians made it clear that they attached no importance to the fortifications in this area. At the last minute Sweden intervened to try to achieve what it had been promised if it joined the war. Sweden wanted to gain the islands, impose a limit on the Russian Baltic fleet and reduce Russian fortifications along the Finnish coast. The allies saw no reason why they should accommodate Sweden when it had refused to help them during the war. The final agreement was that the islands were not to be fortified and that no military or naval establishment was to be maintained on them.

The treaty of Paris

The peace treaty was signed at 12.30 p.m. on Sunday 30 March (the day before the armistice expired) and was greeted by a 101-gun salute from the Invalides. In London the guns were fired at 10 p.m. that evening. It was certainly not a 'victors' peace'. As Bourqueney, the man who had done much to draft the main terms, remarked, 'When you read this treaty, you wonder, who was the loser, who was the victor?'[3] Russia made only one cession of territory around the mouth of the Danube and that was much smaller than it had agreed just six weeks earlier. It lost its special position in the Principalities and Serbia, and its claim to a more general protectorate over the Orthodox population of the Ottoman empire had to be abandoned. However, the close religious and cultural ties remained and Russia's growing power and influence in the Balkans were hardly diminished. The only measure that significantly restricted its power and its ability to pressurise the Ottoman empire was the neutralisation of the Black Sea (although these measures restricted Ottoman power, too). The continuation of the Straits Convention also served Russian interests by making it almost impossible for other states to dominate the Black Sea. But, without stronger measures, this was likely to be no more than a temporary setback.

The British were unhappy. Their military and naval contribution to the war had been far from glorious and they resented the fact that the bulk of the effort had been borne by France, whose armies had achieved most of the allied successes. They blamed others for their problems, as Clarendon told Palmerston even before the treaty was signed:

> We are making a premature peace and another campaign would have given us different results but as we were compelled to accept the Austrian Ultimatum on pain of separating from France there is no use in lamenting it now and we must try to make the best of our position.[4]

Palmerston agreed. He thought the peace 'will not be unsatisfactory though it may fall short of what we would wish'. He believed that Russia would remain a great power and would recuperate, and would then 'place in danger the great interests of Europe'. But, as he reflected philosophically, 'the future must take care of itself'.[5]

Further work

Napoleon always envisaged that the peace conference should act as a European Congress to address wider issues. The other participants were unenthusiastic about the idea. Nevertheless there were five more meetings of the delegates in early April after the peace treaty was signed. These sessions also filled in time between the grand celebratory dinners. On 12 April Napoleon gave a banquet for 140 people at the Tuileries. Two days later the Prefect of the Seine gave an even grander dinner at the Hôtel de Ville in Paris that lasted for seven hours.

One issue that could not be avoided was the future of Italy, because of the presence of Sardinia. This was one of the major reasons why Cavour and the King had brought Sardinia into the war, but they were disappointed by the outcome. Their only tangible gain was the acceptance of Sardinia's increased status through its participation in the conference and by its signature on the treaty. Napoleon still favoured the formation of an Italian confederation (including the Austrian territories), which would be dominated by France, rather than the unification of Italy brought about by Sardinia. Cavour gained nothing else from the conference apart from some discussion of the Italian question. He returned to Turin a disappointed man: 'Peace is signed. The drama is finished and the curtain has fallen without having brought about a solution which would have been materially favourable to us. This is a sad result.'[6]

The Paris conference did, however, produce the first general agreement about the laws of naval warfare and to that extent it marked a major step forward in the development of international law. The subject was introduced by Clarendon at the session on 8 April and a wider scheme was agreed eight days later. The first measure was the abolition of privateering (it had not been used since 1815). It was little more than a formal renunciation of an outdated practice. Originally Clarendon had not wanted to go further than this, but Orlov argued that a single proposal hardly constituted a grand declaration of principles. The British and French therefore agreed to the formalisation of their policy during the war. First, there should be no seizure of enemy goods when they sailed under neutral flags, except for contraband of war. Second, there should be no seizure of neutral goods when they sailed under an enemy flag, unless they were contraband of war. Third, to be legal, blockades had to be effective and not just declared on paper. As we have seen, these ideas were a major departure from previous British policy. They reflected its position as the major trading nation in the world, its belief that it gained from such trade and that it was more effective to pressurise neutrals into carrying out their duties rather than coerce them through a harsh naval regime.

The proposal on privateering was deliberately designed to isolate the United States – they strongly opposed its abolition. After the declaration was agreed at Paris, the Americans approached the Russians for support on the issue but were rebuffed. They made a second proposal to accept the end of privateering in return for the complete protection of private property at sea (including war contraband). This gave such an unbalanced protection of neutral rights at the expense of the interests of belligerents that, although Russia supported the United States (the Russians had no fleet capable of exercising a blockade), both Britain and France refused even to consider the American proposal. The United States therefore refused to sign the Declaration of Paris even though it was accepted by every other important power.

The last subject discussed at the Paris conference was the idea of arbitration. Clarendon raised the subject informally on 6 April and admitted that he was doing so only to appease public opinion. Arbitration to resolve disputes between states was an increasingly popular idea in the mid-nineteenth century. In 1849 the liberal, free-trade advocate Richard Cobden introduced a motion in the House of Commons in favour of arbitration treaties between Britain and all other countries. A few years earlier the Chief Justice of the United States had proposed an International Court of Justice. During the Paris conference the Quaker-run Peace Society sent three delegates to lobby the representatives of all the powers. Article eight of the peace treaty did impose mediation in any dispute between the Ottoman empire and any other power (i.e. Russia) and Clarendon raised the subject formally on 14 April. He proposed that article eight should have general applicability, but subject to the reservation that it could not affect the independence of governments and that they were the sole judges of their interests and honour. The reservation rendered arbitration meaningless, exactly as Clarendon intended. Even this proposal was too much for the other delegates (as Clarendon knew it would be) and in the end the conference did no more than adopt a resolution that it was their 'wish' that states should appeal to friendly arbitration before they resorted to force. With that resounding declaration of principles the conference ended and the delegates returned home.

The armies return

News of the peace treaty reached the Crimea immediately it was signed in Paris, and on 2 April a 101-gun salute was fired. A few days later the Russian commander, General Lüders, gave a celebratory lunch for the French and British commanders and their staffs. The hospitality was returned a couple of days later. On 13 April Pélissier and Codrington reviewed a march past of Russian troops on the Mackenzie Heights. Four days later Lüders reviewed British and French troops.

Once these formalities were complete, the long, complex and boring task of organising the return of the troops, their equipment and supplies back to Britain and France could begin in earnest. There was also the question of the civilian population, in particular the Tartars (traditionally anti-Russian), many of whom had collaborated with the allies. Although the Russians formally agreed to an amnesty, the allies did not trust them to keep to its terms. In the end Codrington placed two transports at the disposal of the Ottoman authorities so that the Tartars could be evacuated to the Dobrudja.

EYE-WITNESS
THE BRITISH ARMY LEAVES THE CRIMEA

Frederick Dallas

6 June: 'You cannot conceive a more utterly desolate scene than a deserted Camp, and it is very sad riding past little huts where one has spent many a jolly hour, now emptying & falling to pieces . . . Two regiments of Guards have gone & the Fusiliers go tomorrow. We shall miss them dreadfully, for I and others spent much of our spare time playing cricket &c at their Camps.'

10 July: 'I really think that at last, we are on the point of starting for home . . . we embark our horses tomorrow, ourselves, they say, the next day . . . We shall probably be the very last to leave this beloved shore . . . [we] landed the first day of the Campaign in the Crimea, and shall go away the last, having not been away for a day.'

The final contingent of French troops left the Crimea on 5 July 1856 – Pélissier was one of the last to embark. The last British troops left a week later on 12 July. The final act of the war was the Russian evacuation of Kars on 6 August.

19

The Impact of the War

Although it is usually regarded as unimportant, the Crimean War was the largest war fought between the end of the Revolutionary and Napoleonic Wars in 1815 and the outbreak of the First World War in 1914. Its casualty toll was higher than the American Civil War, and that war lasted twice as long as the conflict between the allies and Russia. In total probably 650,000 men died, the overwhelming majority from various diseases contracted either at the front or in hospital; during the Crimean War about four times as many men died from disease as from military action. This was the normal ratio for a nineteenth-century war and was the result of poor sanitation and overcrowding leading to lice infestation and polluted drinking water. The two main killers in the war were cholera and typhus.

Of the 650,000 dead almost three-quarters were in the Russian army, which suffered about 475,000 deaths. Because Russian records are so poor it is impossible to analyse the causes of death. On the allied side the French suffered by far the largest number of deaths – 95,000 (of this number, 75,000 men died of disease, most in the bad winter of 1855–56). British deaths were less than a quarter of the French figure, at 22,000, but of these just 4,000 men died in action or of wounds received in battle. Almost half of the British deaths were the result of cholera, diarrhoea and dysentery. Roughly 3,500 died of typhus, typhoid and malaria and half that number from frostbite and scurvy. The number of deaths in the Ottoman army is difficult to calculate because, like the Russian army, its records are so poor. The best estimate is significantly more than double the number of British deaths, probably just over 50,000. On the allied side the smallest number of deaths occurred in the Sardinian army – about 2,000 men. However, only twenty-eight of these were battle casualties; nearly all the rest died of cholera.

The Crimean War was not only the greatest conflict of the nineteenth century, but also the one that first saw the emergence of many of the features that have come to be regarded as typical of 'modern warfare'. There were, however, still some features of what might be called 'old style'. The British army still fought in uniforms that were little changed (except to become even more elaborate) from those of the eighteenth century. The British, for the last time, also tried to recruit foreign mercenaries, just as they had in the limited wars of the previous century. The Russians were still equipped mainly with the musket – the principal infantry weapon for the previous 300 years. The Charge of the Heavy Brigade and the Charge of the Light Brigade at Balaklava were the last significant British cavalry charges in a European war. The war was also a very 'civilised war', even though The Hague and Geneva Conventions were still decades away. Enemy civilians were not interned on the outbreak of war. In Russia allied civilians were left free to help prisoners of war, feed and clothe them and intervene with Russian officials to secure better conditions. British newspapers still circulated freely in Russia. For example, in January 1855 the British prisoners of war held at Kharkov were able to read the *Illustrated London News* of 2 December with its description of the battle of Inkerman. Allied civilians in Russia were still able to correspond with Britain and France. On 16 May 1855 Lieutenant Duff of the 23rd Regiment of Foot passed through Kharkov as a prisoner of war. A French lady living in the city wrote to *The Times*, which was able to publish her letter giving the news that he was still alive on 5 June. British prisoners in Russia were treated very well – at times they were hardly supervised, let alone imprisoned. They were given free access to the towns and cities where they were held, so that they could go out for drinks and go shopping.

These 'older' features were heavily outweighed by the first signs of the new types of warfare. Allied infantry were overwhelmingly equipped with modern, high-velocity, rapid-fire rifles that gave them a decisive technological superiority over the Russian troops. That superiority proved to be crucial in most of the battles in the Crimea. The fighting around Sevastopol very quickly began to look like the warfare on the western front in the First World War – elaborate trench systems, vast artillery barrages that proved only partially effective, and static warfare in which the defenders were worn down in battles of attrition. At sea new types of warfare also emerged. Although sailing ships were still in use, the new steam-powered, screw-propelled warships were the dominant weapons. However, they were still wooden-hulled and this left them vulnerable to fire from forts on land. By the last months of the war the new armoured gunboats, 'floating batteries' and ironclads showed clearly the way ahead for naval warfare.

Other technologies were also seen for the first time. The development of the telegraph had already speeded up diplomatic communications, but by the time the line was extended to the Crimea in the early summer of 1855 military commanders found that they were under much closer supervision from their political authorities at home. The British use of a small railway at Balaklava in the spring of 1855 not only kept the army operational, but demonstrated how important modern supply systems would be in warfare.

The Russian lack of any railways south of Moscow was decisive in restricting their ability to send reinforcements and supplies. The allies could move their troops and supplies far faster by steamboat across the Mediterranean. (Within a decade the ability to move troops by railway would be a decisive factor in European warfare.) The Crimea was also the first major war where 'war correspondents' (in particular William Howard Russell) were important in relaying news of the fighting and in shaping domestic opinion about the progress of the war. (The military and political authorities soon learnt how to restrict and regulate such activities.) For the first time a major campaign was covered by a 'war photographer', Roger Fenton, although, because of the limits of existing technology, he was restricted to taking static scenes and was unable to record the actual fighting.

For such a major war, and such a high level of casualties, the results of more than two years of fighting were very limited. There were two reasons for this. First, allied military strength (in particular that of Britain) was not great enough to inflict a substantial defeat on Russia. This weakness was magnified by the fact that the land campaign took place in a peripheral area of little strategic importance, and by the decision of the Russian fleet to stay in port rather than face certain annihilation by a technologically superior force. It took the allies a year to capture Sevastopol and, although this was enough to give them a limited success, the peace terms were bound to reflect the restricted nature of the war. Second, diplomacy stopped the conflict expanding into a full-scale European war. This was largely the result of Austrian policy – they had their own clear reasons for wanting to avoid such a major conflagration. If France and Austria had not agreed moderate peace terms in the autumn of 1855 and forced the British to accept them, and if the Russians had not accepted the Austrian ultimatum, the 1856 campaign would have seen a much wider war. The major allied attack in the Baltic would have involved Sweden (and probably Denmark) in the assault on Russia. Austria would have opened a new front in Galicia and Poland, and Prussia would almost certainly have had little choice but to join the allies. The United States might well have sided with Russia. Such a war would probably have inflicted a decisive defeat on Russia and led to a major redrawing of the map of central and eastern Europe.

In the mid-nineteenth century the world's two great powers were Britain and Russia. Britain was the main imperial, maritime and trading power, Russia the chief land power. Both were expanding their influence far faster than any other state, and they appeared to be on a course that would lead to conflict over their global ambitions. They were rivals from the Ottoman empire to Persia, Afghanistan and the frontiers of India, to the Pacific and even in the Arctic around Alaska and the north of Canada. Yet the

Crimean War was the only time these two rivals fought each other, and it was limited by the inability of both countries to inflict a significant strategic defeat on the other. By the time, in the late nineteenth century, when the two powers came into much more direct conflict over influence in Central Asia and Persia, they were able to compose their differences and even fight as allies in the First World War.

Because the Crimean War ended before it escalated into a full-scale European war, its immediate effects were limited. However, its longer-term impact was profound. It marked a very clear transition from the relatively stable post-1815 system to the unstable situation of the late nineteenth century, which led to the outbreak of the First World War. The Vienna settlement of 1815 was aimed at containing France and worked through the collaboration of the three conservative powers of Russia, Austria and Prussia and latent British hostility to France. New states such as Belgium and Greece emerged, but the impact of these changes was easily contained. Although the so-called 'Concert of Europe' was weakening by the late 1840s, it was still possible for Russian troops to secure the Habsburgs on their throne in 1849 after the revolutions of the previous year. That 'concert' was shattered by the war, and the diplomacy of the period 1853–56 ended the period of relative stability in Europe. Between 1859 and 1871 there were four wars in Europe that redrew the map and led to the unification of Italy and Germany and the defeat of France.

The destruction of the European system that had contained France since 1815 was the primary aim of Napoleon III and the main reason why he decided to exploit the obscure dispute between the Christian churches in Palestine. By 1855 he had secured most of his objectives – France was allied with Britain, and Austria was deeply estranged from Russia. Once these had been achieved he had little interest in continuing the war, especially after the fall of Sevastopol had provided some military glory. Indeed, by the summer of 1856 France was in its best diplomatic and strategic situation for decades – it was allied to Britain and Austria, and Russia was seeking its support after the war. Within a few years Napoleon had thrown away this advantage. The war with Austria over the future of Italy in 1859 was not some belated price paid for the support of Sardinia in the Crimean War – it was a decision to revise yet again the 1815 settlement to the detriment of Austria. By 1863 Napoleon finally alienated Russia following his support for the Polish revolt. In 1870 he made a disastrous miscalculation and went to war with Prussia. Within months he was back in exile in Britain, and France suffered its worst defeat since 1815 and one that was to shape its anti-German policy for the next ninety years.

The power that gained most from the consequences of the Crimean War was the one that was least involved in it – Prussia. After 1856 it was able to exploit the preoccupation of Russia with internal recovery and reform, and the weakness and isolation of Austria, to achieve a very rapid and large increase in its power. The wars against Denmark and Austria in the mid-1860s ensured that the unification of Germany took place on Prussia's terms, and its overwhelming victory in the Franco-Prussian War of 1870–71 brought about the final unification of Germany. This was a fundamental change in the European balance of power and one that dominated European diplomacy and strategy for the next seventy-five years.

The power that suffered most from the Crimean War was the other major state that did not participate in it – Austria. By the mid-nineteenth century it faced a very difficult situation. The western expansion of Russian power, especially into the Balkans, represented a direct threat to its own interests. It outweighed any joint interest that the two conservative powers had in the maintenance of the political and social status quo. Austria could not allow Russia to be the sole beneficiary of a dismemberment of the Ottoman empire. The emergence of national states in the Balkans would be a direct threat to its multi-national empire. Like Britain and France, Austria had an interest in the preservation of the Ottoman empire as a barrier to Russian expansion and destabilising nationalism, yet it could not afford to fight alongside the two western allies in a war on Russia. It did not have the resources to do so and was unlikely to benefit from any redrawing of the map of central and eastern Europe.

During the Crimean War Austrian policy seemed to be successful. Buol's actions, though opposed by the conservative Habsburg interests that wanted to side with Russia, contained the war and ensured a moderate peace settlement. However, in doing this Austria managed to alienate everybody. Russia felt betrayed after its help in ensuring the Habsburgs stayed on the throne in 1848–49. Both Britain and France resented Austrian interference and its failure to join the war. The British government thought that it would have obtained a much better peace without the Austrians, and Napoleon always regarded Austria as France's prime enemy. Immediately after the Paris conference the three states signed a treaty that was in effect a defensive alliance against Russia and a protection of the Ottoman empire. Austria saw this as highly significant, but both Britain and France regarded the treaty as worthless and had no intention of sticking to its terms. Within months of the end of the Crimean War Austria was dangerously isolated. In 1859 it lost its Italian provinces to a French-inspired war. Russia paid it back for its actions a few years earlier by concentrating a large army in Galicia, so that Austria faced the threat of a two-front war and could not fight effectively in northern Italy. In 1866 Austria was rapidly defeated by Prussia and lost any influence over the future of Germany. In 1867 the empire only survived by turning itself into the 'Dual Monarchy' with a semi-autonomous Hungarian state. The creation of a united Germany dominated by Prussia turned Austria further towards the Balkans and into conflict with Russia. Austria remained isolated until 1879 when it became a subordinate partner to the newly unified Germany.

For Russia the Crimean War demonstrated that its military power was supported by a flimsy social and economic base that could not sustain a major conflict. The war was followed by a period of introspection and the ending of the old idea (prevalent since 1815) that Russia could act as the 'gendarme of Europe' to prop up conservative regimes and oppose revolution. Efforts were concentrated on internal reform. Serfdom was abolished, but not on the grounds that it was economically backward and socially repressive. The aim was to provide a better foundation for army recruitment and the increasing professionalisation of the army. Foreign capital, mainly from France, was used to build a railway system that would increase army mobility. Greater efforts were made to speed up the pace of industrialisation. However, these reforms remained very limited – in the last resort the autocratic Tsarist government was not going to destroy the basis on which its power rested.

The check to Russian power in the Black Sea area lasted for about twenty years. In that period, particularly in the 1860s, Russian expansion was directed into Central Asia and nearly all of the independent Khanates of the region were conquered. This signified a much more direct threat, especially in the longer term, to the 'jewel in the crown' of the British empire – India. The period after the Crimean war marked the real beginning of the 'Great Game': the struggle between Russia and Britain for influence across the region from Persia to Afghanistan and Tibet and into Central Asia. Nobody expected the Black Sea clauses restricting Russian power to last very long after the treaty of Paris. In every European diplomatic crisis for the next fourteen years every state (except Britain) offered support for ending the restrictions in return for a quid pro quo that was important to them at the time. Napoleon III was the first to do so during the talks about a Franco-Russian alliance in 1858–59. He had no real interest in supporting the clauses which always meant much more to the British than the French. Neutralisation of the Black Sea survived until the Franco-Prussian War of 1870–71. Then, with France defeated and occupied, Prussia preoccupied and Britain isolated, the Russians unilaterally repudiated the clauses at the end of October 1870. The states involved made some ritual objections, but nothing concrete happened until a general European conference held in London in early 1871 formally repealed the clauses and gave retrospective sanction to Russian actions.

From the Ottoman perspective, the Crimean War was highly successful.

It ended the threat that Russia would, through exploiting its claims to a protectorate over the Orthodox population, turn the empire into a client state. (This was exactly the reason why Britain and France supported the Ottomans.) The Crimean War was also the only Ottoman success in the long series of conflicts with Russia fought in the hundred years from the late eighteenth century. Not only did the empire not lose any territory, but it even made a small gain through the cession of territory in Bessarabia to Moldavia. The war also brought about a period of twenty years when the threat from Russia was significantly reduced. The problem, from the Ottomans' point of view, was that the pressure from the Russians was replaced by a more general pressure from the European powers. All these powers sought to make gains at their expense – Austria in the Balkans, France in the Levant and the British in Egypt and the Middle East. The peripheral areas of the empire in the Balkans – Serbia, Montenegro and Romania (the Principalities were unified, as the French wanted, in the early 1860s) – continued to edge from autonomy to independence. The pressure for the reform of institutions was also destabilising.

Less than seven years after the abolition of the Black Sea clauses Russia was ready to attack the Ottomans again. This time the French were too weak after their recent defeat by Prussia to consider going to war. The British decided that they had been wrong to fight in 1854 – this time they allowed Russia to defeat the Ottomans and then helped bring about, at the Congress of Berlin, a revision of the settlement they had imposed. The success of this strategy, in which Britain appeared to gain more (not just possession of Cyprus) than it had by fighting, reinforced the view that the Crimean War had been a mistake. The settlement of the late 1870s, however, destabilised the Balkans. It created new states – Serbia, Montenegro, Romania and Bulgaria – all of which had numerous disputes with each other. It also embroiled Austria and Russia in a fatal rivalry that lasted until both states were destroyed in the First World War – a war largely brought about by these Balkan rivalries.

The British were rapidly disillusioned with the Crimean War. Although their military and naval efforts had been spectacularly unsuccessful, they still felt that they should have done better in the peace settlement. They thought they had been betrayed by Austria and, in particular, by France. It was easier to return to their traditional policy of ignoring Europe as much as possible and preparing for a war against their real enemy: France. The Royal Navy paid off all the specialist craft (floating batteries, blockships, gunboats, mortar ships and ironclads) that had been built for the 1856 campaign in the Baltic and returned to the much more congenial policy of concentrating on large battleships optimised for war with the French. With the perennially anti-French Prime Minister Palmerston dominating British politics until his death in 1865, expenditure on fortifications along the Channel coast increased rapidly after the Crimean War.

The British were glad to be rid of what they regarded as the morally decrepit French and the alliance ended almost as soon as the peace was signed. The French could be blamed for Britain not continuing the war on its own – even though that was a strategic impossibility. Clarendon reassured Queen Victoria on the day peace was signed in Paris:

> If we had continued the war single-handed France would feel she had behaved shabbily to us, and would *therefore* have hated us all the more, and become our enemy sooner than under any other circumstances.[1]

By December 1856 the alliance with France had little substance. The British political elite was relieved, as Palmerston told Clarendon: 'We ought . . . to be thankful at having got so much out of the alliance, and to have maintained it so long than to be surprised or disappointed at its approaching end.'[2]

Britain could turn back to isolation and the belief in its moral, social, economic and political superiority to the benighted countries on the European continent. The Crimean War settled into the comforting mythology of the heroism of the Charge of the Light Brigade and the self-sacrifice of Florence Nightingale. Britain could begin to forget its failure in the Crimean War.

Bibliography

Primary sources: manuscript, public

Public Record Office (PRO), Kew
ADM   Admiralty
FO   Foreign Office
WO   War Office
Ministère des Affaires Etrangères, Paris
AE   Archives des Affaires Etrangères

Primary sources: manuscript, private

Aberdeen Papers   British Library, Add MSS
Clarendon Papers   Bodleian Library, Oxford
Codrington Papers   National Maritime Museum
Dundas Papers   National Maritime Museum
Graham Papers   British Library. Add MSS
Keppel Papers   National Maritime Museum
Napier Papers   British Library, Add MSS
Newcastle Papers   University of Nottingham
Palmerston Papers   University of Southampton
Raglan Papers   National Army Museum
Russell Papers   Public Records Office
Seager Papers   National Army Museum
Wood Papers   Borthwick Institute, York

Private papers, printed

Addington, H., The Crimean and Indian Mutiny Letters of the Hon. Charles Addington, 38th Regiment, *Journal of the Society for Army Historical Research*, Vol. 46, 1968, pp. 156–80
Arbusov, Y., Reminiscences of the Campaign in the Crimean Peninsula in 1854 and 1855, *The War Correspondent*, Vol. 19, No. 3, 2001, pp. 40–46, and Vol. 19, No. 4, 2002, pp. 30–35
Barnsley, R., The Diaries of Sir John Hall, Principal Medical Officer in the

Bibliography

Crimea 1854–1856, *Journal of the Society for Army Historical Research*, Vol. 41, 1963, pp. 3–18

Benson, A. & Esher, Viscount, *The Letters of Queen Victoria Vol. III* (London, 1907)

Bentley, N. (ed.) *Russell's Despatches from the Crimea 1854–1856* (London, 1966)

Bonham-Carter, V. (ed.), *Surgeon in the Crimea: The Experiences of George Lawson Recorded in Letters to his Family 1854–1855* (London, 1968)

Bright, J., *The Diaries of John Bright* (London, 1930)

Brisbane Douglas, G. & Ramsay, G., *The Panmure Papers, Being a Selection from the Correspondence of Fox Maule, 2nd Baron Panmure Afterwards 11th Earl of Dalhousie*, 2 vols (London, 1908)

Brown, G., *Memoranda and Observations on the Crimean War 1854–5* (Elgin, 1879)

Burgoyne: See Wrottesley

Clifford, H., *His Letters and Sketches From the Crimea* (London, 1956)

Dallas: see Hargreave Mawson

Duberly, F., *Journal During the Russian War* (London, 1855)

Eckstaedt, C. F. Vitzthum, Count von, *St Petersburg and London 1852–1864*, 2 vols (London, 1887)

Ernst, O., *Franz Joseph as Revealed by His Letters* (London, 1927)

Evelyn, G., *A Diary of the Crimea* (London, 1954)

Fenton: see Gernsheim

Fisher-Rowe, E., *Extracts from Letters written during the Crimean War* (Godalming, 1907)

Foot, M. & Matthew, H., *The Gladstone Diaries: Vol. 4 1848–54* and *Vol. 5 1855–60* (Oxford, 1974 and 1978)

Gernsheim, H. & A., *Roger Fenton: Photographer of the Crimean War. His Photographs and his Letters from the Crimea* (London, 1954)

Goudie, S., *Florence Nightingale: Letters from the Crimea 1854–1856* (Manchester, 1997)

Gough Calthorpe, J., *Letters from Headquarters* (London, 1857)

Hall: see Barnsley

Hargreave Mawson, M., *Eyewitness in the Crimea: The Crimean War Letters (1854–1856) of Lt Col George Frederick Dallas* (London, 2001)

Heath, Admiral Sir L., *Letters from the Black Sea, during the Crimean War 1854–55* (London, 1897)

Hodasiewicz, R., *A voice from within the walls of Sebastopol* (London, 1856)

Horton, K., *One Hussar: The Journal of James Rawlins* (Stourton, n.d.)

Inglesant, D. (ed.), *The Prisoners of Voronesh: The Diary of Sergeant George Newman, 23rd Regiment of Foot, The Royal Welch Fusiliers taken prisoner at Inkerman* (Old Woking, 1977)

Kerr, P. (ed.), *The Crimean War* (London, 1997)

Kohl, J., *Russia* (London, 1844, reprinted New York, 1970)

Koribut-Kubitovich, L., Recollections of the Balaklava Affair of 25 October 1854, *The War Correspondent*, Vol. 19, No. 1, 2001, pp. 28–37

Lambert, A. & Badsey, S., *The War Correspondents: The Crimean War* (Stroud, 1994)

Lawson: see Bonham-Carter

Lysons, D., *The Crimean War from First to Last: Letters from the Crimea* (London, 1895)

Marsay, M., One Woman's Story: With the 19th Foot by Margaret Kirwin, *Newsletter of the Friends of the Green Howard's Regimental Museum*, No. 3, September 1997

Marx, K., *The Eastern Question* (London, 1897)

Naval Records Society, *The Campaigns in the Baltic 1854/1855* (London, 1943/1944)

O'Flaherty, P., *Philip O'Flaherty* (Edinburgh, 1855)

O'Malley, J., *The Life of James O'Malley* (Montreal, 1893)

Oliphant, L., *The Russian Shores of the Black Sea in the Autumn of 1852* (London, 1854, reprinted New York, 1970)

Panmure: see Brisbane

Reid, D., *Memories of the Crimean War: January 1855 to June 1856* (London, 1911)

Russell: see Bentley

Saint Arnaud, L. de, *Lettres du Maréchal Saint-Arnaud*, 2 vols (Paris, 1858)

Strachey, L. & Fulford, R., *The Greville Memoirs, 1814–1860*, Vol. 3 (London, 1938)

Tolstoy, L., *The Sebastopol Sketches* (London, 1986)

Ushakov, M., The Attack by Russian Forces on the Kadykoi Heights on 13 (25) October 1854, *The War Correspondent*, Vol. 20, No. 1, 2002, pp. 12–16

Vincent, J., *Disraeli, Derby and the Conservative Party: Journals and Memoirs of Edward Henry, Lord Stanley 1849–1869* (Hassocks, 1978)

Warner, P., *Letters Home from the Crimea* (Moreton-in-Marsh, 1999)

Wrottesley, G. (ed.), *Life and Correspondence of Field Marshal Sir John Burgoyne*, 2 vols (London, 1873)

Bibliography

Secondary sources: books

Adkin, M., *The Charge: The Real Reason Why the Light Brigade was Lost* (London, 1996)

Alexander, Z. & Dewjee, A., *Wonderful Adventures of Mrs Seacole in Many Lands* (Bristol, 1984)

Allen, W. & Muratoff, P., *Caucasian Battlefields: A History of the Wars on the Turco-Caucasian Border 1828–1921* (Cambridge, 1953)

Anderson, M., *The Eastern Question 1774–1923* (London, 1966)

Anderson, O., *A Liberal State at War: English Politics and Economics during the Crimean War* (London, 1967)

Barker, A., *The Vainglorious War 1854–56* (London, 1970)

Bartlett, C., *Great Britain and Sea Power 1815–53* (Oxford, 1963)

Baumgart, W., *The Peace of Paris 1856: Studies in War, Diplomacy and Peacemaking* (Oxford, 1981)

Baumgart, W., *The Crimean War 1853–1856* (London, 1999)

Bayley, C., *Mercenaries for the Crimea: The German, Swiss and Italian Legions in British Service 1854–56* (Montreal, 1977)

Beskrovny, L., *The Russian Army and Fleet in the Nineteenth Century: Handbook of Armaments, Personnel and Policy* (Gulf Breeze, FL, 1996)

Case, L., *French Opinion on War and Diplomacy during the Second Empire* (Philadelphia, 1954)

Chamberlain, M., *Lord Aberdeen: A Political Biography* (London, 1983)

Compton, P., *Cardigan of Balaklava* (London, 1972)

Conacher, J., *The Aberdeen Coalition 1852–1855: A Study in Mid-Nineteenth Century Party Politics* (Cambridge, 1968)

Conacher, J., *Britain and the Crimea 1855–56: Problems of Peace and War* (London, 1987)

Cooke, B., *The Grand Crimean Central Railway: The story of the railway built by the British in the Crimea during the war of 1854–56* (Knutsford, 1990)

Crowley, T., *Democratic Despot: A Life of Napoleon III* (London, 1961)

Curtiss, J., *The Russian Army under Nicholas I 1825–1855* (Durham, NC, 1965)

Curtiss, J., *Russia's Crimean War* (Durham, NC, 1979)

David, S., *The Homicidal Earl* (London, 1997)

Davison, R., *Reform in the Ottoman Empire* (Princeton, 1963)

Dossey, B., *Florence Nightingale: Mystic, Visionary, Healer* (Springhouse, PA, 1999)

Dowty, A., *The Limits of American Isolation: The United States and the Crimean War* (New York, 1971)

Echard, W., *Napoleon III and the Concert of Europe* (Baton Rouge, 1983)

Erickson, A., *The Public Career of Sir James Graham* (Westport, CT, 1974)

Fuller, W. Jnr, *Strategy and Power in Russia 1600–1914* (New York, 1992)

Gammer, M., *Muslim Resistance to the Tsar: Shamil and the Conquest of Chechnia and Daghestan* (London, 1994)

Gillard, D., *The Struggle for Asia 1828–1914* (London, 1977)

Goldfrank, D., *The Origins of the Crimean War* (London, 1994)

Gooch, B., *The New Bonapartist Generals in the Crimean War: Distrust and Decision-making in the Anglo-French Alliance* (The Hague, 1959)

Greenhill, B. & Giffard, A., *The British Assault on Finland 1854–1855: A Forgotten Naval War* (London, 1988)

Halicz, E., *Danish Neutrality during the Crimean War 1853–1856: Denmark between the Hammer and the Anvil* (Odense, 1977)

Harries-Jenkins, G., *The Army in Victorian Society* (London, 1977)

Harris, S., *British Military Intelligence in the Crimean War 1854–1856* (London, 1999)

Henderson, G., *Crimean War Diplomacy* (Glasgow, 1947)

Hibbert, C., *The Destruction of Lord Raglan: A Tragedy of the Crimean War 1854–55* (London, 1961)

Hopwood, D., *The Russian Presence in Syria and Palestine 1806–1914* (Oxford, 1969)

Jelavich, B., *Russia's Balkan Entanglements 1806–1914* (Cambridge, 1991)

Kofas, J., *International and Domestic Politics in Greece During the Crimean War* (New York, 1980)

Lambert, A., *The Crimean War: British Grand Strategy against Russia 1853–1856* (Manchester, 1990)

Lincoln, W., *Nicholas I: Emperor and Autocrat of all the Russias* (London, 1978)

MacDonagh, O., *Early Victorian Government 1830–70* (London, 1977)

Ma'oz, M., *Ottoman Reform in Syria and Palestine 1840–61* (Oxford, 1968)

Martin, K., *The Triumph of Lord Palmerston* (London, 1962)

Mercer, P., *Inkerman 1854* (London, 1998)

Mitra, S., *The Life and Letters of Sir John Hall* (London, 1911)

Monnier, L., *Étude sur les origines de la guerre de Crimée* (Geneva, 1977)

Mosse, W., *The Rise and Fall of the Crimean System* (London, 1963)

Moyse-Bartlett, R., *Nolan of Balaklava: Louis Edward Nolan and his influence on the British cavalry* (London, 1971)

Munsell, F., *The Unfortunate Duke: Henry Pelham, Fifth Duke of Newcastle, 1811–1864* (Columbia, MO, 1985)

Bibliography

Murphy, D., *Ireland and the Crimean War* (Dublin, 2002)

Palmer, A., *The Banner of Battle* (London, 1987)

Pamuk, S., *The Ottoman Empire and European Capitalism 1820–1913: Trade, Investment and Production* (Cambridge, 1987)

Polk, W. & Chambers, R., *The Beginnings of Modernization in the Middle East* (Chicago, 1968)

Prest, J., *Lord John Russell* (Columbia, SC, 1972)

Puryear, V., *England, Russia and the Straits Question 1844–56* (Berkeley, CA, 1931)

Puryear, V., *International Economics and Diplomacy in the Near East: British Commercial Policy in the Levant 1834–53* (Stanford, 1935)

Riasanovsky, N., *Nicholas I and Official Nationality in Russia* (Berkeley, CA, 1959)

Rich, N., *Why the Crimean War? A Cautionary Tale* (London, 1985)

Royle, T., *Crimea: The Great Crimean War 1854–56* (London, 1999)

Saab, A., *The Origins of the Crimean Alliance* (Charlottesville, 1977)

Saul, N., *Distant Friends: The United States and Russia 1763–1867* (Lawrence, 1991)

Schroeder, P., *Austria, Great Britain and the Crimean War: The Destruction of the European Concert* (London, 1972)

Seaton, A., *The Crimean War: A Russian Chronicle* (London, 1997)

Searle, G., *Entrepreneurial Politics in Mid-Victorian Britain* (Oxford, 1993)

Shepherd, J., *The Crimean Doctors*, 2 vols (Liverpool, 1991)

Smith, F., *Florence Nightingale: Reputation and Power* (London, 1982)

Spiers, E., *The Army and Society 1815–1914* (London, 1980)

Spiers, E., *Radical General: Sir George de Lacy Evans 1787–1870* (Manchester, 1983)

Stanmore, Lord, *Sidney Herbert: Lord Herbert of Lea: A Memoir* (London, 1906)

Strachan, H., *Wellington's Legacy: The Reform of the British Army 1830–54* (Manchester, 1984)

Strachan, H., *From Waterloo to Balaclava: Tactics, Technology and the British Army 1815–1854* (Cambridge, 1985)

Strachey, L., *Eminent Victorians* (London, 1918)

Sweetman, J., *War and Administration: The Significance of the Crimean War for the British Army* (Edinburgh, 1984)

Sweetman, J., *Balaklava 1854* (London, 1990)

Sweetman, J., *Raglan* (London, 1993)

Thomas, D., *Charge! Charge! Hurrah!: A Life of Lord Cardigan* (London, 1974)

Thomas, R. & Scollins, R., *The Russian Army of the Crimean War* (London, 1991)

Ware, T., *Eustratios Argenti: The Greek Church under Turkish Rule* (Oxford, 1964)

Warner, P., *The Crimean War: A Reappraisal* (Ware, 2001)

Wetzel, D., *The Crimean War: A Diplomatic History* (New York, 1985)

Woodham-Smith, C., *Florence Nightingale* (London, 1951)

Woodham-Smith, C., *The Reason Why* (London, 1953)

Secondary sources: articles

Abbreviations:
CEH: Central European History
EcHR: Economic History Review
EHR: English Historical Review
HJ: Historical Journal
JMH: Journal of Modern History
JSAHR: Journal of the Society for Army Historical Research
MM: Mariner's Mirror
TRHS: Transactions of the Royal Historical Society

Abu Jaber, K., The Millet System in the Nineteenth Century Ottoman Empire, *The Muslim World*, Vol. 57, 1967, pp. 212–23

Alaysa, K., The Turco-Russian War and the Crimean Expedition 1853–56, *Revue Internationale d'Histoire Militaire*, Vol. 46, 1980, pp. 72–87

Alder, G., India and the Crimean War, *Journal of Imperial and Commonwealth History*, Vol. 2, 1973–74, pp. 15–37

Anderson, F., The Role of the Crimean War in Northern Europe, *Jahrbücher für Geschichte Osteuropas*, Vol. 20, 1972, pp. 42–59

Anderson, O., The Russian Loan of 1855, *Economica*, Vol. 27, 1960, pp. 368–71

Anderson, O., Further Light on the Inner History of the Declaration of Paris, *Law Quarterly Review*, Vol. 76, 1960, pp. 379–85

Anderson, O., Economic Warfare in the Crimean War, *EcHR*, Vol. 14, 1961–62, pp. 34–47

Anderson, O., Wage Earners and Income Tax, *Public Administration*, Vol. 41, 1963, pp. 189–92

Anderson, O., Loans versus Taxes: British Financial Policy in the Crimean War, *EcHR*, Vol. 16, 1963–64, pp. 314–27

Anderson, O., Great Britain and the Beginnings of the Ottoman Public Debt, *HJ*, Vol. 7, 1964, pp. 47–63

Bibliography

Anderson, O., The Janus Face of Mid-Nineteenth Century English Radicalism: The Administrative Reform Association of 1855, *Victorian Studies*, Vol. 8, 1964–65, pp. 231–42

Anderson, O., The Reactions of Church and Dissent towards the Crimean War, *Journal of Ecclesiastical History*, Vol. 16, 1965, pp. 209–20

Anderson, O., Early Experiences of Manpower Problems in an Industrial Society at War: Great Britain 1854–56, *Political Science Quarterly, Vol. 82, 1967, pp. 526–45*

Anderson, O., The Growth of Christian Militarism in Mid-Victorian Britain, *EHR*, Vol. 86, 1971, pp. 46–72

Armytage, W., Sheffield and the Crimean War, *History Today*, 1955, pp. 473–82

Bolsover, G., Nicholas I and the Partition of Turkey, *Slavonic Review*, Vol. 27, 1948, pp. 115–45

Burroughs, P., *The Human Cost of Imperial Defence in Early Victorian Britain,* Victorian Studies, Vol. 23, 1980, pp. 7–32

Case, L., A Duel of Giants in Old Stamboul: Stratford versus Thouvenel, *JMH*, Vol. 35, 1963, pp. 262–73

Chadwick, G., The Army Works Corps in the Crimea, *Journal of Transport History*, Vol. 6, 1964, pp. 129–41

Collins, T., 'Redan Massy', *JSAHR*, Vol. 42, 1964, pp. 92–95

Curtis, J., Russian Sisters of Mercy in the Crimea 1854–55, *Slavic Review*, Vol. 25, 1966, pp. 84–100

Davis, J., The Bamberg Conference of 1854, *European History Quarterly*, Vol. 28, 1998, pp. 81–107

Duker, A., Jewish Volunteers in the Ottoman-Polish Cossack Units During the Crimean War, *Jewish Social Studies*, Vol. 16, 1954, pp. 203–18

Farmer, H., Bands in the Crimean War, *JSAHR*, Vol. 41, 1963, pp. 19–26

Florescu, R., The Rumanian Principalities and the Origins of the Crimean War, *Slavonic and East European Review*, Vol. 43, 1964–65, pp. 46–67

Gooch, B., The Crimean War: A Review of Recent Documents and Books, *Victorian Studies*, Vol. 1, 1958, pp. 271–79

Gough, B., The Crimean War in the Pacific, *Military Affairs*, Vol. 37, 1973, pp. 199–214

Gray, E., The Stone Frigates of Sevastopol, *History Today*, 1969, pp. 383–96

Hamilton, C., Sir James Graham, the Baltic Campaign and War-Planning at the Admiralty in 1854, *HJ*, Vol. 19, 1976, pp. 89–112

Hamilton, C., The Royal Navy and the French Navy in the 1840s, *Journal of Strategic Studies*, Vol. 6, 1983, pp. 183–94

Hamilton, C., French Naval Policy in the 1840s, *HJ*, Vol. 32, 1989, pp. 686–87

Herder, H., Clarendon, Cavour, and the Intervention of Sardinia in the Crimean War, *International History Review*, Vol. XVIII, No. 4, 1996, pp. 819–36

Herkless, J., Stratford, the Cabinet and the Outbreak of the Crimean War, *HJ*, Vol. 18, 1975, pp. 427–523

Horton, K., The Greatest Engineering Feat of the Crimean War, *The War Correspondent*, Vol. 19, 2001, pp. 13–19

Howard, H., Brunnow's Reports on Aberdeen, *Cambridge Historical Journal*, Vol. 4, 1932–34, pp. 312–21

Howard, H., Lord Cowley on Napoleon III in 1853, *EHR*, Vol. 49, 1934, pp. 502–05

Hurewitz, J., Ottoman Diplomacy and the European State System, *Middle East Journal*, Vol. 15, 1961, pp. 141–52

Hurewitz, J., Russia and the Turkish Straits, *World Politics*, Vol. 14, 1961–62, pp. 605–33

Jonasson, A., The Crimean War, the beginning of strict Swedish Neutrality, and the myth of Swedish intervention in the Baltic, *Journal of Baltic Studies*, Vol. 4, 1973, pp. 244–53

Luxenburg, N., England and the Caucasus during the Crimean War, *Jahrbücher für Geschichte Osteuropas*, Vol. 16, 1968, pp. 499–504

Moon, D., Russian Peasant Volunteers at the Beginning of the Crimean War, *Slavic Review*, Vol. 51, 1992, pp. 691–704

Mosse, W., The Triple Treaty of 15th April 1856, *EHR*, Vol. 67, 1952, pp. 203–29

Mosse, W., Stratford and the return of Reschid Pasha, *EHR*, Vol. 68, 1953, pp. 546–73

Osbon, G., The First of the Ironclads: The Armoured Batteries of the 1850s, *MM*, Vol. 50, 1964, pp. 189–98

Osbon, G., The Crimean Gunboats, *MM*, Vol. 51, 1965, pp. 103–16, 211–20

Parry, J., The Impact of Napoleon III on British Politics 1851–1880, *TRHS*, 6th Series, Vol. 11, 2001, pp. 147–75

Pinson, M., Ottoman Colonization of the Circassians in Rumili after the Crimean War, *Études Balkaniques*, Vol. 3, 1972, pp. 71–85

Pinter, W., Inflation in Russia during the Crimean War, *American Slavic and East European Review*, Vol. 18, 1959, pp. 81–87

Potichnyj, M., The Struggle of the Crimean Tartars, *Canadian Slavonic Papers*, Vol. 17, 1975, pp. 302–19

Robins, C., Lucan, Cardigan and Raglan's Order, *JSAHR*, Vol. 75, 1997, pp. 86–92

Rodkey, F., Ottoman Concerns Over Western Penetration of the Levant 1849–56, *JMH*, Vol. 30, 1958, pp. 348–53

Saab, A., Knapp, J. & de Bourquenny Knapp, P., A Reassessment of French Foreign Policy during the Crimean War based on the Papers of Adolphe de Bourquenny, *French Historical Studies*, Vol. 14, 1985–86, pp. 467–96

Schroeder, P., Bruck versus Buol: Austria's Eastern Policy 1853–5, *JMH*, Vol. 40, 1968, pp. 193–217

Schroeder, P., A Turning Point in Austrian Eastern Policy in the Crimean War: The Conferences of March 1854, *Austria History Yearbook*, Vols. 4–5, 1968–69, pp. 159–202

Schroeder, P., Austria and the Danubian Principalities 1853–56, *CEH*, Vol. 2, 1969, pp. 216–36

Shepherd, J., The Civil Hospitals in the Crimea 1855–56, *Proceedings of the Royal Society of Medicine*, Vol. 59, 1966, pp. 199–204

Stephan, J., The Crimean War in the Far East, *Modern Asian Studies*, Vol. 3, 1969, pp. 257–77

Stone, I., The Falkland Islands and the Crimean War, *The War Correspondent*, Vol. 19, 2001, pp. 42–46

Stone, I. & Crampton, R., The Franco-British Attack on Petropavlosk 1854, *The War Correspondent*, Vol. 19, 2002, pp. 12–17, 42–46

Strachan, H., Soldiers, Strategy and Sebastopol, *HJ*, Vol. 21, 1978, pp. 303–25

Sweetman, J., Military Transport in the Crimean War, *EHR*, Vol. 88, 1973, pp. 81–91

Sweetman, J., Turkish Troops and the Siege of Sevastopol 1854–55, *Army Quarterly and Defence Journal*, Vol. 105, 1975, pp. 203–17

Sweetman, J., Ad Hoc Support Services in the Crimean War 1854–56, *Military Affairs*, Vol. 52, 1988, pp. 135–40

Taylor, A., *John Bright and the Crimean War*, Bulletin of the John Rylands Library, Vol. 36, 1954, pp. 501–22

Temperley, H., The Last Phase of Lord Stratford de Redcliffe, *EHR*, Vol. 47, 1932, pp. 216–59

Temperley, H., Stratford de Redcliffe and the Origins of the Crimean War, *EHR*, Vol. 48, 1933, pp. 601–21, and Vol. 49, 1934, pp. 265–98

Temperley, H., The Alleged Violation of the Straits Convention, *EHR*, Vol. 49, 1934, pp. 637–42

Thomas, D., The Reaction of the Great Powers to Louis Napoleon's Rise to Power in 1851, *HJ*, Vol. 13, 1970, pp. 237–50

Todorova, M., The Greek Volunteers in the Crimean War, *Balkan Studies*, Vol. 25, 1984, pp. 539–63

Urry, J. & Klipperstein, L., Mennonites and the Crimean War, *Journal of Mennonite Studies*, Vol. 7, 1989, pp. 102–16

Vincent, J., The Parliamentary Dimension of the Crimean War, *TRHS*, 5th

Series, No. 31, 1981, pp. 37–49

Walker, F., The Rejection of Stratford by Nicholas I, *Bulletin of the Institute of Historical Research*, 1967, pp. 50–64

Wright, M., General Sir William Fenwick Williams: Defender of Kars, *Army Quarterly and Defence Journal*, Vol. 113, 1983, pp. 43–51

Notes

1. The Reason Why

1. Goldfrank, p. 79
2. Monnier, pp. 22–23
3. FO 195/406, 21.4.53
4. Aberdeen to Russell, 15.2.53, Clarendon Papers C4
5. Aberdeen to Graham, 31.5.53, ibid., pp. 125–26
6. Clarendon to Aberdeen, 9.6.53, ibid.
7. De la Cour to Drouyn, 20.7.53, AE Turquie 314
8. Aberdeen Corres. 1852–55, p. 182
9. Clarendon to Aberdeen, 26.8.53, ibid., p. 197
10. FO 519/169, 12.8.53
11. Ibid., 6.9.53
12. Rich, p. 91
13. Letters of Queen Victoria Vol. II, p. 555, 11.10.53
14. Aberdeen to Russell, 15.2.53, op.cit.
15. John Bright Diary, p. 159, 8.2.54

2. Strategy

1. Spiers, p. 13
2. Ibid., p. 5
3. Clifford, p. 269, 9.10.55
4. *United Services Magazine*, 1853, Vol. II, p. 500
5. T. Martin, *Life of the Prince Consort*, Vol. III, pp. 188–89
6. House of Lords, 31.3.54
7. Clarendon to Aberdeen, 26.6.54, Add MS 43189
8. Aberdeen to Russell, 27.4.54, Add MS 43068
9. Palmerston to Clarendon, 16.1.54, Palmerston Papers GC/CL/552
10. Graham to Clarendon, 1.3.54, Clarendon Papers C14
11. Graham Papers, 22.1.54
12. ADM 1/5626, 7.1.54 (received London, 1.2.54)
13. Graham to Clarendon, 19.2.54, Clarendon Papers C14
14. Memo to Stratford, 22.3.54, Burgoyne, Vol. 2, p. 25
15. Baumgart (1999), p. 72

16. Raglan Papers 6807/283
17. Burgoyne to Raglan, 10.4.54, Burgoyne, Vol. 2, p. 40

3. The Baltic: 1854

1. Greenhill & Giffard, p. 114
2. Ibid., p. 115
3. Kerr, pp. 199–200
4. Lambert & Badsey, pp. 276–85
5. Codrington Papers COD/113/1, 24.4.54
6. Keppel Papers HTN/52a, 27.5.54
7. PRO 30/16/12, 24.4.54
8. Napier Papers, Add MS 40024
9. Naval Records Society, 1854, p. 131
10. Greenhill & Giffard, p. 177
11. Keppel Papers HTN/52a, 6.6.54
12. Lincoln, p. 346
13. Greenhill & Giffard, p. 239
14. Ibid., p. 272
15. Codrington Papers, COD/113/2

4. The War in the East

1. Gooch, p. 78
2. WO 6/74/1, 10.4.54
3. Gooch, p. 81
4. Saint Arnaud, Vol. 2, p. 428
5. *The Times*, 4.11.54
6. Gladstone to Aberdeen, 11.11.53, Add MS 44742
7. Add MS 44778, 22.2.54
8. FO 32/206, 4.6.53
9. Kofas, p. 52
10. Ibid., p. 55
11. FO 32/215, 16.2.54
12. Kofas, p. 55
13. FO 32/215, 6.3.54
14. FO 32/219, 27.7.54
15. Kerr, p. 39
16. Baumgart (1999), p. 37
17. Woodham-Smith (1953), p. 151

18. Murphy, p. 41
19 PRO 30/22/11/D, 22.8.54
20 Palmerston to Clarendon, 25.8.54, Clarendon Papers C15
21 PRO 30/22/11/E, Clarendon to Russell, 18.9.54

5. Varna to the Alma

1. Baumgart (1999), p. 113
2. FO 519/170, 17.6.54
3. Graham to Raglan, 8.5.54, Graham Papers
4. Newcastle to Raglan, 28.6.54, Raglan Papers 6807/282
5. Brown, pp. 15–16
6. Brown to Raglan, 27.7.54, Raglan Papers 6807/292/2
7. Oliphant, p. 186
8. Ibid., p. 178
9. Ibid., p. 186
10 Kohl, p. 113
11. Newcastle to Raglan, 9.11.54, Raglan Papers 6807/283/1
12. Raglan to Newcastle, 26.7.54, Raglan Papers 6807/282
13. Curtiss (1979), p. 303
14. Burgoyne, Vol. 2, p. 73
15. Tylden to Raglan, 10.8.54, Burgoyne, Vol. 2, pp. 55–56
16. Strachan (1978), p. 318
17. Palmerston to Clarendon, 7.9.54, Palmerston Papers GC/CL/570
18. Aberdeen to Palmerston, 3.10.54, Aberdeen Corres. 1854–55, pp. 230–31
19. Clarendon to Russell, 4.9.54, PRO 30/22/11
20. Duberly, p. 66
21. Godman, p. 46, 24.8.54
22. Kerr, p. 50
23. NAM MS 8311-9, 28.9.54
24. Evelyn, pp. 82–83

6. Alma and After

1. Woodham-Smith (1953), pp. 190–91
2. Seaton, p. 121
3. Burgoyne, Vol. 2, pp. 88–89, 21.9.54
4. Ibid., p. 93, 24.9.54
5. Saint Arnaud, Vol. 2, p. 500

6. Gooch, p. 131
7. Russell, pp. 101–02
8. Burgoyne, Vol. 2, p. 102, 8.10.54
9. Raglan to Stratford, 1.10.54, Raglan Papers 6807/291
10. Russell, p. 111
11. Raglan to Stratford, 1.10.54, op.cit.
12. Aberdeen Corres. 1854–55, pp. 225–26, 30.9.54
13. Newcastle to Raglan, 9.10.54, Raglan Papers 6807/283
14. Burgoyne, Vol. 2, pp. 94–104
15. Dundas to Raglan, 17.10.54, Raglan Papers 6807/298
16. Fenton, pp. 1–2

7. Balaklava

1. Raglan to Newcastle, 23.10.54, Raglan Papers 6807/282/2
2. Russell, p. 117
3. Kerr, pp. 78–79
4. Ibid., p. 79
5. Godman, p. 114
6. Lambert & Badsey, pp. 113–17
7. Dallas, pp. 39–41, 27.10.54
8. Clifford, p. 72, 27.10.54
9. www.kelsey-family.demon.co.uk/topics/recall
10. Fenton, p. 17

8. Inkerman

1. F. Wellesley, *The Paris Embassy During the Second Empire*, London, 1925, p. 174
2. Burgoyne, Vol. 2, p. 114
3. Evelyn, pp. 107–08, 8.11.54 and 10.11.54
4. Clifford, pp. 94–98, 8.11.54 and 13.11.54
5. Burgoyne, Vol. 2, p. 124, 15.11.54
6. Ibid., pp. 122–23, 12.11.54
7. Ibid., p. 118, 6.11.54

9. Crimean Winter

1. Russell, p. 138, 8.11.54

2. Eckstaedt, Vol. 1, p. 143
3. Hall Diary, p.11, 26.11.54

10. Crimean Winter: The Response

1. Newcastle to Raglan, 18.11.54, Newcastle Papers NeC 9984
2. Palmerston to Russell, 15.11.54, Baumgart (1999), p. 88
3. Burgoyne, Vol. 2, p. 174, 30.12.54
4. Lambert & Badsey, pp. 81–82
5. Lawson, p. 139, 1.12.54
6. Ibid., p. 140, 17.12.54
7. Hall Diary, 11.1.55, p. 14
8. Lambert & Badsey, p. 80
9. Stanmore, Vol. 1, p. 346
10. Ibid., p. 345
11. Dossey, p. 85
12. Mitra, p. 338
13. Goudie, pp. 36–37, 14.11.54
14. Ibid., pp. 42–43, 5.12.54
15. Ibid., pp. 44–45, 11.1.55
16. Ibid., pp. 46–48, 10.12.54
17. Ibid., pp. 50–51, 15.12.54
18. Ibid., p. 34, 25.1.55
19. Ibid., p. 82, 5.2.55
20. Ibid, pp. 40–41, 25.11.54
21. Dossey, p. 146, 19.2.55
22. Ibid.
23. Goudie, p. 107, 18.3.55
24. Ibid., p. 82, 5.2.55
25. Ibid., p. 112, 16.4.55
26. Ibid., p. 113, 22.4.55
27. Dossey, p. 153
28. Goudie, p. 231, 16.3.56
29. Ibid., p. 165, 19.10.55
30. House of Commons, 6.3.54
31. FO 352/39, 24.12.53
32. House of Lords, 7.4.54
33. Sweetman (1984), p. 8
34. Conacher (1968), p. 498
35. Clarendon to Russell, 2.1.55, PRO 30/22/12A
36. WO 6/70/84

37. WO 1/371/84, 30.1.55
38. Add MS 44745
39. Vincent, p. 127
40. Bright Diary, p. 182, 26.1.55
41. Letters of Queen Victoria, Vol. III, pp. 111–13
42. Ibid., pp. 114–18
43. Add MS 44745, 5.2.55
44. Bright Diary, p. 184, 14.2.55
45. Add MS 44745
46. House of Commons, 24.7.54

11. Peace Rejected

1. Clarendon Papers C31, 15.2.55
2. Palmerston Papers GC/CL/607, 24.3.55
3. FO 519/171, 3.4.55
4. Palmerston Papers GC/CL/627, 30.4.55
5. FO 519/171, 2.5.55
6. Ibid., 4.5.55
7. Ibid.

12. The Wider War

1. Clarendon to Graham, 16.2.54, Graham Papers
2. Ibid., 16.3.54
3. FO 83/2280, 22.3.54
4. Cardwell to Aberdeen, 3.4.54, Add MS 43197
5. FO 98/350, 6.4.55
6. FO 97/344, 9.4.55
7. FO 78/1243, 13.4.55
8. Ibid., 3.9.55
9. Alder, p. 16
10. FO 65/425, 24.3.53
11. Wood to Clarendon, 12.4.54, Clarendon Papers C14
12. Alder, p. 25
13. Ibid., p. 26
14. ADM 1/5629, 15.4.54
15. ADM 1/5657, 23.5.55
16. ADM 1/5672, 11.12.55
17. ADM 1/5657, 1.10.55

18. FO 67/198, 23.3.54
19. Panmure, Vol. 1, p. 124, 7.2.55
20. Ibid., pp. 134–35, 30.3.55
21. Palmerston to Clarendon, 29.8.54, Clarendon Papers C30
22. Saul, p. 201
23. Dowty, p. 58
24. Ibid., p. 153
25. Ibid., p. 204
26. Ibid., p. 207

13. The Baltic: 1855

1. Greenhill & Giffard, p. 311

14. Crimean Spring

1. Curtiss (1979), p. 427
2. Panmure, Vol. 1, pp. 108–09, 24.2.55
3. Ibid., pp. 125–26, 26.3.55
4. Add MS 49562, 7.5.55
5. Raglan Papers 6807/31, 20.1.55
6. Raglan Papers 6807/301, 3.7.55
7. Gooch, pp. 208–09
8. Ibid., p. 216
9. Ibid., p. 217
10. Ibid., p. 218
11. Panmure, Vol. 1, p. 246

15. The Fall of Sevastopol

1. Seaton, p. 194
2. Gooch, p. 225
3. Simpson to Panmure, 30.6.55, Panmure, Vol. 1, pp. 256–57
4. Ibid., p. 295
5. Ibid., pp. 282–83
6. Ibid., pp. 289–91
7. Ibid., pp. 320–21
8. Palmerston Papers GC/CL/677, 8.8.55
9. Panmure, Vol. 1, pp. 316–17, 28.7.55

10. Ibid., pp. 348–49, 14.8.55
11. Seaton, p. 195
12. Ibid., p. 196
13. Panmure, Vol. 1, p. 348
14. Seaton, p. 207
15. Panmure, Vol. 1, p. 361
16. Ibid, p. 376, 4.9.55

16. Stalemate

1. Panmure, Vol. 1, p. 388
2. Ibid., pp. 389–90, 17.9.55
3. Palmerston Papers GC/PA f120, 26.9.55
4. Panmure, Vol. 1, pp. 405–06
5. Ibid., pp. 406–07
6. Ibid., pp. 438–39
7. Clarendon Papers C42, 15.9.55
8. Clarendon Papers C31, 6.10.55
9. Palmerston Papers GC/CL/712, 17.10.55
10. FO 27/1078, 26.10.55
11. FO 519/172, 31.10.55
12. Clarendon Papers C35, 7.11.55
13. Ibid., 16.11.55
14. Panmure, Vol. 2, pp. 87–88

17. The Road to Peace

1. Ernst, p. 78
2. FO 519/217, 28.10.55
3. Clarendon Papers C35, 17.11.55
4. Clarendon Papers C134, 18.11.55
5. FO 519/172, 19.11.55
6. Conacher (1987), p. 147
7. Clarendon to Elliott (Vienna), 20.11.55, Clarendon Papers C134
8. FO 519/172, 20.11.55
9. Clarendon Papers C134, 26.11.55
10. FO 519/172, 28.11.55
11. Conacher (1987), p. 152
12. FO 519/173, 11.1.56
13. Ibid., 7.1.56

14. Ibid., 15.1.56
15. Schroeder, p. 347
16. Palmerston Papers GC/CL/782, 15.5.56

18. The Peace of Paris

1. Baumgart (1981), p. 154
2. Ibid., p. 110
3. Ibid., p. 207
4. Palmerston Papers GC/CL/816, 5.3.56
5. Clarendon Papers C49, 7.3.56
6. Baumgart (1981), p. 90

19. The Impact of the War

1. Letters of Queen Victoria, Vol. III, pp. 234–35
2. Puryear, p. 431, 10.12.56

Eye-Witnesses

4. The War in the East

The voyage to the east: Lawson, p. 31; Godman, p. 12; Dallas, pp. 26–27
The British at Gallipoli: Lawson, pp. 38–41
The British encounter the French army at Gallipoli: Russell, pp. 31, 42
The siege of Silistria: Kerr, pp. 28–29
The French and British at Varna: Godman, p. 19; Clifford, p. 36; Godman, p. 42; Russell, p. 54; Kerr, p. 36; Kirwin, pp. 14–15; Godman, p. 26, Russell, p. 25
Cholera strikes the allied armies at Varna: Lawson, p. 54; Russell, pp. 56–57; Clifford, p. 43; Kerr, pp. 47–48; Godman, p. 38
An attack of cholera: Fenton, pp. 102–03
The great fire at Varna: Lawson, pp. 62–63; Addington, p. 161; Kerr, p. 49

5. Varna to the Alma

Embarkation at Varna: Godman, p. 47; Clifford, p. 46; Lawson, pp. 67–68; Dallas, pp. 31–32
Landing in the Crimea: Russell, pp. 59–60; Evelyn, pp. 79–80; Russell, pp. 64–65
The first days ashore: Evelyn, p. 81; Lawson, p. 70; Dallas, pp. 32–33; Kerr, p. 54
The march south: Lambert & Badsey, p. 56
The night before the battle: Seaton, p. 76

6. Alma and After

The allies attack: Russell, pp. 84–86; Seaton, pp. 82–84
The Russian retreat: Seaton, pp. 92–93, 87, 96–97
After the battle – the wounded: Lawson, pp. 77–78; Lambert & Badsey, p. 66
The flank march: Russell, p. 93; Evelyn, p. 86; Kerr, p. 67
Mackenzie's Farm: Murphy, p. 52; Gough Calthorpe, Vol. 1, pp. 217–18
The British army camp: Heath, pp. 79–80

Waiting to attack Sevastopol: Hall, p. 10; Lawson, pp. 84–85; Dallas, pp. 36–37; Lawson, pp. 85–86
The bombardment: Kerr, pp. 73–74, 75
The aftermath: Dallas, pp. 38–39; Lawson, p. 101; Burgoyne, Vol. 2, p. 111; Dallas, p. 42

7. Balaklava

The Russian attack on the redoubts: Koribut-Kubitovich, p. 32
The Russian attack on the 93rd Highlanders: Koribut-Kubitovich, p. 32
The Charge of the Heavy Brigade: Kerr, pp. 83–84; Godman, pp. 75–76
The Charge of the Light Brigade: www.pinetreeweb.com/13th-balaklava2.htm

8. Inkerman

The British army after Balaklava: Evelyn, pp. 99–100; Godman, p. 80; Lawson, pp. 95–96
The weather: Russell, pp. 132–34
The Russian attack: Kerr, pp. 95–102
The battle: Evelyn, pp. 101–04; Dallas, pp. 44–48
The Russian retreat: Kerr, pp. 103–05; Seaton, pp. 176–77
The aftermath: Russell, pp. 137–38; Fenton, p. 73
The British prisoners: Newman, pp. 3–29

9. Crimean Winter

The British army – early November 1854: Lawson, pp. 102–04; Godman, pp. 86–87
The Great Storm: Russell, pp. 143–48; Evelyn, pp. 109–10; Lawson, pp. 105–06; Kerr, p. 128
The British prisoners leave Simferopol: Newman, pp. 46–51
Balaklava after the Great Storm: Evelyn, pp. 110–11; Russell, pp. 148–49
Winter 1854: the siege of Sevastopol: Lambert & Badsey, pp. 144–46; Godman, pp. 94, 98
The cavalry and the animals: Clifford, p. 105; Godman, pp. 100–01; Dallas, p. 57
The British soldiers: Dallas, pp. 51, 54–55; Kerr, p. 130; Dallas, pp. 58–59
Views about the Generals: Dallas, pp. 49–50; Godman, pp. 105, 113, 116

Christmas in the Crimea: Lawson, p. 111; Newman, p. 105

The Russian army: Kerr, p. 135; Curtiss (1979), p. 338; Tolstoy, pp. 43–44, 52–53

January 1855: the weather: Lawson, p. 109; Godman, p. 121; Dallas, p. 70; Lawson, pp. 113–14

January 1855: the wounded and dying: Russell, p. 161; Godman, p. 128

January 1855: disorganisation: Evelyn, p. 137; Dallas, pp. 61–62, 67

January 1855: views about the army leadership: Lawson, pp. 141–42; Godman, p. 125; Dallas, p. 72; Clifford, p. 163; Dallas, p. 81

January 1855: the British and the French: Godman, pp. 122–23; Lambert & Badsey, p. 157; Dallas, pp. 74–75; Addington, p. 170; Dallas, pp. 68–69, 75

January 1855: the British prisoners: Newman, pp. 116, 120

10. Crimean Winter: The Response

A Russian hospital in the Crimea: Kerr, p. 107

Reform of the British government: The Times, 5.5.55; Dickens, *Little Dorrit*, pp. 111–13

12. The Wider War

The siege of Kars: Kerr, pp. 225–26, 235, 236

14. Crimean Spring

The British army improves: Lambert & Badsey, pp. 159–60, 169; Russell, pp. 165, 175–77; Godman, pp. 131, 145; Lawson, pp. 165–66; Fenton, p. 55

Reaction to the April bombardment of Sevastopol: Godman, p. 151; Kerr, p. 159; Lawson, pp. 169–70; Dallas, pp. 110–11, 113; Kerr, pp. 160–61; Fenton, p. 71

The expedition to Kerch: Fenton, pp. 78–85; Kerr, p. 172

The British prisoners at Voronezh plan to escape: Newman, pp. 204–05

Inside Sevastopol: Kerr, pp. 157, 179; Tolstoy, pp. 83–84

The attack on Sevastopol: early June 1855: Fenton, pp. 91–94

The allied attack: 18 June 1855: Fenton, pp. 97–99; Dallas, pp. 146–48; Kerr, pp. 180–82, 184

18 June: the aftermath: Kerr, p. 184

15. The Fall of Sevastopol

Views about the British military leadership: Dallas, pp. 149–50, 154, 155–56; Godman, p. 147

The British army: summer 1855: Dallas, pp. 151–52, 157, 162, 163, 168–69; Godman, p. 177

The British prisoners move to Odessa: Newman, pp. 210–32

The battle of the Chernaya: Kerr, pp. 191–93; Dallas, pp. 170–71

Sevastopol: late August 1855: Kerr, pp. 187, 208–09

Sevastopol: the final bombardment: Kerr, pp. 210–11

The French attack on the Malakhov: Kerr, p. 216

The British attack on the Great Redan: Fenton, pp. 104–05; Clifford, p. 259; Russell, p. 260

The fall of Sevastopol: Kerr, p. 221; Russell, pp. 260–61; Dallas, pp. 179–80; Clifford, pp. 260–61; Dallas, p. 180

The captured city: Russell, pp. 263–64; Dallas, pp. 181–82

16. Stalemate

The British army after the fall of Sevastopol: Lambert & Badsey, pp. 251, 261; Dallas, pp. 180–82; Clifford, pp. 265–66

The British prisoners are exchanged: Newman, pp. 250–54

The British army: winter 1855–56: Dallas, pp. 194–96, 210–11, 227

18. The Peace of Paris

Armistice in the Crimea: Dallas, pp. 233, 235

The British army leaves the Crimea: Dallas, pp. 240, 250–51, 254–55

Index